THE

GOOD FRIDAY

PRAYER

THE

GOOD FRIDAY

PRAYER

by

Howard Rubenstein

Granite Hills Press™

THE GOOD FRIDAY PRAYER
by
Howard Rubenstein

Published 2012 by Granite Hills Press™
SAN 298-072X
granitehillspress@yahoo.com

ISBN: 978-1-929468-23-2
Library of Congress Control Number: 2012931217

Cover design by Chuck Conners
Cover concept by Howard Rubenstein—Front: after Marc Chagall's *White
Crucifixion*, original in the Art Institute of Chicago; Back: after *Book of
Kells*, folio 183V, Gospel of Mark 15:25–31, original in Trinity College,
Dublin.

Cataloging-in-Publication Data:
    Rubenstein, Howard.
        The good friday prayer / Howard Rubenstein—1st ed.
            p. cm.
        Summary: The author replies to those who would convert him to
            Christianity—Provided by the publisher.
        Includes bibliographical references.
        ISBN 978-1-929468-23-2
        LCCN 2012931217
    1. History of the church 2. Church teachings 3. Church scholarship
    4. Jesus of Nazareth. I. Title.
        2012

Made in the U. S. A.

In Gratitude to

Arius
Michael Servetus
Giordano Bruno
Michel de Montaigne
Thomas Paine
Thomas Jefferson
Pope John Paul I

and
all those who have dedicated their lives
to freedom of thought

For nothing is hid that shall not be made manifest, nor anything secret that shall not be known and come to light.

—Jesus of Nazareth
(Luke 8:17).

CONTENTS

4.   THE FORMATION
OF THE CHURCH   215

5. THE TRUE DOCTRINE   **272**

CELSUS

6. JESUS OF NAZARETH   344

THE

GOOD FRIDAY

PRAYER

PREFACE

It is a mystery to the church that the Jews, who gave Jesus of Nazareth to the world, did not—and do not—believe in him. It is a mystery to me that the church, which adopted a Jew as its Messiah or Christ, and only begotten Son of God, and Son of man, and Savior, and Redeemer, and Lord, and Perfect Man, and God-Man, and God, has for almost two millennia treated the Jews with contempt.

By "church" I usually mean any of the many denominations of Christian churches. For the period from Constantine in the fourth century to the Reformation in the sixteenth, I usually mean the Roman Catholic Church; after the Great Schism of the eleventh century, I sometimes also mean the Eastern Orthodox Church. From the sixteenth century, at the time of the Reformation, to the present, whenever a specific Protestant church is meant, I specify it.

The church has been trying to convert me ever since I was a small boy—for more than seventy years. I am not referring to Christians on street corners carrying signs that read, "The time is fulfilled, and the kingdom of God is at hand. Repent, and believe in the gospel!" I am not referring to year round billboards that announce, "Repent, for Jesus Christ is coming!" or December billboards that proclaim, "Jesus is the reason for the season!" Or those preachers who predict the exact date when the world is coming to an end and so I had better get ready and find Jesus. I am talking about those members of the church who try to convert me one-on-one, such as a very few well-meaning acquaintances, but, much more frequently, strangers who approach me on the street or who unexpectedly appear at my front door. I am also talking about the Church of Jesus Christ of Latter Day Saints which intends to convert me after I am dead. Most especially I am talking about the Roman

Catholic Church, which every Good Friday has its faithful say a prayer for the conversion of the Jews.

Some Christians express surprise or tell me they are offended to learn that other Christians are trying to convert me. I think they are disingenuous, for they, no less than the others, are bound by their faith to believe that without Jesus Christ one is damned. Curiously, those who actively try to convert me have not expressed the least interest in learning why I cannot accept what they believe. So I have decided to write a book to tell them.

My principal source has been the Holy Bible Revised Standard Version (RSV, 1952), but I also used other English translations, as well as the Hebrew Scriptures in Hebrew, the Septuagint (the Hebrew Scriptures translated into ancient Greek), the New Testament in Greek as well as in English, and the Latin Vulgate. Other sources include the writings of the church fathers, the teachings of the Roman Catholic Church, the Talmud, and some writings of the so-called heathen authors. A list of important sources appears in the Selected Bibliography at the end of the book. When a source is used only once, it is identified in the text, not the bibliography. Not all books in the bibliography had a quotation that required citation. Nonetheless, because of their important influence on my thinking, I listed those books.

In Jesus of Nazareth's day, many Jews, in addition to the twelve apostles, accepted and believed in him. One can only guess whether Jews who rejected him used reasoning similar to my own, for there are no extant Jewish documents of the first and second centuries that mention Jesus except the gospels themselves. Unfortunately, the contemptuous tone of the gospels and much of the rest of the New Testament toward the Jews so biases readers against them and their objections to Jesus that it is often difficult to comprehend just what it is that the Jews are saying, though one gets the distinct impression that whatever it is has to be bad or stupid, which was, of course, the intent of the authors. I tried to overcome the contempt and uncover the issues, but it was sometimes difficult. Moreover, the gospels are frequently confusing, starting out in one direction, then going in another, and ending somewhere completely unexpected, leaving the reader bewildered and amazed. Finally, Christianity has changed greatly in its transformation from a small primitive sect of Nazarene Jews to the colossal sophisticated gentile church that we have come to know. The Jews in the gospels do not discuss this transformation, for it had not yet taken place. I, however, discuss it, and therefore go far beyond the limited objections of the Jews of Jesus' day.

In my book, biblical quotations, whether from the Hebrew Scriptures or the New Testament, usually appear in boldface without quotation marks, and quotes by Jesus of Nazareth appear in boldface *and* italics, unless context or special clarity demand standard Roman type with quotation marks.

Until recently, the word *gentiles* appeared in lowercase because the word means simply *the nations*, that is, all the nations except the nation of the Jews. Today the word sometimes appears with a capital *G*, perhaps because some people have mistakenly thought that lowercase was disrespectful. I have not been consistent in usage, but lowercase does not indicate disrespect. I have also not been consistent with other words that have variable capitalization, such as gospel, resurrection, crucifixion, incarnation, god, messiah, etc. Context or personal preference or bias—my own or that of the author being quoted—usually determined whether to use lower case or capitals. For example, an ancient Greek believing in many Gods might, contrary to the Christian convention, capitalize *Gods* but indicate the one *god* with lower case.

For the sake of clarity, I usually represent the Hebrew name of God by the letters *YHVH*, the transliterated form of that name in Hebrew, or by *Lord [YHVH]* or *Lord YHVH*, rather than by the conventional single word *Lord*. I do this because the church uses the word *Lord* not only for the God of Israel but also and especially for Jesus of Nazareth. This creates confusion in those cases where it is unclear which Lord is meant. By indicating as above, I avoid the confusion.

There are scholars who believe Jesus of Nazareth never lived, that he is legendary or mythological. I do not share that view and proceed on the assumption that he really lived. I do this if for no other reason than Christian antisemitism or desire to convert me is real enough and is based on that assumption.

In antiquity, there were many Jews named Jesus, so I call the most famous one and the principal subject of my book by his full name Jesus of Nazareth to set him apart from the others. When context makes it clear to which Jesus I am referring, I call him simply Jesus. Similarly, there probably were many Jews named Matthew, Mark, and John, and more than one gentile named Luke, but aside from John the Baptist and Luke the evangelist and Luke the physician (were the two Lukes the same?), I am unaware of any New Testament personage or author with a distinguishing epithet to set him apart from others. The name Paul is a nickname (his given name was Saul) that means "little one" (he was of short stature; in the USA we might have called such a man "Shorty"), and hard as it may be to imagine a Roman man (*vir*) with that name, it may not be assumed to be unique. The gospels and the New Testament letters and the other writings that are associated with a particular name are generally assumed to have been written by a single author. I usually go along with that assumption, even though, as I just explained, it is not necessarily so.

I never attended divinity school or theological seminary. No one ever suggested that I write a book of this kind. In doing the research and the writing, which spanned more than forty years, I did not consult a single biblical scholar, Jewish or Christian, rabbi, priest, or minister; so I give no formal page of acknowledgment or word of thanks. Some will say that the lack of consultation with experts is the book's greatest weakness; others will say it is the book's greatest strength. Whatever people say, "the Jews"—that well-known generalization and gospel term of contempt—had nothing to do with the book. My wife Judy is the only Jew who helped me, and without her help, I could not have brought the book to completion. She constantly encouraged and nurtured me and also served not only as my publisher but also as my editor, organizing the material, asking questions that required answers, and demanding clarification of every aspect of each draft all along the way. For that I am grateful beyond measure. However, the authorship of the book is mine—the concept, the research, the selection of sources and documents and quotations, the presentation and interpretation, the essays and new ideas—and I take full responsibility for the book, including any factual errors and major omissions it may contain.

A final word: The purpose of the book is to explain why I cannot convert to Christianity. My purpose is not to convert anyone to Judaism. I firmly believe that attempts at conversion, evangelization, or proselytization are not acts of goodness, but on the contrary acts of supreme evil. I myself am a secular Jew and agnostic or whatever one calls someone who believes in God intensely one moment only to disbelieve completely the next.

Howard Rubenstein
San Diego
June 14, 2012

PROLOGUE

THE GOOD FRIDAY PRAYER

Every Good Friday in every Roman Catholic Church, faithful Catholics say a prayer for the conversion of the Jews. Until Vatican Two in the middle of the twentieth century, this prayer went as follows:

> Let us pray also for the perfidious Jews: That the Lord our God may take the veil from their hearts and that they also may acknowledge our Lord Jesus Christ. Let us pray: Almighty and everlasting God, you do not refuse your mercy even to the perfidious Jews; hear the prayers which we offer for the blindness of that people so that they may acknowledge the light of your truth, which is Christ, and be delivered from their darkness. Let us pray through the same Lord Jesus Christ who lives and reigns with thee in the unity of the Holy Spirit, God, forever and ever. Amen.

Some have tried to justify the word *perfidious* on the ground that in Latin, the word means *nonbelieving* as well as *treacherous*. This is a disingenuous argument. Although in Latin the word perfidious may mean *nonbelieving*, its primary meaning in English is *treacherous*. Furthermore, if the church has all along meant *nonbelieving*, why has it invariably chosen to translate the word as *perfidious*? And why is the prayer said on Good Friday, the day of Jesus of Nazareth's crucifixion?

After Vatican Two, in a conciliatory gesture to the Jews, the church changed the language of the prayer. The new version, recited today, is as follows:

> Let us pray for the Jewish people, the first to hear the word of God, that they may continue to grow in the

love of his name in faithfulness to his covenant. Almighty and eternal God, long ago you gave your promise to Abraham and his posterity. Listen to your church as we pray that the people you first made your own may arrive at the fullness of redemption. We ask this through Christ our Lord. Amen.

The word *perfidious* no longer appears and the tone has been sweetened, but the message remains the same: Let us pray that the Jews "may continue to grow" and "arrive at the fullness of redemption" is thinly veiled code for let us pray that the Jews convert.

1. CHURCH TEACHINGS

SALVATION

"NO SALVATION OUTSIDE THE CHURCH"

The church teaches that there is no salvation outside the church:

> It is to be held as a matter of faith that no one can be saved outside the Apostolic Roman Church (Pope Pius IX, *Singulari Quadam*, AD 1854).

> The church declares that she is the one true religion and rejects and condemns all religions and sects that are separated from communion with her (First Vatican Council, AD 1870).

> The Catholic church . . . [is the] necessary means of salvation. . . . She is the pillar and foundation of truth, free and untouched by any danger of error or falsehood. The gift of infallibility . . . has been revealed as an enduring characteristic of the Catholic Church (First Vatican Council, AD 1870).

> It is through Christ's Catholic Church alone, which is the universal help toward salvation, that the fullness of the means of salvation can be obtained (Second Vatican Council, AD 1964).

> [T]he one, holy, catholic and Apostolic church . . . will never be complete until all people and cultures have found their home in her. . . . Membership of the church is necessary for salvation (*The teaching* [*sic*] *of the Catholic Church*, pp. 197–200, AD 1967).

"Outside the Church there is no salvation" [Cyprian].
. . . Hence they could not be saved who, knowing that
the Catholic Church was founded as necessary by God
through Christ, would refuse either to enter it or to remain in it. This affirmation is not aimed at those who
through no fault of their own do not know Christ and
his Church (*Catechism of the Catholic Church*, p. 224,
AD 1994).

The social duty of Christians is to . . . awaken in each
man the love of the true. . . . It requires them to make
known the worship of the one true religion, which sub-
sists in the Catholic and apostolic church (ibid., p. 511).

"For there is no salvation outside the Church," St. Cyp-
rian taught in the third century. The Church has always
taught this doctrine. But this is not a fierce proclamation that those who, through no fault of their own, have
not come to recognize Christ's presence in the Church
. . . will be excluded from salvation. . . . The Catholic
Church [however] is not . . . merely optional. . . . If one
were to recognize the reality of the Catholic faith and
the personal will of Christ to live in it, and yet deliberately disobey . . . he would be turning himself away
from the Savior and salvation (*The Teaching of Christ*,
pp. 179–180, AD 2005).

This view of salvation requires examination.

JESUS TEACHES THE ONE SOURCE OF SALVATION

The gospels do not teach that the church is essential to salvation. The gospels do teach that a belief in Jesus is essential
for salvation. But Jesus taught another source of salvation:

Salvation is from the Jews (Jn 4:22).

Jesus taught he was not necessary for salvation; he taught anyone who speaks badly of him would be forgiven:

> **And everyone who speaks a word against the Son of Man will be forgiven** (Lk 12:10).

THE SALVATION OF CHILDREN

The church teaches that children must be baptized to obtain salvation, but Jesus did not teach that:

> **Let the children come to me, and do not hinder them; for to such belongs the kingdom of heaven** (Mt 19:14; Mk 10:14).

It is evident that the issue of salvation is not as clear-cut as the church leads one to believe. Moreover, we learn immediately that the teachings of Jesus and those of the church can be in conflict.

FAITH OR DEEDS

FAITH OR DEEDS

The Catholic church praises faith and deeds. The Protestant churches led by Calvin and Luther teach that faith is more important than deeds.

The Hebrew Scriptures teach that salvation is dependent on good deeds:

> **I the Lord [YHVH] search the mind and try the heart, to give to every man according to his ways, according to the fruit of his doings** (Jer 17:9–10).

Jesus of Nazareth repeatedly paraphrased the Hebrew Scriptures:

> *You will know them by their fruits. Are grapes gathered from thorns, or figs from thistles?* (Mt 7:16).

> *You will know them by their fruits* (Mt 7:20).

> *Not every one who says to me, "Lord, Lord," shall enter the kingdom of heaven, but he who does the will of my Father* (Mt 7:21).

> *[The Son of man] will repay every man for what he has done* (Mt 16:27).

> "Teacher, what good deed must I do, to have eternal life?" To the young man who asked this question, Jesus answered, *If you would enter life, keep the Commandments* (Mt 19:16–17).

> *[T]he Son of man came not to be served but to serve* (Mt 20:28; Mk 10:45).

> *Why do you call me 'Lord, Lord' and not do what I tell you?* (Lk 6:46).

> [Zacchaeus said,] "Half of my goods I give to the poor, and if I have defrauded anyone of anything, I shall restore it fourfold." Whereupon Jesus exclaimed, *Today salvation has come to this house!* (Lk 19:8–9).

> *I have lived in the midst of you, not as the man that sits at the table, but as the man who serves* (Lk 22:27).

> *The works that the Father has granted me to accomplish—these very works which I am doing—bear witness that the Father has sent me* (Jn 5:36).

Peter said:

> **Jesus of Nazareth . . . went about doing good. . . . And we are witnesses to all that he did both in the country of the Jews and in Jerusalem** (Acts 10:38–39).

> **The Father judges each one impartially according to his deeds** (1 Pet 1:17).

Paul wrote:

> **God will render to every man according to his deeds** (Rom 2:6).

> **It is not those who listen to the Law's commandments who are righteous before God, but those who do them** (Rom 2:13).

> **Brothers, never grow tired of doing good** (2 Thess 3:13).

> **Try hard to be worthy of God's approval by blameless hard work** (2 Tim 2:14–15).

> **All Scripture is inspired by God and profitable for . . . training in righteousness, that the man of God may be complete and equipped for every good deed** (2 Tim 3:16–17).

> **Do not neglect to do good and to share what you have, for such sacrifices are pleasing to God** (Heb 13:16).

James wrote:

> **What does it profit, my brethren, if a man says he has faith but has not works? Can his faith save him? If a brother or sister is ill-clad and lack of daily food, and one of you says to them, "Go in peace, be warmed and filled," without giving then the things needed for the body, what does it profit? So faith by itself, if it has no works, is dead. But someone will say, "You have faith, and I have works." Show me your faith apart from your works, and I by my works will show you my faith** (Jas 2:14–19).

John wrote:

> **Let us not love in word or speech, but in deed** (1 Jn 3:18).

One of Jesus' most famous stories is of the "good Samaritan." Two faithful Jews pass by an injured Jew without helping him, whereas a Samaritan goes out of his way to help. Using the Samaritan as a model of righteous behavior, Jesus says, ***Go and do likewise*** (Lk 10:37). The moral of the story is that people are judged by their deeds. To drive home the point, Jesus reminded his disciples that on Judgment Day, he would separate those who did good deeds—fed the hungry, welcomed the stranger, clothed the naked, and visited the sick and imprisoned—from those who did not. To the first group, he will say: ***Come, O blessed of my Father, inherit the kingdom prepared for you*** (Mt 25:34), whereas to the second he will say: ***Depart from me, you cursed, into the eternal fire*** (Mt 25:41).

MORALITY AND RELIGION

Religion is not associated with morality. Consider the wars fought or the cruelty inflicted on humanity in the name of religion. There is no evidence that atheists are less moral than those who embrace a religion, particularly the Christian one.

Christian missionaries reported their surprise on discovering the goodness of many heathens they had come to convert. Goodness and morality clearly are not dependent on Christianity. Nonetheless, the church teaches there is no morality without the Christian faith. Significantly, Jesus never spoke of the superior morality of faith. Jesus gave the one and only criterion by which to judge whether people were good or evil: *You will know them by their fruits* (Mt 7:16, 20).

GOOD DEEDS WITH ULTERIOR MOTIVES

Martin Luther taught that works done with the ulterior motive of going to heaven were evil. Good deeds had to be done sincerely for their own sake. Those who did them for the reward were going to hell.

Luther neglected to demand the same rigorous requirements of faith, but they surely apply. Faith held with the ulterior motive of going to heaven is evil. Faith has to be held sincerely for its own sake. Those who keep the faith for the reward are going to hell. In other words, anyone who says, "I believe in the Lord Jesus Christ" without sincerely meaning it and solely for the sake of going to heaven is going to hell. Jesus said:

> *Not everyone who says to me "Lord, Lord" shall enter the Kingdom of Heaven, but he who does the will of my Father who is in heaven. On that day many will say to me, "Lord, Lord, did we not prophesy in your name, cast out devils in your name, and do many mighty works in your name?" And then I shall say to*

them, "I never knew you! Depart from me, you evil-doers!" (Mt 7:21–23).

TWO VIEWS OF BELIEF

The Old Testament teaches: **The simple believes every-thing** (Prov 14:15). The New Testament teaches: **He who does not believe is condemned** (Jn 3:18).

According to John, Jesus changed his mind about doing good deeds to attain heaven. Belief in Jesus was paramount:

> *He who believes in the son has eternal life* (Jn 3:36).

> *This is the will of my Father, that everyone who sees the son and believes in him should have eternal life* (Jn 6:40; 10:28).

Christian views on faith vs. deeds are always changing. Even Jesus changed his mind. So let us set aside faith and deeds and ask a new question: Who is going to heaven?

HEAVEN

ARE THE JEWS GOING TO HEAVEN?

Jesus of Nazareth taught that the Jews were going to heaven, and, what is more, they are going to be called "great" there, whereas those who want Jews to convert or abandon the com-mandments will be called "least":

> *Whoever then relaxes one of the least of these com-mandments [of the law of Moses] and teaches men so, shall be called least in the kingdom of heaven, but he*

who does them and teaches them shall be called great in the kingdom of heaven (Mt 5:19–20).

So the Jews are going to get the best positions in heaven, too!

For the church to deny heaven to anyone is arrogant. Hebrew Scriptures teach:

> **You [YHVH] guide me with your teachings, and afterwards you will receive me in glory** (Ps 73:24).

> **The Lord [YHVH] commanded the blessing of life everlasting** (Ps 133).

> **[T]he dust returns to the earth as it was, and the spirit returns to God who gave it** (Eccles 12:7).

> **Many of those who sleep in the dust of the earth will awaken, some to everlasting life** (Dan 12:2).

> **The Lord [YHVH] takes away life and gives life. He sends down to hell, and He can raise the dead up again** (1 Sam 2:6).

> **Thus says the Lord God: Behold, I will open your graves, and raise you from your graves** (Ezek 37:12).

> **The dead shall live! Their bodies shall rise! O dwellers in the dust, awake and sing!** (Is 26:19).

In spite of gospel antisemitism, Paul wrote that the Jews are going to heaven; for God's gifts to the Jews are irrevocable:

> **As regards the Gospel, the Jews are enemies of God for your [the Gentiles'] sake; but as regards election [going to heaven], they [the Jews] are beloved for the**

sake of their forefathers. For the gifts and the call of God are irrevocable (Rom 11:28–29).

CHRISTIAN HEAVEN

Christian heaven is described in the New Testament. In the book of *Revelation*, it is a physical place where the streets are paved with gold and precious stones, and where God lives in a palace with walls of jasper. Surrounding God's kingdom is a tall and impenetrable fence with beautiful gates inlaid with pearls. Peter is the gatekeeper and holds the keys to the Kingdom. In the gospels, Jesus taught that the Father is hosting a heavenly banquet, with Jesus sitting at the Father's right. Also sitting at the banquet table are the Hebrew patriarchs Abraham, Isaac, and Jacob, and all the prophets. We do not learn where the heavenly food supply comes from, probably from the heavenly pastures, orchards, and vineyards. There is no description of the heavenly restrooms.

THE WIDE ROAD, THE WIDE GATE, THE WIDE DOOR

A million faithful frequently traverse the wide road leading to St. Peter's basilica. The pope stands on the balcony or at his window and waves to the crowds in the square below. The square leads to the wide gates and doors of St. Peter's, and the doors open onto the colossal basilica that accommodates the multitudes. Are they going to heaven? Not according to Jesus:

> *Enter by the narrow gate; for the gate is wide and the way is easy, that leads to destruction, and those who enter by it are many. For the gate is narrow and the way is hard, that leads to life, and those who find it are few* (Mt 7:13–14).

> And someone said to [Jesus], "Lord, will those who are saved be few?" And he said to them, *Strive to enter by the narrow door; for many, I tell you, will seek to enter and will not be able. When once the householder has risen up and shut the door, you will begin to stand outside and to knock at the door, saying,* "Lord, open to us." *He will answer you,* "I do not know where you come from." *Then you will begin to say,* "We ate and drank in your presence, and you taught in our streets." *But he will say,* "I tell you, I do not know where you come from. Depart from me, all you workers of iniquity!" *There you will weep and gnash your teeth, when you see Abraham and Isaac and Jacob and all the prophets in the kingdom of God and you yourselves thrust out* (Lk 13:22–28).

Jesus does not seem to allow Roman Catholics into heaven.

RESURRECTION

THE SIGNIFICANCE OF THE EMPTY TOMB

In the Gospels, the High Priest and Pharisees suggest to Pilate that he guard Jesus' tomb lest Jesus' disciples steal his body and then claim his resurrection (Mt 27:62–66). Pilate, seeing the sense in this advice, places guards at the tomb, but they fall asleep. When Mary Magdalene came to the tomb in the morning, she found it empty. Mary, a Jewish believer, came to the same conclusion as the nonbelieving Jews: **They have taken the Lord out of his tomb** (Jn 20:3). It was a reasonable conclusion. She did not conclude that Jesus had been resurrected.

Tomb robbing in Jesus' day was not uncommon. The following ordinance of Caesar Claudius was discovered in Nazareth:

> AN ORDINANCE OF CAESAR
> It is my wish that graves and tombs remain undisturbed. . . . If anyone has information that someone has either destroyed a tomb, or has for any reason removed the corpse, or has maliciously moved it to another place in order to wrong it, or has removed the sealing stone, or any stone, I order that such a one be brought to trial. . . . Let it be absolutely forbidden for anyone to disturb the dead. If this order is not obeyed, I want any offender sentenced to death on the charge of violation of sepulture (The Emperor Claudius, c. AD 50, the translation is paraphrased after Barrett, *The New Testament Background*, p. 15).

What happened to Jesus' body? Let us assume that it was resurrected as the church teaches. What was the status of Jesus' resurrected body?

THE RESURRECTED JESUS
The Pharisees taught that all resurrected bodies would rise in the same flesh in which they had died, however diseased or mutilated. Jesus of Nazareth taught the same:

> *If your hand is your undoing, cut it off! . . . And if it is your eye, gouge it out! It is better to enter the Kingdom of Heaven with one eye than to keep both eyes and be thrown into hell!* (Mk 9:43–49).

When the resurrected Jesus appeared to the apostles, Thomas thought he was seeing a ghost. To prove that he was not a ghost, but flesh and blood, Jesus ordered Thomas to handle him:

> *See my hands and my feet, that it is I myself; handle me and see. No ghost has flesh and bones as you can see that I have* (Lk 24:39).

> **But [Thomas] said to them, "Unless I see in his hands the print of the nails, and place my fingers in the mark of the nails, and place my hand in his side, I will not believe." . . . Then [Jesus] said to Thomas,** *Put your fingers here, and see my hands; and put out your hand and place it in my side* (Jn 20:25–27).

Then to show that the resurrected body, no less than any other living body, needs nourishment, Jesus said:

> *Have you anything to eat?* **They gave him a piece of boiled fish, and he took it and ate it before them** (Lk 24:41–43).

Jesus makes it clear that at resurrection, one rises in the very flesh in which one died, however mutilated or diseased, and one has the same basic needs, such as for food.

GREEKS AND RESURRECTION

The Greeks were great admirers of the human body and were revolted by the church's teachings about resurrection. They would not accept the new religion with a resurrection in diseased or mutilated flesh. So Paul had to invent a new conception of resurrection, without crucified flesh, without holes for Thomas to stick his fingers into; and without the one-eyed, the one-armed, or the eunuchs whom Jesus spoke of. Paul wrote:

> **The body is buried in corruption, [but] is raised in-corruptible . . . It is buried a physical body, [but] it is raised a spiritual body** (1 Cor 15:42–44).

What Paul meant by "a spiritual body" no one then or now knows. Nonetheless, Paul's "spiritual body" was acceptable to the Greeks. In the sixteenth century at the general Council of Trent, however, the church recognized that Paul's spiritual body was nonsense and discredited Paul, calling him a fool without naming him, and decreed:

> We do not believe that we shall rise again in some spiritual body or any other body—as some foolishly maintain—but in that same body in which we live and move and have our being (*Declaration on Justification*, General Council of Trent, AD 1563).

Paul deceived the Greeks about the nature of the resurrected body. But his deception worked.

ETERNAL LIFE WITHOUT RESURRECTION

Many Jews like the Greek philosophers believed that the soul went to heaven without resurrection of the body. Hebrew Scriptures taught:

> **The dust shall return to the earth as it was, and the spirit shall return unto God who gave it** (Eccles 12:6).

HOW TO WIN ETERNAL LIFE

How does one win eternal life according to Jesus of Nazareth? Jesus gives one answer in the gospels according to Matthew and Luke, and a different answer in the gospel of John.

According to Matthew:

> [A young man asked Jesus,] "Teacher, what good deed must I do, to have eternal life?" To the young man who asked this question, Jesus answered, *If you would enter life, keep the Commandments* (Mt 19:16–17).

According to Luke, by the "Commandments" Jesus did not mean only the Ten Commandments. He meant all six hundred thirteen commandments given in the Law. We know that from the following incident:

> Behold, a lawyer stood up to test Jesus saying, "Teacher, what must I do to inherit eternal life?" Jesus said to him, *What is written in the Law? Let me hear how you read it.* And the lawyer answered, "'You shall love the Lord [YHVH] your God with all your heart, and with all your soul, with all your strength, and with all your mind' [Deut 6:5]. And 'You shall love your neighbor as yourself' [Lev 19:18]." And Jesus said to him, *You have answered correctly. Obey these commandments and you will live* (Lk 10:25–28).

The two commandments quoted by the lawyer are not two of the Ten Commandments, but are among the other six hundred thirteen commandments in the Law. These two, according to Jesus, are the most important of all. So much for the church's teaching that Jesus revoked the Old Law and replaced it with a New Law, and that only the Ten Commandments are binding for Christians. Jesus specifically teaches that all the commandments, even the least, must be kept:

Think not that I have come to abolish the law. . . . For truly, I say to you, till heaven and earth pass away, not an iota, not a dot will pass from the law until all is accomplished (Mt 5:17–18).

[The] good news of the Kingdom of God is preached, and everyone enters it violently! But it is easier for heaven and earth to pass away than for one dot of the Law to become void (Lk 16:16–17).

THE PRODIGAL SON
AND AUTHENTIC RESURRECTION

When Jesus of Nazareth began to preach, he taught an authentic resurrection—repentance, forgiveness, and reconciliation.

To illustrate, Jesus told the story of the Prodigal Son who leads a life of debauchery and squanders the fortune his father gave him. But then he repents. He asks his father's forgiveness. (It is not our task to question the son's motivation.) The father not only forgives him but prepares a banquet to celebrate the son's transformation. The father's other son, the good and responsible son, looks on with resentment. The father, sensing this, reassures him, saying, **"Son, don't be resentful. Everything I have is yours. It is fitting now for us all to make merry and be glad because your brother who was dead has come back to life"** (Lk 15:31–32). The moral is clear: Repentance, forgiveness, and reconciliation bring about authentic resurrection: **your brother who was dead has come back to life**.

GRACE

NO GRACE BEFORE JESUS

The church teaches that there was no grace before Jesus Christ:

> [The Old] Law is . . . imperfect. . . . [I]t shows what must be done, but does not of itself give the strength, the grace of the Spirit, to fulfill it. Because of sin, which it cannot remove, it remains a law of bondage (*Catechism of the Catholic Church*, p. 476).

The church therein bears false witness not only against the "Old" Law but also against God:

> Jacob said, **"God has dealt graciously with me"** (Gen 33: 11).

> **The Lord [YHVH], a God merciful and gracious, slow to anger, and abounding in steadfast love and faithfulness, keeping steadfast love for thousands, forgiving iniquity and transgression and sin** (Ex 34:5–7).

> **May the Lord [YHVH] bless you and keep you.**
> **May the Lord [YHVH] make his face to shine upon you and be gracious to you.**
> **May the Lord [YHVH] lift up his countenance upon you and give you peace** (Num 6:25).

> **For the Lord [YHVH] your God is gracious and merciful** (2 Chron 30:9).

But thou art a God ready to forgive, gracious and merciful, slow to anger and abounding in steadfast love (Neh 9:17).

Thou art a gracious and merciful God (Neh 9:31).

Jesus prays:

Father, for such was thy gracious will (Mt 11:26).

DAMNATION

CHURCH OF CURSES AND DAMNATION

The church preaches love of enemy, but it does not practice it. It curses its enemies, in fact, not so much enemies as those who disagree with it. Here are some church curses that remain in effect to this very day (*The teaching of the Catholic Church*). *Anathema sit* is Latin for *Let him be cursed!*

If anyone does not believe that Jesus Christ is truly God and the Blessed Virgin therefore the Mother of God . . . —*anathema sit* (AD 431).

If anyone dares to say the Christ was a man bearing God in him, and not rather in truth the One God . . . —*anathema sit* (AD 431).

If anyone does not express belief in two births of Jesus Christ, one from eternity from the Father, timeless and incorporeal, the other in recent times . . . who came down from heaven and was incarnate from the holy and glorious Mother of God, Mary every-virgin, and was born of her—*anathema sit* (AD 553).

Anyone who does not accept the whole of the Church's tradition, both written and unwritten—*anathema sit* (AD 787).

If anyone shall say that the married state excels the state of virginity or celibacy and that it is better and happier to be united in marriage than to remain a virgin or celibate—*anathema sit* (AD 1563).

If anyone shall say that the assertions of science should be readily accepted and held as true, even when contrary to revealed church doctrine, and that they may not be condemned by the church—*anathema sit* (AD 1870).

The church is also the church of damnation, and these condemnations are still in effect. *Condemnatus sit* is Latin for *May he be damned!* or *May he go to hell!*

If anyone does not truly and rightly believe . . . that the Divine Word came down from Heaven, was incarnate of the Holy Spirit and Mary ever Virgin, became man, was crucified in the flesh of his own free will, suffered, and was buried, and on the third day rose again and ascended into heaven . . . —*condemnatus sit* (AD 649).

If anyone believes the following: The sacrifice made by the blessed Virgin Mary in the Temple on the occasion of her purification—two doves, one as a burnt offering, the other in atonement for sins—is sufficient evidence that she was in need of purification from sins; and also that her son, whom she presented, was also stained by the stain of his mother—*condemnatus sit* (AD 1690).

Regarding the immediately previous condemnation regarding the Virgin Mary and her newborn son, an explanation may be in order. The evangelist Luke wrote:

> **And when the time came for their purification according to the law of Moses, [Mary and Joseph] brought [the infant Jesus] up to Jerusalem to present him to the Lord . . . and to offer a sacrifice according to what is said in the Law of the Lord, "a pair of turtle doves or two young pigeons"** [see Lev 12:6–8] (Lk 2:22–24).

The Jansenists, a group of seventeenth century Catholics, argued that Luke's gospel showed that Mary and Jesus were not free of sin. The church damned the Jansenists:

> The most blessed Virgin Mary from the first moment of her conception was, by the singular grace and privilege of the Almighty God, in view of the merits of Christ Jesus the Savior of the human race, preserved immune from all stain of Original Sin . . . and this is therefore firmly and constantly to be believed. . . . Wherefore, if any persons shall dare to think, which God forbid, otherwise than has been defined by us, let them clearly know that they are condemned (Pope Pius IX, *Ineffabilis Deus* [The Immaculate Conception], AD 1854).

The church thereby also damned Luke, who told the incident.

DAMNATION OF PROTESTANT SCHOLARSHIP

In the late nineteenth and early twentieth centuries, Protestant scholars, greatly influenced by the many contemporary scientific discoveries, decided to examine the New Testament in a scientific light. In 1907, the new scholarship was condemned in the Decree *Lamentabili* (*Articles of Modernism Condemned*). Here are some of the condemned ideas:

- The Gospel parables were contrived by the evangelists and by Christians of the second and third generations after the Crucifixion to explain the poor results of Jesus' preaching among the Jews.

- In many of their accounts, the evangelists narrated not so much the truth as what they thought would, although false, be more helpful to their readers.

- Until the Canon had been defined and constituted, the Gospels were constantly added to and amended. Therefore, there remains no more than a slight and uncertain trace of Christ's teachings.

- St. John's accounts are not really history but a mystical contemplation. . . . The statements contained in his Gospel are theological meditations about the mystery of salvation and devoid of historical truth.

- It is obvious to anyone who is not led by preconceived opinions that either Jesus taught in error the immediate coming of the Messiah or most of his teachings, as contained in the synoptic Gospels, lack authenticity.

ORIGINAL SIN AND EVIL

ORIGINAL SIN: ADAM AND EVE

The church blames Original Sin on Adam and Eve, our original parents. The church says they committed a grave sin by disobeying God, and their disobedience was the Original

Sin. The church is unjust. Adam is our common father and
Eve our common mother. All mankind is descended from
them and owes its very existence to them. Instead of honoring
our mother and father, the church dishonors them and breaks
the Fifth Commandment by unjustly accusing them of trans-
mitting Original Sin.

God forbade Adam from eating the fruit from the tree that
gave man knowledge to discriminate good from evil. Knowing the difference between good and evil was reserved only for
God. Before eating the forbidden fruit, Adam could not have
known the significance of disobedience, because he had not
yet tasted the fruit that would enable him to know it. Only *after* eating the fruit did Adam realize that it was evil to be disobedient.

God must have known that Adam and Eve would one day
eat the fruit, because God created man with curiosity, and God
created the tree. Why did God create the tree if not to pique
their curiosity? Eating the forbidden fruit instantly satisfied
Adam's curiosity and banished his ignorance. Expelled from
the Garden of Eden, Adam and his descendants, in addition to
engaging in physical labor, would soon become engaged in
intellectual work, including pondering the great philosophical
problems: Why did God create evil? Why did God create
mankind? What is the meaning of life? What is the reason for
suffering? Why did God punish mankind so severely? Is there
really a place called heaven similar to Eden? If so, does one
really want to go there only to become bored once more?

If man wants to return to Eden, he must now create his own
garden—his own paradise—through hard work. Sooner or
later, he will come to the realization that God created evil, for
the snake was present in the Garden of Eden before Adam's so-
called fall. That is the great lesson of Eden. Evil like weeds is
always lurking in the garden. There is no way to eradicate it.
Controlling it is a constant challenge.

In the fifth century, Pelagius, a British theologian, left his native Britain to visit Rome. He found that immorality among the clergy was rampant, with all manner of sexual promiscuity. The clergy in Rome defended its behavior by means of the doctrine of Original Sin, saying that mankind was in bondage to lust, had no free will to overcome it, but placed its hope in the saving grace of Jesus Christ. How many priests today use that excuse when engaged in forbidden behavior?

The clergy encouraged Pelagius to join them in their orgies, but he, exerting his free will, refused. He said, how convenient for men to take no responsibility for their behavior and place all blame on the determinism of Original Sin and to rely on the saving grace of Jesus Christ!

Pelagius argued that Adam's sin could not have been passed on to the rest of humanity. Adam's disobedience injured Adam alone. Pelagius also said that lust cannot be sinful because without it there could be no way for mankind to **be fruitful and multiply**. Lust was natural, a gift from God. Adam eventually would have died even if he had not been disobedient. Newborns are innocent; so newborns who die unbaptized have eternal life. Finally, people do not die because of Adam's sin but because God in his goodness and mercy created death. Augustine and the church condemned Pelagius.

THE PROBLEMS OF ORIGINAL SIN

The doctrine of Original Sin has many problems, not the least of which are its conflicts with teachings of Jesus. Jesus taught that children were not stained with Original Sin:

> *Truly, I say to you, unless you turn and become like children, you will never enter the kingdom of heaven* (Mt 18:3).

> *Let the children come to me . . . for to such belongs the kingdom of heaven* (Mt 19:14; Mk 10:14; Lk 18:16).

THE SOUL IS GOOD AND THE BODY IS EVIL

In antiquity, there were Greek philosophers who taught the soul is good and the body is evil. With that philosophy in mind, consider the following: A man picks his nose. If one believed that the soul is good and the body is evil, one might say, "Cut off the finger, or cut off the nose!" Another man is masturbating. One might say, "Cut off the hand!" or . . . . Yet another man is aroused at the sight of a beautiful woman. One might say, "Pluck out the eyes!" or . . . . Jesus of Nazareth said something similar:

> *If your hand is your undoing, cut it off! . . . And if it is your eye, gouge it out! It is better to enter the Kingdom of Heaven with one eye than to keep both eyes and be thrown into hell!* (Mk 9:43–49).

By contrast, the prophet Ezekiel expressed a point of view more typically Jewish:

> **It is the soul that sins, and it is the sinning soul that shall die** (Ezek 18:20).

PAUL AND ORIGINAL SIN

Paul was the first to write of Original Sin although he did not call it by that name: **Sin came into the world through one man [Adam]** (Rom 5:12); **the wages of sin is death** (Rom 6:23). Augustine coined the term Original Sin and extended Paul's notions that Adam passed on his sin to the rest of humanity, and that through divine retribution, Adam lost free will and gained determinism. Augustine taught God punished all mankind further by afflicting it with lust and death: "For it was by the evil use of his free will [freely deciding to be disobedient] that man [Adam] destroyed both free will and himself [and mankind]" (*The Nicene and Post-Nicene Fathers*, First Series, vol. 3, St. Augustine, Enchiridion [Handbook of Faith, Hope, and Love], 9:30, p. 247). Augustine went on to teach that the only cure for Original Sin was the Crucifixion of Jesus Christ and the grace which that bestowed on humanity.

AUGUSTINE'S EVIDENCE FOR ORIGINAL SIN

Augustine provided the following evidence for Original Sin:

> "[T]here is none free from sin, not even the infant who has lived but a day. . . . I have myself observed a baby to be jealous, though it could not speak; it was livid as it watched another infant at the breast. . . . If [as the psalmist says,] "I was brought forth in iniquity, and in sin did my mother conceive me" [Ps 51:7], where . . . or when was I . . . ever innocent? (*Confessions*, chap. 7).

A one-day-old infant can hardly see, let alone be jealous. The baby's instinctual behavior to satisfy its hunger has nothing to do with Adam's disobedience. Animals, including mankind, have the instinct of self-interest and selfishness for the purpose of survival, and either God made them that way, or as a modern biologist would say, the genes program them with those characteristics. Augustine may be excused for his ignorance of genetics, but the modern church may not. For Augustine the choice was to blame God or Adam. Augustine chose to blame Adam, and the Second Council of Orange in 529 declared: "We must, with God's help, preach [Original Sin], and believe it!" [That statement suggests that the church had a hard time believing it.] And fourteen centuries later, in 1950, Pope Pius XII declared:

> Original Sin is a fact. It is the result of a sin committed in actual history by an individual man named Adam, and it is a quality native to all of us simply because it has been handed down by descent from him (*Humani generis*).

DETERMINISM VS. FREEDOM

The church teaches that God has a master plan for the universe. If that is so, then determinism existed before Adam's sin; and God, not Adam, is responsible for man's proclivity to disobedience. The scientific evidence shows that in spite of a prevailing determinism some freedom exists: Electrons sometimes jump at random as they orbit; genetic mutations occur at random; probability theory, of which the Uncertainty Principle is an example, shows the necessary role of chance in the real world; and statisticians speak of "degrees of freedom."

DARKNESS VS. LIGHT

The New Testament extolls light as if it comes from God, and damns darkness as it if comes from the devil. That conflicts with the Old Testament which teaches that God created both light and darkness, and that darkness has a special holiness:

> **I am the Lord [YHVH], and there is no other. I form light and create darkness** (Is 45:6–7).

> **You heard the voice [of God] out of the midst of the darkness** (Deut 5:23).

The Lord [YHVH] has set the sun in the heavens, but has said that he would dwell in thick darkness (1 Kings 8:12).

The Lord [YHVH] has said that he would dwell in thick darkness (2 Chron 6:1).

[God] made darkness his covering round him (Ps 18:11).

EUCHARIST

CANNIBALISM

The church teaches that in the Eucharist the faithful give thanks to the Father for sending the son to be sacrificed for the redemption of the world, whereupon the faithful eat the son. The wooden cross on which Jesus was crucified was the "true" altar on which the Father sacrificed the son; a church altar is merely a symbol of the true altar. The eucharist is a feast, "a Paschal banquet in which Christ is consumed" (*Catechism of the Catholic Church*, p. 334).

The eucharist is based on the following teachings of Jesus:

> *I am the living bread. . . . If anyone eats of this bread, he will live forever; and the bread . . . is my flesh. . . . [H]e who eats my flesh and drinks my blood has eternal life. . . . [H]e who eats me will live* (Jn 6:51–57).

This is cannibalism. And because it was said before an all male audience, it has hints of homosexuality. No wonder, then, that many of the disciples grumbled: **"This is a hard saying. Who can listen to it?"** (Jn 6:60). When Jesus saw the negative reaction the teaching invoked, he told the disciples that they had misunderstood; he had been speaking not literally but figuratively:

> *Do you take offense at this? . . . It is the spirit that gives life, the flesh is of no avail; the words that I have spoken to you are [not flesh and blood but] spirit and life* (Jn 61–63).

But, it was too late: **After this, many of his disciples withdrew and no longer went about with him** (Jn 6:66). Jesus' words were seen as an abomination. For God's Law teaches repeatedly:

> **You shall eat no blood whatever** (Lev 7:26).

> **If any man of the house of Israel or of the strangers that sojourn among them eats any blood, I will set my face against that person who eats blood, and will cut him off from among his people** (Lev 17:10).

> **No person among you shall eat blood** (Lev 17:12).

> **You shall not eat blood** (Deut 12:16; 15:23).

When Jesus saw the many followers who were abandoning him, he turned to the twelve apostles and said: *Do you also want to desert me?* (Jn 6:60–7). Peter, speaking for the twelve, indicated they understood that Jesus had spoken figuratively and that by flesh and blood Jesus meant his words: **Your words are words of eternal life** (Jn 6:67–68). At the end of the lengthy discourse, Jesus reaffirmed that he was speaking figuratively: *I have spoken to you in figures of speech* (Jn 16:25). They accepted Jesus' clarification, for the early church continued to teach: **[It is] necessary . . . that you abstain . . . from blood** (Acts 15:28–29). However, when the church became predominantly gentile and no longer apostolic, it taught that Jesus was not speaking figuratively but literally. Furthermore, the gentile church taught that when it consecrates bread and wine, these substances actually turn into Jesus' flesh and blood. The Council of Trent in the sixteenth century declared:

> Because Christ our Redeemer said that it was truly his body that he was offering in bread, it has always been the conviction of the Church . . . that by the consecration of the bread and wine there takes place a change of the whole substance of the bread into the substance of the body of Christ . . . and of the whole substance of the wine into the substance of his blood. This change the Holy Catholic Church has fittingly and properly called transubstantiation.

Primitive man believed he became what he ate, so cannibals sought out their most powerful enemy. They thought by eating him they, too, would become powerful. The gentiles, perceiving the Jews as their most powerful enemy, adopted the Jews' most powerful representative, Jesus of Nazareth, and ate him. They eat him still.

EATING DIONYSUS

The Greeks who celebrated the mystery religion and worshipped Dionysus, son of Zeus, son of god, ate the god Dionysus. At first his celebrants feasted on wild animals devoured raw, and they believed they were mysteriously feasting on the god's own flesh and blood (portrayed in Euripides' play *Bacchae*). In time, they gave up eating wild animals, but insofar as Dionysus was the god of wine, continued to drink the sacramental wine, which they believed was the god's blood. If the worshippers of Dionysus were to become Christians, they would have to eat Jesus of Nazareth, too. They did. And they do. The sacrament remained. The god changed. Old wine in new skins.

WORSHIPING THE EUCHARIST

The church teaches that at the moment the priest consecrates the bread and the wine, the bread and wine become the Son of God. Therefore, the faithful worship and adore the Eucharist because the consecrated bread and wine have become Christ who is God. The faithful then eat the Eucharist and become united with Christ: "The Sacrament of the Eucharist effects union with Christ" (*The teaching of the Catholic Church*, p. 280). By eating Christ, the faithful become Christ. This belief has serious implications:

- The bread and wine are not Christ until the priest incants the sacred words. Christ does not come until the moment the priest invokes him. Christ, then, is as obedient to the priest as a dog is to its master.
- The faithful by eating the Eucharist eat Christ. Jesus said, ***Do you not see that whatever goes into the mouth passes into the stomach, and is evacuated into the latrine?*** [εἰσ ἀφεδρῶνα ἐκβάλλεται] (Mt 15:17). So Jesus himself tells us part of Christ ends up in the latrine.
- If the Eucharist is Christ, but the faithful have to eat the Eucharist repeatedly, then Christ is not eternal, but only intermittent.
- Bread and wine are not God-made, but man-made. Wheat and grapes are God-made. To make bread and wine, man has to process wheat and grapes. Man has to make the bread and wine of the Eucharist. Since the Eucharist is man-made, Christ is a man-made god.

MARY

MARY "EVER-VIRGIN"

The church teaches curious things about Mary, the mother of Jesus. First and foremost, it teaches that Mary is "ever-virgin" when the gospels teach otherwise:

> **[Joseph] took [Mary for] his wife, but had not intercourse with her until the child was born** (Mt 1:25).

"Until" shows that Joseph had intercourse with Mary after the child was born. Jesus had brothers (Mk 3:31). The word *brothers*, whether in ancient Greek or modern English, means sons of the same mother. Brothers are not cousins or brothers-by-adoption or half-brothers or step-brothers, as the church would have the faithful believe. If Jesus had no brothers, and if Mary had been "ever-virgin," the gospels surely would have said so, that being extraordinarily unique. Instead the gospels say:

> **Is this not the carpenter's son? Is not his mother called Mary? And are not his brothers James and Joseph and Simon and Judas? And are not all his sisters with us?** (Mt 13:55–56).

> **Is this not the carpenter, the son of Mary and the brother of James and Joseph and Judas and Simon, and are not his sisters here with us?** (Mk 6:3).

Moreover, how could Mary's hymen remain intact as Jesus was being born? Anyone who raises that question is deserving of death, according to the church. Indeed, the church tells a tale of a midwife who came to examine Mary to see whether Mary's hymen was intact after she had given birth to Jesus. As soon as the woman inserted her hand into Mary's vagina, she was struck dead for her lack of faith.

Come now, what little boy doesn't think his mother is a virgin? But the little boy grows up!

"MOTHER OF GOD"

The church declared that Mary was the "mother of God." But the Old Testament does not say that God had a mother, and the New Testament does not say that God had a mother. Surely the bible would have said that God had a mother if God had had a mother! Jesus nowhere called Mary "mother of God." Not even the angel of the annunciation, on telling Mary that she was going to have a son, said she was going to become the "mother of God." The angel saluted Mary thus: **Hail, O favored one** (Lk 1:28). The church, not believing that the angel had given his salutation correctly, gave its own version: "Hail Mary, full of grace. . . . Hail Mary, Mother of God. . . ." And in AD 1891, Pope Leo XIII infallibly declared: "Mary, worthy of all praise, is the powerful mother of the all-powerful God."

"POWERFUL MOTHER"

Jewish mothers are well known for their power, and Mary was no exception. Consider her behavior at the wedding at Cana:

> [T]here was a marriage at Cana in Galilee. . . . When the wine ran out, the mother of Jesus said to him, "They have no wine." And Jesus said to her, *O woman! What have you to do with me! My hour has not yet come!* His mother said to the servants [thereby appeasing her angry son by pretending to transfer her power to him], "Do whatever he tells you." Now, six stone jars were

> standing there. . . . Jesus said to [the servants], *Fill the jars with water.* And they filled them up to the brim. He said to them, *Now draw some out, and take it to the steward of the feast*. . . . When the steward of the feast tasted the water now become wine, [he] did not know where it came from, but the servants who had drawn the water knew (Jn 2:1–9).

At first, Jesus scolds his mother, telling her not to order him about; but in the end, Mary gets her way, although she pretends through flattery that it really is Jesus' way. That story shows how easily Mary could manipulate her son and what great power she held over him. As the pope said, Mary is an "all-powerful mother," but not, as he also said, the "mother of the all-powerful God." Mary is the mother of Jesus of Nazareth.

THE ASSUMPTION OF MARY

In 1950, Pope Pius XII declared in the Apostolic Constitution *Munificentissimus Deus* the Assumption of the Virgin Mary. By assumption is meant Mary went to heaven in her physical body:

> By the assumption of the Blessed Virgin, we mean that her body was taken up into heaven after her death. We believe in it 1) because the church cannot teach error. . . . 2) because no one ever claimed to have a relic of our blessed mother's body [neither a finger, nor a breast, nor a lock of hair, nor her hymen]; and surely the apostles, who knew and loved her, would have secured some relic had her body remained upon the earth.
>
> All these arguments and considerations of the church fathers and theologians rest on sacred Scripture for their ultimate foundations. . . . Since our Redeemer is the son of Mary and observed the divine Law most perfectly, he certainly could only honor his beloved

Mother with an honor second only to that given to his eternal Father; and seeing that by preserving her from the corruption of the grave, he could give her such great honor, we must believe that he actually did so.

The fathers thought of the Virgin Mary as the new Eve, who though subject to the new Adam, was still most closely united with him. The struggle which the blessed Virgin endured in common with her son was to end in the glorification of her virginal body. . . .

Thus, from all eternity . . . the august Mother of God is united in a mysterious way with Jesus Christ . . . the noble companion of the divine Redeemer . . . as the crowning glory of her privileges. . . .

Like her Son before her, she conquered death, and was raised body and soul to the glory of heaven where as Queen she shines refulgent at the right hand of her Son. . . (1 Tim 1:17).

Therefore, since the Catholic Church, which the Spirit of Truth actively and infallibly directs in perfecting the knowledge of revealed truth . . . [and] since the bishops of the entire world almost unanimously petition that the truth of the bodily assumption of the blessed Virgin Mary into heaven be defined as a dogma of the divine Catholic faith . . . which truth is founded on sacred Scriptures, we deem the moment ordained in the plan of divine Providence has arrived for us to proclaim solemnly this extraordinary privilege of the Virgin Mary.

We proclaim and define it as dogma revealed by God, that the Immaculate Mother of God, Mary ever Virgin, when the course of her earthly life was finished, was taken up body and soul into the glory of heaven. . . .

As proof for Mary's assumption, the pope gave the following:

> **To the King of the ages, immortal, invisible, the only God, be honor and glory forever and ever** (1 Tim 1:17).

The pope's declaration was "dogma revealed by God." Mary was the "new Eve" united in a mysterious way with her son Jesus Christ, the "new Adam." Something is amiss! Adam and Eve were husband and wife, whereas Mary and Jesus were mother and son! Is this not heavenly incest? The pope further declared, "[F]rom all eternity . . . the august Mother of God is united in a mysterious way with Jesus Christ." How could Mary mysteriously united with Jesus not become incorporated into the Trinity? The pope further asserted that the Virgin Mary, after her assumption, sits at the right hand of her son. The pope, therefore, claimed to be more knowledgeable and more powerful than Jesus, who taught:

> *To sit at my right or left is not for me to grant; it is for those to whom it has already been assigned by my Father* (Mt 20:23; Mk 10:40).

LOVE

LOVE OF ENEMIES: THE SPANISH INQUISITION
The church preaches love, especially love of enemies, but the Spanish Inquisition is but one example to show the church does not practice what it preaches.

During the Spanish Inquisition, when Jews and heretics were burned at the stake in an "act of faith" (*auto-da-fe*) to the glory of God, the priests intoned the following commandment of Jesus:

> *If a man does not abide in me, he is cast forth as a*
> *branch is cast forth and dries up. And the branches*
> *are gathered, thrown into the fire, and burned*
> (Jn 15:5–6).

Why did the church find it necessary to burn nonbelievers at the stake when it had faith they were going to burn eternally in hell? The church apparently did not have enough faith.

GOD LOVES THE JEWS ETERNALLY

God loves the Jews eternally, no matter how grave their sins, for God's love is unconditional and everlasting:

> **In overflowing wrath for a moment I hid my face**
> **from you, but with everlasting love I will have com-**
> **passion on you, says the Lord [YHVH], your Re-**
> **deemer** (Is 54:8).

> **Thus says the Lord: The mountains may disappear,**
> **and the hills; but I shall never stop loving you**
> (Is 54:10).

> **Thus says the Lord [YHVH]: . . . . I have loved you**
> **with an everlasting love** (Jer 31:2–3).

> **Thus says the Lord [YHVH]: Cease your weeping.**
> **. . . Is Ephraim [Israel] still my darling boy? The**
> **child in whom I delight? No sooner do I turn my**
> **back on him, then I think of him. And my heart**
> **yearns for him, so filled am I with tenderness for**
> **him** (Jer 31:16–22).

The love of God for the Jews is the unconditional love of a father for a son. Significantly, the New Testament Father never expressed such love for the Son.

GOD OF WRATH AND JUSTICE

The church teaches that the God of the Old Testament is not a god of love, but a god of wrath and justice. The church bears false witness against God:

> **When I look at your heavens, the work of your fingers, the moon and the stars, which you have established, what is man that you are mindful of him, and the son of man that you care for him?** (Ps 8:34).

> **The Lord [YHVH] is merciful and gracious, slow to anger and abounding in steadfast love. . . . He has not treated us as our sins demand or requited us for our iniquities. As high as the heaven is above the earth, so great is his mercy toward them that revere him** (Ps 103:8–11).

> **O give thanks to the Lord [YHVH], for he is good, for his steadfast love endures forever** (Ps 106:1–2).

> **O give thank to the Lord [YHVH], for he is good, for his steadfast love endures forever** (Ps 107:1).

> **Let them thank the Lord [YHVH] for his enduring love, and for the marvelous things he has done for men** (Ps 107:8).

> **O give thanks to the Lord [YHVH], for he is good, for his steadfast love endures forever. O give thanks to the God of gods, for his steadfast love endures forever. O give thanks to the Lord of lords, for his steadfast love endures forever. . . . endures forever . . . endures forever . . . forever . . . forever . . . forever. . . . O give thanks to the God of heaven, for his steadfast love endures forever** (Ps 136).

> **When Israel was a child, I loved him. Out of Egypt I called my son [Israel]. The more I called my people, the more they ran away. . . . Yet it was I who taught Ephraim [Israel] how to walk. I took them up in my arms** (Hos 11:1 ff.).

Where in the New Testament is there love comparable to this love?

PLURALISM

The church teaches that pluralism among the Christian denominations is a "scandal" because the church is monolithic, catholic, universal.

But the psalmist, the Hebrew prophets, Jesus of Nazareth, and even the church fathers do not agree with the church:

Psalmist:

> **Let the peoples praise thee, O God; let all the peoples praise thee! Let the nations be glad and sing for joy, for thou dost judge the peoples with equity and guide the nations upon earth** (Ps 67:3–5).

Prophets:

> **My house shall be called a house of prayer for all peoples** (Is 56:7).

> **Should I not pity Nineveh, that great [gentile] city?** (Jon 4:11).

> **Have we not all one Father? Has not one God created us all?** (Mal 2:10).

Jesus of Nazareth:

> *Is it not written,* **My house shall be called a house of prayer for all peoples?** (Mk 11:17).

> *In my Father's house are many mansions* (Jn 14:2).

Peter:

> **God shows no partiality. In every nation, anyone who fears him and does what is right is acceptable to him** (Acts 10:35).

Paul:

> **Is God the God of the Jews only? Is he not the God of the Gentiles as well? Yes! Of the Gentiles also, since there is only one God** (Rom 3:29–30).

> **There is no distinction between Jew and Greek. The same God is God of all** (Rom 10:12).

Origen, church father of the third century:

> [A]ny teaching which has had a serious origin, and is beneficial to life, has caused different sects. . . . [S]ince the problems [discussed by philosophers] allow of considerable diversity of opinion, on this account very many sects indeed have come into existence. . . . [Similarly, Christians] interpreted differently the scriptures . . . and sects arose (Chadwick, *Contra Celsum*, 3:12, pp. 135–136).

> If [Celsus] thinks it is a charge against Christianity that there are several sects among Christians, on this analogy would it not be considered a charge against phi-

losophy that among the sects of philosophers there is disagreement? . . . . These are the two sects of Ebionites [Christian Jews], the one confessing as we do that Jesus was born of a virgin, the other holding that he was not born in this way but like other men. What criticism is there in this? (ibid., 5:61, pp. 311–312).

THE LAW

CONTEMPT FOR THE LAW

There is no more civilizing influence than law, and there is no human concept more noble than justice. But the church taught contempt for law and justice on the ground that they were ideas from the outmoded Jewish religion. Love and mercy, not law and justice, characterized the religion of the church. To show its disdain for Judaism, the church dismissed it as "legalistic" and called the writings of Moses "Old Law" or "Old Covenant" or "Old Testament." Jesus of Nazareth wryly asks: *But if you do not believe [Moses'] writings, how will you believe my words?* (Jn 5:47).

The church teaches:

> [The Old] Law is . . . imperfect. . . . [I]t shows what must be done, but does not of itself give the strength, the grace of the Spirit, to fulfill it. Because of sin, which it cannot remove, it remains a law of bondage. . . . The New Law [that of the Gospel] is called a *law of love* because it makes us act out of . . . love rather than from fear; a *law of grace* because it confers the strength of grace to act. . . ; a *law of freedom*, because it set us free from the ritual and juridical observances of the Old Law. . . . The perfection of the New Law consists essentially in the precepts of love of God and neighbor . . . (*Catechism of the Catholic Church*, pp. 476–479).

> The Law of the Gospel fulfills and surpasses the Old Law and brings it to perfection (ibid., p. 481).

The church does not tell the truth. The "precepts of love of God and neighbor" come directly from the "Old Law" (Deut 6:4–5; Lev 19:18). Moreover, God teaches there can be no "New Law," and nothing surpasses the "Old Law":

> **You shall not add to the word which I command you, nor take from it** (Deut 4:2).

> **Everything that I command you, you shall be careful to do; you shall not add to it or take from it** (Deut 12:32).

Jesus said:

> *[S]cripture cannot be broken* (Jn 10:35).

Moreover, the "Old Law" can indeed remove sin and therefore is not a "law of bondage":

> **As a father has compassion on his children, so the Lord [YHVH] has compassion on all who revere him. For he knows how we were made** (Ps 103:13–14).

> **Thus says the Lord [YHVH], though your sins are like scarlet, they shall be as white as snow** (Is 1:18).

Jesus taught:

> *Think not that I have come to abolish the law. . . . For truly, I say to you, till heaven and earth pass away, not an iota, not a dot will pass from the law until all is accomplished* (Mt 5:17–18).

Whoever then relaxes one of the least of these commandments and teaches men so, shall be called least in the kingdom of heaven; but he who does them and teaches them shall be called great in the kingdom of heaven (Mt 5:19).

The Gospel of the Kingdom of God is preached, and everyone enters by means of violence! But it is easier for heaven and earth to pass away than for one dot of the Law to become void (Lk 16:161–7).

And one of the scribes . . . asked Jesus, "Which commandment is first of all?" Jesus answered, *The first is, "Hear O Israel: The Lord [YHVH] is our God, the Lord [YHVH] is one" [Deut 6:4]. The second is this, "You shall love your neighbor as yourself" [Lev 19:18]. There is no other commandment greater than these* (Mk 12:28–31).

A lawyer [said], "Master, what must I do to inherit eternal life?" Jesus replied, *What is written in the Law? Tell me which passages one needs to read!* And the man answered, "You shall love the Lord your God . . . [Deut 6:4–5]. And, "You shall love your neighbor as yourself!" [Lev 19:18]. Jesus said to him, *You have given the right answer! Now do it, and you will live!* (Lk 10:25–28).

THE LAW AND THE PSALMS

Although the church scorns the Law of Moses, it adores the Psalms. But it is not possible to adore the Psalms and scorn the Law, for the psalmist sings:

Put false ways far from me; and graciously teach me thy Law (Ps 119:29).

Godless men utterly deride me, but I do not turn from thy Law (Ps 119:51).

Though the cords of the wicked ensnare me, I do not forget thy Law (Ps 119:61).

Thy Law is my delight (Ps 119:77).

Oh, how I love your Law (Ps 119:97).

I love thy Law! (Ps 119:113).

Thy Law is true (Ps 119:142).

I long for thy salvation, O Lord, and thy Law is my delight (Ps 119:174).

OLD LAW: "INSTRUMENT OF LUST"
The church bears false witness against the Law:

> The Law entrusted to Israel . . . became the instrument of 'lust' (Cf. Rom 7:7). . . . Christ's faithful "have crucified the flesh with its passions and desires" (Gal 5:24) (*Catechism of the Catholic Church*, p. 608).

But the New Law could not help Paul crucify his flesh:

> **For I do not do what I want, but I do the very thing I hate. . . . Wretched man that I am! . . . [W]ith my flesh I serve the law of sin!** (Rom 7:7–25).

And the New Law has not been able to help priests crucify the flesh. Contrary to the teachings of the church and Paul, lust does not come from the Old Law. Lust is part of the natural law so beloved by Paul and written on men's hearts or, as a scientist would say, programed into the DNA. Lust is more powerful than love of God and conquers it, as the church has repeatedly shown.

JUSTICE VS. LOVE

The church teaches that the "Old Law" is a legalistic law of Justice, whereas the "New Law" is a law of Love. To see whether this is so, compare the story of Elijah's would-be disciple Elisha with a similar story of Jesus of Nazareth's would-be disciple.

Old Law:

> **Elisha was plowing his fields when Elijah the prophet passed by. Elisha left his oxen and ran after Elijah the prophet shouting, "Let me kiss my father and mother good-bye, and then I will follow you!" Elijah the prophet responded, shouting, "Go and do it! Who's stopping you?" Whereupon Elisha turned and ran home. . . . After that, Elisha followed Elijah and became his disciple** (1 Kings 19:19–21).

New Law:

> **A man said, "I will follow you Lord, but let me first say good-bye to my family at home." Jesus replied,** *No one who puts his hand to the plow and looks back is fit for the Kingdom of God* (Lk 9:61–62).

Who shows love, Elijah or Jesus?

SOCIAL ISSUES

LIBERATION THEOLOGY

The term "Liberation Theology" was coined during the Catholic Bishops' Conference in Medellin, Colombia, in 1968. At that Conference, the clerics of Latin America wrote a document titled the "Medellin Manifesto," which stated that the church in Latin America would reach out to the poor, work toward ending their exploitation, and strive for social justice. The Vatican considered the Manifesto both Marxist and Jewish, too much in accord with the social concerns of the Old Law, not enough in accord with the New Law which is not concerned with social issues. Had not Jesus said as much?

> ***The poor you have with you always*** (Mt 26:11; Mk 14:7; cf. Jn 12:8).

The Old law, as the church said, is indeed greatly concerned with social issues:

> **You shall not wrong a stranger or be hard on him. You were yourselves strangers in Egypt** (Ex 22:20).

> **You shall do no injustice in judgment; you shall not be partial to the poor or defer to the great, but in righteousness shall you judge your neighbor** (Lev 19:15).

> **When a stranger settles with you in your land, you shall not oppress him. He shall be treated as a native-born among you. And you shall love him as you love yourself. Because you were strangers in Egypt** (Lev 19:34).

**When your brother is reduced to poverty and cannot
support himself in the community, you shall assist
him as you would a stranger or a newcomer, and he
shall live with you** (Lev 25:35).

**You shall not harden your heart . . . against your
needy brother, but you shall open your hand to him.
You shall give him enough to satisfy his needs. You
shall give generously. . . . You shall open wide your
hand to your brother, to the needy, and to the poor**
(Deut 15:7–11).

SLAVERY

Jesus would have performed a great service to humanity had
he preached the evils of slavery and encouraged its abolition.
Instead, Jesus called slavery a blessed state:

> ***Blessed is the slave whom the master on his return
> finds doing the things he is supposed to do*** (Lk 12:43).

Paul, paraphrasing Jesus, said:

> **Bid slaves be submissive to their masters** (Tit 2:9).

It is not surprising, therefore, that the church was the last institution to condemn slavery. In the nineteenth century, the British, by means of powerful warships, put an end to the slave
trade. The church did not praise Britain, a Protestant country,
for its humanitarian act, nor did it condemn the nations, most
of them Catholic, that opposed Britain. The church in fact did
not condemn slavery until early in the 20th century and did so
very quietly. After all, condemnation of slavery conflicted
with the teaching of Jesus.

WOMEN

The church teaches that women are at best the servants of men and at worst their seducers and destroyers.

Paul wrote:

> **Women should keep quiet in church** (1 Cor 14:34).

> **Wives, be subject to your husbands. . . . The man is the head of the woman. . . . [W]omen [must] be subject to their husbands in everything** (Eph 5:22–24).

In the fifteen century, the church published *Malleus Maleficarum* [*Hammer for Dealing with Evildoers*], and this is what it had to say about women:

> Women's carnal lust is insatiable. The vagina is never satisfied; and so, for the sake of satisfying their lust, women will have intercourse with the Devil himself.

It appears that misogyny is the basis for the church not allowing women to become priests, but the church teaches that women cannot become priests because all of Jesus of Nazareth's apostles were men; had Jesus wanted women to be priests, he certainly would have selected a woman apostle. By that reasoning, gentiles cannot become priests because all of Jesus' apostles were Jews; had Jesus wanted gentile priests, he certainly would have selected a gentile apostle.

The church has reserved a unique place in hell for women who have had abortions, an "abominable crime." Those women are wallowing up to their necks in a lake of liquified excrement; standing nearby on the shore, their aborted fetuses silently and perpetually point accusing fingers at them.

CELIBACY

The Old Testament recommends marriage and a life of joy:

> **[A] man leaves his father and his mother and cleaves to his wife, and they become one flesh** (Gen 2:24).

> **Enjoy life with the wife whom you love** (Eccles 9:7–9).

But Jesus taught:

> *The sons of this age marry and are given in marriage; but those who are accounted worthy to attain to . . . the resurrection from the dead neither marry nor are given in marriage* (Lk 20:34–35).

And the church teaches:

> If anyone shall say that the married state excels the state of virginity or celibacy and that it is better and happier to be united in marriage than to remain a virgin or celibate—*anathema sit [let him be cursed]* (AD 1563).

CHURCH TEACHINGS ABOUT THE CHURCH

CHURCH TEACHINGS ABOUT THE CHURCH

Here are some of the things the church has taught about itself:

> Anyone who believes that only God the Father may be called God, and who thus believes only in One God, is

heretical in all things and is, in fact, a Jew! (Creed of the Council of Rome, AD 382).

One who by force, terror, and punishment is brought to accept baptism to avoid harm to himself receives . . . the character of Christianity stamped upon him; and must therefore be held to the observance of the Christian faith since, under the circumstances, he did give his consent, even if not unconditionally (letter of Pope Innocent III to Ymbertus, Archbishop of Arles, AD 1201).

The church is so perfect that it is distinct from all human societies and stands far above them (First Vatican Council, AD 1870).

The Church herself, with her marvelous propagation, eminent holiness, and inexhaustible fruitfulness in everything good, her catholic unity and invincible stability, is a great and perpetual motive of credibility and an irrefutable witness to her divine mission (First Vatican Council, *Dei Filius* 3: DS 3013, AD 1884).

PAPAL INFALLIBILITY

The church teaches that on matters of church doctrine and morals, the pope is infallible:

This See of Holy Peter remains free from all blemish or error. . . . Therefore . . . we teach and define that it is a dogma divinely revealed that the Roman Pontiff, when he speaks *ex cathedra*, is in possession of that infallibility which the Divine Redeemer willed that his church should be endowed for divining doctrine regarding faith and morals. . . . But if anyone—which God forbid!— presume to contradict this our definition—*anathema sit!* [*let him be cursed!*] (First Dogmatic Constitution on the Church of Christ, First Vatican Council, AD 1870).

This dogma conflicts with the early church. Jesus did not think Peter was infallible:

> **[Jesus] said to Peter, *Get behind me, Satan! You are a hindrance to me; for you are not on the side of God but of men* (Mt 16:23; cf. Mk 8:33).**

And Paul did not think Peter was infallible. Paul wrote:

> **When Cephas [Peter] came to Antioch, I opposed him to his face, because he stood condemned (Gal 2:11).**

Paul advises against any doctrine of "infallibility":

> **[L]et any one who thinks that he stands take heed lest he fall (1 Cor 10:12).**

Pope John Paul I wrote in the twentieth century:

> [N]o one is infallible! (Albino Luciani, *Illustrissimi*, from the letters between Albino Luciani and St. Bernard de Clairvaux, 1971, p. 43).

This pope died inexplicably one month into his papacy.

DID JESUS OF NAZARETH FOUND THE ROMAN CATHOLIC CHURCH?

The church teaches that Jesus of Nazareth founded the Roman Catholic Church, but he did not. Jesus was born a Jew, lived his life as a Jew, and died a Jew. Like other Jews of his time, he worshiped in synagogues and in the Temple in Jerusalem. He celebrated the Sabbath, the seventh day, not the "Lord's Day," the first day. He celebrated Passover and Hanukah, not Easter and Christmas. He never worshiped before idols or icons, nor bowed down before them. He never burned incense. He was circumcised according to the Hebrew covenant, which he never abrogated nor taught others to do. He was buried according to Mosaic law, which he never called the "Old Law." He founded no new religion, no new *kehal*, ecclesia or church. He worshiped the God of Abraham, Isaac, and Jacob, and that God alone. His only bible was the Hebrew Scriptures, which was complete of itself and required no additions or amendments. He would have been puzzled by the terms Old Testament, New Testament, Old Law, New Law, Old Covenant, New Covenant, Roman Catholic Church.

Jesus declared, ***Hear O Israel, the Lord [YHVH] is our God, the Lord [YHVH] is one!*** (Mk 12:29 [Deut 6:4]).

JESUS, KING OF ISRAEL FROM THE BEGINNING OF TIME

The church teaches that Jesus of Nazareth is King of Israel of the line of David, and that God had this plan in place from the beginning of time. God himself refutes that church teaching:

> **Since the day that I brought my people out of the land of Egypt, I chose no city in all the tribes of Israel in which to build a House that my name might be there, and chose no man as prince over my people Israel. But now I have chosen Jerusalem, that my name may be there, and I have chosen David to be over my people Israel** (2 Chron 6:5–6).

God says plainly that he did not select David at the beginning of time. Therefore, God had no plan at the beginning of time for Jesus.

HOW TO PRAY
The church teaches the faithful to pray thus:

> Prayer cannot be reduced to the spontaneous outpouring
> of interior impulse. . . . One must . . . learn how to pray
> (*Catechism of the Catholic Church*, p. 637). . . . Prayer
> . . . has access to the Father only if we pray "in the
> name" of Jesus (ibid., 640). . . . The most appropriate
> places for prayer are . . . oratories, monasteries, places
> of pilgrimage, and above all the church (ibid., 647).

But Jesus taught his disciples to pray thus:

> *And when you pray, you must not be like the hypo-*
> *crites; for they love to stand and pray . . . [where] they*
> *may be seen by men. . . . But when you pray, go into*
> *your room and shut the door and pray to your Father*
> *who is in secret; and your Father who sees in secret*
> *will reward you. And in praying do not heap up empty*
> *phrases as the Gentiles do; for they think that they*
> *will be heard for their many words. Do not be like*
> *them* (Mt 6:5–8).

CALLING A PRIEST "FATHER"
The church teaches the faithful to call its priests "Father,"
but Jesus of Nazareth taught:

> *Do not call any man on earth "Father." For you have*
> *one Father, and he is in heaven* (Mt 23:9).

LIFESTYLE OF THE POPE
Jesus of Nazareth was a homeless man who did not know
where he would spend the night or get his next meal. But the
pope, the spiritual leader of the church, lives in luxury and

splendor in the style of a Roman Emperor, in a palace adorned with riches and treasure, surrounded by servants ready to do his bidding, and feasting on the finest fare.

Jesus condemned riches and spectacles. The coronation of a pope with all its splendor did not come to an end until late in the twentieth century when Pope John Paul I refused coronation at his inauguration. That set a precedent for the pope's successors. The funeral of a pope has replaced the coronation as perhaps the greatest show on earth. Papal funerals last for nine days with pomp and pageantry, costing millions of dollars. Dignitaries from around the world are invited, and worldwide television and the press cover the event. Throughout the spectacle, the words of Jesus are assiduously ignored: *Be careful not to make a show of your religion before men. For if you do, no reward awaits you in your Father's house in heaven* (Mt 6:1).

WHAT UNIFIES THE GENTILES?

What unifies the gentiles? What reconciles them? Jesus of Nazareth? No. Paul astutely observed that the one thing that reconciled gentiles was their universal hatred and rejection of the Jews. Paul nonetheless warned that there was no life after death without acceptance of the Jews:

> **Rejection of the Jews brings about reconciliation of the world, but acceptance of the Jews brings about life after death** (Rom 11:15).

WHO ARE GOD'S ELECT?

The church teaches that it is the church that is God's elect. But according to Jesus of Nazareth it is those who fulfill the Old Law's two greatest commandments:

A lawyer [said], "Master, what must I do to inherit eternal life?" Jesus replied, *What is written in the Law? Tell me which passages one needs to read!* And the man answered, "You shall love the Lord your God . . . [Deut 6:4–5]. And, "You shall love your neighbor as yourself!" [Lev 19:18]. Jesus said to him, *You have given the right answer! Now do it, and you will live!* (Lk 10:25–28).

FAITH AND CREEDS

CREEDS

The Roman Catholic Church teaches:

> We begin our profession of faith by saying: "I believe" or "we believe" (*Catechism of the Catholic Church*, p. 13).

> Faith is certain. It is more certain than all human knowledge (ibid., p. 43).

The word *creed* comes from the Latin *credo*, which means "I believe." Creeds are belief systems that by their very name indicate that evidence is not required. Without evidence, however, one cannot speak with confidence, but only with doubt. When one speaks with doubt, one prefaces a statement with "I believe," whereas when one speaks with confidence, as in the case of facts, it is not necessary to preface the statement. One does not say "I *believe* that Rome is the capital of Italy" or "I *believe* that I am hungry" or "I *believe* that 1+1+1=3."

One says, "Rome *is* the capital of Italy" or "I *am* hungry" or "1+1+1=3."

It is of the highest significance that, unlike the church, Jesus of Nazareth and the apostles had no creeds. Jesus proclaimed as a statement of fact:

> ***Hear O Israel, the Lord [YHVH] is our God, the Lord [YHVH] is one!*** (Mk 12:29 [Deut 6:4]).

Jesus never considered God someone to be believed in. Jesus never said, *Credo in unum deum* (*I believe in one God*). Jesus was not dubious about the existence of God. Jesus did not *believe*. Jesus *knew*! Jesus said to the Gentile woman: ***You [Gentiles] worship what you do not know. We [Jews] worship what we know*** (Jn 4:20–22).

The word "believe" appears in the Torah (the first five books of the Bible, Christian as well as Hebrew) only eleven times, and then rarely in association with belief in God. And the Torah is about twice as long as all four gospels combined. By contrast, the word "believe" appears in the gospels eighty-three times, and almost all these "believes" are associated with belief in Jesus of Nazareth! Ironically, John's gospel, whose primary intent was to remove all doubt, contains the largest number of "believes"—fifty-five! John, contrary to his intent, ends up expressing more doubt than any other book in the New Testament.

The church, not having the same confidence in God that Jesus had, not only had a creed, but has composed new creeds over the centuries to keep up with its changing definitions of Christ and God. As the complexity of the definitions increase, so do the creeds. Here are some of the important ones.

APOSTLES' CREED

The Apostles' Creed was written in the third century. It was given its name to give it authority, but there is no evidence that the apostles wrote it. The Apostles' Creed was changed over the centuries, until it reached its present form, perhaps as late as the ninth century:

> I believe in God, the Father almighty, Creator of heaven and earth.
>
> And in Jesus Christ, His only Son, our Lord; who was conceived by the Holy Spirit, born of the Virgin Mary, suffered under Pontius Pilate, was crucified, died, and was buried. He descended into hell; the third day He arose again from the dead; He ascended into heaven, sits at the right hand of God the Father almighty; from thence He shall come to judge the living and the dead.
>
> I believe in the Holy Spirit, the Holy Catholic Church, the communion of saints, the forgiveness of sins, the resurrection of the body, and life everlasting. Amen (*The Teaching of Christ*, p. 516).

TERTULLIAN'S CREED

Tertullian, a church father of the third century, was a man of great faith and wit. He composed the most succinct of all the creeds. Although never said in church, his creed expresses the most faith—the faith that the church teaches "is more certain than all human knowledge":

> The Son of God died; it is by all means to be believed because it is absurd. And He was buried and rose again; the fact is certain, because it is impossible (*The Ante-Nicene Fathers*, vol. 3, Tertullian, On the Flesh of Christ, chap. 5, p. 525).

NICENE CREED

The Nicene Creed is the most famous of the creeds. It was composed in the fourth century during the Council of Nicea, where Jesus of Nazareth was deified by a vote of men. At Nicea, Trinity was not yet called as such, and the Holy Spirit was added almost as an afterthought. Here is the Nicene Creed:

> We believe in one God, the Father Almighty, Creator of all things visible and invisible; and in one Lord Jesus Christ, the Son of God, only-begotten of the Father, that is, of the substance of the Father, God of God, light of light, very God of very God, begotten, not made, being of the same substance with the Father, by whom all things were made in heaven and in earth, who for us men and for our salvation came down from heaven, was incarnate, was made man, suffered, rose again the third day, ascended into the heavens, and He will come to judge the living and the dead. And in the Holy Ghost. Those who say, There was a time when He was not, and He was not before He was begotten, and He was made of nothing (He was created), or who say that He is of another hypostasis, or of another substance (than the Father), or that the Son of God is created, that He is mutable, or subject to change, the Catholic Church anathematizes (Hefele, *A History of the Christian Councils*, pp. 293–295).

Making Jesus a god created great theological problems. Prior to his deification, Jesus had died, been resurrected, and by his death redeemed humanity. Once he was declared a god, however, he could not die because the immortal gods do not die. After Nicea, the church realized that since Jesus was a god, the previous creeds had been erroneous. Jesus had not died as those creeds said; he merely suffered. But if Jesus did not die, there could be no redemption and no resurrection. Without redemption and resurrection, there was no Christianity! It took the church a thousand years to come up with a so-lution, although inadequate, to this difficult puzzle.

The Nicene Creed as formulated at Nicea had not adequately defined and described the Holy Spirit. So another Council was convened in Constantinople in AD 381, at which the Nicene Creed was corrected by expanding the description of the Holy Spirit (interchangeably called the Holy Ghost) and the follow-ing was added:

> And (I believe) in the Holy Ghost, the Lord and giver of life; who proceeds from the Father (and the Son). Who together with the Father and the Son is adored and glo-rified; who spoke through the prophets (*The teaching of the Catholic Church*, p. 425).

Does the Holy Ghost proceed only from the Father or from the Father and the Son? In the church in Spain, the formula "and the son" or filioque was added: the Holy Ghost proceeds from the Father *and the Son*. The Roman Catholic Church in the West liked the formula but did not make it obligatory. That preserved the unity with the Church in the East, which ob-jected to the term. Then in the eleventh century, without con-sulting the eastern church, the western church made the for-mula obligatory which created enormous dissension. This time, with no leader like Constantine to enforce unanimity, the church was rent asunder into Roman Catholic Church and Eastern Orthodox Church. The two churches completely sepa-rated, each side cursing the other and calling it heretical, each side claiming to be acting in accordance with the will of God and inspired by the Holy Ghost. A formula invented by men and based on no information did this.

Meanwhile, the important question, Did Jesus die?, contin-ued to perplex all the churches. That problem defies solution to this day. Shortly we shall continue to explore it.

ATHANASIAN CREED

The church composed the Athanasian Creed, the most comprehensive and sophisticated creed of all, between the late fourth and sixth centuries. This creed more fully addressed the Holy Spirit as one of the three persons of God but denied his role in the begetting of the Son. It is the first creed to mention Trinity. And although it spoke of the two natures of Jesus Christ, human and divine, it did not clearly address the puzzle of whether Jesus died in his humanity. The creed glossed over the matter—going from "he suffered" to he "descended into hell, rose again from the dead"—and therefore inadvertently implied that the suffering Jesus had been buried alive and miraculously exhumed himself. The Athanasian Creed:

> Whoever wishes to be saved must first of all hold the Catholic faith, for anyone who does not maintain this whole and inviolate will surely be lost eternally.
> And the Catholic faith is this, that we worship one God in Trinity, and Trinity in Unity, neither confounding the Persons, nor dividing the substance. For there is one person of the Father, another of the Son, and another of the Holy Spirit. But the godhead of the Father, of the Son and of the Holy Spirit is all one, the glory equal, the majesty co-eternal. As the Father is, so is the Son, and so is the Holy Spirit. Uncreated the Father, the Son uncreated, and the Holy Spirit uncreated. The Father immeasurable, the Son immeasurable, and the Holy Spirit immeasurable. The Father eternal, the Son eternal, and the Holy Spirit eternal. And yet there are not three eternals, but one eternal. Just as there are not three uncreateds nor three immeasurables, but one uncreated and one immeasurable. Likewise the Father is almighty, the Son is almighty, and the Holy Spirit is almighty; yet not three almighties, but one almighty. Thus God the Father, God the Son, and God the Holy Spirit; yet not three gods but one God. Thus the Father

is Lord, the Son is Lord, and the Holy Spirit is Lord; yet there are not three Lords, but one Lord. For as we are compelled by Christian truth to acknowledge that each Person by himself is God and Lord, we are forbidden by the true Catholic religion to say that there are three Gods or Lords. The Father is made by none, nor created, nor begotten. The Son is from the Father alone, not made nor created but begotten. The Holy Spirit is from the Father and the Son, not made nor created nor begotten, but proceeding. So there is one Father, not three Fathers; one Son, not three Sons; and one Holy Spirit, not three Holy Spirits. And in this Trinity none is before or after another, none is greater or less, but all three Persons are co-eternal with one another and co-equal. So that in all things, as has already been said above, both Unity in Trinity and Trinity in Unity are to be adored. Therefore whoever will be saved must believe this of the Trinity.

For eternal salvation it is further necessary that we faithfully believe in the incarnation of our Lord Jesus Christ. The right faith is therefore this: that we believe and confess that our Lord Jesus Christ the Son of God is both God and man; God of the substance of the Father, begotten before time, and man of the substance of his mother born in time; perfect God and perfect man, consisting of a rational soul and human body; equal to the Father in his divinity, less than the Father in his humanity; who, although both God and man is not two but one Christ; one, however, not by the conversion of the Godhead into flesh but by the assumption of manhood into God. Wholly one, not by fusion of substance but by unity of person. For as the rational soul and the body are one man, so God and man are one Christ. Who suffered for our salvation, descended into hell, rose again from the dead on the third day, ascended into heaven, sits at the right hand of the Father, whence he will come to judge the living and the dead. When he comes, all men will rise again with their bodies and give an account of their own deeds, and those who have done good will enter into eternal life, and those who have done evil into eternal fire. This is the Catholic faith, and if anyone shall not faithfully and firmly believe it, he cannot be saved (*The teaching of the Catholic Church*, pp. 428–429).

Jesus had warned:

> *And in praying do not heap up empty phrases as the Gentiles do; for they think that they will be heard for their many words. Do not be like them* (Mt 6:5–8).

THE CREED THAT REFUTES ITSELF

In spite of the Athanasian Creed's assertion that the Father and Son are equal, the Creed itself refutes that assertion four times, each time indicating that the son is less than the Father:

1. "The Father is made by none, nor created, nor begotten. The Son is from the Father alone, not made, nor created, but begotten." The son is *begotten*, but the Father is not. Therefore, the Son is less than the Father.

2. "[The Son is] equal to the Father in His divinity, less than the Father in His humanity." The Son is less than the Father in His humanity. Therefore, the Son is less than the Father.

3. "[The Son] sits at the right hand of the Father." Jesus of Nazareth's conception of heaven is a banquet, where the Father, evidently King and Host, sits at the head of the table, while the Son, evidently the guest of honor, is seated at the Father's right. The seating arrangement reveals that the Son is less than the Father.

4. The very order in which the creed names its three persons—Father first, Son second, Holy Spirit third—indicates that the Son is less than the Father. (And the Holy Spirit is least of all.)

Four times the Athanasian Creed indicates that the Son is inferior to the Father, thereby refuting itself that their "glory [is] equal" and confirming what Jesus said: *The Father is greater than I* (Jn 14:28).

THE CREED THAT OMITS THE VIRGIN MARY AND THE HOLY SPIRIT IN BEGETTING JESUS

The Athanasian Creed omits the Virgin Mary and the Holy Spirit in begetting the Son of God. The Athanasian Creed says, the "Son of God is both God and man; God of the substance of the Father, begotten before time, and man of the substance of his mother, born in time." How could the Son of God be "born" without first being begotten or conceived by his Mother *and* the Holy Spirit? The gospel of Luke says: **And the angel said to her [Mary], "The Holy Spirit will come upon you, and the power of the Most High will overshadow you"** (Lk 1:35). And the previous two creeds, the Apostles' and the Nicene, say, the Son of God "was incarnate by the Holy Spirit with the Virgin Mary and was made man." The Athanasian Creed, therefore, conflicts with Luke and the two previous creeds. Why would church theologians do that? I offer the following explanation:

Arius had argued that "there was a time when the Son was not," which means that the Son, unlike the Father, was not eternal, and was therefore inferior to the Father. The Athanasian Creed attempted to refute Arius's irrefutable argument, even at the cost of denying the gospel of Luke and previous creeds, by stating without reasons that the Son was "begotten before time," which the authors of the Creed thought was synonymous with eternal. However, begotten before time is not synonymous with eternal. It is impossible for the Son to be eternal if he was begotten, even if he was begotten before God created time.

And how is it possible that Mary is the Mother of God, when she did not exist before time?

Finally, it does not really matter whether the Son was begotten before or after God created time, because in the last analysis, by being begotten, the Son cannot be eternal. The Son could not have existed before he was begotten. Therefore, as Arius said, the Son, unlike the Father, is not eternal, and is inferior to the Father.

CREEDS FROM THE SIXTH
THROUGH THE THIRTEENTH CENTURY

The Nicene Creed and the Athanasian Creed held sway through the twelfth century. Both creeds made a point of saying that Jesus of Nazareth suffered but neither said he died. How was the puzzle of his death or non-death going to be resolved?

PROFESSION OF FAITH OF THE FOURTH GENERAL
LATERAN COUNCIL, AD 1215

In the thirteenth century, church theologians wrote a new creed that the church believed was the solution to the puzzle whether Christ died. The Profession of Faith of the Fourth General Lateran Council of AD 1215 said that Christ died in his humanity but not in his divinity. In addition to the puzzle's solution, although inadequate, as we shall see, the creed gives a clear exposition of the Eucharist and states that Christ was both priest and victim. That is, Christ sacrificed Christ, for the salvation of humanity.

To return to the puzzle, for the first time since the Apostles' Creed of the third century, a creed said that Jesus not only suffered but died. His death, however, was a highly qualified one. Jesus died in his humanity but lived on in his divinity. That "solution," however, raised new questions that have never been resolved:

1. Jesus died in his humanity but lived on in his divinity. Isn't that so of all righteous people who have immortal souls?

2. Of what significance was Christ's dying in his humanity, when he never ceased living in his divinity? What was his sacrifice? How did it differ from that of other righteous people?

3. Jesus was dead in his humanity only from Friday afternoon to Sunday morning—hardly long enough to be considered worthy of being a redeeming death for all humanity forever and ever.

4. Can a human sacrificial death redeem anyone when human sacrifice is a barbaric practice of primitive man long ago outlawed by civilized nations?

Here is the Profession of Faith of the Fourth General Lateran Council:

> We firmly believe and simply confess that there is only one true God, eternal, immeasurable and unchangeable, incomprehensible, almighty and ineffable, Father, Son and Holy Spirit: three persons indeed but one essence, substance or wholly simple nature: the Father from no one, the Son from the Father alone, and the Holy Spirit equally from both: and without beginning, always, and without end; the Father generating, the Son being born, the Holy Spirit proceeding; consubstantial, co-equal, co-omnipotent and co-eternal; one origin of all things: the Creator of all things visible and invisible, spiritual

and corporal. Who by his almighty power created both orders of creation out of nothing from the beginning of time, the spiritual and corporeal, that is the angelic and the earthly, and then the human order which being constituted of spirit and body is as it were common to both. For the devil and other wicked spirits were indeed created by God good by nature, but they became evil of themselves. Man indeed sinned at the suggestion of the devil. This holy Trinity, undivided in its common essence but distinct in the properties of the Persons, first communicated its doctrine of salvation to the human race to Moses and then to the holy prophets and to others of his servants according to the most perfect plan for the times.

And finally the only-begotten Son of God Jesus Christ, incarnate by the whole Trinity working in common, conceived of Mary ever a Virgin by the cooperation of the Holy Spirit, made true man, composed of a rational soul and a human body, one person in two natures, showed the way of life more clearly. That very same *(person)* although immortal and impassable in his divinity became passible and mortal in his humanity; he suffered on the wood of the cross for the salvation of mankind and died, descended into hell, rose from the dead, and ascended into heaven: but he descended in the soul and rose in the body; but ascended equally in both. . . .

There is indeed one universal Church of the faithful, outside which no one at all is saved. In it the same Jesus Christ is at once priest and victim, whose body and blood are truly contained in the Sacrament of the altar under the species of bread and wine, the bread being transubstantiated into the body by the divine power, and the wine into the blood, so that we receive of his what he received of ours to complete the mystery of unity . . . . (*The teaching of the Catholic Church*, pp. 430– 432).

PROFESSION OF FAITH
OF MICHAEL PALEOLOGUE, AD 1274, VALIDATED
AT THE COUNCIL OF FLORENCE, AD 1431–45

The church, realizing the two natures—one human and the other divine—had not been resolved by the Profession of Faith of the Fourth General Lateran Council, adopted yet another creed later in the thirteenth century called the Profession of Faith of Michael Paleologue (AD 1274).

Michael Paleologue was a Byzantine emperor, a member of the Eastern Orthodox church who tried in vain to unify the Eastern Orthodox and the Roman Catholic churches. He agreed to convert to Roman Catholicism provided that church adopted his profession of faith. The pope agreed and Paleologue converted. But the church was uncomfortable accepting a creed of the Eastern Orthodox church. And so, to give the creed the Roman Catholic stamp of approval, it was validated unchanged in its relevant portion at the Council of Florence, AD 1431–1445, as if it had always been a Roman Catholic Creed.

Michael Paleologue's Profession of Faith was presumably an advance in solving the puzzle of Christ's death and non-death, but it was not. And so, most of the faithful have never heard of it. The Paleologue Profession is as follows:

> We believe in the Holy Trinity. . . . We believe in the *Son of God* himself, the Word of God, eternally born of the Father, . . . equal with the Father in divinity, born in time of the Holy Spirit and Mary ever a Virgin, with a rational soul, having two births, one eternal birth from the Father, the other temporal from his mother; true God and true man, real and perfect in both natures; . . . in and from two natures, that is, divine and human natures, in the unity of one person; in divinity impassable and immortal, but having in his humanity truly suffered with bodily suffering for us and for our salvation; that

> he died and was buried, and descended into hell, and
> the third day rose again from the dead in a true resur-
> rection of the body; that on the fortieth day after his
> resurrection he ascended into heaven with the body in
> which he rose again and with his soul; that he is seated
> at the right hand of God the Father. . . (*The teaching of
> the Catholic Church*, pp. 432–435).

This creed did not solve the problem of the man Jesus' sacrifice for humanity. He was dead in his humanity only three
days, at best a token sacrifice. And he did not die at all in his
divinity. How then was he the Redeemer that took away the
sins of the world?

THE TRIDENTINE PROFESSION OF FAITH, AD 1564 (THE CHURCH LOYALTY OATH)

The church has a loyalty oath, which it administers to clergy
or influential laity who are suspected of not being sufficiently
faithful. Anyone who refuses to take the oath does so under
pain of excommunication and eternal damnation. The oath,
formulated in 1564, is remarkable in completely skirting the
two natures of Jesus Christ and is called the Tridentine Profession of Faith:

> . . . . I acknowledge the sacred Scripture according to
> that sense which Holy Mother Church has held and
> holds, to whom it belongs to decide upon the true sense
> and interpretation. . . .
> I embrace and receive all things and every single thing
> that were defined and declared by the sacred Council of
> Trent concerning *original sin*. . . .
> I hold unswervingly that there is a *purgatory*. . . ;
> likewise that the *Saints* reigning with Christ are to be
> venerated and invoked . . . and that their relics are to be
> venerated. I firmly assert that images of Christ and of

> the ever-virgin Mother of God, as well as of other
> Saints, are to be possessed and retained and that due
> honour and veneration should be accorded them. . . .
> And at the same time I condemn, reject and anathema-
> tize all things contrary thereto and whatever heresies
> have been condemned, rejected and anathematized by
> the Church.
> This true Catholic belief without which no one can be
> saved, which I here freely profess and truly hold, I
> [Name], promise, vow and sear by the help of God to
> hold and confess entire and undefiled most constantly
> to the last breath of life . . . so help me God and these
> holy Gospels of God (*The teaching of the Catholic
> Church*, pp. 436–438).

It is worth comparing the Tridentine Profession of Faith with
the command given by Peter, whom the church considers the
first pope:

> **Tend the flock of God that is in your charge not by
> constraint but willingly . . . not by domineering over
> those in your charge, but being examples to the flock**
> (1 Pet 5:2–4).

MODERN CATECHISM

Ever dissatisfied with its inability to explain the two natures
of Jesus Christ—in spite of the oversimplification, if not glib-
ness, of the formula "he died in his humanity but not in his
divinity"—the church has kept defining and redefining the
concept of the Man-God over the centuries. Because the pro-
liferation of creeds was becoming embarrassing if not scandal-
ous, the church stopped creating them but concentrated on
catechism. Catechism also uses many words, for there is no
economy of words or definitions in church doctrine. Occam's
razor is never used. It cannot be used when dealing with im-

possible and incredible premises, which need to be woven and rewoven into tapestries of greater complexity. The best one can do is to call these extravagant works of philosophy and theology, comparable to the astronomy of Ptolemy, "economical" and move on. The church's magisterium keeps teaching about the two natures but without ever adequately explaining them. The latest attempt appeared in the authoritative catechism of 1976, modified in 2005:

Jesus Is Truly Man
In [Jesus'] passion the reality of His humanity was clearly evident. . . . He suffered the sharp physical pain of scourging and crucifixion; and He truly died. . . .

The humanity of Jesus is overwhelmingly important . . . because through His humanity He redeemed us. . . .

Jesus Is Truly God
The Catholic faith steadfastly professes that Jesus is literally and truly God. . . .

This is the good news of Christian faith; that He who is almighty, the eternal Lord of all . . . "dwelt among us" (Jn 1:14) in the visible humanity. . . .

Jesus Is One Person
Jesus is human and Jesus is God; but Jesus is one Person. . . . He took to Himself a human nature in time, and He remains a man forever. But it is one Person, Jesus Christ, who is both God and man.

This the faith has always proclaimed. The same Christ who was born of Mary and who suffered for us is also God. . . .

He created in the womb of Mary a human nature. . . . When this human nature began to be, a new person did not begin to be; rather, the eternal Son of God then began to live in a new nature, in a humanity. . . .

Our Lord Jesus Christ is One Person. He is truly God, and in his divine nature dwells eternally with the Father. . . . He is man as well: "He has truly been made one of us, like us in all things except sin (cf. Heb 4:15)". . . . His humanity is united with His divinity. . . . He who is the Son of God is this Man. This Man, Jesus, is God. . . .

Because Jesus is one Person who lives in two distinct natures, one can truthfully say of the Son of God. . . . He suffered and died in His human nature, and He is God, and so we may say that God suffered and died. This is literally true, although in His divine nature Jesus could not and did not suffer. The sublime truth that Jesus is one Person, though He is both God and man, reveals much of the greatness of God's generosity in the incarnation. . . .

"Not a Human Person"
Catholic teaching states that Jesus is one Person, and that a divine Person, "one of the Holy Trinity." Thus Jesus is "not a human person." . . .

This person, Jesus, *is* human. . . . But when we say He is not a human person, we are using the word "person" in its technical meaning of "distinct intelligent being." Jesus is not a being *distinct* from the Person who is the son of God.

The point here is this: Jesus is not divided. There is no human person "Jesus" who would be other than the Person who is the eternal Son of God. In fact, this is the joyful good news of Christianity; that this Man Jesus, the One who could be seen, He who walked this earth, He is my God. . . . To this man Jesus we are personally known and related, because He is no mere human person, but a true man who is the Son of God.

It is because this man Jesus is not a separate created person that He is rightly adored as God. . . .

The Son of God Humbled Himself
    To say that God is humbled is not to speak a myth. . . .
For it is a fact; it is the saving truth that is at the heart of
faith. In Christ God Himself has become man. . . . He
who made us became visible among us; His divinity
indeed is not visible, but it is He Himself who is visible
in His humanity. . . . The One who is poor and small
and humbled in our midst is our God.

The Glory of His Manhood
Jesus, the Son of God, is in His human nature perfect
man. He is fully God and fully man. . . (*The Teaching
of Christ: A Catholic Catechism for Adults*, pp. 78–85).

The Catechism, like the Athanasian Creed, denies a role for
the Holy Spirit in begetting Jesus. The Athanasian Creed acknowledged the role of the Virgin Mary only in giving birth to
Jesus Christ without her conceiving or begetting him. The
Catechism says the man Jesus Christ was "created in the womb
of Mary." How creation took place without conception or begetting is not explained.

The two natures of Jesus Christ have not been explained in
over a thousand years of trying to explain them. And the reason they cannot be explained is they are inexplicable. They are
inexplicable because they are impossible and incredible.

> **As the dreams increase, the empty words grow
> abundantly. All that is required is to revere God!**
> (Eccles 5:7).

> **The more words, the more vanity!** (Eccles 6:11).

MANY GODS CALLED ONE GOD

RATIONALIZATION
One may say $1+1+1 = 1$, but that would not make it so. The answer is 3, even if the respondent insists he is infallible.

TWO GODS CALLED "THE FATHER"
The church asserts a belief in one God called the Father, but by its teachings reveals it actually believes in two gods called the Father. The church teaches that the God of the Old Testament, who is called the Father, is a tribal god of justice and legalism, a god of wrath and vengeance. This is the God who gave Moses the everlasting "Old Law" to which not one word could be added or taken away. The church's God of the New Testament is called the Son, and although a separate person from the Father, is nonetheless identical to him, a universal god, a god of love, forgiveness, mercy, and grace. The church's New Testament Father, the church teaches, canceled the "Old Law" and gave Jesus a "New Law." Clearly the Father of the Old Testament is different from the Father of the New Testament even though the church teaches that both Fathers are the same Father.

TRINITY
The church believes in three divine persons, Father, Son, and Holy Spirit, but not wanting to be polytheistic, calls its three persons one god named *Trinity*. The church believes that this definition of God is not only true but absolutely and infallibly true. Well, some believe the earth is flat. Some believe the moon is made of green cheese. Those who hold such beliefs

do so with sincerity and faith, but faith and sincerity do not make a false belief true.

Jesus of Nazareth did not believe in a god named Trinity. At no time did Jesus say: "I am one person in the Trinity, equal with the Father, and of the same substance." Jesus said, *Hear O Israel, the Lord [YHVH] is our God, the Lord [YHVH] is one!* (Mk 12:29 [Deut 6:4]).

THE EVER-CHANGING TRINITY

The church teaches that God is immutable, and yet the God that is called Trinity is always changing. The church teaches that a spiritual Son descended from heaven, was made incarnate as Jesus of Nazareth through Mary by the Holy Spirit, lived about thirty years on earth, and then in crucified flesh ascended into heaven:

> The Father's power . . . introduced his Son's humanity, including his body, into the Trinity (*Catechism of the Catholic Church*, p. 169).

After Jesus' ascension, what had once been an entirely spiritual, pure, and divine Trinity became an incarnate, crucified, and human Trinity as well. The Trinity thus became grotesque and corrupt. The grotesqueness and corruption grew worse.

Church dogma declares that at the end of Mary's life, she was assumed into heaven in her flesh and was united with her son, Jesus. Thereby, Mary had to have become another member of the Trinity, which was now a Quaternity, a god that contained not only Jesus' crucified flesh but also Mary's old woman's flesh.

The Trinity grows more grotesque and corrupt. Athanasius proclaimed:

> For the Son of God became man so that we might become God (ibid., p. 116).

Augustine proclaimed:

> Let us rejoice then and give thanks that we have become not only Christians, but Christ himself. . . . Marvel and rejoice: we have become Christ! (ibid., p. 210).

Thomas Aquinas proclaimed:

> The only begotten Son of God, wanting to make us sharers in his divinity, assumed our nature, so that he, made man, might make men gods (ibid., p.116).

Pope Gregory the Great similarly proclaimed:

> Our redeemer has shown himself to be one person with the holy Church (ibid., p. 210).

The entire church becomes part of God! And the church proclaims today:

> The Church is one with Christ (ibid., p. 210). Christ . . . loved the Church as his Bride. . . ; he joined her to himself as his body (ibid., p. 218).

So the Trinity became a Quintinity—Father, Son, Holy Ghost, Mother of God, and Church. By its ever-changing definitions, the church, instead of glorifying God, has made a mockery of God.

HEXITY

The book of Genesis teaches that at the time of creation **God created man in his own image, in the image of God he created him; male and female he created them** (Gen 1:27). God says he is male and female, for he created them in his own image. So the Nicene fathers ought to have invented, instead of a Trinity of three males, a Hexity of three males and three females—Father, Son, Holy Spirit (male); Mother, Daughter, and Holy Spirit (female). Not six substances, but one substance. Not six gods, but one god. *Credo in unum deum.*

TRINITY CONFLICTS WITH BIBLE

The deification of Jesus of Nazareth with the subsequent creation of the Trinity had grave consequences. Those who voted for deification ignored the biblical warnings:

Scripture:

> **God is not a man who lies** (Num 23:19).

Prophets:

> **Cursed is the man who trusts in a man** (Jer 17:5).

Jesus:

> *What is exalted among men is an abomination in the sight of God* (Lk 16:15).

Paul wrote:

> **The time is coming when people will not endure sound teaching but, having itchy ears, will turn to teachers that teach them what they want to hear,**

> **will turn away from listening to the truth and wander into mythology** (2 Tim 4:3–4).

> **They exchanged the glory of the incorruptible God for the likeness of an image of corruptible man. . . . They exchanged the truth about God for a lie. And they worshipped and served the creature rather than the Creator** (Rom 1:23–25).

TRINITY AND ISLAM

By the eighth century, a new monotheistic religion was born. If, as the church teaches, Christianity brought Judaism to completion, then Islam, as Muslims teach, corrected, perfected, and purified Christianity.

The Koran states that Muhammad was "the messenger of Allah and the Seal of the Prophets" which Muslims interpret to mean that Muhammad confirmed the prophets and was the last prophet and that Islam is the final and perfect religion. The Koran declares that Allah or God is one, and those who teach Trinity lead their people astray and are painfully doomed:

> Say: O People of the Scripture! [A title usually of both Jews and Christians, but in this case clearly only Christians.] Come to an agreement between us and you: that we shall worship none but Allah, and that we shall ascribe no partner unto Him, and that none of us shall take others for lords beside Allah (*The Family of Imran*, v. 64).

> They indeed have disbelieved who say: Lo! Allah is the Messiah, son of Mary (*The Table Spread*, v. 17).

They surely disbelieve who say: Lo! Allah is the Messiah, son of Mary. The Messiah (himself) said: O Children of Israel, worship Allah, my Lord and your Lord. Lo! whoso ascribeth partners unto Allah, for him Allah hath forbidden Paradise. His abode is the Fire. For evil-doers there will be no helpers.

They surely disbelieve who say: Lo! Allah is the third of three; when there is no God save the One God. If they desist not from so saying, a painful doom will fall on those of them who disbelieve.

Will they not rather turn unto Allah and seek forgiveness of Him? For Allah is Forgiving, Merciful.

The Messiah, son of Mary, was no other than a messenger, messengers (the like of whom) had passed away before him. . . . (*The Table Spread*, vv. 72–75).

Say: O People of the Scripture! Stress not in your religion other than the truth, and follow not the vain desires of folk who erred of old and led many astray, and erred from a plain road (*The Table Spread*, v. 77).

And when Allah saith: O Jesus, son of Mary! Didst thou say unto mankind: Take me and my mother for two gods beside Allah? he saith: Be glorified! It was not mine to utter that to which I had no right. If I used to say it, then Thou knewest it. Thou knowest what is in my mind, and I know not what is in Thy Mind. Lo! Thou, only Thou art the Knower of Things Hidden. I spake unto them only that which Thou commandedst me, (saying): Worship Allah, my Lord and your Lord. (*The Table Spread*, vv. 116–117*).*

MICHAEL SERVETUS

The Reformation championed by Martin Luther and John Calvin in the sixteenth century achieved the severance of many Christians from the influence of the pope and the Vatican, but the Reformation did not significantly affect Christian dogma in general and the Trinity in particular. The Trinity had met its first great opposition by Arius before and during the Council of Nicea in the fourth century. After Nicea, the Trinity as a definition of god went essentially unchallenged until Michael Servetus began to write about it in the sixteenth century.

Michael Servetus was a Catholic physician who wrote theological tracts expressing the judgment that Luther and Calvin had not been sufficiently revolutionary in reforming the church, for they had allowed the doctrine of Trinity, which Servetus found incredible, to stand unchallenged. In 1531, Servetus published "On the Errors of the Trinity," in which he wrote, "Not one word is found in the whole Bible about the Trinity, nor about its Person, nor about an Essence, nor about a unity of Substance, nor about one Nature of three beings." And in 1552, he published "Christianity Restored," in which he stated that at Nicea, Christianity had been corrupted with pagan doctrines; and he challenged both Catholics and Protestants to return to the purity of their origins.

In June 1553, Servetus was condemned in absentia by the Council of Lyon for heresy, and was sentenced to burning at the stake. In August, he passed through Geneva, where Calvin lived, and under Calvin's orders was arrested and charged with thirty-nine counts of heresy and blasphemy. He stood trial before the Geneva city council, where the unanimous verdict was guilty of "heresies and horrible, execrable blasphemies against the Holy Trinity, against the Son of God, against the baptism of infants and the foundations of the Christian religion." He was again sentenced to the stake, to be burned to ashes along with his books for trying "to infect the world with stinking, heretical poison." His last request was to to have an audience with Calvin, but Calvin refused. On October 27, 1553, Michael Servetus was burned at the stake.

It is important to note that at the time of Servetus's execution, Protestants took pride in having no laws of capital punishment for religious dissenters, so in executing Servetus, the Geneva council broke the law. Michael Servetus was the first person to be executed as a heretic on the authority of a Protestant leader, and his death was the first to invalidate the Protestant boast of "religious toleration."

2. CHURCH SCHOLARSHIP

COMPLAINTS OF PAUL AND EUSEBIUS

The earliest complaint that Christians tampered with the gospels came from Paul. Paul said that although there was only one gospel, many gospels were sprouting up, and these others were false—even if an angel from heaven were to preach one of them (Gal 1:8).

Educated heathens also charged Christians with tampering with and falsifying the gospels; the most famous of the heathens was the philosopher Celsus (see *The True Doctrine*).

Church fathers continued to make the same complaint. Eusebius, a church father and historian, accused the church as late as the fourth century of falsifying the gospels. Eusebius complained about the rate at which new and falsified gospels were multiplying:

> If anyone will take the trouble to collect their several copies [of the same gospel] and compare them, he will discover frequent divergencies. . . . A large number [of copies] are obtainable [for such a comparison], thanks to the emulous energy with which disciples copied the "emendations" or rather perversions of the text. . . . The impertinence of this misconduct can hardly be unknown even to the copyists. Either they do not believe that the inspired Scriptures were spoken by the Holy Spirit—if so, they are unbelievers; or they imagine that they are wiser than He [the Holy Spirit]—if so, can they be other than possessed? They cannot deny that the impertinence is their own, seeing that the copies are in their own handwriting, that they did not receive the Scriptures in such a condition from their first teachers,

and that they cannot produce any originals to justify their copies. Some of them have not even deigned to falsify the text, but have simply repudiated both Law and Prophets, and so under cover of a wicked, godless teaching have plunged into the lowest depths of destruction (Eusebius, *The History of the Church*, 5:28, pp. 237–238).

THE CHURCH BECOMES ALL-POWERFUL

The early church was weak until the Emperor Constantine founded the Roman Catholic Church after the Council of Nicea in the fourth century, whereupon the church became more powerful than the Son, more powerful even than the Father. How did that happen? The evidence suggests that sometime during the fourth century, church redactors had Jesus transfer his power and the Father's to the church:

> *I will give to you [Peter] the keys of the kingdom of heaven, and whatever you bind on earth shall be bound in heaven, and whatever you loose on earth shall be loosed in heaven* (Mt 16:19).

> *If you forgive the sins of any, they are forgiven. But if you retain the sins of any, they are retained* (Jn 20:22–23).

SPURIOUS ENDINGS OF MATTHEW AND MARK

The endings of the canonical gospels of Matthew and Mark are spurious—added during the third or early fourth century. Not one of the early church fathers cites those endings.

Mark's ending underwent several changes before it received the church's final stamp of approval. The earliest gospel of Mark ended thus:

> **Mary Magdalene, Martha the mother of James, and Salome fled from the tomb; for trembling and astonishment had come upon them; and they said nothing to anyone, for they were afraid** (Mk 16:8).

Sometime during the fourth century a new ending was added:

> **But they reported briefly to Peter and those with him all that they had been told. And after this, Jesus himself sent out by means of them, from east to west, the sacred and imperishable proclamation of eternal salvation.**

Sometime between the fifth and ninth centuries, the above ending was deleted and yet a new ending, the final canonical ending, was added:

> **Now, when the Lord Jesus rose early on the first day of the week, he appeared first to Mary Magdalene. . . . But when the apostles heard that he was alive and had been seen by her, they would not believe it. After this he appeared in another form to two of them . . . and they went back and told the rest, but they did not believe them. Afterward he appeared to the eleven apostles as they sat at table; and he scolded them for their unbelief. . . . and he said to them, *Go unto all the world and preach the Gospel to the whole creation. He who believes and is baptized will be saved; but he who does not believe will be condemned.* . . . So then the Lord Jesus, after he had spoken to them, was taken up into heaven, and sat down at the right hand of God. . .** (Mk 16:9–20).

The church evidently liked this one, for there were no further changes.

SPURIOUS LETTERS OF PAUL

Most scholars consider the following letters of Paul to be forgeries: the first and second letters to Timothy, the letter to Titus, and the letter to the Hebrews. The letters to the Ephesians, Colossians, and the second letter to the Thessalonians are highly dubious. The letter to the Hebrews was considered spurious as early as the second or third century. Eusebius reported that the church father Origen wrote, "But who wrote the epistle [letter to the Hebrews] is known to God alone" (Eusebius, *The History of the Church*, 6:25, p. 266).

Changes were made in that letter after the Council of Nicea in the fourth century. Evidence for this is that in the voluminous patristic literature before Nicea, there is not a single reference to the uniquely extraordinary and incredible statement contained in Hebrews chapter one verse eight: "But of the Son, [God] says, 'Thy throne, O God, is forever and ever'" (Heb 1:8). God nowhere in the Hebrew Scriptures, nor in the gospels, nor anywhere else in the New Testament makes such a statement. It is not credible that Paul, an authority on Judaism, could have God make such a statement to the Hebrew Christians and expect them to believe it. And yet today it is the principal text to prove that Jesus is God (*The Teaching of Christ*, p. 80). The church thereby teaches that no matter that the letter to the Hebrews is spurious, no matter that Paul did not write it, no matter that God did not say it, the letter to the Hebrews, along with all of Paul's letters, must be believed. Consequently, letters of Paul, authentic or spurious, are included in the canonical Christian bible.

LORD

LORD

In the Hebrew Scriptures, God's name, יהוה (transliterated as YHVH) is generally translated into English as Jehovah or Yahweh. Jews are forbidden to speak God's name aloud—it is ineffable—and when they come to that name in the text, they recite a substitute word, usually *Adonai*, which in Hebrew and Aramaic means *Lord*. This practice dates from antiquity and continues to the present day.

When the Hebrew Scriptures were translated by Jews into Greek (the *Septuagint*) in the third century BC, Greek was considered a profane language. As a result, the name YHVH was not translated into Greek by ΙΑΩ, which is God's name in Greek, but instead by Κύριος (*Kyrios*), which is the Greek word for Adonai or Lord.

Apart from Scriptures, the word Lord among the Jews of antiquity also meant an honored or distinguished man—such as a king, a priest, a wealthy man, a landowner, a scholar, and a master or teacher; it was also a title of respect for a stranger or a guest. When the Jewish followers of Jesus addressed him as Lord, they used that title to mean Master or Teacher or Rabbi (see John 6:25); there is no evidence that the apostles or the early disciples ever considered Jesus the same as YHVH or the Lord YHVH.

By the fourth century AD, Greek had become the sacred language of the church. After Jesus had been deified at the Council of Nicea, the word Kyrios in the Septuagint created confusion; the church interpreted the word not only as meaning YHVH, but especially Jesus Christ. The church today teaches that the word Lord proclaims Jesus' divinity:

Out of respect for the holiness of God, the people of Israel [the Jews] do not pronounce his name. In the reading of Sacred Scripture, the revealed name (Yhwh) [sic] is replaced by the divine title "Lord" (in Hebrew *Adonai*, in Greek *Kyrios*). It is under this title that the divinity of Jesus will be acclaimed: "Jesus is Lord" (*Catechism of the Catholic Church*, p. 57).

JEROME AND YHVH

In the fifth century, Jerome created a Latin translation of the Hebrew Scriptures. Jerome wanted his translation to be faithful to the Hebrew, but Augustine advised against it on the ground that all the errors and mistranslations in the Greek Old Testament, the *Septuagint*, were now so familiar after centuries of church usage as to be considered sacred. It was better, Augustine argued, to translate Greek errors into Latin than to translate authentic Hebrew into Latin, for to eliminate the errors would introduce changes that would undermine the faith. Jerome at first was reluctant to take Augustine's advice, for he was determined to translate from the source; he even engaged rabbis to help him.

Soon Jerome encountered problems, probably the greatest of which was God's name, יהוה (YHVH) in the Hebrew Scriptures, but Κύριος (Lord) in the Septuagint.

The Hebrew Scriptures contain the declaration commonly referred to as the "Shema," which is the Hebrew word for "Hear," the first word of the declaration. The Shema is the most important declaration of the Jews, and the one which devout Jews want to have on their lips when they die. The Shema confirms two ideas: YHVH is God, and YHVH is One. Here is the Shema as *written* in Hebrew Scriptures hybridized with English transliteration to show the name of God in context. *Eloheinu* means "our God," and *Echod* means "One."

Shema Yisrael, יהוה Eloheinu, יהוה Echod.

Here is the identical verse as *spoken*:

Shema Yisrael, Adonai Eloheinu, Adonai Echod.

Here is the same verse translated into English designed to be *written* or *spoken*:

> **Hear O Israel, the Lord is our God, the Lord is One.**
> (Deut 6:4).

That is exactly how the Revised Standard Version renders it. It must be remembered, however, that when Jews then and now, including Jesus, said and say Adonai or Lord they meant and mean YHVH and only YHVH.

Here is the Shema as written in the Greek Septuagint hybridized with English to show the substitute word for the name of God, Kyrios (Lord), in context:

> **Hear O Israel, Κύριος is our God, Κύριος is one.**

Notice that the Septuagint Greek contains the substitute word **Κύριος** and not **ΙΑΩ** the name of God. It was as if the Jewish translators of the Septuagint considered God's name too sacred to write in any language except Hebrew.

When Jerome translated the Hebrew Scriptures into Latin, he went along with Augustine. Jerome did not use the name of God, **יהוה**, which appears in the Hebrew source, but the Greek word **Κύριος**, which appears in the Septuagint. The translation of **Κύριος** into Latin is ***Dominus***. In choosing ***Dominus*** rather than ***JHVH*** or ***IHVH***, Latin for the name of God, Jerome did not make a faithful translation but rather, as Augustine advised, a translation that was good for the faith.

Jesus called the Shema the first and most important of all the commandments (Mk 12:29), and Jesus had to have had in mind the Shema written with the name of God, **יהוה**. And yet this, the first of all, is never said in church, even as *Kyrios*, *Dominus*, or *Lord*. Why not? The Shema reveals that YHVH is the Lord referred to and that the Trinity is irreconcilable with the Shema's clear and resounding message.

PEACE ON EARTH

"PEACE ON EARTH, GOOD WILL TO MEN"

The earliest version of one of the most beloved verses in the New Testament is found in canonical Luke. It tells of the wondrous night when an angel and a multitude of the heavenly host, praising God, sang to shepherds:

> **Glory to God in the highest! And peace on earth, good will to men!** (Lk 2:14).

That is often referred to as the "Angel Song." It is the clearest and most succinct formulation of Hebrew messianic expectations. It is the *good news*, the *gospel*. Those Jewish shepherds were led to believe that, with the birth of Jesus of Nazareth, the Kingdom of God with everlasting peace on earth had begun! How soon the shepherds were to be disappointed!

In the fifth century, Jerome, the final redactor of the New Testament, knew that the Angel Song was a principal stumbling block to Jewish acceptance of Jesus. The Angel Song simply had not come to fulfillment with Jesus. So Jerome searched and "found" a book with a version of the Angel Song that pleased him even though it was fraudulent. The prefatory letters name Jerome as its author! In the book, which scholars call the "Gospel of Pseudo-Matthew" (*The Ante-Nicene Fathers*, vol. 8, p. 374), angels sang new words in their song: "Glory to God in the highest, and on earth peace to men of good pleasure." What does that mean? Perhaps Jerome himself did not know, so he turned to a well-known forgery called the "First Epistle of Pope Pontianus" (ibid., p. 623), which gave the following Angel Song: "Glory to God in the highest, and on earth peace to men of good will." That message was so qualified and bereft of fulfillment of messianic prophecy as to be meaningless. Jerome evidently believed it was better to have a meaningless Angel Song than one that would discredit Jesus.

Cyril of Alexandria, a contemporary of Jerome who outlived him by twenty years, wrote the most famous scholarly commentary on the gospel of Luke of that time. In the commentary, Cyril did not mention either Pseudo-Matthew or Pope Pontianus. Cyril quoted only the oldest know version: **Peace on earth, good will to men** (Cyril, Sermon 2 from the *Commentary upon the Gospel of Luke*, Syriac, M5 12, 165).

In the seventeenth century, when the King James men were translating the bible, they rejected Jerome's preferred Angel Song and reintroduced the ancient version. Later scholars, although generally critical of Jerome's scholarship, did not criticize Jerome for his selection of a known fraudulent Angel Song. The scholars even approved it, probably for the same reason Jerome had. Many bibles today give the fraudulent version in the text while the older messianic version is relegated to a footnote or not mentioned at all. One may well ask: what does it matter when Luke's gospel by his own admission was not a witnessed account, but a compilation of other authors' writings? Well, it may not matter in the overall evaluation of

Luke's gospel, but it does matter in evaluating the scholarship of redactors of the canonical gospels.

THE NEW ENGLISH BIBLE

In 1946, the Church of Scotland approached the other churches in Great Britain with the idea of undertaking a "completely new" translation of the Bible, employing a "contemporary idiom" rather than traditional biblical English. The finest scholars, representing many of the best British universities, were assembled to engage in the project. A panel of literary advisers was also assembled whose task it was to rigorously scrutinize all translations.

The work was to be so meticulous that when the scholars could not say with certainty which of two or more possible meanings was intended in any particularly difficult passage, the scholars agreed to select "the most important" for the main text and to give the alternative meanings in the footnotes. The enterprise took almost twenty-five years. At last, in 1970, *The New English Bible with the Apocrypha* was published jointly by the Oxford University Press and the Cambridge University Press.

This Bible was prepared under the auspices of the Church of England, the Church of Scotland, the Congregational Church of England and Wales, the Council of Churches for Wales, the Irish Council of Churches, the London Yearly Meeting of the Society of Friends, the Methodist Church of Great Britain, the Presbyterian Church of England, the Baptist Union of Great Britain and Ireland, the British and foreign Bible Society, and the National Bible Society of Scotland.

It is illuminating to see how these distinguished scholars translated three famous gospel passages:

The first example: Luke 2:14, *The Angel Song*.

Angels announce to shepherds: **And peace on earth, good will to men** (καὶ ἐπὶ γῆς εἰρήνη, ἐν ἀνθρώποις εὐδοκία). This statement, often called the "Angel Song," is the message of the ages and is the earliest known version of the song. Most importantly, it is the only messianic one, and therein discredits Jesus. So the New English scholars, like Jerome, preferred one of the forgeries: "Peace on earth to men of good will." And they gave that version in their main text, but in an altered and even more qualified way: "and on earth his peace for men on whom his favour rests." The word *his* is not present once either in the most ancient version or in either of the two forged versions, but in the New English version the word *his* appears twice! Moreover, even though the scholars gave the ancient version in a footnote, they altered it, making it resemble one of the false versions through an awkward word order and again by inserting the word *his* twice. They changed "peace on earth, good will to men" to "on earth his peace, his favour towards men."

The second example: Matthew 19:12, *Castration to win heaven*.

This verse had hitherto not presented any difficulty in meaning. Jesus, whether in Greek or Latin or King James English, recommends self-castration to win heaven:

> *There are eunuchs who have been so from birth and there are eunuchs who have been made eunuchs by men. And there are eunuchs who have made themselves eunuchs for the sake of the Kingdom of Heaven* (Mt 19:12).

The New English scholars found the verse problematic, not in its meaning but in its message. Self-castration to attain heaven? Jesus is asking too much! To make Jesus reasonable, this is how the New English scholars translated it:

> While some are incapable of marriage because they were born so, or were made so by men, there are others who have themselves renounced marriage for the sake of the Kingdom of Heaven.

The scholars gave no footnote. They simply castrated the original text.

   The third example: Mark 3:21, *Jesus is "out of his mind."*
That Jesus' family or friends considered Jesus out of his mind has understandably been difficult for believers for almost two millennia. Here is the RSV translation, generally considered a scholarly translation:

> **When his friends heard of it, they went out to seize him, for they said, "He is beside himself"** (Mk 3:21).

"Beside himself" is an edulcoration. The passage in Greek is:

> **καὶ ἀκούσαντες οἱ παρ᾽ αὐτοῦ ἐξῆλθον κρατῆσαι αὐτόν ᾽ ἔλεγον γὰρ ὅτι ἐξέστη.**

The last phrase **ὅτι ἐξέστη** means "He is out of his mind."
Jerome translated this passage into Latin thus:

> **Et cum audissent sui, exierunt tenere eum: dicebant enim: Quoniam in furorem versus est.**

The last phrase **Quoniam in furorem versus est** means "He is raving mad."

The Greek **οἱ παρ' αὐτοῦ** or Jerome's Latin **sui** means literally "those belonging to him." So either "his family" or "his friends" or even "his family and/or friends" would be a faithful rendering. The Greek says:

> **When his family and/or friends heard of it** [the disturbances Jesus was creating]**, they went out to seize him, for they said, "He is out of his mind."**

Many monks during the Middle Ages were so upset by the passage that they deleted it from their personal copies. Modern translators have typically sweetened the verse, as the RSV's "he is beside himself."

The New English scholars went beyond the limits even of a highly free translation. They translated the phrase thus:

> When his family heard of this, they set out to take charge of him; for people were saying that he was out of his mind.

The New English scholars replaced the pronoun "they," whose antecedent is "his family and/or friends," with the noun "people," absent from the Greek, and thereby changed the meaning of the sentence completely. It was no longer Jesus' family and friends who were saying he was out of his mind; it was the "people." *People?* Which *people?* The only "people" were "the Jews." This alteration accomplished two things for the faith: it restored Jesus to sanity while at the same time it increased hatred of the Jews. In the footnote, the New English scholars restored the pronoun "they" and omitted the noun "people," thereby implying that the scholars really had a choice of two different ancient manuscripts and that they selected for the main text the more authoritative one. But the one they selected was in fact the one that they themselves had written, the one with the noun "people."

Now, if, in the twentieth century, a distinguished body of scholars with impeccable credentials could make such extravagant changes in the gospels when they knew others were watching, we cannot begin to imagine how many changes were made between the second and fifth centuries when redactors thought no one was watching.

JAMES

JAMES, BROTHER OF JESUS

The church has revised its history repeatedly, none more egregiously than when it exchanged James, the first bishop and pope, for Peter, who was never a bishop, never a pope.

James was the brother of Jesus of Nazareth. He was the first bishop of the Jerusalem church, the very first church. Bishops in those days were called "popes." Jerusalem, having the first bishop, had the first pope. James was the most beloved of the leaders of the early church, and he was known as "James the Just" and "James the Righteous."

JESUS DESCRIBES HIS SUCCESSOR

Jesus of Nazareth described his successor:

> **A jealous dispute broke out among the Apostles— which of them was to be regarded as the greatest. Jesus said to them, *The Kings of the Gentiles lord it over their people, and those in authority are called "benefactors." Not so with you. Rather, let the greatest among you become as the least, and let the leader become the one who serves* (Lk 22:24–26).**

In the non-canonical gospel of Thomas, considered by many scholars to be closer to the original apostolic gospel than any of the four canonical gospels, Jesus speaks with great admiration of his brother James and appoints him, not Peter, as his successor:

> The disciples said to Jesus, "We know that you will be leaving us. Who is to be our leader?" Jesus responded, "Wherever you are, you are to go to James the Just, for whose sake heaven and earth came into being" (Saying #12).

Eusebius in the fourth century wrote:

> James, the Lord's brother . . . had been elected by the apostles to the episcopal throne at Jerusalem (Eusebius, *The History of the Church*, 2:23, p. 99).

Eusebius provides lists of the bishops or popes of the early church. Eusebius gives four lines of bishops, the first from Jerusalem, the second from Rome, the third from Antioch, and the fourth from Alexandria. James was first in Jerusalem; Linus first in Rome; Euodius, first in Antioch; and Annianus first in Alexandria. Peter's name is not on any of the lists. The first fifteen bishops had their See or Chair or Cathedra in Jerusalem. They were all Jews. The succession of Jerusalem bishops came to an end in AD 135 by an edict of the Roman Emperor Hadrian, who, after the final unsuccessful uprising of the Jews, banished all Jews from Jerusalem. Hadrian did not distinguish Christian Jews from faithful Jews. Eusebius wrote:

> [U]p to Hadrian's siege of the Jews [AD 135], there had been a series of fifteen bishops [in Jerusalem]. All are said to have been Hebrews in origin. . . . At that time their whole church consisted of Hebrew believers who

had continued from apostolic times down to the later siege in which the Jews, after revolting a second time from the Romans, were overwhelmed in a full-scale war. . . . [T]hat meant the end of bishops of the Circumcision (ibid., 4:5, p. 156).

JERUSALEM AND ROME

FROM JERUSALEM TO ROME

By the fourth century, the Jerusalem church with its succession of bishops starting with James the Just was moribund. Alexandria was intellectually vibrant, but, in spite of the Roman persecutions, the church saw its future in Rome, the "eternal city" and the "hub of the universe." The center of Christianity had to be transferred from Jerusalem to Rome. But how? Jesus had never been to Rome. Although Paul went to Rome, he had never known Jesus, so Paul could not provide the link between the two cities. There was no evidence that John had been to Rome, and, moreover, it appeared that he had spent the remainder of his life in Greece.

So the church turned to Peter. Peter knew Jesus, and the latter years of Peter's life were unknown. That very obscurity would make him a perfect candidate for inventing traditions and forging the necessary link between Jerusalem and Rome.

Gospel redactors inserted Jesus' famous appointment into the gospel: *I tell you, you are Peter [Rock], and on this Rock I will build my church* (Mt 16:18). This statement, known as the Petrine text, had not been referred to by a single church father before the fourth century. That the text is a forgery is strongly supported by the fact it is not found in the Gospel of Mark, which was based on the preaching of Peter. If Peter had been so greatly valued by Jesus, Mark above all would have recorded it. The Petrine text achieved two goals: it destroyed the old link between Jesus and James. It forged the new link between Jesus and Peter. To make the Petrine text concrete, the church had to invent the "tradition" that Peter went from Jerusalem to Rome. It based that tradition on the following:

Peter wrote his first letter to disciples in the diaspora—in Pontus, Galatia, Cappadocia, Asia, and Bithnia. At the end of his letter, almost as a postscript, Peter mentioned that his wife sent regards from Babylon. The church assumed that if Peter's wife was in Babylon, Peter had to have been there, too. Then the church made another assumption: by Babylon Peter really meant Rome. And that is how the church brought Peter to Rome! Once the church transferred Peter to Rome, the church made up yet another tradition: the Romans crucified Peter upside down! That touch of specificity gave the tradition authenticity. With that tradition in place, the church went on to say that Peter, who had never been a bishop and had never been to Rome, was the first bishop and first pope of the "apostolic" Roman Catholic Church!

What was meant by "You are Peter, and on this rock I will build my church"? The redactors speaking for Jesus meant that the church would be built of righteous men such as Peter. It did not mean that the church would be built of stone or on stone. Paul wrote, "Do you not know that you are God's temple?" (1 Cor 3:16) and again "For we are the temple of the living God" (2 Cor 6:16). This was the same building material that Isaiah spoke of:

> **[L]ook to the rock from which you were hewn,**
> **and to the quarry from which you were digged.**
> **Look to Abraham your father**
> **and to Sarah who bore you** (Is 51:1–2).

ST. JOHN LATERAN, THE CATHEDRAL OF ROME VS. ST. PETER'S BASILICA

After Constantine established the Roman Catholic Church, the Lateran family, one of the wealthiest in Rome, donated their home, a magnificent mansion, to the now recognized community of Christians. Christians could now safely build churches. Previously they had to meet secretly in homes. The Lateran mansion became the first Christian cathedral in Rome and was named, in honor of the emperor, the Cathedral of Constantine. Constantine built a church on Vatican Hill, which he called St. Peter's Basilica. But St. Peter's Basilica had neither the stature nor the importance of the Cathedral of Constantine. A cathedral is the seat of a bishop and therefore the highest church among churches whereas in the fourth century a basilica was merely a church.

After Constantine's death, the Cathedral of Constantine was renamed the Cathedral of Christ the Savior. Later, perhaps to diminish its importance as St. Peter's Basilica was increasing in importance, it was renamed the Cathedral of St. John the Baptist. In time the Cathedral of St. John the Baptist was given its present name—the Cathedral of St. John Lateran, a name that honors both the Baptist and the Lateran family.

The earliest Christian churches were called basilicas. A basilica to the Romans was an architectural term, not an ecclesiastical one, and Roman architects applied it to the form used for a public building, usually a law court. Christians did not want to design their meeting houses after Roman and Greek temples (although exceptions were made) and the basilica, a Roman public building, was more acceptable to them. Thus, the basilica became the dominant architectural form for a church. When a basilica held the seat (*kathedra* in Greek) of a bishop, it was called a cathedral, an ecclesiastical term. Most basilicas remained simple churches through the early Dark Ages. Sometime during the Middle Ages, a few great basilicas were elevated to the stature of cathedrals by papal fiat. St. Peter's Basilica in Rome was one.

"ON THIS ROCK I WILL BUILD MY CHURCH"

Another tradition arose about Peter in Rome: that Peter was buried on the very site where Constantine had built St. Peter's Basilica. Some argued that was impossible because Peter by tradition was the first bishop of Rome and ought to have been buried beneath St. John Lateran's Cathedral, the seat of the bishop of Rome. To resolve the dispute, the church invented yet another tradition. Peter's head was buried at St. John Lateran's, but his body was buried at St. Peter's. Traditions do not end there.

Pope Pius XII was a very concrete thinker. In 1939, the pope approved archeological digs beneath St. Peter's Basilica to prove that St. Peter's bones were actually buried there—that Jesus had literally built his church on Peter, except for his skull which was beneath the cathedral of St. John Lateran's.

The digs began in the grottoes beneath the Basilica where many popes were buried. For the next ten years, despite World War II, the digs continued. The foundation walls of the original St. Peter's Basilica built by Constantine were discovered, and below them, an ancient heathen Roman necropolis or city of the dead, with narrow streets leading to doorways of burial houses with chambers built of giant stones ten to fifteen feet long and decorated with mosaics and frescoes. Some of the chambers contained funeral urns and marble sarcophagi. A mosaic of the Greek god Apollo, the sun god, was found in one. Catholic archeologists, in order "to give the mosaic a Christian meaning," called the mosaic an "allegory for Christ, our Sun god."

Directly under the altar of the original St. Peter's Basilica was found a small shrine believed by faithful archeologists to be on the burial ground of Peter, although like the Apollo mosaic, the shrine was heathen. Adjacent to the shrine was a red wall. A chunk of plaster, presumably from this wall, was found nearby bearing the inscription in Greek "Petros eni." Greek scholars could make nothing of it, but the Catholic archeologists insisted it was an important announcement and meant, "Peter is inside!" When the faithful archeologists relayed this news to the pope, he was ecstatic. On searching inside the shrine, however, no bones were found. Indeed, nothing at all was found. An irreverent archeologist quipped, "Peter was not at home."

In 1956, archeologists returned to the red wall. Inexplicably this time they uncovered bones. On examination, the bones were those of goats, cows, horses, and sheep, as well as a few assorted human bones from different people. The digs ended in great disappointment.

Then, in 1964—completely inexplicably—a set of bones turned up in a storeroom within the Vatican! The Vatican claimed that these bones had come from a repository "near" the red wall. But no archeologist took responsibility for finding the bones, nor for transferring them from the red wall deep in the earth to the storeroom upstairs. Experts were called to examine the bones. The experts confirmed that the bones came from a single person, but among the fragments were twenty-nine fragments of skull. That finding was highly problematic because Peter's skull had long been a relic in the Cathedral of St. John Lateran. The pope dismissed this argument saying, of what possible significance were a few fragments of skull when it was the absence of most of the skull that was of real importance. No one dared ask, Whose bones were these? Could anyone of faith doubt they were Peter's?

Nonetheless, a skeptic in the group had sufficient courage to ask the pope how the bones got from the red wall deep in the earth to the store room so high above it. The bones, the skeptic said, were, therefore, *within* St. Peter's, not *beneath* it. If the bones were Peter's, then St. Peter's Basilica was not built upon Peter. The pope was silent.

In the summer of 1968, Pope Paul VI made the announcement to the world that the bones of St. Peter had been unearthed from beneath St. Peter's basilica, thereby "proving" the church's long-standing belief that Christ had built his church on Peter!

Surely one day someone of the faithful will come forward for the good of the faith and confess that he was the one who carried the bones of St. Peter from the small shrine near the chunk of plaster saying, "Petros eni" deep in the earth up to the Vatican storeroom. That person ought to be greatly rewarded for strengthening the church's foundation of truth.

RELICS

MANY AND VARIED RELICS

The church loves relics and teaches the faithful to venerate them. A relic is allegedly the bodily part or remnant or personal belonging or site associated with Jesus, the Virgin, a saint, or a martyr. Not a single relic has been shown to be authentic. We have already discussed the relics of St. Peter's skeleton and his skull, and their locations. Here are some other famous relics and their locations:

Bits and pieces of the "true" cross or the "holy" cross—the one on which Jesus of Nazareth was crucified—may be found in many churches. John Calvin wrote, "There is no town, however small, which does not have a bit of it. . . . There is no abbey so poor as not to have a specimen."

The entire skull of John the Baptist is in Rome, but many skull parts are in other locations: A set of frontal bones is in

Spain; a second set in Malta; the occipital bone in Nevers, France; an entire jaw in Besancon, France; a partial jaw in Paris; and various other parts in various other cities. An arm of his is in Sienna. And the very finger with which he once pointed at Jesus is in Besancon—and also Toulouse, as well as in Lyons, Bourges, Florence, and also just outside Maseon. Moreover, his ashes may be found in Genoa and in Rome.

The entire body of Andrew the apostle is in Melfi. But another body of his is in Toulouse. And one of his feet is in Aix, his skull in Rome, his shoulder in Grisgon; and other body parts elsewhere.

The body of Mary Magdalene is in Vesoul near Auxerre— and another body of hers is in San Maximin of Provence.

Jesus' foreskin, called the "Holy Prepuce," is in Coulombs Abbey, France; another may be found in Charroux; and a third in Rome; and elsewhere. However, many popes discouraged visits to the Holy Prepuce, wherever it may be, lest nonbelievers suspect believers of "prurient interest" not to mention calling into question the church's discouraging circumcision.

The tail of the donkey that Jesus rode in his triumphal entry into Jerusalem on Palm Sunday is reported to be "somewhere" in Italy.

Tears of Jesus are in three cities in France—Vindon, Treves, and Orleans.

According to church tradition, the Archangel Michael always carried a dagger until he accidentally dropped it during the annunciation. Michael's dagger may be found in Carcassonne—and also in Tours.

Mary's engagement ring from Joseph is in Rome.

A set of fragments of bones of the three Magi are in Germany, another set in Milan.

Jesus' baby blanket is in Germany, his cradle in Spain.

Mary's milk is in several locations. John Calvin wrote: "It cannot be necessary to enumerate all the places where it

[Mary's milk] is shown. Indeed, the task would be endless, for there is no town, however small, no monastery or nunnery, however insignificant, which does not possess it."

The wine that Jesus made from water at the wedding of Cana, is in France. John Calvin wrote, "Once a year they give a wine-tasting to any who bring an offering."

Bread from the feeding of the five thousand is in Rome—and also in Spain.

Bread from the Last Supper is also in Spain. A carving knife to slice the Passover Lamb is in France. Small bottles of wine from the Last Supper are sold in a gift shop on the shores of the Sea of Galilee. The towel with which Jesus dried the apostles' feet is in Rome; the same towel bearing an imprint of Judas' footprint is in Germany.

Of all the many relics, the most famous is the shroud of Turin. The shroud's extraordinary fame rests on the belief that it was the sole witness to the Resurrection.

SHROUD OF TURIN

The shroud of Turin presumably has the figure of a crucified man etched into the cloth. Believers insist that the man is Jesus of Nazareth. The etching came about because Jesus' body emanated supernatural heat at the instant of his resurrection.

Most nonbelievers consider the shroud a hoax. In 1988, to settle the issue, the Vatican agreed to the carbon dating of the shroud, but with the following rules: If the shroud dated from the first century, whatever its origin, the church would conclude that the shroud "proved" the resurrection. But if it dated from a later date, the church agreed to call the shroud a hoax.

Carbon dating was performed in a meticulous manner. Sampling was done under the auspices of Vatican observers. Each of three samples was sent to three distinguished universities—Arizona, Oxford, and Zurich. Carbon dating was performed in laboratories at those universities by highly reputable scientists each working secretly and independently. After the analyses were completed, all three universities reported their findings, which were published in 1989 in *Nature*, the most prestigious of scientific journals. The article reported that each university obtained the same result and each reached the same conclusion: The shroud dated from the Middle Ages—the thirteenth or fourteenth century. The shroud of Turin was a hoax.

The Vatican and other men of faith refused to accept the results and abide by the rules. At first some in the Vatican said, what does one expect when the tests were performed by Jews in Jewish universities! Other Vatican critics, more tempered, said that the sample was taken not from the shroud itself but from a medieval patch skillfully woven into the shroud, and the patch went undetected when the samples were obtained. Others said, even if the samples had been taken from the shroud itself and not from a patch, what would that prove; for what, after all, is a scientific study compared with faith?

Most agreed it was pointless to repeat the study. If the results of a new investigation confirmed the original results, men of faith would find yet new reasons to reject the findings. Faith demands that the shroud of Turin prove the resurrection. No scientific study could ever challenge that. Carbon dating had been a waste of time and money. "Faith is certain. It is more certain than all human knowledge" (*Catechism of the Catholic Church*, p. 43).

ALLEGORY

THE DEEPER MEANING
The church teaches that everything about Jesus Christ may be found in the Old Testament if one reads that book, not at its

literal and superficial level but at a profound and spiritual level:

> One can distinguish between two *senses* of Scripture; the literal and the spiritual, the latter [including] . . . the allegorical. . . . We can acquire a more profound understanding of events by recognizing their significance in Christ; thus the crossing of the Red Sea [by Moses and the Hebrews in their flight from Egypt] is a sign or type of Christ's victory and also of Christian Baptism. . . . The Old Covenant [gives] prefigurations of what [God] accomplished in the fullness of time in the person of his incarnate Son. . . . Christians therefore read the Old Testament in the light of Christ crucified and risen (*Catechism of the Catholic Church*, pp. 33–34).

One of the church's most famous allegories is the *Song of Songs* (*Song of Solomon*) which, at its literal level, is a straightforward love poem between a man and a woman. The church has taught for over a millennium that *Song of Songs* is much more than a love poem between a man and a woman— that at a deeper and spiritual level, it is a love poem between Jesus Christ and his bride the church. Today's church seems to be in conflict over whether the poem is allegorical. *The Catholic Encyclopedia* makes the following statement: "At the present day most non-Catholics are strongly opposed to [an allegorical] exposition; on the other hand most Catholics accept the allegorical interpretation" (*The Catholic Encyclopedia*, AD 1913, 1917, 2009 cyberspace edition). Recent catechism (*Catechism of the Catholic Church*, AD 1994; *The Teaching of Christ*, AD 2004) makes no reference to an allegorical interpretation of the *Song of Songs*. The reader will understand why, when the poem is presented as an allegory between Christ and his bride the Church.

SONG OF SONGS (Excerpted)

CHURCH. (*Speaking to Jesus Christ.*)
> O that you would kiss me
> with the kisses of your mouth!
> For your love is better than wine. . . .

JESUS CHRIST. (*Speaking to the Church.*)
> Behold, you are beautiful, my beloved;
> behold, you are beautiful. . . .
> As a lily among brambles,
> so is my love among maidens.

CHURCH.
> As an apple tree among the trees of the wood,
> so is my beloved among young men.
> With great delight I sat in his shadow,
> and his fruit was sweet to my taste. . . .
> O that his left hand were under my head,
> and that his right hand embraced me! . . .
> Behold, he comes,
> leaping upon the mountains,
> bounding over the hills. . . .
> My beloved speaks and says to me:
> "Arise, my love, my fair one,
> and come away . . .
> Arise, my love, my fair one,
> and come away. . . .
> Let me see your face,
> let me hear your voice,
> for your voice is sweet,
> and your face is comely. . . ."

> My beloved is mine, and I am his. . . .

Upon my bed by night
I sought him whom my soul loves;
I sought him, but found him not;
I called him, but he gave no answer. . . .
When I found him whom my soul loves,
I held him, and would not let him go. . . .

JESUS CHRIST.
Behold, you are beautiful, my love,
behold, you are beautiful! . . .
Your eyes. . . . Your hair. . . . Your teeth. . . .
Your lips are like a scarlet thread,
and your mouth is lovely. . . .
Your cheeks are like halves of a pomegranate. . . .
Your neck. . . . Your two breasts. . . .
You are all fair, my love;
there is no flaw in you. . . .

You have ravished my heart . . .
you have ravished my heart
with a glance of your eyes. . . .
How sweet is your love . . .
how much better is your love than wine. . . .

CHURCH.
I had put off my garment,
how could I put it on? . . .
My beloved put his hand to the latch,
and my heart was thrilled within me.
I arose to open to my beloved. . . .
I opened to my beloved,
but my beloved had turned and gone. . . .
I sought him, but found him not;

I called him, but he gave no answer. . . .
I am sick with love. . . .

My beloved is all radiant and ruddy,
distinguishable among ten thousand.
His head . . . his locks. . . .
His eyes. . . . His cheeks. . . .
His lips. . . . His arms. . . .
His body is ivory. . . .
His legs are alabaster columns. . . .
His speech is most sweet
and he is altogether desirable.
This is my beloved, and this is my friend. . . .
I am my beloved's and my beloved is mine. . . .

JESUS CHRIST.
Turn away your eyes from me,
for they blind me. . . .
Who is this that looks forth like the dawn,
fair as the moon,
bright as the sun. . . .

How graceful are your feet in sandals,
O queenly maiden!
Your rounded thighs. . . .
Your navel. . . . Your belly. . . .
Your two breasts. . . .
Your neck. . . . Your eyes. . . .
Your nose. . . . Your head. . . .
How fair and pleasant your are,
O loved one, delectable maiden!
You are stately as a palm tree
and your breasts are like its clusters.
I say I will climb the palm tree

and lay hold of its branches.
Oh, may your breasts be like clusters of the vine,
and the scent of your breath like apples,
and your kisses like the best wine. . . .

CHURCH.
I am my beloved's, and his desire is for me.

JESUS CHRIST.
Come, my beloved,
let us go forth into the fields. . . .
Let us go early to the vineyards. . . .
There I will give you my love. . . .

Love is as strong as death,
and passion as cruel as the grave.
Its flashes are flashes of fire. . . .
Many waters cannot quench love,
neither can floods drown it. . . .

The reader can readily appreciate why the Catholic Church today is in conflict over whether the *Song of Songs* is an allegory between Christ and his church. Let us continue to investigate other allegories about which the Church is not in conflict.

THE MANY BRIDES OF CHRIST

The church teaches that the church is the bride of Christ. The church also teaches that Mary, the Mother of God, is the bride of Christ. And the church teaches that nuns and priests are the brides of Christ. In teaching those things, the church is teaching that Jesus Christ is a polygamist.

PASCHAL LAMB: SACRIFICIAL VICTIM FOR THE CRUCIFIXION

The church teaches that the sacrifice of the Paschal Lamb (Ex 12:1–13) is an allegory for the Crucifixion. That cannot be so for many reasons:

- The Paschal lamb's blood was used not to take away sins, but as a paint to mark doorways to show the angel of death that Jews lived there and to pass over and spare them. Jesus of Nazareth's blood was not used to mark doorways, and his death never spared Jews from the angel of death. Quite the contrary.
- The Paschal lamb had to be without blemish. A bruise or scratch would render the victim unacceptable. Roman scourging and torturing of Jesus prior to his crucifixion would have rendered him unacceptable as a holy sacrifice.
- A blood sacrifice was acceptable only by obtaining the blood at the hands of the high priest when he slit the victim's throat with a sharp knife. Death by crucifixion was an unacceptable and abominable sacrifice.
- Human sacrifice, particularly that of one's own children, was unacceptable to God. That was demonstrated to Abraham and all the Jews once and for all at the time of the binding of Abraham's son Isaac.
- The Hebrew Scriptures teach that one man's death cannot atone for another man's sins.
- Jesus himself along with the prophets taught that sacrifice was not pleasing to God.

GOAT OF GOD

The Jewish holiday to take away sins is Yom Kippur, the Day of Atonement, which comes in the autumn. The animal to take away sins during the Day of Atonement was the goat. At other times of the year, the blood of oxen and sheep were acceptable. Lambs were used to take away sins, but only as burnt offerings. Lambs were most frequently used to purify women after childbirth, to cleanse lepers, as peace offerings, to dedicate a new altar, and as a sacrifice for inadvertent transgressions of omission. The only lambs acceptable for such sacrifices, however, were females. How then could Jesus of Nazareth be the Lamb of God?

On the Day of Atonement in the autumn, a Goat of God took away the sins of Israel (Lev 16:30). Unable to make Jesus the Goat of God because he died in the spring, John invented the **Lamb of God who takes away the sins of the world** (Jn 1:29).

Some may ask, what about the paschal lamb, wasn't that a blood sacrifice? It was indeed, but its purpose was not to take away sins. The blood of the lamb at Passover was to paint the posts and lintels on houses in which Jews lived as a sign for the angel of death to pass over those houses. That sacrificial blood saved the Jews simply because they were Jews. Whether they were sinners or not had nothing to do with the story. Therefore, how could the slaying of the paschal lamb be an allegory for the crucifixion of Jesus of Nazareth?

ABRAHAM BINDING ISAAC:
THE FATHER SACRIFICING THE SON

The Jews considered the death of a child the greatest of human losses. The Egyptians felt similarly. When the Hebrews wanted to depart from Egypt, it was only the death of Pharaoh's son that made Pharaoh relent and allow the Hebrews to leave (Ex 5:22–23).

God puts Abraham to the test, telling him he must sacrifice his son Isaac (Gen 22:1–19). Abraham binds Isaac and prepares to sacrifice him, but at the last minute God intervenes and prevents that sacrifice, and Abraham sacrifices a ram (not a lamb) instead of his son. God thereby taught that human sacrifice must never take place, particularly that of one's own son. Moreover, God thereby teaches that such sacrifice is so abhorrent that even if God himself commands someone to sacrifice a human being, especially his own son, then God must be disobeyed. That is the true test. Even devotion to God has its limits; when these limits are passed, devotion becomes abomination.

Nonetheless, the church teaches that the binding of Isaac was a prefigurement or allegory for the sacrifice of Jesus of Nazareth by the Father. The church further teaches that the Father showed greater love than Abraham because the Father actually sacrificed his son! How could the Jews possibly believe such theology when to them it was an abomination? Moreover, Hebrew Scriptures taught that human sacrifice was not only unholy but in fact murder and therefore could not redeem sins. YHVH said to Moses:

> **Say to the people of Israel, any man of the people of Israel . . . who gives any of his children to Molech** [a heathen god who demanded sacrifice of one's own children] **shall be put to death . . . because he has given one of his children to Molech, defiling my sanctuary** (Lev 20:1–3).

> **When you come into the land which the Lord [YHVH] your God gives you, you shall not learn to follow the abominable practices of those nations. There shall not be found among you any one who burns his son or his daughter as an offering** (Deut 18:9–10).

Although Abraham passed God's obedience test, he did not pass God's morality test. If Abraham had refused to sacrifice his son, Abraham would have passed the morality test. Only God's intervention prevented Abraham from failing the morality test. The Father of the New Testament in killing his own son failed that morality test.

DID GOD WANT THE CRUCIFIXION?

The central doctrine of the church is that the crucifixion of Jesus of Nazareth was the sacrifice that took away the sins of the world. But the psalmist, the prophets, and Jesus himself tell us that doctrine is false because sacrifice does not take away sins.

The psalmist:

> **Sacrifice and offering you [YHVH] do not desire** (Ps 40:6).

> **God has no delight in sacrifice** (Ps 51:16).

> **The sacrifice acceptable to God is a broken spirit; a broken and contrite heart** (Ps 51:17).

The prophets, Isaiah, Ezekiel, Hosea, and Jeremiah:

> **I [YHVH] do not delight in the blood of . . . lambs** (Is 1:11).

> **Bring me [YHVH] no sacrifices! They are in vain!** (Is 1:13).

> **He who slaughters an ox is like him who commits murder; he who sacrifices a lamb is like him who breaks a dog's neck. . . . These have chosen to do things their own way, and their soul delights in their abominations** (Is 66:3).

I [YHVH] have no desire for any man's death! (Ezek 18:32).

I [YHVH] desire mercy, and not sacrifice (Hos 6:6).

Your burnt offerings are not acceptable to me, nor are your sacrifices pleasing to me [YHVH]! (Jer 6:20).

When I [YHVH] brought your forefathers out of Egypt, I gave them no commandments about whole offerings and sacrifices. I said not a word about such things. . . . But they did not listen, they paid no heed and persisted in disobedience, with evil and stubborn hearts (Jer 7:4–18, 22).

Jesus:

> *Go and learn what this means,* **"I desire mercy and not sacrifice"** (Mt 9:13).

> *And if you had understood what this means,* **I desire mercy and not sacrifice,** *you would not have condemned the innocent!* (Mt 12:6–7).

Paul:

> **When Christ came into the world, he said,** *Sacrifices and offerings You have not desired. . . . In burnt offerings and sin offerings You have taken no pleasure* (Heb 10:5).

The so-called sacrifice of Jesus on the cross was not a sacrifice. It was an execution. Jesus' execution redeemed no one's sins except perhaps his own.

The church teaches:

> The end does not justify the means. Thus the condemnation of an innocent person cannot be justified as legitimate means of saving the nation (*Catechism of the Catholic Church*, p. 434).

The church itself teaches then the crucifixion of an innocent man cannot be justified as a legitimate means of saving humanity.

THE WAY TO REDEMPTION AND SALVATION

The Hebrew scriptures teach that the way to redemption and salvation is through repentance and good works. Paul reiterated this: **[If you are looking for salvation,] turn to God and perform deeds worthy of . . . repentance** (Acts 26:20).

King David loved Bathsheba, a married woman. To possess her, David arranged for the murder of her husband. When David realized the magnitude of his sins—adultery and murder—he did not go to the temple priest to make sacrifice. He threw himself entirely on God's mercy. And God forgave him (2 Sam 12:11–13). Evidently, sacrifices are not necessary to take away sins, and the God of the Old Testament is not so merciless and unforgiving as the church teaches. It is clear that God does not require sacrifice to take away sins.

EVERYONE DIES FOR HIS OWN SINS

The church teaches that the Father sent his son to be sacrificed to take away the sins of the world. But the Hebrew Scriptures teach that no man can take away another man's sins:

> **Every man shall be put to death for his own sin** (Deut 24:16).

. . . every man shall die for his own sin
(2 Kings 14:6).

. . . every man shall die for his own sin
(2 Chron 25:4).

. . . everyone shall die for his own sin
(Jer 31:30).

No man can redeem his brother
(Ps 49:8).

PAUL AND SACRIFICE

Paul wrote that only the shedding of blood was an acceptable sacrifice for atonement of sins: **Without the shedding of blood, there is no forgiveness of sins** (Heb 9:22). Paul was justifying the shedding of blood during the crucifixion, but there were ways other than the shedding of blood to take away sins: **And he shall bring [as much fine flour as he eats in a day] to the priest, and the priest shall take a handful of it as its memorial portion and burn this on the altar, upon the offerings by fire to the Lord [YHVH]; it is a sin offering** (Lev 5:12). Paul did not inform the gentiles that tossing a handful of flour on the altar fire was as effective as the crucifixion. It is reasonable to think he assumed that the gentiles would not have converted knowing that.

ANCIENT BELIEFS

At the time when Jesus of Nazareth lived, people were ignorant of many commonplace facts known today by ordinary people. Ancient people believed the earth was flat, that it was at the center of the universe, and that the sun revolved around the earth. Those people were also superstitious. They believed that a person's disease was punishment for his sins, that catastrophes were God's wrath for the community's sins, and that sacrifice appeased the gods. But today, most people know that the earth is not flat and is not at the center of the universe, and the sun does not revolve around the earth. Disease and catastrophe are not divine retribution but natural events. And sacrifice neither appeases the gods nor takes away sins. Sacrifice is a barbaric practice of primitive man.

THE SUFFERING SERVANT:
ALLEGORY FOR JESUS DURING HIS PASSION

The church maintains that the Suffering Servant described by the prophet Isaiah, especially in Isaiah chapters 42, 43, 44, and 53, was a prefigurement for Jesus of Nazareth. That cannot be so because Isaiah's Suffering Servant was not sacrificed and did not die. His suffering came to an end, whereupon he prospered and begot many children. How then could the Suffering Servant be an allegory for Jesus of Nazareth? But there are several other reasons why Isaiah's Suffering Servant cannot be Jesus of Nazareth:

1.   God calls the Servant "my" servant and puts his spirit upon his servant so that he will bring justice to the gentiles:

> **Behold my servant, whom I uphold;**
> **my chosen, in whom my soul delights;**
> **I have put my spirit upon him,**
> **he will bring forth justice to the nations** (Is 42:1).

The Suffering Servant cannot be Jesus because God did not call Jesus "my" servant, and Jesus did not bring justice to the nations (the gentiles). Although Matthew said (Mt 12:15–18) Jesus fulfilled this prophecy by healing people in secret, that is a desperate and inappropriate attempt to make Jesus fulfill a prophecy he did not fulfill.

2.   God commands the Suffering Servant not to preach in the street. God through Isaiah recognized that those who preached in the street were emotionally disturbed, and their message could not be believed. Credible preachers preached in synagogues and the temple:

> **He will not cry or lift up his voice,**
> **or make it heard in the street. . . .**
> **I am the Lord [YHVH], I have called you**
> **in righteousness . . . a light of the nations** (Is 42:2–6).

The Suffering Servant cannot be Jesus because Jesus was frequently heard preaching in the street.

3.   God says that men shall die for the Suffering Servant, not that the Suffering Servant shall die for men:

> **Because you are precious in my eyes,**
> **and honored, and I love you,**
> **I give men in return for you,**
> **peoples in exchange for your life** (Is 43:4).

The Suffering Servant cannot be Jesus because not one of his apostles or any man of Jesus' time was willing to die for him. So the church turned things around and had Jesus die for men.

4.   God speaks of the offspring of the Suffering Servant:

> **I will bring your offspring from the east,**
> **and from the west I will gather you;**
> **I will say to the north, Give [them] up,**
> **and to the south, Do not withhold [them];**

> **bring my sons from afar,**
> **and my daughters from the end of the earth**
> (Is: 43:5–6).

This Suffering Servant cannot be Jesus because he had no children. They cannot be metaphorical children, because they are actual "offspring" ["seed" in the original Hebrew] of the servant.

5.   Isaiah says that those who make images are "nothing," and those who pray to images and call them god have no sense, no understanding, "no knowledge":

> **All who make idols are nothing** (Is 44:9). . . . **But Israel is saved by the Lord [YHVH] with everlasting salvation. . . . They have no knowledge who carry about their wooden idols, and keep on praying to a god that cannot save** (Is 45:9–20).

The church, like the heathen gentiles before it, encourages its faithful to bow down before images and pray for salvation; but Isaiah says, they pray and "keep on praying to a god that cannot save." Isaiah here may apply to Jesus, but not because he is the Suffering Servant, but because he is the "god that cannot save." "But Israel is saved by the Lord with everlasting salvation."

6.   God calls "my servant" not "Jesus" but "Israel" and "Jacob" and redeems him for his transgressions:

> **Remember these things, O Jacob,**
> **and Israel, for you are my servant;**
> **I formed you, you are my servant;**
> **O Israel, you will not be forgotten by me.**
> **I have swept away your transgressions**

> **like a cloud, and your sins like mist;**
> **return to me, for I have redeemed you** (Is 44:21–22).

God calls the servant specifically Jacob and Israel, which are synonyms for the same group, the Jews. God does not call the servant Jesus. Moreover, Israel has need of redemption, which God grants repeatedly. Does Jesus have need of redemption?

7.   God asks, who can believe that this unsightly plant—a metaphor for the Jewish people—took root and thrived in the desert?

> **For he grew up before him like a young plant,**
> **and like a root out of dry ground;**
> **he had no form or comeliness**
> **that we should look at him,**
> **and no beauty that we should desire him** (Is 53:2).

The church is unwilling to say that Jesus "had no form or comeliness" or that he was, in a word, ugly.

8.   Isaiah says the Suffering Servant was afflicted for our transgressions, and we were healed by the striped wounds that the whip cut on his back:

> **He was despised, and rejected by men;**
> **a man of sorrows, and acquainted**
> **with grief [disease],**
> **and as one from whom men hide their faces;**
> **he was despised, and we esteemed him not.**
> **Surely he has borne our griefs [diseases]**
> **and carried our sorrows;**
> **yet we esteemed him stricken,**
> **smitten by God, and afflicted.**
> **But he was wounded for our transgressions,**
> **he was bruised because of our iniquities:**

> **upon him was the chastisement that made us whole,**
> **and with his stripes we are healed** (Is 53:3–5).

This cannot be Jesus because Jesus was not repeatedly afflicted. Afflicted with what? The Hebrew says "with diseases," but Christian bibles traditionally translate this as "with grief." Moreover, even though the servant was whipped, he was not crucified, and did not die. Although Jesus was whipped, he was also crucified, and most importantly he died. The church teaches that it was Jesus' death in his humanity that brought about the salvation of mankind.

9.   Isaiah says the Suffering Servant did not complain during his suffering. Not only did he not complain, but he did not even open his mouth:

> **[T]he Lord [YHVH] laid on him the iniquity of us**
> **all. He was oppressed, yet he opened not his mouth;**
> **like a lamb that is led to the slaughter,**
> **and like a sheep that before its shearers is dumb;**
> **so he opened not his mouth** (Is 53:6–7).

This cannot be Jesus because Jesus opened his mouth to complain and pray often during his final ordeal.

10.   The servant suffers because of the "transgressions of my people" Israel:

> **By oppression and judgment he was taken away;**
> **and as for his generation, who considered**
> **that he was cut off out of the land of the living,**
> **for the transgression of my people?** (Is 53:8).

This cannot be Jesus because the church says Jesus died for the sins of the world, not just Israel.

11. The servant's grave was prepared for him with the rich and the wicked even though he was without deceit:

> **And they made his grave with the wicked**
> **and with a rich man in his death,**
> **although he had done no violence,**
> **and there was no deceit in his mouth** (Is 53:9).

This cannot be Jesus because Jesus was not without deceit (Mt 13:44; Jn 7:2–10).

12. The preparation of a grave was in vain, for the Suffering Servant did not die:

> **Yet it was the will of the Lord [YHVH]**
> **to bruise him; he has put him to grief**
> **[to crush him by disease];**
> **when he makes himself an offering for sin,**
> **he shall see his offspring,**
> **he shall prolong his days,**
> **the will of the Lord [YHVH]**
> **shall prosper in his hands;**
> **he shall see the fruit of the travail of his soul**
> **and be satisfied;**
> **by his knowledge shall the righteous one,**
> **my servant, make many to be accounted righteous;**
> **and he shall bear their iniquities** (Is 53:10–11).

This cannot be Jesus because the Suffering Servant was afflicted, but did not die. (This extends and develops ideas expressed above in 8 and 10.) Although a grave had been prepared for the servant, such preparations were in vain, for he did not die. God intervened and saved him. And the servant went on to live a long and prosperous life, with endless generations of children. Is this Israel or Jesus? The question has become foolish.

JONAH: ANOTHER ALLEGORY FOR THE PASSION

The story of Jonah is Jesus' allegory for the passion, an allegory that the church does not discuss. The reasons will become evident.

Jonah is called by God to save the wicked gentile city of Nineveh from destruction. But Jonah is not interested in helping gentiles; so he books passage on a ship sailing in the opposite direction from Nineveh. During the voyage, a violent storm comes up, threatening to capsize the ship. Jonah, convinced that the storm is God's wrath on him, informs the crew of his disobedience to God and tells them the only way to save themselves is to throw him overboard. He argues that one man's life is a small price to pay to save all the others. The sailors, righteous men, are reluctant to toss Jonah overboard, for they consider that murder. In a quandary, they pray: "We beseech thee, O Lord, let us not perish for [taking] this man's life, and lay not on us innocent blood; for thou, O Lord, hast done as it pleased thee." Thereupon they throw Jonah overboard. The storm abates; the ship and men are saved. Jonah is swallowed by a giant sea monster, but after spending three days in its belly, he is vomited up and washed ashore. In the end Jonah does what God wanted him to do in the first place. He goes to Nineveh and preaches repentance to the gentiles; the people repent and are saved from destruction.

Jesus saw the Jonah story as an allegory for his own Passion (Mt 12:40). Jonah (now Jesus) is the cause of the storm (the turmoil in Jerusalem because of the things Jesus was saying and doing). Was Jesus' disobedience to God that he, like Jonah, did not want to preach repentance to the gentiles? We never learn. We only learn that the way to save the ship (the

Jewish nation) and the sailors (the Jewish leaders) is for the sailors to throw Jesus overboard (turning him over to the Romans for crucifixion). It is better that one man be sacrificed than the entire nation. The sailors (the Jewish leaders) toss Jonah overboard (hand Jesus over to Pilate for crucifixion). Prior to tossing him overboard, did the Jewish leaders pray, "We beseech thee, O Lord, let us not perish for [taking] this man's life, and lay not on us innocent blood; for thou, O Lord, hast done as it pleased thee"? The gospels do not say. In any event, Jesus is crucified and dies. The storm abates, and the Jewish nation is saved. Yes, not destroyed but saved! Judea's destruction did not occur until forty years after the Crucifixion and it happened for political reasons, not religious ones.

The allegory does not end there: Jesus says that just as Jonah was three days in the belly of the "fish" and then restored to life, Jesus will be three days in the earth and then restored to life. It follows that the resurrected Jesus, like Jonah, will go on to preach through his disciples to Nineveh (the gentiles).

The church does not like the allegory because it implies that Jesus like Jonah had sinned by being disobedient to God. Furthermore, the allegory implies that the crucifixion was divine punishment for Jesus' sin.

DID MOSES PROPHESY THE COMING OF CHRIST AND THE DESTRUCTION OF NONBELIEVERS?

Jesus said, *for he [Moses] wrote of me* (Jn 5:46), but Jesus never said where Moses wrote of him. Peter, however, seemed to know, for he said that Moses prophesied not only the coming of Jesus Christ but also the destruction of nonbelievers:

> **Moses said, "[YHVH] The Lord God will raise up for you a prophet from your brothers as he raised me up. You shall listen to him in whatever he tells**

> **you. And it shall be that every soul that does not listen to that prophet shall be destroyed from the people"** [Deut 18:18–19] (Acts 3:20–23).

Peter, however, was bearing false witness. He took the line out of context. Moses' very next line is:

> **But the prophet whosoever shall impiously speak in my name a word which I have not commanded him to speak, and whosoever shall speak in the name of other gods, that prophet shall die** (Deut 18:20).

Peter omitted that line because, in fact, Jesus died. Did Jesus speak words that God had not commanded him to speak and therefore was rightly condemned and crucified?

PORPHYRY: A HEATHEN CRITIC OF ALLEGORY

Porphyry, a third century Greek philosopher and heathen, wrote a treatise in fifteen volumes on the fallacies of Christianity. The church burned all copies. Unfortunately, unlike the case of Origen and Celsus, there are no surviving rebuttals by a church father. Only a fragment remains of Porphyry:

> [Some Christians] resorted to interpretations which cannot be reconciled or harmonized with the [Jewish] Scriptures. . . . "Enigmas" [Allegories?] is the pompous name they [these interpreters] give to the perfectly plain statements of Moses, glorifying them as oracles full of hidden mysteries, and bewitching the critical faculties by their extravagant nonsense. . . . This absurd method must be attributed to Origen, . . . whose fame . . . of these theories is widespread (Eusebius, *The History of the Church*, 6:19, p. 258).

Eusebius, speaking for himself writes:

> Such are the allegations made by Prophyry . . . against
> the Christians. He tells the truth about Origen's teach-
> ing (ibid., 6:19, p. 259).

DANGERS OF ALLEGORY AND PREFIGUREMENT

The church speaks of the entire Old Testament as an allegory or a prefiguration of the New Testament. That is a dangerous game to play. Someone could say that the following
passage from the Old Testament was an allegory for the
church:

> **We have made a covenant with death, and with**
> **Sheol we have an agreement . . . for we have made**
> **lies our refuge, and in falsehood we have taken shel-**
> **ter** (Is 28:15).

A passage from the Old Testament Apocrypha could also be
interpreted as an allegory for the church:

> [Y]ou have conquered all who went before, ruling over
> the whole world and holding it in the grip of fear and
> harsh oppression. You have lived long in the world,
> governing it with deceit and with no regard for truth.
> You have oppressed the gentle and injured the peaceful,
> hating the truthful and loving liars; you have destroyed
> the homes of the prosperous, and razed to the ground
> the walls of those who had done you no harm. Your
> insolence is known to the Most High, and your pride to
> the Mighty One (*The New English Bible with Apocry-*
> *pha,* 2 Esdras 11:40–43).

3. CHRISTIAN PROBLEMS

WHO KILLED CHRIST?

WHO KILLED CHRIST?

Who killed Christ? That may be the most frequently asked question in the Western world. And yet the question ought never to have arisen. The church should all along have been teaching that the question is irrelevant when, as Paul wrote and the church teaches:

Christ loved us and gave himself up for us (Eph 5:2).

That is the very core of Christian theology. The celebration of the mass of the Catholic church and Eastern Orthodox church is based on it. And yet, all the while the church was celebrating mass and saying, "Christ died for our sins," it was saying, "The Jews killed Christ," or, as if that were possible, "The Jews killed God."

QUESTIONS AND ANSWERS

Query: Who killed Socrates?
Answer: A few powerful Greeks.

Q: Who killed Julius Caesar?
A: A few powerful Romans.

Q: Who killed Joan of Arc?
A: A few powerful Catholics.

Q: Who killed Jesus of Nazareth?

A: The Roman governor along with a few powerful Jews. No, not the Roman governor. A few powerful Jews. No, not a few powerful Jews. All the Jews living then. No, not all the Jews living then. All the Jews collectively who ever lived and ever will live!

People clearly feel differently about the Jews than about the Greeks or the Romans or the Catholics or the Roman governor.

SIGNIFICANCE OF THE CRUCIFIXION

The evangelist Luke posed a profound question: **Was it necessary that the Christ should suffer these things?** (Lk 24:25–26). Luke does not answer his question, but others answered for him. John wrote:

> **For God so loved the world that he gave his only son** (Jn 3:16–17).

Paul wrote:

> **Christ died for our sins** (1 Cor 15:3).

> **Christ loved us and gave himself up for us** (Eph 5:2).

In the early twentieth century, Pope Pius X proclaimed:

> Mary gave her flesh for the birth of the only begotten Son of God so that in a human body the Victim Jesus was made ready for the salvation of the world. Mary's task went further: to cherish and nourish the Victim and to bring him at the appointed time to the Altar. . . . As the Son's life drew to its end, there, at the foot of

Jesus' cross, stood his mother, not overwhelmed by sorrow, as you might think, but rejoicing, because her only son was sacrificed for the salvation of the human race (Pope Pius X, from the encyclical *Ad Diem Illum*, AD 1904).

Towards the end of the twentieth century, Vatican Two taught:

Christ underwent his passion and death freely, and out of infinite love because of the sins of all men, so that all may obtain salvation. This the church has always held (*Nostra Aetate*, AD 1974).

The church's answer to Luke's question is, Yes, the crucifixion was necessary. The Father planned it and executed it for the salvation of humanity, and Christ was a willing victim. This "the church has always held." And yet. . . .

IS KILLING JESUS OF NAZARETH THE SAME AS KILLING CHRIST?

The church teaches and, in its own words, "has always" taught that Jesus of Nazareth "underwent his . . . death freely . . . so that all may obtain salvation." And yet, the church taught and in some places continues to teach that the Jews killed Christ. Which was it?

If Jesus was not the Christ, then the Jews did not kill Christ. Whoever was responsible executed a man, but not the Christ. If Jesus, however, was the Christ, then "the Jews"—a phrase implying all the Jews—did not kill him because all of his early followers were Jews: his mother Mary, the twelve apostles, and the entire new sect of Nazarene Jews. They most certainly did not kill Jesus or the Christ.

DID JESUS DESERVE TO BE EXECUTED?

The church teaches that the Jewish leaders thought Jesus of Nazareth was a blasphemer, and blasphemy under Jewish law was a crime deserving of death. But Jesus wasn't a blasphemer, not by the Jewish definition of blasphemy:

> **You shall not take the name of the Lord [YHVH] your God in vain** (Ex 20:7; Deut 5:11).

> **[W]hoever blasphemes the Name of the Lord [YHVH] shall be put to death; the entire congregation shall stone him** (Lev 24:16).

> Anyone charged with blasphemy is not considered guilty of blasphemy unless he utters the very name of God [which is YHVH] (*The Mishnah*, Sanhedrin 7:5).

Jesus never uttered the ineffable name of God, YHVH. Like his fellow Jews, Jesus used the substitute word *Adonai* or *Lord*. Hebrew Scriptures proclaim: **Hear O Israel: YHVH our God, YHVH is one** (Deut 6:4). When Jews say this aloud they say, "Hear O Israel, the Lord our God, the Lord is one." Jesus said the same: ***Hear O Israel: The Lord our God, the Lord is one*** (Mk 12:29).

A less common substitute word for the name of God is *Power*. (Those who speak Yiddish will recognize that word as *Gevalt*, as in *Oy, Gevalt!*) Jesus, on one occasion, used the word *Power* in place of YHVH: ***But I tell you, hereafter you will see the Son of man seated at the right hand of Power and coming on the clouds of heaven.* Then the high priest tore his robe and said, "He has uttered blasphemy"** (Mt 26:63–66; cf. Mk 14:61–64). However, the Council concluded that the high priest's allegation was unfounded. Jesus had said Power not YHVH. The Council exonerated Jesus and released him.

Blasphemy is a religious crime, not a political one. Roman law did not require someone accused of a religious crime to have a Roman trial. Had Jesus been found guilty of blasphemy, the Jewish Council would have stoned him to death without involving the Roman authorities.

MULTITUDES OF JEWISH BELIEVERS

THE MANY JEWISH FOLLOWERS OF JESUS

During the lifetime of Jesus of Nazareth, his mother, all the twelve apostles, and most of his disciples were Jews. A few of his well-known Jewish followers included John the Baptist, John's father Zechariah and his mother Elizabeth, Joseph of Arimathea, Simon of Cyrene, and Nicodemus. But Jesus had multitudes of Jewish followers who were unnamed:

> **Most of the crowd [of Jews] spread their garments on the road, and others cut branches from the trees and spread them on the road. And the crowds that went before him and that followed him shouted, "Hosanna to the son of David! Blessed is he who comes in the name of the Lord! Hosanna in the highest!"** (Mt 21:8–9).

> **And many [Jews] spread their garments on the road, and others spread leafy branches which they had cut from the fields. And those who went before and those who followed cried out, "Hosanna! Blessed is he who comes in the name of the Lord! Blessed is the kingdom of our father David that is coming! Hosanna in the highest!"** (Mk 11:8–10).

> **[A]ll the multitude [of Jews] was astonished at his teaching** (Mk 11:18).

And Jesus returned . . . to Galilee . . . and he taught in their synagogues and was glorified by all (Lk 4:14–15).

As [Jesus] was now drawing near, at the descent of the Mount of Olives, the whole multitude of [Jewish] disciples began to rejoice and praise God (Lk 19:37–38).

And there followed him a great multitude of the [Jewish] people and of women who bewailed and lamented him (Lk 23:27).

And all the multitudes [of Jews] who assembled to see the sight, when they saw what had taken place, returned home beating their breasts (Lk 23:48).

When the great crowd of Jews learned that Jesus was there, they came. . . . [for] many of the Jews were . . . believing in Jesus (Jn 12:9–11).

The next day a great crowd [of Jews] who had come to the feast heard that Jesus was coming to Jerusalem. So they took branches of palm tress and and went out to meet him, crying, "Hosanna! Blessed is he who comes in the name of the Lord, even the King of Israel!" (Jn 12:12–13).

There were even Pharisees and members of the Jewish council who supported Jesus:

At that very hour some Pharisees came and said to Jesus, "Get away from here for Herod wants to kill you!" (Lk 13:31).

Even the Jewish council was not unanimously against Jesus (Lk 23:50).

The gospels relate how Jewish leaders, knowing how popular Jesus was with the Jewish multitudes, were afraid to arrest him:

But when they [the chief priests and the Pharisees] tried to arrest him, they feared the multitudes [of Jews], because they held him to be a prophet (Mt 21:46).

Then the chief priests and the elders of the people gathered in the palace of the high priest, who was called Caiaphas, and took counsel together in order to arrest Jesus by stealth and kill him. But they said, "Not during the [Passover] feast, lest there be a tumult among the people" (Mt 26:3–5).

And they [the leaders] tried to arrest him, but feared the multitude (Mk 12:12).

And [Jesus] was teaching daily in the temple. The chief priests and the scribes and the leaders of the people sought to destroy him; but they did not find anything they could do, for all the people hung upon his words (Lk 19:47).

So [Judas Iscariot] . . . sought an opportunity to betray him . . . in the absence of the multitude (Lk 22:6).

After the crucifixion, multitudes of Jews continued to be followers of Jesus. James, the head of the Jerusalem Nazarenes (the Jewish believers), said to Paul, the apostle to the Gentiles:

You see, brother, how many thousands there are among the Jews who are believers (Acts 21:20).

The church prefers to ignore the many Jews who were believers and speak as if all the Jews were nonbelievers, thereby justifying collective antisemitism.

THE TOMB OF JOSEPH OF ARIMATHEA

When Jesus of Nazareth was taken down from the cross, his body was not thrown into the potter's field with the rest of the paupers. He was placed instead in the tomb of a rich Jew. The tomb is essential to the story because the resurrection could not be told without it. But the church does not teach the faithful that, nor does it teach that the tomb was donated by a Jew who was a member of the Jewish council.

> **There was a man named Joseph from the Judean town of Arimathea. He was a member of the council, a good and righteous man, who had not consented to the council's purpose and deed, and he was looking for the Kingdom of God. He went to Pilate and asked for the body of Jesus. Then he took it down [from the cross] and wrapped it in a linen shroud and laid it in a rock-hewn tomb** (Lk 23:50–54).

JEWISH MOBS

"HIS BLOOD BE ON US AND ON OUR CHILDREN"

His blood be on us and on our children (Mt 27:25) is the infamous curse of the Jews gathered in Pilate's courtyard upon themselves and their posterity. How many Jews were assembled in that courtyard? A hundred? A thousand? Ten thousand? If ten thousand, what percentage of all the Jews then in Jerusalem would that number represent? Historians estimate that about three million Jews came to Jerusalem for the Passover in those days. Ten thousand of three million represents less than 1% of all the Jews in Jerusalem. That means more than 99% of the Jerusalem Jews, not to mention 100% of the Jews in the Diaspora who had not come to Jerusalem, were not shouting "Crucify him!" and were not cursing themselves for doing so.

"CRUCIFY HIM!"

On Palm Sunday, several days before the incident in Pilate's courtyard, multitudes of Jews were waving palm fronds enthusiastically and shouting "Hosanna!" as Jesus entered Jerusalem riding on an ass. A day or so later, two days before the Passover, the Jewish leaders were afraid to do anything to Jesus out of fear that the multitude of Jews who loved Jesus would create an uprising:

> **It was now two days before the Passover and the feast of Unleavened Bread. And the chief priests and the scribes were seeking how to arrest him by stealth, and kill him; for they said, "Not during the feast, lest there be a tumult of the people"** (Mk 14:1–2).

And yet, the very next day, a Jewish mob appeared in Pilate's courtyard shouting, **Crucify him!** (Mt 27:22; Mk 15:8–14; Lk 23:13–21). John says it was not a mob but only the chief priest and officers (Jn 19:6). No matter. To the church it became *all* the Jews of *all* time. "Collective guilt" was the church's term.

BARABBAS: THE SECOND PRISONER

**Now at the feast [of the Passover] the [Roman] gov-
ernor [Pilate] was accustomed to release for the
crowd any one prisoner whom they wanted. And
they had then a notorious prisoner called Barabbas.
The crowd asked for the release of Barabbas. As for
Jesus called the Christ, they all said, "Let him be
crucified." Then Pilate released for them Barabbas**
(Mt 27:15–26).

On Palm Sunday, a few days before the above incident, the
gospels describe multitudes of adoring Jews. What happened
during the few days between Palm Sunday and the day before
Passover to make the adoring multitudes turn into a hateful
mob? Nothing. But over a few centuries something happened
to the church and also to the gospels.

It is reasonable to assume that in the original apostolic gospel the same adoring multitudes of Palm Sunday also appeared
in Pilate's courtyard, demanding Jesus' release. Pilate adamantly refused, and sentenced Jesus to death. But, by the
middle of the second century, the church and the Romans faced
a major problem. Many Romans had converted to Christianity
from their religion of the Olympian gods. Something had to be
done to the gospels to improve the unfavorable depiction of the
Romans who killed Jesus while at the same time negating the
favorable portrayal of the Jews who were trying to save Jesus.

To achieve the transformation was relatively easy; all the
redactors had to do was invent a second prisoner with the same
name as Jesus of Nazareth but in a disguised form. The name
the redactors chose was a hellenized Aramaic one, Barabbas.
That name to Romans and Greeks ignorant of Aramaic would
be devoid of meaning. This was one of the greatest obfusca-
tions of all time, and it achieved its objective.

This so-called "second" prisoner, Barabbas, had a first name, but insofar as it is possible that name has been kept hidden. One may find it only with difficulty in some gospel translations. Most translators of the gospels prefer to perpetuate the obfuscation by simply calling him Barabbas. What was his first name? Barabbas's first name was Jesus (Mt 27:15).

The name Jesus Barabbas is a hellenized version of the Aramaic name Jeshua Bar-Abba. One frequently translates a foreign name into Greek by adding a final *s*. Thus, Judah becomes Judas, Isaiah becomes Isaias, Jeshua becomes Jesus, and Bar-Abba becomes Barabbas. What does Barabbas or Bar-Abba mean? It means *son of the Father*. Son of the Father is synonymous with son of God.

Barabbas = Jesus Barabbas
Jesus Barabbas = Jesus Bar-Abbas (hellenized Aramaic)
Jesus Bar-Abbas = Jesus Bar-Abba (Aramaic)
Jesus Bar-Abba = Jesus son of the Father
Jesus son of the Father = Jesus son of God
Jesus son of God = Jesus of Nazareth
∴ Barabbas = Jesus of Nazareth!

The Jewish mob was indeed shouting, "Release Jesus Barabbas! Release Jesus, son of the Father." In other words, the mob was shouting for the release of Jesus of Nazareth! Who was shouting "Crucify him!"? We shall see.

There is no evidence of a prisoner named Barabbas or comparable incident in any gospel before the late second or early third century, and there is no evidence that the Romans or the Jews had a custom of releasing a prisoner during the Passover.

An ancient apocryphal text titled the "Acts of Pilate" also tells the Barabbas incident, but with significant differences (*New Testament Apocrypha*, Acts of Pilate, pp. 449–459;

J. Rendel Harris, *The Homeric Centones and the Acts of Pilate*, London: C. J. Clay and Sons, Cambridge University Press Warehouse, 1898). The major differences are: the mob of Jews hostile to Jesus are henchmen of the high priest and the council; in addition to that mob, multitudes of weeping Jews headed by Nicodemus appear before Pilate, vigorously supporting and defending Jesus, testifying that he was a good man and a doer of good and wonderful deeds. On seeing these multitudes of Jews, Pilate said to the hostile council, "Not all the multitude wishes him to die." It is worth noting too, that as in the gospel account, the twelve apostles are not among the multitudes. Finally, without ambiguity, it is Pilate who pronounces sentence upon Jesus and delivers him to his own soldiers for scourging and crucifixion: "I have decreed that you should first be scourged according to the law of the pious emperors, and then hanged on the cross." In the *Acts of Pilate*, then, we have a Christian work that gives an account of the passion that markedly conflicts with the gospel accounts as we know them.

In conclusion, there was only one prisoner who appeared before Pilate that fateful day, and he was Jesus Barabbas. But there were two mobs: one, the high priest's henchmen shouting "Crucify him!"; the other, the multitudes of Jews shouting "Release him!" To vilify all the Jews, the gospel redactors fused the two conflicting groups into one, invented the second prisoner, and had the Jews shouting Crucify Jesus! and Release Barabbas! Pilate released no one that fateful day. He sentenced to death by crucifixion the one and only Jesus Barabbas, who was Jesus of Nazareth.

KING OF THE JEWS

KING OF THE JEWS

"King of the Jews" was the title given to Jesus of Nazareth, sometimes seriously, at other times mockingly. The three wise men searching for the baby Jesus, inquired earnestly, **Where is the child who was born to be King of the Jews?** (Mt 2:2). But the Roman soldiers said mockingly, **"Hail! King of the Jews!"** (Mt 27:27). Whether in earnest or derision, Jesus became the King of the Jews. The King of the Jews became the god of the Christians.

TWO QUESTIONS ABOUT THE KING OF THE JEWS

1. Why is Jesus King of the Jews to everyone but the Jews?

2. Why is Jesus King of the Jews but not King of the Gentiles?

INRI: JESUS OF NAZARETH, KING OF THE JEWS

Jesus of Nazareth was crucified by the Romans, and the charge against him was INRI, an acronym for *Iesus Nazareth Rex Iudaeorum* [Jesus of Nazareth, King of the Jews] (Mt 27:7; Mk 15:26; Jn 19:19). To be King of the Jews was a grave civil crime, treason against Rome, punishable by crucifixion. Only the emperor could appoint a king in the Roman provinces. The emperor had not selected Jesus as king. The emperor probably had never heard of Jesus.

JESUS OF NAZARETH, KING OF THE JEWS
A PLAY IN ONE ACT

Characters
>JESUS OF NAZARETH, so-called King of the Jews
>PONTIUS PILATE, Roman Governor of Judea

Time: First century, c. AD 33
Scene: The Roman Governor's Palace, Jerusalem

PROLOGUE

JESUS. (*Enters.*) You are about to see my encounter with Pontius Pilate, the Roman governor, in his palace in Jerusalem. Before you do so, I must remind you of one of my most important teachings. Remember it, for your salvation depends on it! "Let what you say be simply 'Yes' or 'No.' Anything more than this comes from evil." Matthew, chapter 5, verse 37. (*Exits.*)

THE PLAY

At Rise: JESUS *is standing before* PILATE.

PILATE. Jesus of Nazareth, are you the King of the Jews?

JESUS. (*Not responding.*)

PILATE. (*Louder.*) Jesus of Nazareth, are you the King of the Jews?

JESUS. (*Not responding.*)

PILATE. (*Louder; annoyed.*) Jesus of Nazareth! Are you the King of the Jews?

JESUS. You have said so.

PILATE. (*Angry.*) Are you the King of the Jews?

JESUS. Is that your own idea or have others suggested it to you?

PILATE. (*Angrier.*) Answer the question! Are you the King of the Jews?

JESUS. My kingship is not of this world!

PILATE. (*Triumphant.*) So! You *are* a king!

JESUS. *You* say I am a king.

(PILATE *winces and slowly shakes his head. Curtain.*)

EPILOGUE

PILATE. (*Enters.*) Our play is over. Well now, I ask you, is this man, Jesus of Nazareth, King of the Jews? Let what you say be simply, "Yes" or "No."

(PILATE *stares intently but briefly at the audience, then he swiftly exits. Black-out.*)

The End

WAS JESUS CRUCIFIED?

The New Testament is not unanimous in stating that Jesus died by crucifixion. There are five statements in the New Testament that say Jesus was hanged from a tree; three are said by Peter and two by Paul.

The statements of Peter:

> **The God of our fathers raised Jesus whom you [the High Priest and the Council] killed by hanging him on a tree** (Acts 5:30).

> **They put him to death by hanging him on a tree** (Acts 10:39).

> **Jesus himself bore our sins in his body on the tree, that we might die to sin and live to righteousness** (1 Pet 2:24).

The statements of Paul:

> **And when they** [The Jewish leaders and the Roman rulers] **had fulfilled all that was written of him, they took him down from the tree, and laid him in a tomb** (Acts 13:29).

> **Christ redeemed us from the curse of the law, having become a curse for us—for it is written, "Cursed be everyone who hangs on a tree"** (Gal 3:13).

So which was it? Hanging or crucifixion?

"A HANGED MAN IS ACCURSED BY GOD"

The Old Testament states: **a hanged man is accursed by God** (Deut 21:22–23). If Jesus was hanged, Jesus was accursed by God. Paul gives the curse a positive spin (see above,

Gal 3:13). Jesus, in taking God's curse of hanging upon himself, removed the curse from his followers. Paul's interpretation did not please the church. How could Christians worship a hanged man, accursed by God? Crucifixion became the official cause of death.

WHO KILLED CHRIST?

WHO KILLED CHRIST ACCORDING TO HISTORY?

Who killed Christ according to history? There is only one historical document concerning this death. It was written in the early second century by the Roman historian Tacitus:

> Christ, the founder of the name [Christians], had undergone the death penalty in the reign of Tiberius, by sentence of the procurator Pontius Pilate, and the pernicious superstition was checked for a moment, only to break out once more, not merely in Judaea, the home of the disease, but in the capital itself [Rome], where all things horrible or shameful in the world collect and find a vogue (Tacitus, *Annals* 15:44).

Significantly, although Tacitus despised the Jews, he placed no blame on them for the crucifixion. He does not even mention them. Tacitus places the responsibility entirely on the Roman governor Pontius Pilate. Moreover, Tacitus implies that in crucifying Christ, Pilate acted responsibly, Christ being the author of "a most mischievous superstition."

WHO KILLED CHRIST ACCORDING TO CHRISTIAN THEOLOGY?

"Who killed Christ" according to Christian theology? In theology, God killed Christ and Christ was a willing victim:

> **For God so loved the world that he gave his only son, that whoever believes in him, should not perish, but have eternal life. For God sent the son into the world . . . that the world might be saved through him** (Jn 3:16–17).

In AD 1551 the Council of Trent declared:

> [Christ] our Lord and God was once and for all to offer himself to God the Father by his death on the altar of the cross.

The church also teaches that Christ killed Christ. The Profession of Faith of the Fourth General Lateran Council, AD 1215, states:

> Jesus Christ is at once priest and victim, whose body and blood are truly contained in the Sacrament of the [Eucharist] (*The teaching of the Catholic Church*, p. 431).

The church teaches today:

> Christ offering himself once for all a spotless victim to the Father (*Catechism of the Catholic Church*, p. 391).

THE FATHER SACRIFICES THE SON

The church teaches that the episode in the Old Testament of Abraham binding his son Isaac in preparation to sacrifice him was a prefigurement for the crucifixion. But that cannot be so because Abraham did not sacrifice his son. At the last moment, God intervened and prevented it. This was to teach the Jews that human sacrifice was forbidden; it was an abomination. The church, however, teaches that God is more loving than Abraham; whereas Abraham did not sacrifice his son, God actually did sacrifice his son. I think a father who sacrifices his son is not a god but a monster, and unworthy of being worshiped.

WHO KILLED CHRIST ACCORDING TO JESUS OF NAZARETH?

When Jesus of Nazareth stood before Pilate, Pilate said to him:

> **Surely you know that I have the authority to release you and I have the authority to crucify you** (Jn 19:10).

Jesus replied:

> *You would have no authority over me if it had not been granted to you from above* [from God]*. And therefore, the deeper guilt lies with him* [either God or the chief priest predetermined by God to do this] *who handed me over to you* (Jn 19:11).

Jesus tells Pilate that if anyone is to be held responsible, it is God, not Pilate. Jesus earlier had placed responsibility not only on God but also on himself:

The Father loves me because I lay down my life. . . .
No one takes it from me. I am laying it down of my
own free will. I have the right to lay it down. . . . This
charge I have received from the Father (Jn 10:17–19).

It would seem that Jesus committed suicide because the father charged him to do so, and the father committed filicide because that was his will.

JESUS' PROPHECY:
THE GENTILES WILL KILL JESUS

Jesus prophesied that the Jewish leaders would find him guilty but the Romans, after humiliating and whipping him, would kill him:

[The] Son of man will be delivered to the chief priests
and the scribes, and they will condemn him to death,
and deliver him to the Gentiles; and they will mock
him and spit upon him, and scourge him, and kill him
(Mk 10:33–34).

[The Son of man] . . . will be delivered to the Gentiles,
and he will be mocked and shamefully treated and spit
upon; they will scourge him and kill him
(Lk 18:31–33).

JESUS COULD HAVE ESCAPED

There were times when Jesus of Nazareth provoked the Jewish leaders to the point of arresting or murdering him, but he always managed to escape:

And they . . . led him to the cliffs of the hill on which
the city was built that they might cast him down

headlong [and kill him]. But [Jesus] passed through the midst of them and walked away (Lk 4:24–30).

Again they tried to arrest him, but he escaped from their hands (Jn 10:39).

During the passion, however, Jesus said he no longer wished to escape:

> *Do you think that I cannot appeal to my Father? He would at once send me more than twelve legions of angels [who would instantly come and save me]* (Mt 16:53).

Jesus gave himself up freely because to die, Jesus said, was what he was sent to do.

WHO KILLED CHRIST ACCORDING TO MATTHEW?

Matthew fulfills Jesus' prophecy that the Gentiles will humiliate and torture and crucify him:

> **Then the governor's [Pontius Pilate's] soldiers took Jesus into the praetorium, and they gathered the whole battalion before him. And they stripped him and put a scarlet robe upon him; and plaiting a crown of thorns, they put it on his head, and put a reed in his right hand. And kneeling before him, they mocked him, saying, "Hail! King of the Jews!" And they spat upon him, and took the reed and struck him on the head. And when they had mocked him, they stripped him of the robe, and put his own clothes on him, and led him away to crucify him** (Mt 27:26).

WHO KILLED CHRIST ACCORDING TO MARK?

Mark tells the passion story similarly to Matthew—as a fulfillment of Jesus' prophecy. Before crucifying him, the gentiles humiliated, whipped, and tortured him:

> So Pilate . . . having whipped Jesus, delivered him to be crucified. And the soldiers led him away, and took him inside the governor's palace; and they called together the whole battalion. And they clothed Jesus in a purple cloak, and plaiting a crown of thorns, they placed it on his head. And they began to salute him thus, "Hail, King of the Jews!" And they struck his head with a reed, and spat upon him, and they knelt down in homage to him. And when they were finished mocking him, they stripped him of the purple cloak, and put his own clothes on him. And they led him out to crucify him (Mk 15:15–20).

WHO KILLED CHRIST ACCORDING TO LUKE?

Luke, the only gentile evangelist, wrote much later than Matthew or Mark, during the middle of the second century, when the church had become mostly gentile. One ought not be surprised at finding Luke's gospel to be a pro-Roman and antisemitic version of the passion story. Earlier in Luke's gospel, Jesus prophesied that he would be handed over to the gentiles, who would mock him and torture him and spit upon him and scourge him and kill him (Lk 18:31–33). Earlier still, Luke had portrayed Pilate as vicious and responsible for the murder of Galilean Jews and then shamefully mixing their blood with the blood of Roman sacrificial animals (Lk 13:1).

During the passion, however, canonical Luke portrays an altogether different Pilate, one who is sympathetic, kind, gentle, and conciliatory. And contrary to Jesus' prophecy, Pilate does not whip Jesus, nor do his soldiers humiliate him; Luke has the high priest and his cohorts do that. Moreover, Luke would have us believe that Pilate executed Jesus not because that was what God and Jesus wanted or even what Pilate himself wanted, but only because that is what the Jews wanted. In canonical Luke, we see the hand of a pro-Roman antisemitic redactor at work. Luke told us at the onset of his book that he was not a witness and that he was dependent on earlier sources. But there are no pro-Roman antisemitic works on which Luke based his passion. Evidently, Luke's passion was a forgery. Here is the passion in canonical Luke:

> **Pilate then called together the chief priests and the rulers and the people, and said to them, "You brought me this man as one who was perverting the people; after examining him before you, behold, I did not find this man guilty of any of your charges. . . . nothing deserving death has been done by him; I will therefore chastise him and release him."**
>
> **But they all cried out together, "Away with this man, and release to us Barabbas"— a man who had been thrown into prison for an insurrection started in the city, and for murder. Pilate addressed them once more, desiring to release Jesus; but they shouted out, "Crucify, crucify him!" A third time he said to them, "What evil has he done? I have found in him no crime deserving death; I will therefore chastise him and release him." But they were urgent, demanding with loud cries that he should be crucified. And their voices prevailed. So Pilate gave sentence that their demand should be granted. He released the man who had been thrown into prison for insurrection and murder, whom they asked for; but Jesus he delivered up to their will** (Lk 23:13–25).

WHO KILLED CHRIST ACCORDING TO JOHN?

John alludes to Jesus' prophecy by saying that Jesus' prophecy was going to be fulfilled (Jn 18:31–32; 19:1–3). John relates that Jesus was going delivered to the gentiles to be mocked, scourged, and killed:

> **Pilate said to [the crowd of Jews], "Take him yourselves and judge him by your own law." The Jews said to him, "It is not lawful for us to put any man to death." This was to fulfill the word which Jesus had spoken to show by what death he was to die** (Jn 18:31–32).

> **Pilate took Jesus and scourged him. And the soldiers plaited a crown of thorns and put it on his head, and arrayed him in a purple robe; they came up to him, saying, "Hail, King of the Jews!" and struck him with their hands** (Jn 19:1–3).

John then relates that Pilate sought to release Jesus, but the Jewish leaders made him reconsider:

> **[Then] Pilate sought to release [Jesus]. . . . [Pilate] said to the Jews, "Here is your King! . . . Shall I crucify your King?" The chief priest answered, "We have no king but Caesar." Then [Pilate] handed him over to them to be crucified** (Jn 19:12–16).

John's vague phrase "handed him over to them" implies that Pilate handed Jesus over to the Jewish leaders, but it can only mean to the Roman soldiers because John had earlier referred to Jesus' prophecy which stated clearly that he would be handed over to the gentiles who would crucify him (Jn 18:31–32). Moreover, the Romans executed by crucifixion, the Jews did not. The Jews executed by stoning.

WHO KILLED CHRIST ACCORDING TO
THE COPTIC ORTHODOX CHURCH?

Culpability for the crucifixion of Jesus of Nazareth was a great problem for the church during the second century. For the very gentiles who had humiliated, tortured, and crucified Jesus were now worshiping him; while the Jews, to whom and for whom, the Father sent Jesus, were increasingly rejecting him. It was essential that gospel redactors diminish Roman culpability and augment Jewish guilt.

The Coptic Orthodox Church teaches that Pontius Pilate, by washing his hands of Jesus' death (Mt 27:24), exonerated himself of the crucifixion. Jesus, however, had condemned hand washing precisely because it did not wash away the evil in one's heart. The Coptic church ignores Jesus' condemnation of hand washing. The church also said that Pilate gave the order to crucify Jesus only because the Jews bribed him, even though there is no mention of bribery in the gospels. The Coptic church apparently believes that Pilate's acceptance of a bribe was not a crime. The only crime was the Jews offering the bribe. The Jews duped Pilate, and the high priest pressured him. Pilate's whipping of Jesus and his soldiers' mocking and humiliating him were overlooked as crimes.

The Coptic church so adores Pilate that it denies any gospel account that shows Pilate as cruel, and ignores the historical account by Philo, a Jewish historian and contemporary of Pilate, who wrote:

> Pilate was one of the emperor's lieutenants. He had been appointed governor of Judea. . . . He was a man of a very inflexible disposition, and very merciless. . . . He feared [that the Jews] might actually send an embassy to the emperor and might impeach him with highly specific charges about the way in which he ran his government; for example, his corruption, his insolence, his plundering of particulars of the government;

and his habit of insulting people, his cruelty, his continual murders of people without trying them first and without offering any charges against them, and his never-ending, gratuitous, and most grievous inhumanity (Philo, *Embassy to Gaius*, 38:299–303).

The Coptic Orthodox Church canonized Pilate. The church celebrates the feast day of St. Pontius Pilate on June 25.

WHO KILLED CHRIST ACCORDING TO THE GREEK ORTHODOX CHURCH?

The Greek Orthodox Church, in its sacred liturgy and traditions, teaches and practices antisemitism. The Greek church burns Judas Iscariot in effigy at Easter time in a ceremony called the "Burning of Judas." The Greek Ministry of Tourism features the "Burning of Judas" as a tourist attraction to encourage visitors to come to Greece at Easter time. During Holy Week, the Greek Orthodox church in its sacred liturgy reviles the Jews as "Theoktoni" ("God-killers"). Vatican Two had no ameliorating influence on the Eastern Orthodox Church. In the Great Thursday liturgy, recited during Holy Week, after the eleventh gospel reading, the Greek Orthodox church prays for never-ending vengeance on the Jews for killing God:

> [T]he swarm of God-killers, the lawless people, the Jews. . . . Give them, Lord, their requital.

What motivates the Orthodox church to revile the Jews with the most incredible, impossible, and evil epithet of all? Perhaps the following short play will explain it.

I LOVE YOU
A PLAY IN ONE ACT

Characters
  God
  The Eastern Orthodox Church
  The Jews (a nonspeaking character)

GOD: (*Turning to the Jews and raising his hands to bless them.*)

> **The Lord your God has chosen you to be a people for his own possession out of all the peoples that are on the face of the earth. It was not because you were more numerous than any other people that the Lord set his love upon you and chose you, for you were the fewest of all the peoples. But it is because the Lord loves you** (Deut 7:6–8).

EOC: How can you say that you love the Jews? The Jews killed you!

GOD: (*To the Jews.*) I love you.

EOC: How can you tell the Jews that you love them? They killed you.

GOD: (*To the Jews.*) I love you.

EOC: Stop it! They killed you! They are God-killers! Stop saying that you love them! Besides, you're dead! They killed you!

GOD: (*To the Jews.*) I love you.

EOC: You don't know what you're saying! The Jews killed you! Give them their just requital! Kill them all for killing you!

GOD: (*To the Jews.*) I love you, my darling child, my delight, my servant. I love you. When your enemies revile you, they revile me. Whoever hates you, hates me.

EOC: The Jews killed you! Don't you hear us? Don't you care about us? Don't you love us?

GOD: (*To the EOC.*) I love you.

EOC: (*Misunderstanding.*) How can you say that, when they killed you? We love you! Tell us that you love us! Oh, please tell us that!

GOD: (*To the EOC.*) I love you. I've always loved you. I'd love you more if you didn't preach hate.

EOC: Oh, what's the use? Let us pray: O God, take revenge on the God-killers! Kill them! Kill them all! We ask this in Christ's name.

THE END

WHO KILLED CHRIST ACCORDING TO
THE TALMUD?

Why did the church devote so much energy to finding a Jewish book that showed that the Jews and only the Jews killed Jesus of Nazareth, when such a book existed and the church was well acquainted with it? Why did the church, during the Middle Ages, confiscate and burn the Talmud? Why does the church today refuse to engage in dialogue with the Jews regarding the Talmud?

The first and earliest book of the Talmud is called the Mishnah. It existed in an orally transmitted form from the second century BC until the middle of the second century AD when it was codified and written down. Surprisingly, however, Jesus of Nazareth or, as Jews usually referred to him, Jesus the Nazarene, is not mentioned. To the Pharisees and rabbis who formulated the Mishnah, Jesus made no impact. It was as if he had never existed.

Subsequent books of the Talmud were written during the Dark Ages, from the end of the third century through the eighth. There are in fact two Talmuds, one written in Babylon, the other in Jerusalem. My subsequent discussion of the Talmud is based largely on the translation and interpretations by talmudic scholar Peter Schäfer (see Selected Bibliography). The Babylonian Talmud specifically refers to Jesus the Nazarene, and I shall discuss only the Babylonian Talmud. The Jerusalem Talmud has references to Jesus, but they are veiled, and to discuss veiled references is beyond the scope of this book (the interested reader may consult Schäfer). Schäfer explains why the references were veiled: Jerusalem during the Dark Ages was dominated by Christians, who enacted antisemitic legislation that restricted Jewish religious and political freedom. The Jews in Jerusalem, therefore, could not safely write analytically or critically about either Jesus or Christianity. However in Babylon, where Zoroastrianism was the prevalent religion, Jews had political and religious freedom; it was Christians who were persecuted, not for their religion, but for the suspicion they were spies for Rome.

Because the latter books of the Talmud were written several centuries after Jesus' death, references to him represent not history but medieval rabbinic thinking about him based on the New Testament and church teachings about him. It was as if the talmudic rabbis were saying, you, the Church, insist that we Jews killed Christ. And even if we didn't, it doesn't matter to you, because you persecute us as if we did. Because by persecution and torture you force us to confess we killed him, we shall give you our reasons for doing so:

According to the Talmud, Jesus the Nazarene was the bastard son of a loose woman and her lover, either a Roman soldier or the man to whom she was engaged, Joseph the carpenter. When Jesus grew up, he was a disobedient, disrespectful, and failed rabbinic student, sexually promiscuous and blatantly open about it, a sorcerer-healer, and a supreme evil-doer, "accursed by God," and he rightly deserved to die. The Passion story as narrated in the gospels, although placing responsibility for the crucifixion on the Romans, nonetheless places blame, shame, and guilt on the Jews. We talmudists, by contrast, place full responsibility for the execution of Jesus on the Jewish leaders, and we do so without blame, shame, or guilt. The death sentence was just. Jesus got what he deserved. In addition to his disgraceful life, Jesus did some highly evil things: He claimed to be the Messiah or the Christ, when he was not. He claimed to be the one and only Son of God, when he was not. He was an impostor and a charlatan. He was that kind of prophet who prophesied events that had already taken place. He ridiculed the purity laws of the Pharisees, did healing through sorcery, and with his five disciples [Five is puzzling. Were the talmudists saying Christians made up the number twelve to be parallel with the twelve tribes of Israel. Were the talmudists thereby impugning the veracity of the gospel accounts in their entirety?] led many Jews astray by encouraging them to become idolators through worshiping him when the Torah expressly forbids worshiping a man, for men tell lies: **God is not a man, that he should lie** (Num 23:19). Jesus lied. And Isaiah prophesied the fate of those who, like the king of Babylon, aspired to Godhead:

> **How you are fallen from heaven, O Morning Star, Son of the Dawn! How you are cut down to the ground. . . . You said in your heart: "I will ascend to heaven, above the stars of God. . . . I will make myself like the Most High." But you are brought down to the nether world, to the depths of the Pit** (Is 14:12–15).

The punishment for idolatry was death. Jesus received the punishment he deserved.

According to Jewish law, the severest crimes—blasphemy and idolatry—were accursed by God. To show that a criminal was accursed by God, he was hanged: **[A] hanged man is accursed by God** (Deut 21:23). It was the Jewish custom, prior to execution, for the judges to send forth a herald calling for witnesses to come forward to defend the accused. Although Jesus had five disciples, not one of them came forward to defend him. Accordingly, he was executed.

What specifically defined Jesus' idolatry? First and foremost, the talmudists said, Jesus promised his followers that if they ate his body and drank his blood, they would have eternal life. For the Jews, eating blood is forbidden; it is an abomination. Second, God alone gave eternal life.

The gospels say that after Jesus died, the Jewish leaders were concerned that a fraudulent resurrection would be accomplished by the disciples; they would steal the body from the tomb (Mt 27:62–66). Well, the talmudists said, that is exactly what happened.

Finally, the Talmud teaches that although all Jews have a place in the world to come, Jesus of Nazareth was an exception. He had no place in the world to come. Eternal life awaited him most certainly, but not the kind he promised and expected. He is not sitting in heaven, as he foretold, at the right hand of the Father, but is in hell, where he sits forever in a pool of boiling excrement. And all those who believe in him share the same fate.

Schäfer suggests the following link between Jesus' punishment and his teaching: Jesus taught that eating with unclean hands did not defile a man, for whatever one eats turns to excrement, and passes into the latrine; therefore, it is not that which enters the mouth that defiles a man; it is that which leaves the mouth—a man's evil words:

> ***Do you not see that whatever goes into the mouth passes into the stomach, and so passes on?*** ["Passes on" is an edulcorated translation for "is evacuated into the latrine" as explained earlier (see Eucharist). ***But what comes out of the mouth proceeds from the heart, and this is what defiles. For out of the heart come evil intentions . . . false witness, slander. These are what defile a person, but to eat with unwashed hands does not defile*** (Mt 15:17–20).

Jesus was wrong to ridicule the hand washing rule of the Pharisees, but he was right when he said that the words one speaks defile. Jesus spoke the following defiling words:

> ***[H]e who eats my flesh and drinks my blood has eternal life. . . . [H]e who eats me will live*** (Jn 6:54–57).

> *I am the resurrection and the life. He who believes in*
> *me, even though he die, yet shall he live, and whoever*
> *lives and believes in me shall never die. Do you be-*
> *lieve this?* (Jn 11:25–26).

Do you believe this? No, the talmudists did not believe this. Only God gives eternal life. If someone eats Jesus, some of what is eaten turns into excrement and is evacuated into the latrine. So whoever consumes Jesus body and blood goes to hell, and sits eternally with their master in a pool of their own boiling excrement.

In conclusion, the Talmud denies that the Jews killed Christ. It readily admits, however, that the Jewish authorities killed Jesus the Nazarene, who claimed to be the Christ but was not. The Jewish leaders rightfully executed Jesus; for he was one of the most evil Jews who ever lived, accursed by God. He received his just reward. And so will his followers.

There were periods in the Middle Ages when the church burned the Talmud. The church also saved a few, which may be found in the Vatican library.

Some Christian scholars dismiss the Talmud as a polemic that slanders and libels "our Lord," as if the Talmudists had no right to engage in polemic, but the New Testament and the church have always had that right to engage in polemic where the Jews were concerned. Other Christian scholars dismiss the Talmud on the ground that it was written so many centuries after Jesus lived that it contributes nothing to an understanding of the historical Jesus. Perhaps it contributes more than those scholars are willing to admit. One scholar dismisses the Talmud on the ground that there is nothing in it that in the least resembles "our Lord," so the Talmud must be referring to another Jesus!

In summary, the church teaches that without Jesus one goes to hell, whereas the Talmud teaches that with Jesus one goes to hell. Who is telling the truth?

SOME ABSURDITIES

THE DEATH OF ZEUS
The heathens who lived on Crete boasted that Zeus died on that island. Poets and philosophers asked, If Zeus is god, how can Zeus be dead? And if Zeus is dead, how can Zeus be god? To save the ancient religion from that criticism, many heathens concluded that the Cretans were liars.

THE JEWS AS HIGH PRIESTS
If Jesus of Nazareth was the sacrificial Lamb of God to take away the sins of the world, and if the Jews sacrificed the Lamb of God, then the Jews ought to be considered the high priests of God, worthy of the church's highest praise, instead of its greatest scorn. The church, however, insists that Jesus himself was the high priest who sacrificed himself, a willing victim, to take away the sins of the world.

At the Lateran Council of 649, the church decreed:

> If anyone does not truly and rightly believe . . . that . . . the divine Word [Jesus] . . . was crucified in the flesh of his own free will . . . *condemnatus sit* [may that person be damned].

PREDESTINATION AND THE CRUCIFIXION
Free will is nowhere at work in the Passion. The Father's will determines the whole story. Pontius Pilate, the Roman

soldiers, the Jewish Council, the high priest, and Judas Iscariot are all actors in the service of the Father's will.

Jesus prophesied that it was the Father's will that the Gentiles crucify him. Anyone who tried to intervene and prevent the Crucifixion was evil and thwarting God's will. When Peter tried to spare Jesus, Jesus angrily shouted: *Get behind me, Satan* (Mt 16:23).

The author of Acts says:

> **[F]or truly in the city [of Jerusalem] there were gathered together against your holy servant Jesus, whom you anointed, both Herod and Pontius Pilate, with the Gentiles and the peoples of Israel, to do whatever your hand and your plan had predestined to take place** (Acts 4:24–28).

All those centuries of bloodshed and murder over an event that the church teaches was predestined by God for the salvation of mankind!

ONE PERSON REDEEMING ANOTHER

A certain man was convicted of a massacre of innocent people. The judge pronounced sentence—death. No sooner was the sentence pronounced than a man in the courtroom jumped up and shouted, "I want to die for that man's sins. Release him and kill me!" The judge said, "How would justice be served by killing the wrong man?" How was justice served by the death of Jesus of Nazareth?

CHRIST KILLED THE JEWS

A popular slogan among antisemites has been "Kill a Jew for Christ!" And alas, too often they were willing murderers. Those who say, "The Jews Killed Christ" have it backwards.

The Jews didn't kill Christ. Christ killed the Jews. (Lk 19:27; cf. Hitler, *Mein Kampf*, p. 65).

CHRISTIAN ANTISEMITISM

"OUR LORD" IS A JEW

Jesus of Nazareth was a Jew who came from the Jews for the Jews. The church has never forgiven Jesus and the Jews for that.

"JUDAIZERS"

Jesus taught: *Think not that I have come to abolish the Law and the Prophets* (Mt 5:17). From this teaching, Peter and James taught that to become a Christian, one first had to become a Jew. Paul disagreed, and so did the early gentile church, which said that those who taught such things were "Judaizers," a term of great contempt.

THE GREAT CRIME OF THE JEWS

Was the Jewish leaders' participation in the execution of Jesus of Nazareth the great crime of the Jews? No. The great crime of the Jews was rejecting Jesus as the Messiah. Rejection is one of the most painful of all human emotions and may evoke the most malignant form of revenge. Not a single Christian has felt the pain of the crucifixion, but every Christian has felt the pain of rejection. Jews without having to say a word constantly remind the church they think it has accepted a false christ, worships a false god, and practices a false religion. That hurts. It hurts so much the church has felt the great need to convert the Jews. To convert them is to annihilate them bloodlessly. To annihilate them one way or another is to remove the pain of rejection.

"SLAVONIC" JOSEPHUS

It had long been the church's goal—particularly the Eastern Orthodox Church—to prove that the Jews and only the Jews were responsible for the death of Jesus of Nazareth. That the Father sent the Son to take away the sins of the world and that Jesus died of his own free will to accomplish this end was only theology. Antisemitism was more expedient than theology.

Josephus was the Jewish historian who lived at the time of the Roman conquest of Jerusalem. In the Middle Ages, a "new" version of Josephus appeared, not in Jerusalem, not in Rome or Greece, but incredibly in Central Europe inhabited by Slavs where antisemitism was particularly virulent. It was called the "Slavonic" Josephus.

Early Christian interpolators had Josephus attribute the fall of Jerusalem to the martyrdom of James the Just, brother of Jesus. Origen in the third century, was puzzled by that. Josephus subsequently was redacted, and the fall of Jerusalem was attributed to the crucifixion of Jesus of Nazareth.

Slavonic Josephus went further. Slavonic Josephus attributed the fall of Jerusalem to *the killing of God* by the Jews, not only the Jews of Jerusalem, but all the Jews everywhere, and not only those who lived at the time of Jesus, but all the Jews who ever lived or who ever would live. This version was so extravagant that even the church called it a forgery.

THE TWELFTH "BENEDICTION"

In ancient synagogues, "Eighteen Benedictions" were recited in the liturgy. One of those, the twelfth, was not a benediction, but a curse. The twelfth benediction antedated Christianity by two centuries, so it could not have been composed with the Christians in mind.

The twelfth benediction went as follows:

> For the renegades [Jews who collaborate with the enemy], let there be no hope. And may the arrogant kingdom [the Kingdom of the Greeks, which oppressed the Jews of Judea at the time of the Maccabees during the second century BC, before the Roman conquest] soon be rooted out in our days, and the *minim* [Jewish apostates to the heathen Greek religion] perish as in a moment, and be blotted out from the book of life, and may they not be inscribed with the righteous. Blessed art thou, O Lord, who humbles the arrogant.

After the Nazarene sect came into being in the first century AD, faithful Jews applied the word *minim* to all Jewish apostates, including converts to the Nazarene sect. In time, to lend the curse more specificity, the phrase "and the Nazarenes" was added to the word *minim.*

The church was pleased to find one Jewish curse and considered it equivalent to the many church curses on the Jews. So important was the twelfth benediction that Christian seminaries and schools of theology, which otherwise teach little about Judaism, unfailingly teach the twelfth benediction to show that the synagogue taught hatred of Christians. Those seminaries fail to teach, however, that the twelfth benediction was a curse only on Jewish converts to Christianity. It was not a curse on born Christians or on the church or on Christianity.

The twelfth benediction is defunct and has not been recited for centuries. All church curses on the Jews in canon law, however, remain in effect.

JUDENSAU

The church of the Middle Ages taught that the Jews did not eat pork because they worshipped the female pig—*Judensau* [*Jew Sow*]—which was their Christ. Because of Jewish adoration of the sow, the Jews feasted not on her flesh and blood but on her milk and excrement.

The church no longer teaches that, but the medieval teaching may still be seen in Christian art—in sculpture and paintings. Jews are shown sucking milk from the sow's teats, alongside the piglets, while a rabbi is kneeling expectantly by the sow's anus, his mouth wide open, eagerly awaiting the falling onto his tongue of the freshly emerging excrement.

Images of the *Judensaw* may be seen in the following churches and cathedrals—most of them in Germany where antisemitism fanned by Martin Luther was particularly virulent: Bamberg Cathedral, Brandenberg Cathedral, Cologne Cathedral, Magdeburg Cathedral, Regensburg Cathedral, and Wittenberg parish church, Martin Luther's very own church. Outside of Germany, these images are found in Metz Cathedral, France; Basel Cathedral, Switzerland; and Uppsala Cathedral, Sweden.

HITLER AND THE CHURCH

Adolph Hitler, the leader of Nazi Germany, was a Roman Catholic. Although he and the Nazis were responsible for the murder of millions of Jews, the church has never condemned them; the church never excommunicated Catholic Nazis for crimes against humanity. Instead, the church followed the recommendation of Saint Thomas Aquinas who, in the thirteenth century, wrote:

> Heretics deserve not only to be separated from the church by excommunication but also to be shut off

from the world by death (*Summa Theologica*, ii Q. xi, article III).

The Fourth Lateran Council decreed:

> Catholics who . . . devote themselves to the extermination of heretics shall enjoy the same indulgence and privilege as those who go to the Holy Land (Decrees of the Fourth Lateran Council, AD 1215).

GOD'S LOVE FOR THE JEWS

Another source of church antisemitism is God's love for the Jews as expressed in the Old Testament and particularly in the Prophets. Nowhere in the gospels nor anywhere in the New Testament, does God express such love for the gentiles. Jesus of Nazareth calls the gentiles "dogs." This is what God has to say about the Jews:

> **The Lord your God has chosen you to be a people for his own possession out of all the peoples that are on the face of the earth. It was not because you were more numerous than any other people that the Lord set his love upon you and chose you, for you were the fewest of all the peoples. But it is because the Lord loves you** (Deut 7:6–8).

> **But you, O Israel, my servant, you, O Jacob, whom I have chosen. . . . I have called you my servant, have chosen you. . .** (Is 41:8–9).

> **You are precious in my eyes and honored, and I love you** (Is 43:1–4).

> **I betroth you to myself forever. I betroth you . . . in tender love** (Hos 2:19).

The Lord said to Israel, I love you (Mal 1:1).

Nothing upsets a child so much as the thought that a parent may love a sibling more. In trying to convert the Jews, the church evidently wants the Jews to forsake God's singular love of them. Adolph Hitler interpreted the word *chosen* (Deut 7:6, above) to mean that God made the Jews not only his favorites but also the most powerful people on earth. And so, Hitler feared them. Hitler wrote:

> When, over long periods of human history, I scrutinized the activity of the Jewish people, suddenly there rose up in me the fearful question whether inscrutable Destiny, perhaps for reasons unknown to us poor mortals, did not, with eternal and immutable resolve, desire the final victory of this little nation [of Jews]. Was it possible that the earth had been promised as a reward to this people that lives only for this earth? Have we an objective right to struggle for our self-preservation, or is this justified only subjectively within ourselves? (Hitler, *Mein Kampf*, p. 64).

This statement demolishes the so-called racial inferiority theory regarding Hitler and the Jews and shows that Hitler's antisemitism did not originate in contempt, but in extraordinary admiration. The statement shows, too, how deeply religious Hitler was. He feared that the Jews really had a connection with the power of the universe and through that connection had acquired supernatural power. These are not the words of an atheist or a pagan. Moreover, in speaking of the Jews as "this people that lives only for this earth," Hitler intimates his devotion to Christian heaven.

In *Mein Kampf* [*My Struggle*], Hitler asks the question that consumed his entire political life and defined the core of his political philosophy: Have I not the right to fight to make the earth free of the Jews in order to save the earth for the Christians? And what Hitler referred to as "my struggle," he saw as a noble enterprise that avenged the Lord Jesus Christ. Hitler wrote:

> <u>By defending myself against the Jew, I am fighting for the work of the Lord</u> [underlining is Hitler's] (Ibid., p. 65).

What was the "work of the Lord?" The Lord Jesus defined it:

> ***But as for these enemies of mine who did not want me to reign over them, bring them here, and slay them before me!*** (Lk 19:27).

NAZI ANTISEMITISM: CHRISTIAN ANTISEMITISM

Hans Küng, a church theologian, wrote in the twentieth century about Christian antisemitism. Father Küng said that church persecution of the Jews culminated in the Holocaust:

> The church preached love while it sowed the seeds of murderous hatred. It proclaimed love, while it prepared the way for atrocities and death. And these acts were perpetrated against the compatriots and brothers of him who taught the church, "What you did to one of the least of these, my brothers, you did to me" (Mt 25:40) (Kung, *The Church*, p. 184).

> Nazi anti-Semitism . . . would have been impossible without the preceding 2,000 years of "Christian" hostility to the Jews. . . . [N]one of the anti-semitic measures of the Nazis were new. The use of special clothing as a distinguishing mark, exclusion from certain professions, banning of mixed marriages, seizing of Jewish

goods, expulsion and concentration camps, burning and butchering—all these things existed in the "Christian" Middle Ages and during the "Christian" Reformation (Ibid., p. 185).

The following are some Christian writings that support Father Küng's statement:

Paul wrote in the first century:

> **[The Jews] killed the Lord Jesus and the Prophets, drove us out, displease God, and oppose all men. . . . But God's wrath has come upon them forever** (1 Thess 2:14–15).

Saint John Chrysostom wrote in the fourth century:

> The synagogue . . . is a theater, a whore house, a den of thieves, a den for wild animals, . . . raving mad Jews! . . . The Jews killed the son of your Master. . . . Will you so dishonor him as to respect and cultivate his murderers, the men who crucified him? (*Eight Homilies Against the Jews*).

The church decreed in the thirteenth century:

> Catholics who . . . devote themselves to the extermination of heretics shall enjoy the same indulgence and privilege as those who go to the Holy Land (Decrees of the Fourth Lateran Council, AD 1215).

Martin Luther wrote in the sixteenth century:

> What then shall we Christians do with this damned, rejected race of Jews? . . . Since they live among us, and we know about their lying, blasphemy, and cursing,

> we cannot tolerate them, if we do not wish to share in
> their lies, curses, and blasphemy. . . . We must prayer-
> fully and reverentially practice a merciful severity (Lu-
> ther, *On the Jews and Their Lies*).

Luther went on to define "merciful severity"—the burning of Jewish homes, schools, and synagogues; the burning of Jewish prayer books and Torah scrolls; the prohibition of rabbis from teaching and holding religious services; the confiscation of Jewish property; and enforced hard labor on Jewish youth. Luther further advocated the expulsion of all Jews from Germany, but realizing that may not be possible, advised:

> If that advice of mine [expulsion of the Jews from
> Germany] does not suit you, then find something better
> [that is, their murder and annihilation] so that you and
> we may all be free of our insufferable satanic bur-
> den—the Jews! (ibid.).

Luther's writings became Hitler's handbook.

Ashamed of Christian antisemitism, the church has tried to separate itself from the Nazis by teaching that Hitler was godless and that Nazis were pagans. While some of the Nazis advocated a form of Nordic mythology, they did not abandon Christianity. On Sundays, many went with their families to the Lutheran or the Roman Catholic church.

It is commonly taught that Hitler's war against the Jews was fought on racial and not on religious grounds, that he saw the Jews as an inferior race; and that Hitler, in trying to annihilate them, was practicing a form of eugenics. This is not so. Hitler was in awe of the Jews and regarded them as superior. Hitler was a Christian, and there is no evidence he ever turned from Christianity. He claimed in *Mein Kampf* that his war against the Jews was a religious war not a political one. He said he was acting in accordance with the will of the Creator and he was fighting for the work of the Lord Jesus Christ:

> I am acting in accordance with the will of the Almighty Creator. <u>By defending myself against the Jew, I am fighting for the work of the Lord</u> [underlining is Hitler's] (Hitler, *Mein Kampf*, p. 65).

I have cited words of some very famous Christians—Paul, John Crysostom, the Fourth Lateran Council of the Roman Catholic Church, Martin Luther, and Adolph Hitler. But none of their words were as hateful as those of the master himself, Jesus of Nazareth, who tells a parable that concludes:

> ***But as for these enemies of mine who did not want me to be their king. Bring them here and slay them before me!*** (Lk 19:27).

If anyone is looking for sacred authority for Christian antisemitism, look no further. The Holocaust was spelled out by Jesus. The historian Werner Keller wrote:

> With the rise of Christianity, the daughter religion of Judaism, a new, powerful, and inexorable enemy of the Jews appeared. Paganism had destroyed the political existence of the Jews. Now the time was approaching when victorious Christianity would attempt . . . to stamp out their spiritual existence as well. . . . The Jews were to find their cruelest enemy in Christianity, which owes its origins to Judaism, derives its highest ethical doctrines from the spirit and thought of the great sons of Israel, sings the Psalms, and repeats the ancient prayers of the Jews. Christianity, having risen to power in the secular state, did everything it could to break the spirit of the Jews and to convert them. Judaism became for Christians the "unholy cult" of a damned "blasphe-

mous nation," the members of which were condemned as "God-killers" and "Christ-killers" (Keller, *Diaspora: The Post-Biblical History of the Jews*, p. 72).

THE SILENT CHURCH: POLITICALLY CORRECT ANTISEMITISM

The church was silent during the Holocaust. Today the church defends its silence by claiming silence was the most effective shield for saving Jews. That is not credible.

Radical Moslems today claim there is no evidence of a historic Jewish presence in Jerusalem or Palestine. The church again is silent, even though it knows how frequently Jerusalem is mentioned in the New Testament (over a hundred times), as is Judea, the land of the Jews (over forty times), the Jewish temple (over a hundred times), and the Jews, especially the Jew named Jesus of Nazareth (countless times), whereas the name Palestine does not appear once.

The gospels refer repeatedly to Jesus of Nazareth's preaching in synagogues in Judea as well as in the Galilee, and refer to his many visits to Jerusalem and the Jewish temple. The Arch of Titus, which stands in the Roman forum and dates from the first century shows carved in stone the conquest of Jerusalem with Jewish slaves bearing the trophies of the Jewish temple into Rome.

In spite of the overwhelming evidence showing a Jewish presence in Judea and Jerusalem and the temple mount during the first century, extremist Moslems maintain that there is no evidence of a Jewish presence in Judea or Jerusalem. The church listens to these statements in silence, which is, after all, the politically correct thing to do. Why take sides when it is more expedient to deal even-handedly? To be even-handed in this case, however, is to support a lie. When the church does not speak of the Jewish presence in Judea and Jerusalem and of the temple and the temple mount, the church is denying Jesus of Nazareth who lived there and died there. And for the church to deny Jesus, by its own teaching, is to deny its own salvation.

THE GIFT FROM THE JEWS

The gifts to humanity from the Jews in all areas of human endeavor are unparalleled. The church ought to praise the Jews continuously at least for one gift, Jesus of Nazareth.

LIMITS OF ANTISEMITISM

Antisemitism has its limits. No antisemite has ever called Jesus Christ, "Kike!"

GOSPEL ADMIRATION OF THE JEWS

The New Testament, allegedly a book of love, is largely a book of hatred where the Jews are concerned. Even so, there are a few verses that express extraordinary admiration of the Jews. The church ignores those verses, and the faithful hardly know of them:

> **Simeon took [the baby Jesus] up in his arms, praised God, and said, "He is a light for revelation to the Gentiles and for glory to thy people Israel"** (Lk 2:32).

Jesus said:

> *You [Gentiles] worship what you do not know. We [Jews] worship what we know. Salvation is from the Jews* (Jn 4:22).

Paul wrote:

> **They are the Israelites, and to them belong the sonship, the glory, the covenants, the giving of the Law, the worship, and the promises. To them belong the patriarchs, and from them in the flesh came the Christ** (Rom 9:4–5).

> **Are they Hebrews? So am I** (2 Col 11:22).

Paul, explaining Gospel antisemitism, wrote:

> **As regards the Gospel, the Jews are enemies of God for your [the Gentiles'] sake; but as regards election [going to heaven], they are beloved for the sake of their forefathers. For the gifts, and the call of God are irrevocable** (Rom 11:28–29).

Peter, after castigating a group of Jews for "crucifying Christ," ends his rebuke lovingly:

> **For the promise is to you** (Acts 2:22).

As regards election, I am beloved! The promise is to me! I would be a fool to convert.

DIVINE RETRIBUTION

THE FALL OF JERUSALEM

In AD 70, Jerusalem was conquered and destroyed by the Roman Empire. The church taught that this was divine retribution against the Jews for the crucifixion. That theological interpretation of history became more important to the church to prove the divinity of Jesus than did his resurrection. The resurrection was witnessed by no one, but the fall of Jerusalem was witnessed by the whole world.

MALACHI'S PROPHECY

The Messiah (the Christ) was to bring an end to discord between parents and children. Malachi prophesied that if a man appeared and, instead of promoting harmony between parents and children, increased discord between them, and the people believed in that man, God would smite and curse the land:

> **And he will turn the hearts of fathers to their children and the hearts of children to their fathers, lest I come and smite the land with a curse** (Mal 4:5).

Did Jesus promote harmony between parents and children? No, quite the contrary. Jesus said:

> *Do you think that I have come to give peace on earth? No, I tell you, but rather divisiveness! . . . Father against son, son against father, mother against daughter, daughter against mother!* (Lk 12:49–53).

> *I have come to set a man against his father, and a daughter against her mother* (Mt 10:34–36).

> *If anyone comes to me and does not hate his own father and mother . . . he cannot be my disciple* (Mt 14:26–33; cf. Lk 14:26).

Was Jesus the Messiah? Hardly. Malachi implies that Jesus was the anti-Christ, who caused God to smite the land with a curse.

HEATHEN INTERPRETATION

In the second century, a heathen Greek philosopher by the name of Celsus gave a different interpretation for the fall of Jerusalem. The church father Origen reports Celsus's words:

> [T]hey [the Jews] suffered . . . through those who followed Jesus and believed him to be the Christ. . . . [A] revolt against the community led to the introduction of new ideas [contrary to those in the Law given by Moses] (Chadwick, *Contra Celsum*, 3:5, p. 131).

Celsus's interpretation was that the fall of Jerusalem was divine retribution not for the Jews who plotted against Jesus or who "killed Christ," but for the Jews who believed that Jesus was the Christ. Celsus's interpretation was consistent with Malachi's prophecy above and the word of God that follows:

> **But if . . . you . . . are drawn away to worship other gods and serve them, I declare to you this day, that you shall perish; you shall not live long in the land which you are going over the Jordan to enter and possess. . . . I have set before you life and death, blessing and curse; therefore choose life, that you and your descendants may live, loving the Lord [YHVH] your God, obeying his voice, and cleaving to him; for that means life to you and length of days, that you may dwell in the land which the Lord [YHVH] swore to give to your fathers, to Abraham, to Isaac, and to Jacob** (Deut 30:17–20).

Jerusalem and Judea fell as divine retribution not for the Crucifixion, but because so many Jews turned to a new god, to Jesus of Nazareth.

THE EMPEROR HADRIAN

For several generations following the AD 70 destruction of Jerusalem and the Temple, many Jews remained in the Judean countryside, and many of them conducted a relentless guerrilla war against the Romans. In AD 135 the Roman Emperor Hadrian put down the rebellion and crushed the Jews completely. Hadrian expelled them from Jerusalem and Judea, and issued an edict forbidding them from ever entering the city and the land again. He ordered that a temple to Jupiter be built in Jerusalem on the site where the Temple had stood, changed the name of Jerusalem to Aelia Capitolina, a city that was to remain forever free of Jews, and changed the name of the nation from Judea, which means the land of the Jews, to Palestina, which means the land of the Philistines, the people, Hadrian's historians told him, who had dwelled in the land before the Jews.

Hadrian's hatred of the Jews had nothing to do with love of the Christians, for he did not distinguish between Christians and Jews. He asserted that his conquest showed how weak was their god compared with the gods of the Romans. The church teaches that Hadrian's conquest came about to punish the Jews. But Hadrian dealt a wound so great to the Christians in Jerusalem that the nascent church there transferred its center first from Jerusalem to Alexandria and finally to Rome. During that transition, Christianity went from a Jewish sect to a new heathen religion.

THE FALL OF ROME

In AD 410, shortly after Christianity became the religion of the Roman Empire, Rome experienced the horror she had so often inflicted on others. She was sacked by the warlord Alaric and his Visigoths. It was the first time in its long history that Rome was invaded, let alone conquered. Alaric's victory was swift and complete. The news of Rome's fall spread quickly around the world. Jerome was in Bethlehem in Judea at the time. Jerome exclaimed:

> My voice sticks in my throat; and as I dictate, sobs choke my utterance. The City which had taken the whole world was itself taken! (Letter 127).

The fall of Rome marked the beginning of the end of the Roman Empire. In AD 455, the final blow was delivered by Gaiseric and his Vandals. There followed wave upon wave of barbarian invasion. The empire's cities were sacked and her countryside wasted. On September 4, 476, the last Roman emperor was deposed, and the Roman Empire ceased to exist.

THE FALL OF JERUSALEM COMPARED WITH THE FALL OF ROME

The church taught that the fall of Jerusalem was divine retribution that showed God's displeasure toward the Jews for their rejection or killing of Jesus Christ, whereas the fall of Rome showed God's love of the Christians for their endurance and fortitude.

Roman heathens, however, said the Roman Empire fell as divine retribution for Constantine's sin in rejecting the Roman gods and replacing them with the Christian god, and Jerusalem fell for the same reason.

CALAMITIES ON THE JEWS VS. CALAMITIES ON THE CHRISTIANS

When the church speaks of calamities on the Jews, it calls them divine retribution or God's wrath upon the Jews. Paul wrote, **God's wrath has come upon [the Jews] at last!**

(1 Thess 2:16). However, when the church speaks of calamities on the Christians, it says that God has bestowed upon the Christians laurel crowns of victory! Eusebius wrote, "[B]y their heroic endurance of every kind of torture and every form of death, [Christian martyrs] were wreathed with the crowns laid up with God" (Eusebius, *The History of the Church*, 6:1, p. 239).

THE STAR OMEN

Josephus, who witnessed the fall of Jerusalem, reported that just before the city fell, "a star stood over the city" and "foretold the coming desolation." The people regarded the star as an omen for good. Josephus despaired that no one heeded the star for what it was, an omen of doom:

> [The people] neither heeded nor believed in the manifest portents that foretold the coming desolation but . . . disregarded the plain warnings of God. So it was when a star . . . stood over the city (Josephus, *The Jewish War*, Book VI, pp. 288–289).

Earlier in that century, a star stood over Bethlehem. Then, too, the people regarded the star as an omen for good:

> **Lo, the star which [the three wise men] had seen in the East went before them, till it came to rest over the place where the child was. When they saw the star, they rejoiced exceedingly** (Mt 2:9–10).

DIASPORA

The church taught that the Dispersion of the Jews, the Diaspora, was also divine retribution, even though the Diaspora had taken place before Jesus of Nazareth was born. Josephus reported that the Greek geographer and historian Strabo, who lived a century before Jesus, said this of the Jews in the Diaspora:

> The Jewish people has already made its way into every city, and it is not easy to find any place in the habitable world which has not received this nation and in which it has not made its power felt (Josephus, *Jewish Antiquities*, Book 14, line 115, p. 509).

Josephus, speaking for himself, wrote:

> The Jewish people is densely interspersed among the native populations of every part of the world (Josephus, *The Jewish War*, Book 7, line 43, p. 517).

Jesus said:

> ***Where I am, you cannot come.*** **The Jews said to one another, "Where does this man intend to go that we shall not find him? Does he intend to go to the Dispersion [Diaspora]"** (Jn 7:34–35).

Paul who wrote and preached before the fall of Jerusalem reported synagogues in all the cities of the world that he visited: Salamis (Acts 13:5); Antioch (13:14); Iconium (14:1); Thessalonica (17:1–2); Beroea (17:10); Athens (17:16–17); Corinth (18:1–4); Ephesus (18:19).

About AD 40, thirty years before the fall of Jerusalem, King Agrippa wrote in a letter to the emperor Caligula:

> While Jerusalem is my native city, she is also the mother city not of one country, Judea, but of most of the others by virtue of the colonies of Jews sent out at various times to the neighboring lands—Egypt, Phoenicia, Syria—and lands lying far away—Pamphylia,

Cilicia, most of Asia [the Middle East], . . . Europe, Thessaly, Boeotia, Macedonia, Aetolia, Attica, Argos, Corinth, and most of the nicest parts of the Peloponnese. And not only are the mainlands full of Jewish communities, but also the most highly esteemed islands—Euboea, Cyprus, Crete. As regards the countries beyond the Euphrates . . . they all—Babylon and the other satrapies where the land is highly fertile—have Jewish inhabitants (Philo, *Embassy to Gaius*, lines 281–2).

God, speaking through his prophet Isaiah, long before Jesus was born, promised:

I will make an everlasting covenant with [the Jews]: Their descendants shall be known among the nations, and their offspring in the midst of the peoples [gentiles]; all who see them shall acknowledge them, that they are a people whom the Lord [YHVH] has blessed (Is 61:8–9).

Clearly the Diaspora had nothing to do with the crucifixion.

THE DESTRUCTION OF THE TEMPLE

The church taught that the temple was destroyed as divine retribution for the crimes of the Jews against Jesus. What the church does not teach is that God never wanted a temple in the first place. God is everywhere, so what need has God of a house? God said that repeatedly:

Would you build me a house to dwell in? I have not dwelt in a house since the day I brought up the people of Israel from Egypt to this day (2 Sam 7:5–6).

> **Heaven is my throne and the earth my footstool;
> what is the house which you would build for me, and
> what is the place of my rest?** (Is 66:1).

Moreover, God did not want sacrifices performed in the temple
or elsewhere:

> **For in the day that I brought [the children of Israel]
> out of the land of Egypt, I did not speak to your fa-
> thers or command concerning burnt offerings and
> sacrifices. But this command I gave them, 'Obey my
> voice, and I will be your God, and you shall be my
> people; and walk in all the way that I command you,
> that it may be well with you.' But they did not obey
> . . . but walked in their own counsels and the stub-
> bornness of their evil hearts, and went backward
> and not forward** (Jer 7:22–24).

Sacrifice was the barbarian practice of primitive man, a step
backward for civilization. In vain the Temple. In vain sacrifices. In vain the Crucifixion.

SALVATION OF THE JEWS
AFTER THE CRUCIFIXION

Had God been angry at the Jews for the crucifixion and
wished to punish them for it, he would have done so immediately rather than waiting forty years when it would have been
impossible, except by the irrational, to make an association.
One does not punish a man for something he did as a child and
expect him to learn something from it.

God had the opportunity to punish the Jews shortly after the
crucifixion, but he did not do so. Josephus reports the following episode that occurred in AD 41, soon after the crucifixion:

The insolence of the Emperor Caligula surpassed all bounds. He even defied destiny. He wished to be considered a god, and to be greeted as one . . . and his impiety extended even to Judea. In fact, he sent Petronius [the governor of Syria] with an army to Jerusalem to install in the Temple statues of himself. In the event that the Jews refused to allow it, Caligula's orders were to put the recalcitrants to death and to reduce the whole nation to slavery. But God's care intervened. . . .

The Jews assembled with their wives and children in the plain of Acre and implored Petronius first to have regard for the Law of their fathers, and next for themselves. He yielded temporarily . . . left the statues and his troops at Acre and advanced into Galilee, where he summoned the people, including their leaders, to the town of Tiberias. There he talked at length of Roman power and the fate of the Emperor's enemies. Furthermore, he pointed out the rashness of their request. All nations subject to Rome . . . had erected in every one of their cities statues of Caesar, along with those of the other gods. That the Jews alone should oppose this practice was a serious insult, tantamount to revolution.

When the Jews appealed to their Law . . . that they were forbidden to place an image of a god, let alone a man, not only in their Temple but even in any unconsecrated spot throughout their country, Petronius replied, "But I, too, must obey the law of my master. If I transgress it and spare you, I shall be put to death, and justly so. War will be made upon you by him who sent me, not me. For, like you, I must obey commands."

At this the crowd cried out that they were ready to endure anything for their Law. Petronius, after calming them, said, "Will you even go to war with Caesar?" The Jews replied that twice daily they offered sacrifices on behalf of Caesar and the Romans, but that if he was determined to set up these statues, then he must first sacrifice the entire Jewish nation; and they presented themselves, wives and children, ready for the slaughter. These words filled Petronius with astonishment . . . at the incomparable devotion of this people to their religion and their unflinching resignation to death. And so, for the time being, he dismissed them, reaching no decision.

During the ensuing days . . . he used entreaty one minute, advice the next, but most often threats, holding over their heads the power of Rome, the fury of Caligula, and the order he had to carry out. . . . When he realized that none of this would induce the Jews to budge, and as he saw that the country was in danger of remaining unplanted, for it was seed time, and the people had already wasted fifty days waiting for him [to reach a decision], he finally called them together and said, "It is better that I risk it. Either, with God's help, I shall prevail over Caesar and have the satisfaction of saving myself as well as you; or, if his fury is aroused, I am ready, on behalf of the lives of so many, to lose my own." With that he dismissed the multitude, who showered blessings upon his head. Collecting his troops, he left Acre and returned to Antioch. From there he sent a report to Caesar concerning his expedition into Judea and the entreaties of that nation; and he added that, unless Caligula wished to destroy the entire country with all its people, he ought to respect their Law and revoke his order.

To this dispatch Caligula replied in no measured terms, threatening to put Petronius to death for his delay in carrying out orders. However, it so happened that the bearers of this message encountered a storm at sea that kept them immobile, while other messengers, who brought the news of Caligula's death, had swift passage. So Petronius received the news of Caligula's death twenty-seven days before he received the letter conveying his own death warrant (Josephus, *The Jewish War*, Book 2, lines 184–204).

For those who give theological interpretations to historical events, one could say, based on the episode reported above, that God did not punish the Jews after the crucifixion. God saved them! It was not until AD 70, at which time the Jewish Christians had established a church in Jerusalem and had begun to worship, in addition to the one God YHVH, a new god, that God, because of their great sin, destroyed Jerusalem.

ISRAEL

THEODOR HERZL AND THE VATICAN

When Theodore Herzl in the nineteenth century conceived the idea of recreating a Jewish state in Palestine, he went to the Vatican with the hope of receiving the Pope's support. The Pope refused to see him but sent his representative, Secretary of State Cardinal Merry del Val. The meeting was brief. The Cardinal said simply, "The Vatican cannot support your proposal because the Jews are in fact doomed to perpetual dispersion and wandering for the crime that they committed in biblical times." In so saying, the Vatican once more rejected the word of God: **I will give you and your descendants after you the land of your sojournings, all the land of Canaan, for an everlasting possession** (Gen 17:7–8) and also rejected the teaching of Paul: **For the gifts and the call of God are irrevocable** (Rom 11:28–29).

CREATION OF THE STATE OF ISRAEL

> **Who has heard such a thing?**
> **Who has seen such things?**
> **Shall a land be born in one day?**
> **Shall a nation be brought forth in one moment?**
> **For as soon as Zion was in labor**
> **she brought forth her sons. . . .**
> **Rejoice with Jerusalem, and be glad for her,**
> **all you who love her;**
> **rejoice with her in joy,**
> **all you who mourn over her** (Is 66:8–10).

For almost two millennia, the church taught that the Jews lost Jerusalem and Judea, the Land of the Jews, as divine retribution for their role in the crucifixion of Jesus of Nazareth. If the Jews lost their land because they had participated in the greatest of all sins, what is the significance of their reinheritance? Does it mean that God has at last forgiven the Jews or does it mean that God never blamed them?

"STATEMENT TO OUR FELLOW CHRISTIANS" 1973

In 1973, the National Council of Churches of Christ in collaboration with the National Conference of Catholic Bishops convened and published the document called "A Statement to Our Fellow Christians." The Statement said that Judaism had not been replaced by Christianity; that Judaism is not inferior to Christianity; that Christians should be eternally grateful to the Jews for permitting Christians to obtain salvation through the Jew Jesus:

> The ministry of Jesus and the life of the early Christian community were thoroughly rooted in the Judaism of their day, particularly in the teachings of the Pharisees.

The Christian church is still sustained by the living faith
of the patriarchs and prophets, kings, and priests,
scribes and rabbis, and the people whom God chose for
his own. Christ is the link (Gal 3:26–29) enabling the
Gentiles to be numbered among Abraham's offspring;
and therefore fellow heirs with the Jews according to
God's promise. . . . The singular grace of Jesus Christ
does not abrogate the covenantal relationship of God
with Israel (Rom 11:1–2). In Christ, the church shares
in Israel's election without superseding it. . . . For our
spiritual legacy and for all that the Jews have done for
the whole human race, we Christians are grateful to
God and to the people whom God has chosen as a special instrument of his kindness. . . . Unfortunately
many Christians have assumed that the validity of Judaism ended with the beginning of Christianity, the rejection of Jesus as Messiah marking the dissolution of the
covenant. This assumption conflicts sharply with
Paul's declaration that God did not annul his promises
to the Chosen people since God never takes back his
gifts or revokes his call (Rom 11:28–29). . . . In the
words of St. Paul, They are Israelites and to them belong the sonship, the glory, the covenants, the giving of
the law, the worship, and the promises; to them belong
the patriarchs; and of their race according to the flesh is
the Christ (Rom 9:4–5).

The Statement spoke thus about the state of Israel:

The validity of the state of Israel rests on moral and
juridical grounds. It was established in response to a
resolution of the United Nations General Assembly
after termination of the British Mandate. However,
involved in the potentially explosive political conflict in
the Middle East is a theological question that demands
careful scrutiny. What is the relationship between "the
people" and "the land"? What is the relationship be-

tween the Chosen People and the territory comprising the present state of Israel? There is no Christian consensus on these questions. Genesis explicitly affirms a connection between the people and the land (Gen 15:18) and even within the New Testament certain passages imply such a connection. Therefore, Christians who see Israel as something more than a political state are not wrongly theologizing politics by understanding the existence of the Jewish state in theological terms. They are merely recognizing that modern Israel is the homeland of a people whose political identity is sustained by the faith that God has blessed them with a covenant. . . .

Israel's anxiety about national defense reflects the age-old human yearning for security, the anxiety of a people whose history has been a saga of frightful persecutions climaxed by the Holocaust of six million men, women, and children. Against such a tormented background, is it surprising that the Jewish people should want to defend themselves? It would be quite unrealistic and unjust to expect Israel to become a sort of heavenly society of which more is expected than of other nations. This does not mean that Christians must endorse every policy decision by the Israeli government. Most Jews, both within Israel and without, do not do so. Rather, Christians must refrain from the type of criticism that would use the failure of Israel to live up to the highest moral standards as an excuse to deny its right to exist. Such a view could be a double standard, one not applied to any other nation on earth.

As Christians, we urge all nations in the world (our own nation, Israel, and the Arab states included) to recognize that there is no way to secure lasting peace based on the balance of military power and the use of fear as a deterrent. Rather, the only road leading to peace is trust in

and understanding of neighbors and partners. We urge
the church to attend its role as agent of reconciliation.

The Statement had no impact on mainstream Christianity.
And most of those who wrote it ended up denying it or doing
nothing to implement it. Only fundamentalist Christians took
it seriously and implemented it.

ISAIAH AND THE BIRTH OF THE STATE OF ISRAEL

Many in the church consider the creation of the state of Israel the greatest miracle since biblical days. Isaiah prophesied:

> **And the Lord's [YHVH's] ransomed people will re-
> turn and come to Zion with jubilant sons and ever-
> lasting joy** (Is 35:10).

> **Thus says the Lord [YHVH]: Zion says, The Lord
> [YHVH] has forsaken me, my God has forgotten me.
> But can a woman forget the infant at her breast? Or
> a loving mother the child of her womb? Yes! Even
> they forget. But I shall not forget you** (Is 49:14–15).

> **Thus says the Lord [YHVH]: The days are coming
> when men shall no longer swear by the living God
> who brought Israel out of Egypt, but by the living
> God who brought the descendants of the Israelites
> back . . . from all the lands to which he dispersed
> them to live once more on their own soil** (Jer 23:7–8).

> **Hear the word of the Lord [YHVH], O Gentiles, and
> declare it to the coastlands far away: He who scat-
> tered Israel will gather him up, and will keep him as
> a shepherd keeps his flock** (Jer 31:10).

THE KORAN AND THE LAND OF ISRAEL

In the Torah, God said to Abram (later Abraham): **I will give you and your descendants after you the land of your sojournings, all the land of Canaan, for an everlasting possession** (Gen 17:7–8). In the Koran, Allah, through the Prophet Muhammad, says:

20. And (remember) when Moses said until his people: O my people! Remember Allah's favour unto you, how He placed among you Prophets, and He made you kings, and gave you that (which) He gave not to any (other) of (His) creatures.

21. O my people! Go into the holy land which Allah hath ordained for you. . . .

44. Lo! We did reveal the Torah, wherein is guidance and a light (*The Table Spread*).

137. And We caused the folk who were despised [the Jews] to inherit the eastern parts of the land and the western parts thereof which We had blessed. And the fair word of the Lord was fulfilled for the Children of Israel because of their endurance; and We annihilated (all) that Pharaoh and his folk had done and that they had contrived.

138. And We brought the Children of Israel across the sea, and they came unto a people who were given up to idols which they had. They said: O Moses! Make for us a god even as they have gods. He said: Lo! ye are a folk who know not.

139. Lo! as for these, their ways will be destroyed and all that they are doing is in vain.

140. He [Moses] said: Shall I seek for you a god other than Allah when He hath favoured you above (all) creatures?

141. And (remember) when We did deliver you from Pharaoh's folk who were afflicting you with dreadful torment (*The Heights*).

2. We gave unto Moses the Scripture, and We appointed it a guidance for the Children of Israel, saying: Choose no guardian beside Me. . . .

104. And We said unto the Children of Israel after him: Dwell in the land; but when the promise of the Hereafter cometh to pass we shall bring you as a crowd gathered out of various nations (*The Children of Israel*).

12. When before it [the Koran] there was the Scripture of Moses [the Torah], an example and a mercy; and this is a confirming Scripture in the Arabic language, that it may warn those who do wrong and bring good tidings for the righteous (*The Wind-curved Sandhills*).

In the Koran, Allah states that He not only revealed the Torah to the Jews, but is now confirming it. Anwar Sadat, a devout Muslim, believed the Koran. He recognized Israel and her God-given right to exist forever. For that, Moslem fanatics assassinated him.

VATICAN TWO

THE CHURCH AND THE HOLOCAUST

Between 1939 and 1945, those European Christians who called themselves Nazis and those Christians who did not consider themselves Nazis but who collaborated with them murdered six million Jews, almost 50% of all the Jews then living among them. Many of those Christians were disappointed. They had hoped to murder them all.

Today there are Christians who deny that Christians ever did such things. Others say, yes, these murders took place, but on a much smaller scale. Still others say, yes, the murders took place, but they were not committed by Christians, but by pagans.

For several years after World War II, the church was silent regarding the meaning of the Holocaust. The church was in conflict, the reactionaries saying that God was still punishing the Jews for killing Christ, the liberals saying that interpretation was impossible because it would show that the Christian God was not a God of grace, as traditionally represented, but on the contrary was unloving, unforgiving, cruel, and merciless. The liberals prevailed, and the Vatican decided it was time to right two thousand years of church antisemitism culminating in the Holocaust. Pope John XXIII, convened the Second Vatican Council (Vatican Two). He called Christian persecution of the Jews during those two millennia the "second crucifixion." The pope wanted the church to ask forgiveness and composed a prayer for that purpose. He said that the souls of the faithful for two millennia depended on it. But the reactionaries would not hear of it.

Until Vatican Two, the church had taught that the Gospel of Jesus Christ supplanted the Law as revealed by Moses and that Judaism was an anachronistic if not a dead religion. Prior to the Enlightenment, the church had taught that the Jews, regardless of their own wishes and wherever and whenever it was possible, should be baptized, should be made to abandon the Law, and brought by conversion, however violently, into the church. It did not matter that Jesus had taught:

> *Think not that I have come to abolish the law. . . . For truly, I say to you, till heaven and earth pass away, not an iota, not a dot will pass from the law until all is accomplished* (Mt 5:17–18).

> *The Gospel of the Kingdom of God is preached, and everyone enters by means of violence! But it is easier*

*for heaven and earth to pass away than for one dot of
the Law to become void* (Lk 16:16–17).

PAGAN NAZIS: CHRISTIAN NAZIS

To exonerate itself of any guilt in the Holocaust, the church asserted that Adolph Hitler and the Nazis were pagans, not Christians. This is not true. Although some Nazis did promote a form of Nordic mythology as portrayed in Richard Wagner's operas, most of them remained good Lutherans or Catholics, who, whenever they could, went to church on Sundays with their families. Then, too, the most common Nazi symbol was the cross. The swastika itself is a cross. Traditional Latin and Greek crosses appeared throughout Nazi Germany. They were on Nazi medals of honor and they decorated Nazi war planes.

The church even claims it was actively anti-Nazi, but there is little evidence for that. More evidence shows the church was pro-Nazi. For example, the church did not excommunicate a single Catholic Nazi—except Joseph Goebbels, and that because he married a Protestant.

POPE JOHN XXIII AND SECOND VATICAN COUNCIL

Pope John XXIII convened the Second Vatican Council in 1962, ostensibly to help the church better adapt to the modern world. The pope defined and clarified what he meant when he said that the church in the modern world was sorely deficient in love of God and love of neighbor. The real reason, however, was left unspoken. The Holocaust had occurred, the pope believed, because of the church's hateful teachings about the Jews.

The goal of Vatican Two was to rectify church teachings and to bring about reconciliation with the Jews; to bring about ecumenism among Catholics and Protestants, and even with non-Christians, or at least to engage in dialogue with them; and to modernize church thinking about women and birth control.

Vatican Two had limited success. It published fifty-three documents of which four accomplished more or less the objectives. Those four concerned human dignity and dialogue with non-Christians. The Latin title of the four indicates the opening words of the document and not its content. In brackets are the common titles that reflect the content:

> *Unitatis Redinteratio [Decree on Ecumenism]*, 1964;
> *Dignitatis Humanae [On Religious Liberty]*, 1965;
> *Humanae Personae Dignitatem [On Dialogue with Unbelievers]*, 1968;
> *Nostra Aetate [On the Relationship of the Church to non-Christians]*, 1965, 1974.

These documents were revolutionary because they spoke of two things the church had never spoken of in its two thousand year history—the dignity of all human beings, as opposed to the contempt it had previously held for non-Catholics, and dialogue with nonbelievers, as opposed to the monologue it had formerly forced upon them.

Recognizing that the church's belief in its own "absolute truth" was an impediment to dialogue, the documents said:

1) The dogma of absolute truth must be suspended for the sake of dialogue. The church acknowledged that truth may come from sources outside the church and may even "demolish" its own beliefs.
2) Dialogue must proceed without "manipulation, dogma, or coercion, but must rather obey the rules of truth and liberty."
3) Reason must be a prerequisite for faith, and individual Catholics must reexamine their own beliefs.
4) Men should be free to choose their own religious values and spirituality.

These rules appeared Jeffersonian in nobility and idealism, but in reality they were disingenuous. Unbeknownst to those with whom the church was engaging in dialogue, the church secretly continued to maintain that its teachings alone held absolute truth. Therefore, the actual goal of dialogue was to convert to the one true religion those with whom the dialogue was undertaken. Because of that hidden agenda, which soon became apparent, Vatican Two was largely destined to fail in its efforts to achieve ecumenism and meaningful dialogue. The reactionaries dealt the death blow when they insisted on inserting the following disclaimers into two of the documents:

> It is through Christ's Catholic Church alone, which is the universal help toward salvation, that the fullness of the means of salvation can be obtained (*Unitatis Redinteratio* [*Decree on Ecumenism*], AD 1964).

> While the religious freedom which men demand in fulfilling their obligation to worship God has to do with freedom from coercion in civil society, it leaves intact the traditional Catholic teaching on the moral duty of individuals and societies towards the true religion and the one Church of Christ. . . . The love of Christ urges [Catholics] to treat with love, prudence and patience those who are in error or ignorance with regard to the faith (*Dignitatis Humanae*, [*On Religious Liberty*], AD 1965).

After the Second Vatican Council ended, Vatican reactionaries decided that the Council had been misguided and was indeed heretical. The movement to revoke Vatican Two and restore Vatican One has been steadily gaining momentum.

NOSTRA AETATE

Of the fifty-three documents of Vatican Two, the one with the greatest impact was *Nostra Aetate* [*On the Relationship of the Church to non-Christians*], 1965, 1974. Curiously, it is the only document commonly called by its Latin name, perhaps because that name is short and poetic with a nice cadence. The principal purpose of *Nostra Aetate* was to rectify two thousand years of hateful church teachings about Judaism and the Jews. *Nostra Aetate* states:

> As this sacred synod probes the mystery of the Church, it remembers the spiritual bond that ties the people of the New Covenant to Abraham's stock [the Jews]. . . . The Church, therefore, cannot forget that she received the revelation of the Old Testament through the people with whom, in that loving kindness that words cannot express, God deigned to conclude the ancient covenant. Nor can she forget that she draws sustenance from the root of that well-cultivated olive tree on which the branches of the gentiles have been grafted (Rom 11:17–24).

> The Church keeps ever before her eyes, the words of the Apostle [Paul] about his kinsmen [the Jews]: "Theirs is the sonship and the glory and the covenants and the law and the worship and the promises. Theirs are the patriarchs, and from them in the flesh comes the Christ" (Rom 9:4–5). . . . Furthermore, she recalls that the apostles, the Church's foundation stones and pillars (Acts 21:14; Gal 2:9), sprang from the Jewish people as did most of the early disciples. . . . Jerusalem did not recognize the time of her visitation (Lk 19:44), nor did the Jews in large numbers accept the Gospel; indeed, not a few opposed its dissemination (Rom 11:28). Nevertheless, now as before, God holds them most dear

for the sake of the patriarchs. He has not withdrawn his gifts of calling. . . (Rom 11:29).

True, the Jewish authorities and those who sided with them pressed for the death of Christ (Jn 19:6). Still, what happened in his passion cannot be attributed without distinction to all the Jews then alive. Nor can it be attributed to the Jews of today. . . . One thing remains: Christ underwent his passion and death freely, and out of infinite love because of the sins of all men, so that all may obtain salvation. This the Church has always held (*Nostra Aetate*, AD 1974).

"The Guidelines on Religious Relations with the Jews," 1974, designed to clarify *Nostra Aetate* and make it teachable in catechism, stated:

The step taken by the Council finds its historical setting in circumstances deeply affected by the memory of the persecution and massacre of Jews which took place in Europe just before and during the Second World War.

Although Christianity sprang from Judaism, taking from it certain essential elements of its faith and divine worship, the gap dividing them was deepened more and more, to such an extent that Christian and Jew hardly knew each other. . . .

This seems the right moment to propose, following the guidelines of the Council, some concrete suggestions . . . .

The Old Testament and the Jewish tradition founded upon it must not be set against the New Testament in such a way that the former seems to constitute a religion of only justice, fear, and legalism, with no regard for love of God and neighbor. Compare Deuteronomy

6:5 ["And you shall love the Lord your God with all your heart and with all your soul and with all your might"] and Leviticus 19:18 ["You shall love your neighbor as yourself"] with Matthew 22:34–40 [And a lawyer asked Jesus . . . "Teacher, which is the great commandment in the Law?" And Jesus said to him, "You shall love the Lord your God with all your heart and with all your soul and with all your mind. This is the great and first commandment. And a second is like it. You shall love your neighbor as yourself. On these two commandments depend all the Law and the prophets."

Jesus was born of the Jews as were his apostles and a large number of his disciples. . . .

Nostra Aetate was completed in 1965, but it was not published until 1974. What caused the delay? During those nine years, the conservatives and reactionaries who opposed it, deleted portions, changed others, and altered many of the catechismal guidelines. Some of the deleted portions stated:

• Judaism was a living religion that endures forever.

• Christians should ask pardon of their Jewish brothers for the crimes committed against them, for the persecution and moral pressures brought against the Jews for almost 2,000 years. Pope John XXIII composed these ideas into a prayer that he wrote for the entire church. The Vatican, however, refused to make the prayer public and has gone to great lengths to keep it hidden from the faithful and from the world.

- All intent of proselytizing and conversion of the Jews was henceforth excluded.

- Christians were called upon to understand and respect the religious significance of the link between the Jewish people and the land of Israel. The land of Israel was a gift from God, and as such this gift could not be revoked. "For the gifts and the call of God are irrevocable" (Rom 11:29).

Pope John XXIII, along with many liberal priests, thought that even if those statements had been allowed to stand, the document would have been inadequate. They argued as follows:

The document said that the "Jewish authorities pressed for the death of Christ" when it ought to have said, "some of the Jewish authorities pressed for the death of Christ." The gospels tell of Jewish authorities who supported Christ, among them Joseph of Arimathea, a member of the council.

The document made no mention of the central role of Pontius Pilate and the Romans in the crucifixion. Antisemitic church men long maintained that the Jewish leaders bribed Pilate to crucify Jesus. The document was expected to address this assertion by stating it had no foundation, and by saying that even if Pilate executed Jesus as a result of a bribe, how would that exonerate Pilate? Finally, the document said nothing of the significance of Pilate's charge "INRI, Jesus of Nazareth King of the Jews," where being a king not appointed by Rome was treason against Rome, deserving, according to Roman law, of death by crucifixion.

The document failed to say forthrightly that the New Testament was antisemitic in large part to make the new religion, Christianity, attractive to Gentiles, and to make the mother religion, Judaism, unattractive, by portraying the Pharisees in a negative light instead of teaching that Jesus' most important teachings came directly from the Pharisees. Paul had long ago written what the Vatican Two's reactionaries refused to write: "As regards the Gospel, [the Jews] are enemies of God for your [the Gentiles'] sake" (Rom 11:28).

Pope John XXIII pleaded that a public confession of the church's great sin against the Jews must not be deleted from the document. The pope argued that the church for 2,000 years had been crucifying the Jewish people in what John called a "second crucifixion," a mortal sin that would deny Christians salvation. The pope's plea went ignored.

THE PENITENTIAL PRAYER OF POPE JOHN XXIII

In 1963, shortly before he died, Pope John XXIII retired to his private chapel and said the penitential prayer he had composed for the entire church. He said the prayer alone and in private and to save his own soul:

> . . . . We now acknowledge that for many, many centuries blindness has cloaked our eyes so that we no longer could see the beauty of thy chosen people and no longer recognize in its face the features of our first-born brother. We acknowledge that the mark of Cain is upon our brow. For centuries, Abel lay low in blood and tears because we forgot thy love. Forgive us the curse that we wrongfully pronounced upon the name of the Jews. Forgive us that by crucifying them we have crucified you for the second time. For we knew not what we did. . . .

POPE JOHN PAUL I

THE FORGOTTEN POPE

Although Pope John Paul II is well-known, hardly anyone remembers his predecessor Pope John Paul I, born Albino Luciani.

One month after becoming pope, John Paul I suddenly and inexplicably died. During the month of his papacy, he had been popular with the people but not the Vatican. The cause of his death was never established because the Vatican refused an autopsy. Several books have been written alleging that he was murdered by the Vatican (see Selected Bibliography). Suggested motivations included his anti-mafia stance at a time when the Vatican was involved financially with the mafia; his ecumenical ideas that included not only Christians but everyone; his simple, straightforward, and folksy style; his desire to change church liturgy; and his revolutionary if not heretical ideas.

In his Angelus Message September 10, 1978, Pope John Paul I said, God "is our Father, even more He is our Mother." Later he said he was alluding to Isaiah 49:14–15. Albino Luciani, before becoming pope, wrote: "[N]o one is infallible!" (Albino Luciani, *Illustrissimi*, letters between Albino Luciani and St. Bernard de Clairvaux, 1971). Here are others of his revolutionary writings:

ALADDIN'S WONDERFUL LAMP

Albino Luciani liked telling the story of Aladdin and his magic lamp:

A magician hires Aladdin to find a lamp in a cave. Aladdin finds the lamp, but realizing it possesses magic, refuses to give it up. The magician seals Aladdin inside the cave. Aladdin accidentally rubs the lamp, and a genie comes forth promising to grant Aladdin whatever he wishes. Aladdin asks to be set free, to be given a palace, and to marry a princess. His wishes are granted.

The magician, on discovering the empty cave, devises the following scheme to locate Aladdin and retrieve the lamp: He will go through the streets disguised as a peddler shouting, "New lamps for old!" The princess, Aladdin's wife, falls for the scheme. In Aladdin's absence, she finds the old lamp and hands it over to the magician, who exchanges it for a new tin lamp, shiny but worthless. Luciani wrote:

> The teachers tell their pupils the fairy tale of Aladdin and his magic lamp. . . . [A magician] goes through the streets, crying: "New lamps for old!" It looks like an excellent deal, but instead it is a fraud. Aladdin's credulous wife falls for it. In her husband's absence, she goes to the attic, takes the lamp, whose wondrous powers she knows nothing about, and hands it over to the magician. The rascal carries it off, leaving in exchange all his lamps of tin, shiny but worthless. . . . [E]very now and then a magician comes along, philosopher or politician as he may be, and offers to trade merchandise. Watch out! The ideas offered by certain "magicians," even if they shine, are tin, a human matter, lasting only a day! What they call old and outdated ideas are often ideas of God, of which it is written that not even a comma will pass away! (Albino Luciani, *Illustrissimi*, letter to Felix Dupanloup, 1974, pp. 225–226).

Luciani in the last sentence is paraphrasing Jesus, who said: ***For truly, I say to you, till heaven and earth pass away, not an iota, not a dot, will pass from the law*** (Mt 5:18). Is not Luciani saying that the Jews would be foolish to convert? To trade the Old Testament for the New was like trading old lamps for new.

DOUBTS

Although Albino Luciani expressed love of Jesus, under cover of quoting an Italian poet, Luciani expressed doubt about Jesus' divinity:

> I believe in God the Father Almighty. But . . . have you some doubt? Keep it to yourself (Ibid., letter to Andreas Hofer, 1974, p. 250).

As for Jesus' humanity, Luciani was concerned about Jesus' emotional volatility. The gospel tells the following story:

> **And seeing in the distance a fig tree in leaf, [Jesus] went to see if he could find anything on it. When he came to it, he found nothing but leaves, for it was not the season for figs. And he said to it, *May no one ever eat fruit from you again.* . . . [Next] morning, they saw the fig tree withered away to its roots. And Peter said to him, "Master, look! The fig tree which you cursed has withered"** (Mk 11:12–21).

Luciani alluded to this incident:

> Let us not be like neurotic patients who want cherries in autumn and grapes in spring! (Albino Luciani, *Illustrissimi*, letter to St. Francis de Sales, 1972, p. 108).

A NEW WAY TO CELEBRATE GOD

Albino Luciani expressed love of the Roman Catholic Church, but he wished to a create a new way of celebrating and worshiping God, one in which the ancient and outdated rituals and traditions of the church were stripped away and replaced with celebrations worthy of God:

> [If only we could strip away] the concept of God from the guises, at times ingenuous and caricatural, in which an agrarian and pre-scientific civilization had dressed it. But it is a hard job (Ibid., letter to Marconi, 1974, p. 208).

Luciani told the following story to show how outdated traditions come about:

> A town councillor, just nominated, sees a municipal guard keeping daily watch over some benches in the park. A waste, the official thinks. It would be explicable if he were guarding the Bank of Italy, but not a dozen humble benches! He decides to investigate, and he discovers . . . what? Years before, the garden benches had been freshly painted. To keep people from getting stained with fresh paint, a guard—by municipal order—was stationed in that place. The council then forgot to withdraw that order. The pain dried, and the policeman remained there, guarding . . . nothing! (Ibid., from letters between Albino Luciani and St. Bernard, Abbot of Clairvaux, 1971, p. 37).

Luciani observed how traditions hold people in a grip so tight that however convincing is the new evidence to refute them, it is nearly impossible for most people to give up the traditions. He related an incident from *The Pickwick Papers* by Charles Dickens:

> But here you are, President Pickwick, kneeling before a carved stone. . . . "Good heavens!" you exclaim, and you rub the stone with your handkerchief; you discern

some letters on the surface; you have the immediate, distinct sensation that this must be a very ancient anti-quarian find; and you buy the stone from the owner. . . . You . . . with the erudition that distinguishes you, write a pamphlet offering twenty-seven different readings of the inscription. . . . [S]eventeen learned societies, na-tional and foreign, elect you honorary member, in rec-ognition of your discovery.

But then what? Doesn't an envious antagonist turn up in the form of the member Blotton? He carries out a field trip, questions the man who sold you the stone, and reports to the club. The stone, true, is very ancient, but the inscription is recent, made by the very man who sold the stone. . . . The club's reaction is immediate: Blotton is ejected for his presumption and his defama-tion; gold-rimmed spectacles are voted and offered to President Pickwick as a mark of approbation and es-teem; a motion of censure is passed by the seventeen societies against Blotton. . . .

[C]ertain hard heads seem harder than diamond: they never give in, they cling to a mistaken opinion in the teeth of all evidence to the contrary. "Give a nail to a stubborn man," the axiom goes, "and he'll drive it home with his head!" . . . .

[Y]ou risk espousing a certain idea not because it is recognized as true, but because it is the idea of the group. . . . [P]eople go passively where the others go, feathers borne by the wind. . . . (Albino Luciani, *Illus-trissimi*, from the letter To the Four Members of the Pickwick Club, 1972, pp. 66–70).

He expressed a similar idea in a letter to St. Bernard:

[Prudence is hardly] the attitude of those who stub-bornly refuse to face evident realities and fall into ex-cessive rigidity and integralism becoming . . . more monarchist than the king, more papist than the pope.

This happens. There are those who, having mastered an idea, bury it and continue to preserve it, to defend it jealously for their whole lives, never reexamining it, never checking to see what it has become after so much rain and wind, after the storms of events and changes. (Ibid., from letters between Albino Luciani and St. Bernard, Abbot of Clairvaux, 1971, p. 36).

ECUMENISM

Albino Luciani dreamt of an ecumenism that included not only Christians, but everyone, all under One God, our Father:

We are all in the same boat, filled with peoples now brought closer together both in space and in behavior; but the boat is on a very rough sea. If we would avoid grave mishaps, the rule must be this: all for one and one for all. Insist on what unites us and forget what divides us (Ibid., letter to Charles Dickens, 1971, pp. 7–8).

[P]rogress with human beings who love one another, considering themselves brothers, children of a single God the Father, can be something magnificent. Progress with human beings who do not recognize God as a universal Father becomes a constant danger (Ibid., letter to Gilbert K. Chesterton, 1971, p. 15).

Albino Luciani, Pope John Paul I, died under mysterious circumstances after serving only one month of his papacy. Many thought he was murdered. The Vatican was the principal suspect.

4. THE FORMATION OF THE CHURCH

THE NEW SECT OF JUDAISM

THE NAZARENES, THE KEHAL, AND THE WAY

The earliest congregation of what was later to be called "the church" consisted only of Jews who called themselves Nazarenes in honor of the hometown of their leader, Jesus of Nazareth. This congregation was called *kehal* in Hebrew and *ecclesia* or *synagogue* in Greek. The Nazarenes' only Scriptures, which they shared with normative or faithful Jews, were the Hebrew Scriptures, called by Jesus of Nazareth "Scripture" or "Scriptures" and by Christians today the "Old Testament." The Nazarenes considered themselves a sect of Judaism (Acts 24:5) and called their sect not Christianity but "the Way" (Acts 9:2; 19:9; 19:23; 22:4; 24:22).

The congregation of Nazarenes had no "New Testament." Relying on the promises of Jesus, they expected the world to end imminently, and therefore they had no need to write anything down. They were certain that before they died, they would see the coming to its close of the old age with its endless wars, tyrannies, and kingdoms and the beginning of the new age of God's kingdom on earth with everlasting peace.

The Nazarenes prayed in the Temple in Jerusalem and in the synagogues throughout Judea and the Galilee along with the normative Jews, for they did not consider themselves members of a new religion but rather Jews for whom the Messiah had come in the person of Jesus of Nazareth.

CHRISTIANS, CHURCHES, AND CHRISTIANITY

When Jesus of Nazareth spoke of *ecclesia*, he did not mean *church*, a new institution with him at the head. *Ecclesia* in Jerusalem in Jesus' day meant *congregation of Jews* and was synonymous with *kehal* or *synagogue*. After Jesus died, his disciples spoke of ecclesia as a congregation of righteous Jews *and* gentiles, an all-inclusive congregation similar to the one of which King Solomon spoke when he dedicated the Temple:

> **Hear the prayers of your servant and your people Israel. . . . Likewise, when a Gentile, who is not of your people Israel, comes and prays . . . hear his prayer** (1 Kings 8:23–43).

God himself spoke of an all inclusive congregation when he said through the prophet Isaiah:

> **My House shall be called a house of prayer for all peoples** (Is 56:7).

By the time Paul was preaching in the city of Antioch in the diaspora in the middle of the first century, the members of the *kehal* or congregation were no longer calling themselves Nazarenes but Christians, and their Jewish sect not the Way but Christianity. This change reflected the elevation in status of the Way from a sect to an independent religion consisting less of Jews and more of gentiles. The congregation no longer called their *kehal* by that Hebrew name but by its Greek translation *ecclesia*. The traditional Jews continued to call their congregation *kehal* or by its Greek translation *synagogue*. Ecclesia and synagogue, Christianity and Judaism, had gone their separate ways.

Christians in Jerusalem were meeting in a building that would much later be called a cathedral, which means the seat of a bishop. The Jerusalem cathedral was the first, but it was not a grand cathedral like those of Europe that we see today dating from the Middle Ages. The bishop of Jerusalem, the first bishop, was James, the brother of Jesus.

In Rome, in the diaspora, in the first through third centuries, Christians met secretly in private homes, for they were in constant fear of religious persecution by the heathen Romans. In the fourth century, after Constantine made Christianity the state religion of the Roman Empire, Christians were free to worship openly, and with Constantine taking the lead, they began to build houses of worship. Ecclesia then became more than a congregation of Christians. The word also took on its modern meaning of a building housing Christian worship.

The word *ecclesia* continued to be used in the Greek and Latin speaking countries and is still used there. But in northern Europe during the Middle Ages, the word *church* came into usage. *Church* was derived from the Greek 'η κυριακός (*hay kyriakos*) which means *belonging to the Lord*, where the word Lord meant Jesus Christ.

PAUL, APOSTLE AMONG THE GENTILES

PAUL AND JUDAISM

Paul called himself "apostle to the gentiles," but a more apt term is "apostle *among* the gentiles" because in the diaspora he preached to Jews as well as to gentiles although predominately the latter. Paul quickly discovered that to win converts among the gentiles, he had to forego the Mosaic commandments regarding dietary laws, circumcision, and keeping the Sabbath, even though Jesus of Nazareth, a devout Jew, had kept them all. In time, however, the church, to justify its abandonment of the Mosaic commandments, would teach that it was Jesus who had revoked them, even though he had not.

"ALL THINGS TO ALL MEN"

Paul wanted both Jews and Gentiles to become Christians, and to this end he became "all things to all men." To be all things to all men, one needs to be duplicitous, and Paul boasted of his duplicity:

> **To the Jews I have become like a Jew to win Jews . . . to those without the Law [the Gentiles] I have become like a man without any law. . . . I have become all things to all men that I might save them [all]** (1 Cor 9:29; 10:33).

Paul wrote to the Christians in Rome:

> **Now I am speaking to you Gentiles: Inasmuch then as I am the Apostle to the Gentiles, I exaggerate my ministry in order to make my fellow Jews jealous, and thus save some of them** (Rom 11:13–15).

Who can trust a man who boasts of his duplicity?

THE GOSPEL OF THE SON OF GOD

The core of Paul's teaching was the gospel or good news of the Son of God. The gospel of the Son of God was different from the gospel of God as told by the prophets, which concerned a Messiah who would inaugurate God's reign with eternal peace on earth. The gospel of the Son of God concerned Jesus Christ, his sacrificial death, his resurrection, and his promise of eternal life. That was a new gospel, and it replaced the Gospel of God told by the prophets and expected by the Jews.

JESUS' SACRIFICIAL DEATH

Paul wrote that under God's Law as revealed by Moses, only the shedding of blood was an acceptable offering for atonement of sins: **Without the shedding of blood, there is no forgiveness of sins** (Heb 9:22). Paul, however, was not telling the truth. There were acceptable sacrifices other than the shedding of blood: **The priest shall take a handful of cereal . . . and burn it on the altar. . . . It is an offering for sins** (Lev 5:12). What Greek would become a Christian if he learned that burning cereal was as acceptable to God as the blood from the crucifixion?

Moreover, Paul knew that crucifixion was an abominable sacrifice under God's Law as revealed by Moses. In order for a blood sacrifice to be acceptable, the victim had to be without blemish, had to be killed without torture—instantaneously—through the slitting of the throat with a sharp knife by the high priest. Crucifixion as sacrifice was an abomination for several reasons: the victim, already wounded through whipping and torture, was severely blemished; the victim's blood was obtained through oozing wounds, not from the blood vessels of the neck; the execution was painful and slow, lasting over several hours, and was itself a severe form of torture; death was carried out by profane executioners, not holy priests; and most important of all, the victim was human, which God had forbidden. None of these things did Paul tell his gentile audience.

PAUL'S TEACHINGS ABOUT RIGHTEOUS JEWS

Paul, early in his ministry, gave multiple proofs that Jews were going to heaven without belief in Jesus Christ:

> **He is not a real Jew who only looks like one. . . . He is a Jew who is a Jew within. . . . Praises for those who are Jews within, for they come not from men but from God!** (Rom 2:26–29).

> **They are the Israelites, and to them belong the sonship, the glory, the covenants, the giving of the Law, the worship, and the promises. To them belong the patriarchs, and from them in the flesh came the Christ** (Rom 9:4–5).

> **I ask, then, has God rejected his people? By no means! I myself am an Israelite, a descendant of Abraham, a member of the tribe of Benjamin. God has not rejected his people whom he knew from the beginning. . . . So I ask, have they stumbled so as to fall? By no means! But through their trespass, salvation has come to the Gentiles** (Rom 11:1–11).

> **But if some of the branches [wicked Jews] of the olive tree [the religion of the Jews] were broken off, and you, a wild olive shoot [righteous Gentiles], were grafted in their place to share the richness of the olive tree [religion of the Jews], do not boast about the [grafted] branches [righteous Gentiles]. If you do boast, remember, it is not you that support the root [Christianity does not nurture Judaism], but the root that supports you [Judaism is the mother religion and nourisher of Christianity]** (Rom 11:17–18).

> **As regards the Gospel, the Jews are enemies of God for your [the Gentiles'] sake; but as regards election**

[going to heaven], they are beloved for the sake of their forefathers. For the gifts and the call of God are irrevocable (Rom 11:28–29).

When writing to the Romans, Paul spoke well of the Jews, probably because he found many Roman Jews receptive to his message. And when writing to the Corinthians, Paul expressed pride in being a Jew himself: **Are they Hebrews? So am I! Are they Israelites? So am I!** (2 Cor 11:22). But when writing to the Thessalonians, Paul hurled curses because he was poorly received by them.

THESSALONIKA

In the diaspora, Paul did not lose an opportunity to try to convert Jews as well as Gentiles. In Thessalonika—later called Salonika and today called Thessaloniki—he met Jews who offered him great resistance.

Jews had lived in Thessalonika since the third century BC, and Paul found a large and thriving Jewish community there. Paul preached in the synagogue about Jesus Christ, the resurrected messiah, on three consecutive Sabbaths. The Jews had never heard of a resurrected messiah, and they were not expecting one. They were expecting a messiah to bring about the resurrection of all the righteous dead and to establish the Kingdom of God with eternal peace on earth. The Jews of Thessalonika were polite to Paul on the first two Sabbaths, but by the third Sabbath, they had had enough. They told him his messiah was not theirs, they did not wish to hear about him again, and Paul should leave and never return. Paul was so enraged that he spewed hateful statements—a curse, really—not only on the Jews of Thessalonika but on the Jews everywhere and forever:

[The] Jews . . . killed both the Lord Jesus and the prophets, and drove us out, and displease God, and oppose all men. . . . But God's wrath has come upon them forever! (1 Thess 2:14–16).

In spite of Paul's curse, the Jews of Thessalonika continued to live there peacefully and prosperously with their gentile neighbors—dwindling heathen and increasing Christian—for two millennia until the middle of the twentieth century. Among the Christians, however, the peace was tenuous; for Paul's curse had become part of the Christians' holy book, and the Christians were growing in number. Jews continued to flourish throughout all Greece, and many from other lands immigrated there for a better life. By the end of the fifteenth century, Thessalonika contained one of the largest Jewish communities in Europe, mainly because of the great influx from Spain after the Catholic monarchs Isabella and Ferdinand expelled the Jews in 1492. Between the fifteenth and the twentieth centuries, as more and more countries became receptive to Jews, the Jewish population in Thessalonika dwindled but continued to prosper. In 1940, the Jews of Thessalonika numbered about 50,000.

The Germans entered Thessalonika, at that time called Salonika, in April, 1941. That Easter season, as in all previous ones and continuing to this very day, the Greeks burned Judas in effigy. During the sacred liturgy of the Greek Orthodox Church, Orthodox priests reminded the people as they do today of Paul's statement that the Jews "killed the Lord Jesus." The priests go far beyond Paul by saying the Jews killed God and calling the Jews *Theoktoni* or "God killers."

By the summer of 1942, the Germans had enslaved all able-bodied Jewish men. By December 1942, the Germans turned the ancient Jewish cemetery containing a half-million graves into a quarry. Using Jews as forced labor, the Nazis turned gravestones into paving stones for streets and for seats of latrines. A ghetto-camp was created near the railway station to be used as a corral for people. Three hundred empty cattle cars were waiting on the sidetracks to transport the "animals" to the slaughter houses.

In March 1943, the first shipment was dispatched. Jews were crammed into cars overloaded to twice capacity. The doors were locked shut. The train began to move on its way to Auschwitz. Every three days this scene was repeated. The Jews were told they were on their way "to start a new life in a distant region" and most of them believed it; for conditions in the camp at Salonika made the prospect of any change seem one for the better. In August 1943, the last of the Jews were rounded up and placed in cars. That was the nineteenth convoy and the last shipment. Salonika was now Jew-free. In the short period of five months, the entire Jewish community which dated from the third century BC was gone. Disappeared. Vanished. Fifty thousand Salonikan Jews were deported to Auschwitz and 94% were murdered there. General Alexander Loehr, Commander of the German army in Salonika, marveled. Something unheard of anywhere else in Europe had happened in Salonika. Nowhere else—not even in Germany and Poland—had there been such complicity with the Nazis from the local citizens. It was as if the people of Thessalonika were taking it upon themselves to implement Paul's curse.

The Jews of Athens, Zakynthos, and Volos fared better. The local bishops, priests, and town officials—in defiance of Orthodox Christian teachings—protected their Jews. It is worth noting that whenever in Europe Christian clergy intervened on behalf of the Jews, the Jews fared better. But wherever clergy, as in Thessalonika, Corfu, and Rhodes, condemned its Jews as "God killers" deserving of a murder sanctioned by God, the townspeople eagerly collaborated with the Nazis.

In 1946, General Loehr was hanged as a war criminal for crimes against humanity. But the bishop, priests, and ordinary citizens of Salonika went about their daily business. No one made a case against them. And in 1947, when the United Nations partitioned the British territory of Palestine into two parts, one to be a Jewish state and the other to be an Arab state, Greece was the only European nation to vote against partition.

Today at Easter time, the Greek Orthodox Church continues to burn Judas in effigy. The Greek National Tourist Bureau advertises Judas as a major tourist attraction: *Come to Greece at Easter time and see the Burning of Judas!* At Easter time, too, the Orthodox Church continues to call the Jews "God-killers" in its sacred liturgy and prays to God never to cease punishing the Jews for killing Him. If there is a hell, what fate awaits the Greek Orthodox Church and its faithful?

REDEMPTION UNDER THE LAW

The Hebrews had clear teachings of redemption long before the birth of Jesus of Nazareth. When God created man, the man he created was weak and sinful. So, God had mercifully implemented the mechanisms of repentance and redemption. When Paul taught that Judaism lacked repentance and redemption, and therefore required **"perfect confirmation to the Law"** (Gal 3:10–12) and that sinners under the Law were damned (Rom 3:25), he was not telling the truth. Paul was an authority on the Law, so he was deliberately misleading the Gentiles in teaching not only that but also that only faith in Jesus Christ brought forgiveness and redemption. Paul pretended that God had not taught the Jews, **If your sins are like scarlet, they shall become white as snow** (Is 1:16).

PAUL'S OPINION OF WOMEN

Paul had a low opinion of women, which probably contributes to the church's low opinion of them. Paul wrote:

> **The head of a woman is her husband** (1 Cor 11:3).

> **A man ought not to cover his head in church since he is the image and glory of God, but woman is the glory of man. (For man was not made from woman, but woman from man.) Neither was man created for woman, but woman for man** (1 Cor 11:7–10).

> **Women should keep silence in the churches. For they are not permitted to speak, but should be subordinate. . . . If there is anything they desire to know, let them ask their husbands at home. For it is shameful for a woman to speak in church** (1 Cor 14:34–35).

PAUL'S "THORN IN THE FLESH"

Paul confessed to having a defect that made him sin against his will and brought him endless torment: **A thorn was given me in the flesh** (2 Cor 12:7). Whatever the sin was, he said it gave him no hope under the Law. Paul does not specify the sin, but drops many clues that indicate it was homosexuality. The Old Testament prohibited homosexuality. Jesus of Nazareth, however, did not condemn it, and there is evidence, as we shall see, that he may even have engaged in it. Most importantly, Paul taught that Jesus forgave all sins, and therefore would forgive that one, too.

Paul said he engaged in sinful behavior against his will, and he makes an outrageous statement about the Law. He writes that if the Law had not outlawed covetousness, it would never have occurred to him to be covetous; it is precisely because the

Law forbids covetousness that Paul became covetous! Paul says:

> **If it had not been for the Law, I should not have known sin. I should not have known what it is to covet, if the Law had not said, You shall not covet. But sin found opportunity in the commandment and wrought in me all kinds of covetousness! And if there were no Law, sin would lie dead** (Rom 7:7–9).

Paul is saying that if the Law had not prohibited coveting, he never would have coveted. The implication is, if the Law had not outlawed homosexuality, it would never have occurred to Paul to engage in it. The Law then is to blame for his torment! Paul then compares the prohibitions in the Law—those commandments that begin with "You shall not"—with the prohibitions in the marketplace. In the market, one sign says, "Do not handle the merchandise!" Another says, "Do not touch!" Another says, "Do not taste!" Another, "No free samples!" All these signs, contrary to their intent, make Paul want to handle, touch, and sample! In short, the merchants would do better without those signs, and the Law would do better without its prohibitions (Col 2:20–23).

Paul goes on to tell us that it was his flesh that made him sin. His lust, his desire, was so overwhelming he "was sold under sin [became a prostitute?]." There was no hope for him under the Law:

> **[T]he law is spiritual; but I am carnal, sold under sin. I do not understand my own actions. For I do not do what I want, but I do the very thing I hate** (Rom 7:14–15).

Only the grace of Jesus Christ can save him:

> **I delight in the Law of God in my inmost self, but I see in my members [sexual organs] another law at war with the law of my mind, and making me captive to the law of sin which dwells in my members. Wretched man that I am! Who will deliver me from this body of death! Thanks be to God through Jesus Christ our Lord! I myself serve the Law of God with my mind, but with my flesh I serve the law of sin! There is therefore now no condemnation for those who are in Christ Jesus** (Rom 7:22–25; 8:1).

Paul, had preached that the righteous Jew is saved without Jesus Christ. Now he tells us that the sinning Jew along with all the gentiles can be saved only through the saving grace of Jesus Christ. Having found a mechanism to forgive his own sin, unforgivable under the old religion, Paul founded a new religion.

SINS THAT DISQUALIFY PEOPLE FROM HEAVEN

Paul lists the sins that deny people entrance to the Kingdom of heaven without Jesus Christ:

> **Do you not know that the unrighteous will not inherit the kingdom of God? Do not be deceived; neither the immoral, nor idolaters, nor adulterers, nor homosexuals** ["homosexuals" is the usual translation, but it is imprecise. Paul, in fact, mentions two different terms for homosexuals: μαλακοὶ (*malakoi*) which means "soft men," and ἀρσενοκοῖται (*arsenokoitai*) which means "men who sleep with men"], **nor thieves, nor the greedy, nor drunkards, nor revilers, nor robbers will inherit the kingdom of God. And such were some of you. But you were washed, you were**

sanctified, you were justified in the name of the Lord Jesus Christ and in the Spirit of our God (1 Cor 6:9–11).

That Paul used two terms for homosexuals shows his preoccupation with that behavior as well as, in this context, his contempt for it.

PAUL'S NEW RELIGION

It is evident that Paul founded the new religion called Christianity because he practiced a sin that was unforgivable under the Law but was forgivable with a belief in the grace of Jesus Christ.

The problem with Paul's new religion of complete forgiveness is that it negates personal responsibility, particularly when a sin harms others, for example, children or those with disabilities such as mental retardation or blindness. Paul doesn't deal with that. Neither does he deal with the problem of people continuing to repeat their sin—and continuing to harm others. Is there grace from Jesus Christ under those circumstances? Is Jesus' grace without bounds? If so, what would motivate recidivist sinners to cease sinning? On this the church is silent.

THE GOSPEL

THE GOSPEL: THE GOOD NEWS

The "gospel" means the "good news." The nature of the good news has changed at least three times since it was first announced by the Hebrew prophets: the gospel of God, announced by the prophets; the gospel of the Son of God, announced by Paul (and thereafter modified); and the gospel of the Incarnation, announced by the church. In addition to the good news, the term gospel has been applied to the four canonical interpretive biographies of Jesus of Nazareth which comprise the first books of the New Testament.

THE GOSPEL OF GOD

The gospel of God was the original good news that the Hebrew prophets announced: God's Kingdom with eternal peace on earth had come at last, with the Lord YHVH reigning from Zion:

> **O thou that tellest good tidings**
> **[good news, the gospel] to Zion,**
> **Get thee up into the high mountain;**
> **O thou that tellest good tidings to Jerusalem,**
> **Lift up thy voice with strength;**
> **Lift it up, be not afraid;**
> **Say unto the cities of Judah:**
> **Behold your God!** (Is 40:9–10).
>
> **How beautiful upon the mountains**
> **are the feet of him who brings good tidings,**
> **who publishes peace** (Is 52:7–10).
>
> **Behold, on the mountains**
> **the feet of him who brings good tidings,**
> **who proclaims peace!** (Nah 1:15).
>
> **Glory to God in the highest!**
> **And on earth, Peace!** (Lk 2:14).

John the Baptist preached the gospel of God:

> **Repent for the Kingdom of heaven is at hand!** (Mt 3:6).

And Jesus preached the gospel of God:

> **Repent for the Kingdom of heaven is at hand!**
> (Mt 4:17).

> **Jesus came into Galilee, preaching the gospel of God, and saying:** *The time is fulfilled, and the kingdom of God is at hand; repent and believe in the gospel* (Mk 1:14–15).

Those who repented would be saved, whereas those who continued in their evil ways would be destroyed. The end of times and Judgment Day were at hand. But John and Jesus were mistaken, for nothing happened. What were Jesus' followers to do?

THE GOSPEL OF THE SON OF GOD

Because Jesus did not fulfill the gospel of God, Paul changed the definition of gospel. He exchanged the gospel of God for the gospel of the Son of God: Jesus Christ was resurrected from the dead, and his redeeming death brought grace—forgiveness and eternal life—to those who believed in him:

> **The beginning of the gospel of Jesus Christ, the Son of God** (Mk 1:1).

> **Paul, a servant of Jesus Christ, called to be an apostle, set apart for [literally,** *cast out* **or** *set aside***] the gospel of God which he promised beforehand through his prophets in the holy scriptures, the gospel concerning his Son . . . designated Son of God . . . by his resurrection from the dead . . . through whom we have received grace** (Rom 1:1–6).

Paul preached the gospel of the Son of God in Greek to the gentiles and the Jews in the diaspora, and Peter preached the gospel of the Son of God in Aramaic to the Jews of Jerusalem. Other than the language in which they preached and the group to whom they preached, the gospel they preached was the same. Paul made a point of stating that, and the entire New Testament speaks only of *one* gospel. The word *gospels* in the plural does not appear in the New Testament. This indicates, too, that there was only one interpretive biography of Jesus of Nazareth, also called gospel, even though today there are four. Which one is authentic? Significantly, too, none of the four canonical gospels preaches the gospel of the Son of God as clearly as Paul stated it in his letter to the Romans (above).

At first the gospel of the Son of God (later also called the gospel of God, although that one must not be confused with the gospel of God proclaimed by the prophets) was preached by word of mouth. There was no need to write it down because the disciples trusted Jesus when he said the world was coming to an end imminently. Two millennia have passed, and the world has not come to an end, although many people since Jesus' day have said it would, some even giving an exact date. Nonetheless and without any doubt, one day the world as we know it will come to an end, but that will have nothing to do with anything Jesus said or did. Sooner or later everything comes to an end.

Paul wanted to be sure that he was preaching the same gospel to the gentiles that James and Peter were preaching to the Jews, so he *wrote* his gospel down and made a special trip to Jerusalem to have James, Peter, and John, whom Paul called the "pillars" of the church, review and verify his Greek translation. He laid out his gospel before them. The pillars read it and approved it. Whereupon Paul could return to the gentiles confident that everyone, whether preaching in Aramaic or Greek, was preaching one and the same gospel:

> I laid before [James, Peter, and John] . . . the gospel
> which I preach among the Gentiles, lest somehow I
> should be running or had run in vain. . . . [And]
> those, I say, who were of repute [James, Peter, and
> John] added nothing . . . but on the contrary, when
> they saw that I had been entrusted with the gospel to
> the uncircumcised, just as Peter had been entrusted
> with the gospel to the circumcised . . . James and
> Cephas [Peter] and John, who were reputed to be
> pillars, gave to me . . . the right hand of fellowship
> (Gal 2:2–9).

Paul, on returning to the diaspora, discovered that many un-
authorized gospels were appearing and being preached. It is
not clear whether he was talking about different interpretations
of the grace of Jesus or different biographies about Jesus. In
either event, Paul sternly warned that every one of those gospels—"even if an angel from heaven should preach" it—was
false and was not to be believed. Moreover, Paul cursed all
those who preached the new gospels:

> But I am afraid . . . your thoughts will be led astray
> . . . if you accept a different gospel from the one you
> accepted (2 Cor 11:4).

> I am astonished that you are so quickly . . . turning
> to a different gospel—not that there is another gos-
> pel, but there are some who . . . want to pervert the
> gospel. . . . But even if . . . an angel from heaven
> should preach to you a gospel contrary to that which
> we preached to you, let him be accursed. As we have
> said before, so now I say again, if anyone is preach-
> ing to you a gospel contrary to that which you re-
> ceived, let him be accursed (Gal 1:6–9).

THE GOSPEL OF THE INCARNATION

Jesus of Nazareth preached the gospel of God.   Paul preached the gospel of the Son of God.   The church today teaches the gospel of the Incarnation: God humbled himself and took on flesh to become a man to dwell among mankind:

> The Catholic faith steadfastly professes that Jesus is literally and truly God. . . .   This is the good news of Christian faith; that He who is almighty, the eternal Lord of all . . . "dwelt among us" (Jn 1:14) in the visible humanity (*The Teaching of Christ: A Catholic Catechism for Adults*, p. 79).

> [T]his is the joyful good news of Christianity; that this man Jesus, the One who could be seen, He who walked this earth, He is my God (ibid., p. 84).

Paul wrote:

> **They exchanged the glory of the incorruptible God for the likeness of an image of corruptible man. . . . They exchanged the truth about God for a lie. And they worshipped and served the creature rather than the Creator** (Rom 1:23–25).

> **As we have said before, so now I say again, if anyone is preaching to you a gospel contrary to that which you received, let him be accursed** (Gal 1:9).

THE FOUR CANONICAL GOSPELS

THE FOUR INTERPRETIVE BIOGRAPHIES OF JESUS OF NAZARETH, EACH CALLED "GOSPEL"

Paul died in Rome around AD 65, executed by the Romans. In AD 70, Jerusalem fell to the Romans. By then James, the first bishop (bishops were called popes in those days) and the brother of Jesus, had died; his successor was a man called Simeon. The Romans made no distinction between normative Jews and Nazarene Jews and slaughtered Jews indiscriminately. They took the fittest back to Rome in chains. Some escaped by going into hiding or fleeing Jerusalem.

There is no evidence that Mary, Jesus' mother, ever left Jerusalem, where she probably died. Nonetheless, the Christians in Greece, not knowing her at all, invented many legends about her, including her moving to Greece and spending her last days there. Orthodox Christian Greeks claim even to have discovered her home in Greece. They assiduously ignore, however, that their beloved Virgin Mary was Jewish.

Although Peter visited many places in Asia Minor, he did so before the fall of Jerusalem, and there is no evidence, in spite of a church tradition to the contrary, that Peter ever went to Rome or that he died away from Jerusalem.

The only thing we know about Matthew's gospel is that it was written in Hebrew. Jerome in the fifth century had several Hebrew gospels to choose from, and perhaps apostolic Matthew was among them.

A Jew named Mark said he heard Peter preaching the gospel in Aramaic, and Mark later translated Peter's gospel, as best he could remember it, into Greek. It is not known how closely Mark's writing came to Peter's preaching. Canonical Mark is the only gospel to call itself the gospel (Mk 1:1). Canonical Matthew was probably based on canonical Mark, as modern scholars believe, as well as on apostolic Matthew.

After the fall of Jerusalem, John apparently fled to Asia Minor, became an apostle to the gentiles, and lived to be an old man in Greece. Late in the first or early in the second century, he wrote a theological treatise in Greek. John did not consider his treatise a gospel and did not call it by that name. In fact, he never used the word gospel in his book. Because of its highly controversial Christology at the time, John's treatise was slow to gain acceptance. Once accepted, however, the church called it a "gospel."

As late as the middle of the second century, Luke, in his own words, undertook "to compile a narrative" about the life of Jesus. Luke did not call his compilation a gospel. He did not conceal that he had plagiarized from other writers but openly boasted that he had done so. Luke said that in making such a compilation he was not alone, for many of his contemporaries were compiling similar narratives:

> **Inasmuch as many have undertaken to compile a narrative . . . as they were delivered to us by those who from the beginning were eyewitnesses and ministers of the word, it seemed good to me also, having followed all things closely for some time past, to write an orderly account** (Lk 1:2).

Luke's narrative began when Jesus was an adult. However, to satisfy those who wanted an account of Jesus' infancy, redactors later added the nativity story—the author and source of this enchanting and famous work of fiction is unknown. The episode of Jesus at the age of twelve celebrating Passover in Jerusalem was taken almost verbatim from the infancy gospel of Thomas. The two stories, the nativity and the boy Jesus celebrating Passover, are told in chapters one and two of canonical Luke. These chapters are known to be later additions because none of the early church fathers cited them, not even Clement of Alexandria, the greatest scholar of Luke of the third century, who wrote extensive commentary about Luke's gospel.

If one were to follow Paul's advice, all four canonical gospels would be rejected. Even if parts of them were based on the original apostolic biography of Jesus, they contain so much that was added subsequently that it is almost impossible to extract the original. Thomas Jefferson in the eighteenth century may have been the first to identify that problem. Jefferson compiled what he considered the authentic sayings of Jesus and discarded everything else, miracles and all, as trash. Modern scholars have been trying to do something similar.

In the fifth century, when Jerome began his translation of the bible into Latin, he had so many gospels to choose from—a few in Hebrew and many in Greek—that he had difficulty making his selection. Ancient gospels, hitherto unknown, have continued to be discovered, most recently the gospel of Thomas and the gospel of Judas. The church, however, relied exclusively on Jerome's selection. Today's four canonical gospels in Greek, far from being the original sources, are translations of Jerome's Latin gospels. After Jerome died, changes in the canonical gospels continued to be made. Regarding the gospels translated into modern languages, changes in meaning, as we have seen (see Church Scholarship), continue to be made as recently as the twentieth century.

MATTHEW

ORIGINS OF MATTHEW'S GOSPEL

The earliest reference to the gospel of Matthew is found in the writings of an elder of the church named Papias who lived in the second century. Eusebius reported Papias's statement:

> Matthew wrote the oracles [sayings] in the Hebrew
> language, and everyone interpreted them as he was able
> (*The Nicene and Post-Nicene Fathers*, Second Series,
> vol. 1, Eusebius, Church History, 3:39, p. 173).

We learn that those who translated Matthew from Hebrew into
Greek were not skilled translators. We have no idea how many
errors were introduced in that translation.

Apostolic Matthew's book, unlike canonical Matthew, contained only Jesus' sayings. It had no miracles—no star of
Bethlehem, no virgin birth, no resurrection.

In the third century, church fathers, on discovering that apostolic Matthew lacked miracles, accused the Jerusalem ecclesia composed entirely of Jews of having deleted the miracles.
It is both curious and significant that Christian scholars have
not accused Christians of having added the miracles.

MARK

ORIGINS OF MARK'S GOSPEL

The presbyter Papias gave the earliest reference to Mark's
gospel. Papias reported that Mark had accompanied Peter and
heard him preach "the gospel." The gospel Peter preached was
probably the same as Paul's gospel of the Son of God. Significantly, Mark is the only evangelist to call his book a gospel.
After Peter and Mark separated, Mark wrote down and translated into Greek whatever he could remember of Peter's
preaching. Mark's gospel ought rightly to be called Peter's
gospel as remembered, translated, and adapted by Mark.
Eusebius gives Papias's account:

> Mark, who had been Peter's interpreter, wrote down
> carefully, but not in order, all that he remembered of the

> Lord's sayings and doings. For he had not heard the
> Lord or been one of His followers, but later, as I said,
> one of Peter's. Peter used to adapt his teaching to the
> occasion, without making a systematic arrangement of
> the Lord's sayings, so that Mark was quite justified in
> writing down some things just as he remembered them.
> For he had one purpose only—to leave out nothing that
> he had heard, and to make no misstatement about it
> (Eusebius, *The History of the Church*, 3:39, p. 152).

How could Mark not make mistakes? He was making from
memory (how long after Peter preached?) a hearsay account of
the life of Jesus, delivered in a haphazard manner, "adapted"
for the occasion, and translated from oral Aramaic into written
Greek.   Moreover, it is known that Mark's gospel was to
change over time—most notably, the deletion of the secret behavior of Jesus and the addition of the last twelve chapters—
before Jerome received the gospel and transformed it into canonical Mark. There are no references to the last twelve chapters in the patristic literature prior to the Nicene Council.

"SECRET MARK"

Secrecy is a peculiar characteristic of canonical Mark. Notably, Jesus of Nazareth wanted to keep his messiahship a secret. That was highly bizarre when the Messiah was expected
to proclaim the good news to the whole world. Jesus succeeds
in hiding his identity from everyone except—amazing to say—
demons and devils, who instantly identify him as the Messiah!

Canonical Mark has two elliptical episodes that left scholars
puzzled until recently.   Both concern Jesus' relationship to
young men. The first:

Just before Jesus entered Jerusalem, a young man [from
Bethany?] ran up to Jesus, knelt before him, and called him
"good." **And Jesus, looking upon him, loved** [*agape* in the

past tense] **him** (Mk 10:21). Christian scholars have agreed among themselves, and it has become a convention, that whenever in the New Testament the Greek word *agape* (love) appears, it can have only one meaning, namely "brotherly love," even though the word in other writings in antiquity has the full spectrum of meanings of the word, including erotic love. Canonical Mark continues:

> **[Jesus] entered Jerusalem, and went into the temple; and when he had looked round at everything, as it was already late, he went out to Bethany with the twelve. On the following day . . . they came from Bethany. . . . to Jerusalem** (Mk 11:11–15).

According to canonical Mark, Jesus went to Jerusalem, but didn't find whomever he was looking for in the temple so he went to Bethany. On the following day he left Bethany and returned to Jerusalem. This strange detour generates several questions: Whom was Jesus looking for? Was it the young man whom Jesus loved? Did Jesus and the young man have a plan to meet in the temple? If so, what kept the young man from the meeting? Why did Jesus go to Bethany for lodging when he was already in Jerusalem and was planning to return to Jerusalem the next day? The detour to Bethany seems purposeless—unless the purpose had been deleted from canonical Mark. The evidence, which follows, indicates that the purpose of the detour to Bethany had indeed been deleted.

In the twentieth century, a letter written in the third century by Clement of Alexandria was discovered. In his letter, Clement wrote the missing parts of the Bethany story which he said came from the "Secret Gospel of Mark" (also known as "Secret Mark"):

> And they come into Bethany. And a certain woman whose [young] brother had died [No wonder he didn't show up at the temple!] was there. And, coming, she prostrated herself before Jesus and says to him, "Son of David, have mercy on me." But the disciples rebuked her. And Jesus, being angered, went off with her into the garden where the tomb was, and straightway a great cry was heard from the tomb. And going near Jesus rolled away the stone from the door of the tomb. And straightway, going in where the youth was, he stretched forth his hand and raised him, seizing his hand. But the youth, looking upon him, loved him and began to beseech him that he might be with him. And going out of the tomb they came into the house of the youth, for he was rich. And after six days Jesus told him what to do and in the evening the youth comes to him, wearing a linen cloth over his naked body. And he remained with him that night, for Jesus taught him the mystery of the kingdom of God. And thence, arising, he returned to the other side of the Jordan. . . . And he [Jesus] comes into Jericho. And the sister of the youth whom Jesus loved and his mother and Salome were there, and Jesus did not receive them (Smith, *Clement of Alexandria and a Secret Gospel of Mark*, p. 447).

The implications are that the detour to Bethany was not purposeless. And when Jesus left Bethany after six days he did not return to Jerusalem but went to the other side of the Jordan and then to Jericho. Some scholars have stated that the episode shows that Jesus and the youth were physically intimate. Jesus refused to meet with the boy's mother, sister, and Salome. Was he ashamed to do so?

The second incident, this one described in canonical Mark, takes place in the Garden of Gethsemane:

> **And immediately, while [Jesus of Nazareth] was still speaking [in the Garden of Gethsemane], Judas came, one of the twelve, and with him a crowd with swords and clubs, from the chief priests and the scribes and the elders. Now the betrayer had given them a sign, saying, "The one I shall kiss is the man. Seize him and lead him away safely." And then [Judas] came and went up to [Jesus] at once and said, "Master!" And he kissed him. And [the soldiers] laid hands on him and seized him. . . . And [the apostles present with Jesus] forsook him, and fled** (Mk 14:51–52).

Why would a sign be necessary to identify Jesus when he was already well known to the authorities as a troublemaker? Why should the sign be a kiss? Scholars of "Secret Mark" suggest that the kiss of Judas was a diversionary tactic by the redactor of canonical Mark to avert one's attention from another kiss, a passionate one between Jesus and the young man from Bethany—or perhaps another young man. After Jesus is seized, canonical Mark says:

> **And a young man followed [Jesus], with nothing but a linen cloth about his body; and they seized [the young man], but he slipped out of the linen cloth and ran away naked** (Mk 14:43–53).

Some scholars conclude from these two incidents—one in "Secret Mark," the other in canonical Mark—that the early church, drawing an intolerable conclusion, removed the Bethany episode from canonical Mark. The Gethsemane episode apparently was allowed to stand because it is merely suggestive, and a single episode does not carry the weight of two.

LUKE

ORIGINS OF LUKE'S GOSPEL

The early church fathers did not refer to a gospel according to Luke. And Luke himself says that his book was not original, but was a compilation of material from earlier sources who were "eyewitnesses":

> **Inasmuch as many have undertaken to compile a narrative of the things which have been accomplished among us, just as they were delivered to us by those who from the beginning were eyewitnesses and ministers of the word, it seemed good to me also, having followed all things closely for some time past, to write an orderly account** (Lk 1: 1–3).

The earliest reference to Luke did not occur until the middle of the second century when Marcion, a gnostic and antisemite, mentioned and favored that gospel, presumably because Luke was the only gentile of the four evangelists. Marcion also favored Luke's book because it began when Jesus was a grown man; Greek gods came to earth already grown, not as infants or children. (That probably will strike people today as strange because canonical Luke begins with chapters one and two which tell the nativity story.) The church decided that Marcion had excised the nativity story from his copy of Luke because he did not like the idea of a god coming to earth as a newborn and also he found the story too Jewish—for example, it announced the gospel of God rather than the gospel of the Son of God. The church condemned Marcion as a heretic.

The evidence, however, indicates that Marcion did not excise the nativity story but that redactors later added it. Clement of Alexandria, a third century church father with a reputation for impeccable scholarship as well as being considered the greatest authority on Luke at that time, did not describe the nativity story in Luke. Because of Clement's high reputation, the church never accused Clement of having deleted chapters one and two. The church merely ignored this important fact.

The first time a nativity story was mentioned in Luke was also in the third century, when Origen, a church father, described it. Did Origen or a contemporary of his write it? Another late reference (between AD 170 and the fourth century) to Luke called the Muratorian canon fragment says:

> The third book of the Gospel is that according to Luke. Luke, the physician, when, after the Ascension of Christ, Paul had taken him to himself as one studious of right, wrote in his own name what he had been told, although he had not himself seen the Lord in the flesh. He set down the events as far as he could ascertain them, and began his story with the birth of John [the Baptist] (Canon Muratorianus, Fragments of Caius, *Ante-Nicene Fathers*, vol. 5, p. 603).

The fragment was probably a forgery to give the first two chapters of Luke authority. John the Baptist's birth as well as Jesus' birth are described in chapters one and two of canonical Luke. The author of the fragment says that the author of Luke's gospel was the physician friend of Paul's. But that is not credible because Paul and the author of Luke were separated by almost a century. Paul did not know Jesus, but Paul did know Peter and John who had known Jesus. Luke the physician friend of Paul's could have heard about Jesus from Paul. But the Luke who was the author of the gospel implies he knew of Jesus only through documents delivered to him. Furthermore, Paul cursed new gospels and gave no reason to make an exception for Luke. Although the original author of Luke says he was writing a narrative based on earlier works, there is no early work that gives a nativity story, nor do any of the early church fathers allude to one. The evidence indicates that the nativity story was written by redactors after canonical Luke first appeared, not that Marcion or Clement deleted it.

JOHN

ORIGINS OF JOHN'S GOSPEL

John was probably a young teenager, at the time of the crucifixion and was very old when his "gospel" was written. Like Matthew and Luke, John did not call his book a gospel. John called his book a mystical treatise or revelation—not to be confused with the last book of the Christian bible, called *Apocalypse* or *Revelation*.

If John lived into his nineties, then his gospel could have been written as late as the early second century. If we are to believe the Muratorian fragment, at the time that John's gospel was written, several bishops had gathered with John. He had no intention of writing a gospel, even though the bishops encouraged him to do so. He agreed to writing a mystical revelation, however, on the following conditions: The revelation had to be a joint enterprise by all of them. It was not to be an historical account or a collection of sayings, but rather a writing down of the things that came into all of their minds, or were *revealed* to them, after a three-day fast. The bishops agreed.

During the first day of the fast, the apostle Andrew, who was present and had to have been older than John, reported that during the previous night it had been *revealed* to him that at the end of the fast, John alone should narrate to the others whatever came into his head and that John should be the sole author of the work. Here is an account of that meeting:

> The fourth gospel is that of John, one of the disciples.
> When his fellow disciples and bishops entreated him,

he said, "Fast with me for a period of three days; and let us recount to each other whatever may be revealed to us." On the same night, it was revealed to Andrew, one of the Apostles, that John should narrate all things in his own name, as they came to mind (Canon Muratorianus, Fragments of Caius, *Ante-Nicene Fathers*, vol. 5, p. 603).

JOHN'S GOSPEL

John's treatise does not contain the word gospel. The contents were revealed to John in old age after going for three days without food or water. This book was slow to gain acceptance in the church. Luke's book, although written later, was accepted earlier. As Christology advanced in the church, however, John's book, being the most advanced in Christology, gained greater acceptance, and ended by becoming the most important theological "gospel" of them all.

John had been a pillar in the Jerusalem church along with James and Peter. Matthew's and Mark's gospels were filled with doubt. John did not want to write another doubt-filled book. God had given John a special mission—to do whatever was necessary to remove all doubt and make believers of everyone:

> **There was a man sent from God, whose name was John. He came for testimony, to bear witness to the light, that all might believe through him** (Jn 1:6–7).

The word "believe" occurs about ten times in each of Matthew, Mark, and Luke, whereas it appears about a hundred times in John. Moreover, unlike the mere witnesses in the other three gospels, John's are *true* witnesses. Although the Old Testament requires that important events be witnessed by the entire community of Israel, John requires only one witness—presumably himself.

Old Testament:

> **All the great and terrible deeds Moses performed he did in the sight of all the people of Israel** (Deut 34:12).

John:

> **This is vouched for by an eye witness whose testimony is to be trusted. He knows that he speaks the truth so that you too may believe** (Jn 19:35–6).

John's gospel ends:

> **But there are also many other things which Jesus did; were every one of them to be written, I suppose that the world itself could not contain the books that would be written** (Jn 21:25).

Such an extravagant statement demeans the credibility of the whole book and only serves to increase the doubt the book intended to dispel.

John, unlike the other evangelists, is self-aggrandizing although he admits, almost grudgingly, that Jesus was greater than he. Jesus, according to John, was greatly taken with John, too. John repeatedly speaks of Jesus of Nazareth's "beloved disciple," and most scholars assume that disciple was John:

> **One of his disciples, whom Jesus loved, was lying close to the breast of Jesus** (Jn 13:23).

> **. . . the other disciple, the one whom Jesus loved** (Jn 20:2).

> **That disciple whom Jesus loved** (Jn 21:7).

> **. . . the disciple whom Jesus loved, who had lain close to his breast at the supper** (Jn 21:20).

The other evangelists do not confirm a "beloved disciple," although they do describe Jesus' encounters with young men Jesus loved (*agape*). Why does John paint a picture almost of a Greek symposium, and why is he so ambiguously coy about his relationship with Jesus? Perhaps so that he could say to Jews, who would be intolerant of any implication of a symposium, that he was not the "beloved disciple," whereas he could say to Greeks, who would be tolerant, that John was to Jesus what a beloved young man was to a philosopher.

John also says that he had special influence with the High Priest; John was able to gain admittance to the palace of the High Priest whenever he wished. John does not explain the purpose of his gaining admission to the High Priest's palace.

John, by writing his book later than Matthew and Mark, could not only develop the theology they barely had, but also add incidents they lacked. John says that he was the only apostle present at the Crucifixion, another claim not supported by any other evangelist. It was at the Crucifixion, too, that John developed a special relationship with Jesus' mother, a relationship that Jesus himself endorsed. John become a special son of Mary to take Jesus' place.

John frequently compares himself with Peter, and in those comparisons John has himself superior. His competitiveness with Peter is sometimes childish. For example, on the first Easter morning, on hearing the news of Jesus' empty tomb, John and Peter make a dash to the tomb, not so much to witness its emptiness as to see who was the faster runner. John wins!

After the fall of Jerusalem, John escaped to the diaspora. By then, he had become like Paul an apostle to the gentiles. John makes Jesus more divine than the other writers. For example, Matthew, Mark, and Luke have Jesus celebrating the first night of Passover during the last supper. John makes the last supper a day earlier, the day before the Passover, so that Jesus, by his crucifixion, becomes the Passover sacrifice, the Lamb of God, which, John claims, takes away the sins of the world.

John's gospel is notorious for its antisemitism, in large part created through his phrase "the Jews," delivered with great contempt. Nonetheless, John, a Jew himself, must have experienced antisemitism among the Greeks, for his gospel also contains one of the most philosemitic statements found in Christian literature.

JOHN, PHILOSOPHER AND THEOLOGIAN

Although John demonstrated some philosophical ability in defining Jesus Christ, he showed no such ability in portraying God:

> **For God so loved the world that he gave his only Son, that whoever believes in him should not perish but have eternal life** (Jn 3:16).

Contrast that with John's following statement:

> **Do not love the world or the things in the world. If anyone loves the world, love for the Father is not in him** (1 Jn 2:15).

If John actually believed that God sent his Son out of love for the world, John ought to have said, "Love the world and the things in the world as the Father loves the world. If anyone does not love the world, love for the Father is not in him." Instead, John said the very opposite, thereby negating his very own theology which is the core of Christianity.

Many other statements of John are bizarre, irrational, or conflictual. Consider this chain of statements:

> **Jesus and his disciples went into the land of Judea; there he remained with them and baptized. John [the baptist] also was baptizing** (Jn 3:22–3).

> **Jesus was . . . baptizing more disciples than John** (Jn 4:1).

> **Jesus himself did not baptize, but only his disciples** (Jn 4:2).

"THE JEWS"

Perhaps no phrase in western literature has generated as much antisemitism as the New Testament phrase of generalization "the Jews." It is used as contemptuously as if it were a curse word. And no one uses that phrase more often than John—ten times as often as any of the other three evangelists! Here are examples:

> **The [cured] man went away and told the Jews that it was Jesus who had healed him. And this was why the Jews persecuted Jesus, because he did this on the sabbath** (Jn 5:15–18).

> **After this Jesus went about in Galilee; he would not go about in Judea, because the Jews sought to kill him** (Jn 7:1).

Yet for fear of the Jews no one spoke openly of him (Jn 7:13).

The Jews then said to him, "You are not yet fifty years old, and have you seen Abraham?" Jesus said to them, *Truly, truly, I say to you, before Abraham was, I am.* So they took up stones to throw at him; but Jesus hid himself, and went out of the temple (Jn 8:57–59).

The Jews took up stones again to stone him. Jesus answered them, *I have shown you many good works from the Father; for which of these do you stone me?* The Jews answered him, "We stone you for no good work but for blasphemy; because you being a man, make yourself God" (Jn 10:31–33).

[Jesus] said to the disciples, *Let us go into Judea again.* The disciples said to him, "Rabbi, the Jews were but now seeking to stone you, and you are going there again?" (Jn 11:7–8).

Joseph of Arimathea, who was a disciple of Jesus, but secretly, for fear of the Jews, asked Pilate that he might take away the body of Jesus (Jn 19:38).

In all the above cases it is obvious that only a few Jews were involved; and yet John blames them all. Could anyone but an antisemite believe, for example, that every Jew on the face of the earth took up a stone against Jesus? It's not as if John didn't know the difference between "the Jews" and "some Jews." John's purpose probably was to detract from the fact that Jesus and Mary were also Jews, and to a large degree, he achieved that purpose.

"SOME JEWS"

The church and Christians throughout the ages have latched onto John's hostility to "the Jews" to justify persecution and murder of Jews. Curiously, however, the very same John who appears to be so antisemitic can also be even-handed. Significantly, the church does not teach his even-handedness. John tells us that the Jews fell into two groups—those who believed in Jesus and those who did not:

> While some Jews said, "He is a good man," others said, "No, he is leading the people astray" (Jn 7:12).

> Some of the [Jews] of Jerusalem therefore said, "Is not this the man whom they seek to kill? . . . Can it be that the authorities really know that this is the Christ?" . . . Many of the people believed in him; they said, "When the Christ appears, will he do more signs than this man has done?" (Jn 7:25–31).

> When they heard [Jesus'] words, some of the people said, "This is really the prophet." Others said, "This is the Christ." But some said, "Is the Christ to come from Galilee?" . . . So there was a division among the people over him (Jn 7:40–43).

> Jesus then said to the Jews who had believed in him, *If you continue in my word, you are truly my disciples, and you will know the truth, and the truth will make you free* (Jn 8:31–32).

> Some of the Pharisees said, "This man is not from God, for he does not keep the sabbath." But others said, "How can a man who is a sinner do such signs?" There was a division among them (Jn 9:16).

> There was again a division among the Jews. . . .
> Many of them said, "He has a demon, and he is
> mad; why listen to him?" Others said, "These are
> not the sayings of one who had a demon. Can a de-
> mon open the eyes of the blind?" (Jn 10:19–21).

> Many of the Jews . . . believed in him; but some of
> them went to the Pharisees and told them what Je-
> sus had done (Jn 11:45–46).

> Many of the Jews were going away and believing in
> Jesus (Jn 12:11).

"SALVATION IS FROM THE JEWS"

John can be not only even-handed, but even philosemitic.
John has a gentile woman identify Jesus as "a Jew":

> There came a woman of Samaria to draw water.
> Jesus said to her, *Give me a drink.* . . . The Samari-
> tan woman said to him, "How is that you, a Jew, ask
> a drink of me, a woman of Samaria?" (Jn 4:7–9).

Then Jesus and the woman have a discussion during which
Jesus says to her:

> *You [gentiles] worship what you do not know; we
> [Jews] worship what we know, for salvation is from
> the Jews* (Jn 4:22).

Jesus is called a Jew, and Jesus says salvation is from the Jews.
The church ignores these verses.

LAST SUPPER RITUAL: WASHING FEET

Hand washing was part of Jewish tradition. No meal could begin unless the people at table had washed their hands beforehand. The Passover meal includes a ceremonial washing of hands. The master of the meal (today called "the leader of the seder") receives a pitcher, basin, and towel, and proceeds to wash and dry his hands, and the participants do the same.

Jesus of Nazareth, however, scorned hand washing on the grounds that it did not wash the heart (Mt 15:1–20). Jesus' admonition, however noble, did not improve human spirituality and had a disastrous effect on the public health. Hand washing was never meant by the Pharisees to remove sins; it was merely an extension of the commandment to bathe.

Today hand washing is recognized as one of the greatest of preventive public health measures against the spread of communicable disease. The Jews were not aware of that in ancient days. The implications of hand washing for the public health were not discovered until the nineteenth century.

But if Jesus had been sent by God, he would have commended the Pharisaic practice of hand washing, not scorned it. He thereby could have saved countless lives instead of contributing to countless deaths.

In John's book, Jesus takes the Jewish tradition of hand washing and stands it on its head, thereby creating a new tradition—the washing of feet, which neither washes away sins nor affords benefit to the public health. After Jesus receives the customary pitcher, basin, and towel, he startles everyone by rising from table, stripping, and standing naked before the astonished apostles. He then wraps the towel around his waist, takes the pitcher and basin, and proceeds to wash the feet of the apostles (Jn 13:1–15).

To exchange the washing of hands for the washing of feet set the public health back two thousand years. Moreover, the

washing of male friends' feet while standing naked before
them may appear noble to the church but homoerotic to others.

CALLING GOD "FATHER"

John says that the Jews wanted to kill Jesus because he
called God "Father."

> **This was why the Jews sought all the more to kill
> [Jesus], because he . . . called God his father, making
> himself equal with God** (Jn 5:16–28).

John is not telling the truth. First of all, calling God Father
did not make oneself equal with God and was not grounds for
execution. Moreover, what John fails to tell his Greek audience is that the Jews repeatedly called God "Father" or "our
Father." Many ancient Hebrew prayers begin, "Our Father in
heaven" [*Avinu shebashamyim*]. Here are examples from Hebrew Scriptures:

> **Blessed art thou, O Lord [YHVH], God of Israel,
> our Father, for ever and ever** (1 Chron 29:10).

> **Thou [YHVH] hast said, . . . "[David] shall cry to
> me, 'Thou art my Father, my God, and the Rock of
> my salvation'"** (Ps 89:3, 26).

> **Thou, O Lord [YHVH], art our Father, our Re-
> deemer from of old** (Is 63:16).

> **And the Lord [YHVH] said, . . . "Return, faithless
> Israel. . . . I thought how I would set you among my
> sons. . . . And I thought you would call me, 'My Fa-
> ther'"** (Jer 3:11–12, 19).

John knew these things, for John was a Jew. He was simply stirring up trouble. Antisemitism was expedient to the church and good for the faith.

THE FALL OF THE NAZARENES IN JERUSALEM AND THE RISE OF THE CHRISTIANS IN ROME

A SMALL JEWISH SECT
BECOMES A GREAT GENTILE RELIGION

Jerusalem fell to the Romans in AD 70. The community of Nazarenes in Jerusalem, which had been led by James the Just, a brother of Jesus of Nazareth, nearly collapsed at the same time. The Romans did not discriminate between Nazarenes and normative or faithful Jews.

Josephus attributed the fall of Jerusalem to the defiant stand against Rome by the Jewish leaders. Christian interpolators later gave the fall of Jerusalem theological significance; they inserted into Josephus the interpretation that Jerusalem fell as retribution by God because of the martyrdom of James the Just at the hands of the Jewish leaders. Later redactors, probably on Origen's suggestion, changed the reason from martyrdom of James the Just to that of Jesus of Nazareth. The church liked that interpretation. And until Vatican Two, the Roman Catholic church taught that Jerusalem fell because the Jews killed Christ. Unaffected by Vatican Two, the Eastern Orthodox church continues to teach that. This teaching has brought nearly two thousand years of Christian persecution of the Jews.

Before Jerusalem's fall, Paul had gone to Rome and begun the gentile church there. After Jerusalem's fall, Alexandria, Egypt, which had the largest Jewish community in the dias-

pora, became the most important center of the church, and remained so through the third century. It was not until the fourth
century, when the Emperor Constantine, himself a new convert
to Christianity, converted the Roman Empire to the new religion, that Rome became the center of the church.

GOD OF THE CHRISTIANS PRIOR TO THE COUNCIL OF NICEA

Justin Martyr, a church father of the second century, wrote:

> There will be no other God . . . nor was there from eter-
> nity any other . . . but He who made and disposed all
> this universe. Nor do we think that there is one God for
> us, another for you, but that He alone is God who led
> your fathers out of Egypt with a mighty hand and an
> outstretched arm. Nor have we trusted in another, for
> there is no other, but in Him whom you [Jews] also
> have trusted, the God of Abraham, and Isaac, and Jacob
> (*The Ante-Nicene Fathers*, vol. 1, Dialogue with Try-
> pho, chap. 11, p. 199).

Origen, a church father of the third century, wrote:

> Attend to the God of the universe, and to Jesus the
> teacher of the doctrines about Him (Chadwick, *Contra
> Celsum*, p. 179).

Tertullian, another church father of the third century wrote:

> Christ is also God (*The Ante-Nicene Fathers*, vol. 3,
> p. 221).

Heathens ridiculed the many sects of "catholic" and "ortho-dox" Christians. Origen gave the following responses to the heathen philosopher Celsus:

> [A]ny teaching which has had a serious origin, and is beneficial to life, has caused different sects. . . . [S]ince the problems [discussed by philosophers] allow of considerable diversity of opinion, on this account very many sects indeed have come into existence. . . . [Similarly, Christians] interpreted differently the scriptures . . . and sects arose (ibid., pp. 135–136).

> If [Celsus] thinks it is a charge against Christianity that there are several sects among Christians, on this analogy would it not be considered a charge against philosophy that among the sects of philosophers there is disagreement? . . . . These are the two sects of Ebionites [Christian Jews], the one confessing as we do that Jesus was born of a virgin, the other holding that he was not born in this way but like other men. What criticism is there in this? (ibid., pp. 311–312).

To church fathers like Tertullian, Jesus of Nazareth was more than a teacher and more than a man, and more than a messiah or christ. He was a god. But the ever-gnawing question throughout the churches was, if Jesus was a god, was he a god equal to the Supreme God? The question was tearing the church apart. It had to have an answer.

THE CONVERSION OF CONSTANTINE—NOT PEACE BUT THE SWORD

In the fourth century, the Emperor Constantine was converted to Christianity not by the Hebrew prophetic messianic dream of everlasting peace but by Christ's triumphant call:

I have come not to bring peace, but the sword (Mt 10:34). Constantine was impressed. Christ was Constantine's kind of god.

Constantine reported that he had a vision in which Christ said to him, "By this sign, conquer!" The sign was the cross, which has the same form as a sword (both are instruments of death). Constantine used the sign of the cross as an amulet and insignia on his standards. To Constantine, Jesus was a new god of war, displacing the heathen god Mars or Ares. Constantine vowed that if Christ was true to his word and Constantine won his next battle, he would make Christianity the universal or catholic religion of Rome. Constantine took up the sword and the cross, won the battle, and kept his vow. Constantine made Christianity the official religion of the Roman Empire.

But in the emperor's mind, Jesus was not equal with the Supreme God. Jesus was not even equal with the emperor himself. Throughout the City, Constantine had colossal statues of himself set up in public squares in which the emperor's image was holding a miniature image of Jesus in his right hand, as if to say, the world must never forget it was Constantine who made Christ what he is.

DEIFICATION BY VOTE OF MEN

Voting was the standard procedure among the Romans to deify a man. Eusebius wrote:

> [T]he old law still held good that no one could be regarded by the Romans as a god unless by vote and decree of the senate. . . (Eusebius, *The History of the Church*, 2:2, p. 75).

Then Eusebius reported what Tertullian "an expert in Roman law" had to say on the subject:

> [T]here was an old decree that no one should be conse-
> crated a god by an emperor till he had been approved
> by the senate. . . . Godhead is conferred by human ap-
> proval. If a god does not satisfy man, he does not be-
> come a god (ibid., 2:2, pp. 75–76).

Seneca, the Roman philosopher who lived during the early
Christian period—his brother had presided over Paul's trial in
Rome—was so appalled by the voting procedure for deifica-
tion that he satirically called the procedure *pumpkinification*.
The implication was: As men vote to turn someone into a god,
so could they vote to turn him into a pumpkin.

THE COUNCIL OF NICEA, AD 325:
ARIUS VS. ATHANASIUS

In Egypt, early in the fourth century, when Alexandria was
still the center of Christianity, a great struggle was taking place
among those who called themselves "Catholic" and "Orthodox" to settle the questions: Was Jesus of Nazareth a god?
And if a god, was he a lesser god or of the same stature as the
Father? In Antioch, many Catholic and Orthodox Christians
considered Jesus to be, in the word of John the evangelist, the
Logos. They interpreted *Logos* the same way the philosopher
Philo had defined him, as the bridge between the spiritual and
the materialistic worlds.

The controversy was brought to a head in AD 319 by two
men, Arius and Athanasius. Arius was an elder and Athanasius
a deacon in the cathedral of Alexandria. Alexander was the
pope (also called bishop), and vacillated between the views of
the two men in his church, and finally sided with Athanasius.

Athanasius was the champion of deification of Christ, Son
of God. Athanasius insisted that the Son was equal with the
Father and co-eternal with him. Arius, on the other side, was

the champion of the one God, the Father; Arius said the Son of God was human, divine only as the Father's interpreter. Henry Chadwick, a twentieth century church historian, summarized Arius's point of view thus:

> The son who is tempted, suffers, and dies, however exalted he may be, is not to be equal to the immutable Father beyond pain and death. If he is other than the Father, he is inferior (Chadwick, *The Early Church*, p. 124).

Socrates Scholasticus, a church historian of the fifth century, wrote:

> Arius, possessed of no inconsiderable logical acumen . . . . [said,] "If . . . the Father begat the Son, he that was begotten had a beginning of existence; and from this it is evidence that *there was a time when the Son was not*" [this is the crux of the dispute and I put it in italics whenever it appears.]. . . . [H]e excited many to a consideration of the question; and thus from a little spark a large fire was kindled. . . . [C]onfusion everywhere prevailed; for one saw not only the prelates of the churches engaged in disputing, but the people also . . . . Christianity became a subject of popular ridicule, even in the very theatres (*The Nicene and Post-Nicene Fathers*, Second Series, vol. 2, Ecclesiastical History, pp. 3–5).

Theodoret, another fifth century church historian, wrote:

> Arius . . . affirmed that the Son of God is merely a creature or created being, adding the famous dictum, *"There once was a time when [the Son] was not."* . . . Arius . . . organized a gang to fight against Christ, denying His divinity, and declaring Him to be on a level

with other men. . . . They maintain the ungodly doctrine entertained by the Greeks and the Jews concerning
Jesus Christ (*The Nicene and Post-Nicene Fathers*,
Second Series, vol. 3, Ecclesiastical History, pp. 34–
35).

Theodoret quotes a letter from Arius to his friend Eusebius,
Bishop of Nicomedia:

[I have been] unjustly persecuted by Alexander, the
Pope [Bishop of Alexandria]. . . . He has driven us out
of the city [Alexandria] as atheists. . . . [And along
with me] all the bishops of the East have been condemned because [we] say that *God had an existence
prior to that of His Son. . . .* The heretics [Athanasians]
threaten us with a thousand deaths. But we say . . . *the
Son, . . . before He was begotten, was not. . . .* We are
persecuted because we say that *the Son has a beginning
but that God is without beginning* (ibid., p. 41).

The dispute raged. The emperor, Constantine, was afraid it
made the church a laughing stock to the world, and he was
embarrassed by it. Constantine wrote to the cathedral of Alexandria:

You know that philosophers, although they all adhere to
one system, are yet frequently at issue on certain points.
. . . Yet, they are recalled to harmony of sentiment by
the uniting power of their common doctrines. . . . [T]he
Divine commandment in all its parts enjoins on us all
the duty of maintaining a spirit of concord. . . . And
this I say without in any way desiring to force you into
entire unanimity. . . . For we are not all of us like-
minded on every subject, nor is there such a thing as
one disposition and one judgment common to all alike
(*The Nicene and Post-Nicene Fathers*, Second Series,

vol. 1, Eusebius, Life of Constantine, 2:71, pp. 517–518).

The emperor showed remarkable fairness but no appreciation of the gravity of the theological issues. He was concerned mainly with appearances—how the church appeared to the outside world. In spite of his measured words, dissension between the two men and those who sided with them grew ever more intense and bitter. Constantine tried again; he sent another letter to Alexandria:

> [W]e ought to confine [our opinions] to our own consideration, and not incautiously bring them forth in public assemblies, nor thoughtless confide them to the ears of everybody. . . . No cause of difference has been started by you bearing on any important precept . . . nor has any new heresy been introduced by you. . . . [Y]ou thus pertinaciously contend with one another about matters of small or scarcely the least importance. . . . [when] there is but one faith among you (Socrates Scholasticus, *The Nicene and Post-Nicene Fathers*, Second Series, vol. 2, pp. 6–7).

The second letter achieved no better results. And so Constantine called the First Ecumenical Council—the very name [ecumenical then meant "of the Whole Civilized World"] shows that the emperor was looking for a harmonious and peaceful resolution.

The following facts concerning the Council of Nicea, I obtained from the classical work on the subject by the leading scholar in the field, Charles Joseph Hefele (*A History of the Christian Councils*, pp. 231–355). Hefele reconstructed a description of the proceedings from multiple sources and documents of the time. It is interesting to note that there are no minutes of the Council of Nicea, and according to Hefele, there never were. The only written documents are the Creed, the twenty Canons and the Synodal Decree, including fixing the date of Easter. In the year AD 350, a friend asked Athanasius what took place at Nicea. Athanasius gave no answer. Presumably if Proceedings had existed, he surely would have known and would have directed his friend to them. It seems reasonable that the emperor, who had been so greatly humiliated and embarrassed by public ridicule of the many different "Catholic" and "Orthodox" definitions of God, decided that no minutes would be kept; or perhaps they did exist, but he destroyed them by fire in the presence of all, as he had destroyed the mutual complaints of many of the participants leveled against each other; for such documentation would only serve to reveal that the church weaves its theology from rancorous disagreement and not, as Constantine and the church liked to say, from the unanimity inspired by the Holy Spirit.

The Council took place in AD 325, in the city of Nicea, today called Iznik located in Turkey. There were about three hundred bishops in attendance plus their entourage. The emperor had generously provided for everyone's passage from home to Nicea, and also for board in Nicea. The bishops and their attendants had gathered by late May and were already engaging in heated discussions even though the official opening of the Council did not occur until the arrival of the emperor on June 14. Proceedings continued through late July when the emperor brought the Council to its official close by hosting a lavish banquet, during which he gave every participant a gift. Afterwards, the emperor departed, but the bishops lingered until the end of August.

During the Council, a mixture of rancorous shouting matches and calm discussion characterized the proceedings. Each side accused the other of heresy. At first more bishops sided with Arius than with Athanasius, but most of the bishops remained silent. It is evident from this alone that at the start of the Council most of the Catholic or Orthodox bishops did not yet believe that Christ was God.

No progress was made in drawing up a creed until the Athanasians proposed the following phrase: The Son was "from God," a formula that the authors believed demolished Arius's assertion that the Son was "from nothing" or had no prior existence. The Athanasians were surprised to see that the followers of Arius readily accepted the "from God" formula.

All might have ended in unanimity and harmony as the emperor wished had not the Arians then made a fatal mistake. Instead of accepting the formula without comment, they announced, "We are willing to accept the formula 'from God,' for all is from God, we and all creatures." Whereupon the Athanasians found it necessary to discard "from God" and propose a new formula incompatible with Arius's argument: They now said the Son was of the "*substance*"—οὐσία (*ousia*)—of the Father, and of the "*same substance*" or "*consubstantial*"—ὁμοούσιος (*homoousios*)—with the Father.

Arius and his followers objected that these words did not exist in the bible; and what is more, the word *substance* conjured up not a spiritual construct of God but a material one. Origen, the church father of the previous century, had in fact used the word *substance* to describe matter: "[M]atter underlies every body—a substance convertible or changeable or divisible in all its parts. . . . [S]ubstance never exists without a quality. . . . [That] which underlies bodies, and which is capable of quality, is discovered to be matter" (*The Ante-Nicene Fathers*, vol. 4, De Principiis, p. 379).

Constantine, who hitherto had expressed no understanding of the theological issues, now expressed delight with the word *consubstantial*. It seems that an Athanasian had caught the emperor's ear and "helped him understand the question more thoroughly." And so, if the Nicene fathers had had any intention of choosing a word more spiritual than *substance*, the emperor's enthusiasm for that word must have ended that intention, especially when Constantine expressed a deeper understanding of substance than many of the bishops; for he explained to everyone that the word did not signify that within God was a material substance that was capable of being divided between Father and Son; for material characteristics cannot be attributed to purely spiritual beings, no matter what the word otherwise implied.

Eusebius reported that Constantine's presence had a profound influence on those in attendance. How could it be otherwise? Constantine was the emperor. He had paid for everyone's passage to Nicea and for their board while there. He was present during the proceedings; he was an active participant; and everyone knew that he wanted the Council to end in unanimity. And now that the emperor strongly favored the Athanasian view, supporters of Arius melted away. Those bishops, fearing for their jobs and the perquisites that went with them, became supporters of Athanasius, as did those who had been silent. Eusebius of Nicodemia [not to be confused with the Eusebius often quoted in this book, whose full name was Eusebius of Caesarea], one of the leading bishops and hitherto a principal supporter of Arius, suddenly renounced his support of Arius, and begged Constantine not to depose him as bishop. Constantine expressed surprise at the bishop's cowardice.

It was evident that the Athanasians, with the word *homoousios*, had won the contest. The emperor asked that a creed be composed and written down. Eusebius of Caesarea was the scribe. He wrote a variant of the eventually agreed upon creed, but he purposefully left out the words *ousia* and *homoousios*. The emperor reminded him, however, to include those words. (The Nicene Creed is given in the section Faith and Creeds.) The emperor's appreciation for the Creed as other than a unifying force, however, is suspect. For as a compromise, he suggested to three bishops, who hitherto had been supporters of

Arius and who hesitated to sign the Creed, that they insert by their signatures the word *homoiousios*, which means of a "similar substance," not *homoousios*, which means of the "same substance."

The Nicene Creed had in its conclusion Arius's views clearly stated—and anathematized—and it gave the Holy Spirit short shrift (this was corrected in subsequent Councils). The emperor asked all the bishops who agreed with the Creed—he expected unanimity—to sign it, and threatened non-signers with deposition and banishment. Arius, although a principal participant in the Council, being only an elder, was ineligible to sign, as was Athanasias, who although the other principal, was only a deacon.

The Creed was signed by most of the bishops. The exact number of signatories is not known, but the most reliable figure seems to be two hundred twenty-eight. If there were about three hundred bishops at the Council, an often quoted number, and about two hundred thirty signed, then about seventy did not sign. If there were three hundred eighteen bishops, as many believe, then the number of those not signing was about ninety. Whatever the exact number of those men not signing, they were very brave indeed, for they stood to lose everything. Constantine, however, did not carry out his threat in most cases, but he immediately banished Arius and his two leading supporters, ordered Arius's books burned, and threatened on pain of death all who concealed them. Some, who had signed the Creed, were nonetheless deposed and banished by Constantine because they openly objected to the treatment of Arius and his followers. It is always a pleasure to encounter men of moral courage and integrity, unsung heroes.

The Athanasian victors went on to assert that nothing new had been accomplished in Nicea, that the Athanasian view had been that of the apostles at the beginning of the church, and therefore the Nicene church and its religion—with almost no

resemblance to the sect of Jewish apostles and their religion—was "Catholic," "Orthodox," and "Apostolic."

Other matters, at least as important as the new definition of
God, emerged from Nicea. Constantine firmly united church
and state. The Catholic Church, now being the religion of the
Roman Empire, became the Roman Catholic Church. And
Rome became the new center of Christianity.

AFTERMATH OF NICEA

Immediately after the vote, the victorious Athanasians seized
power and called themselves "Orthodox" and "Catholic" and
"Apostolic," and cursed the Arians and said they were guilty of
that greatest of heresies, which became known as the "Arian
heresy." Had Constantine sided with the supporters of Arius,
the church probably would be speaking of the "Athanasian
heresy."

Ironically, Constantine, who, for the sake of unanimity, and
because of his powerful presence, had forced the church—
without sword, bloodlessly—to become Athanasian, remained
an Arian to the end. He never once spoke of Trinity, and the
title *God* or *Almighty God* or *Supreme God*, he reserved exclusively for the Father. Constantine wrote:

> I am most certainly persuaded that I myself owe my
> life, my every breath, in short, my very inmost and se-
> cret thoughts, entirely to the favor of the Supreme God
> (*The Nicene and Post-Nicene Fathers*, Second Series,
> vol. 1, Eusebius, Life of Constantine, Book 2, chap. 29,
> p. 507).

EUSEBIUS ON JESUS AS GOD

Jesus of Nazareth as God was a difficult god for many to accept. There is every reason to think, from the evidence presented earlier, that many who signed the Creed did not believe it. Eusebius of Caesarea, the church historian who had drawn up the first draft, written down the final version, and signed the Creed, later described Christianity not as a new and separate religion but as an off-shoot of Judaism, and he described Jesus as the one who brought the God of the Jews to the gentiles.

The emperor would not have been pleased with such statements, not so much because of Eusebius's minimizing the person of Jesus in Godhead, but because of his homage to the Jews and Judaism. For Constantine had repeatedly expressed the view, especially in the discussions concerning the date on which to celebrate Easter, that Christianity must be separated completely from the Jews and their religion. Eusebius, however, wrote:

> [The church must] guard against any inclination to think of our Saviour and Lord Jesus Christ as novel . . . [or] from imagining that His teaching either was new and strange. . . .

> But although we certainly are a youthful people and this undeniably new name of Christians has only lately become known among all nations, nevertheless our life and mode of conduct, together with our religious principles, have not been recently invented by us, but from almost the beginnings of man were built on the natural concepts of those whom God loved. . . . The Hebrews are not a youthful people, but are respected by all men for their antiquity and are known to all. Now the spoken and written records of this people embrace men of a very early age, scarce and few in number, but at the same time outstanding in religious devotion, righteousness, and all other virtues. . . . Hence, you will find that

those men, God's beloved, were even honored with the appellation of Christ, according to the word which says of them: "Touch not my Christs, and among my prophets commit no mischief" [Ps 105:15]. Obviously, we must regard the religion proclaimed in recent years to all nations through Christ's teaching as none other than the first, most ancient, and most primitive of all religions, discovered by Abraham and his followers, God's beloved [Jews]. . . .

What then is to prevent us from admitting that we, Christ's followers, share one and the same life and form of religion with those [the Jews] who were dear to God so long ago? Thus the practice of religion as communicated to us by Christ's teaching is shown to be not modern and strange but, in all conscience, primitive, unique, and true (Eusebius, *The History of the Church*, 1:4, pp. 45–49).

The church did not like Eusebius's words and continued to distance itself and Christianity as far as it could from the Jews and Judaism, its mother religion.

BISHOP THEODORE ON JESUS AS GOD

As late as the fifth century, Bishop Theodore of Mopsuestia, who began his career in full agreement with the Nicene Creed, ended his career by saying Christ ought not to have been deified, for he was not a god "identical" with God, except in the way any loving son is in accord with his father. Furthermore, although Christ's singular frailty proved his humanity, his miraculous powers in no way proved his divinity, but merely showed that God was working through him the way God had worked through Moses, Elijah, and many other righteous men. The church called Theodore a "madman" and declared him a heretic.

NESTORIUS ON MARY AS "MOTHER OF GOD"

In the fifth century, the church declared that because Jesus was God, Mary, his mother, must be "Mother of God." Nestorius, a monk from Antioch, asked, how can Mary be the "Mother of God" when it has never been shown that her son was God? She should be called the "Mother of Christ."

> When many had declared that Christ was God, Nestorius said: "I cannot term him God who was two and three months old. I . . . shall in future come no more among you." . . . [After this] blasphemy against the Son of God, they deposed him (*The Nicene and Post-Nicene Fathers*, Second Series, vol. 2, pp. 171–172).

The church, however, but did not condemn him as a heretic and taught that Nestorius, after all, had never said that Christ was *not* God.

THE KINGDOM OF GOD:
CONSTANTINE'S VS. AUGUSTINE'S

To Jesus of Nazareth and his fellow Jews, the messianic Kingdom of God was YHVH's kingdom established on earth. Jesus promised the arrival of that kingdom during his disciples' lifetime. But the kingdom did not come. And so, many disciples abandoned the Nazarene movement. Those who remained insisted that the kingdom was coming imminently. The first century ended, but the kingdom did not come. The second century ended, but the kingdom did not come. The third century ended, but the kingdom still did not come.

When, in the fourth century, the Emperor Constantine converted the Roman Empire to Christianity, Constantine declared that the Kingdom of God had at last come, for the Kingdom of God was the Empire itself. Constantine, with Christ's help, had established it. Even the church accepted Constantine's definition, so confident was it that Rome was eternal.   But soon things started to go wrong.

Shortly after Constantine's death, the Roman Empire began to die.   The church was perplexed and disturbed.   Constantine's achievements on behalf of Christianity had never been surpassed: Jesus of Nazareth had been deified, the Trinity had been created, the Roman Catholic Church had been established, and the Kingdom of God had been inaugurated.   But in spite of these remarkable achievements, the Empire was dying.   What could explain it?

For those who kept the ancient Greco-Roman religion, only one conclusion was possible.   The true gods—Zeus, Hera, Apollo, and the other Olympians—were punishing Rome for Constantine's betrayal of them: The emperor had sinfully replaced the Olympian gods with the false gods of the Jews and Christians.   The argument was so powerful that Christianity might well have come to an end had it not been for the counter argument of one of the church fathers, Augustine.

Augustine lived in the century following Constantine and was determined to save Christianity from the wrath of the heathen gods, and this is how he did it: He declared that Constantine had been mistaken in calling the Roman Empire the Kingdom of God.   There were two Kingdoms—the Kingdom of God and the Kingdom of Satan.   The Kingdom of God was the church, and whoever was not part of the church belonged to the Kingdom of Satan.   Therefore, the Roman Empire was part of the Kingdom of Satan.   Christ came to destroy Satan and his kingdom, and that was happening.   Rome was coming to an end.   But the church, the Kingdom of God, would never die.

5. THE TRUE DOCTRINE

CELSUS

Roman persecution of Christians during the first three centuries of Christianity is famous. One readily thinks of Paul's execution in Rome, Christians being fed to the lions in the Colosseum, not to mention Peter's traditional death in Rome where he was crucified upside down. Tacitus, the Roman historian of the second century, wrote:

> Christus [Christ], the founder of the name [Christian], had undergone the death penalty in the reign of Tiberius, by sentence of the procurator Pontius Pilatus [Pilate], and the pernicious superstition was checked for a moment, only to break out once more, not merely in Judaea, the home of the disease, but in the capital itself [Rome], where all things horrible or shameful in the world collect and find a vogue. First, then, the confessed members of the sect were arrested; next, on their disclosures, vast numbers were convicted, not so much on account of arson [setting Rome afire] as for hatred of the human race. And derision accompanied their end: they were covered with wild beasts' skins and torn to death by dogs; or they were fastened on crosses, and when daylight faded, were set on fire to serve as lamps by night (Tacitus, *Annals*, 15:44, pp. 283–285).

Origen, the church father of the third century, whose famous work we are about to discuss, wrote:

> [A]lthough the Romans have wanted to do much against the Christians to prevent their further existence, they have not been able to achieve this (Chadwick, *Contra Celsum*, 5:50, p. 304).

In spite of the historical accounts, once the church was firmly established in the fourth century, with its center in Rome and membership consisting mostly of Romans, the church ceased teaching that the gentiles persecuted Jesus, and his followers, and the new religion, but began teaching instead that it was the Jews, and only the Jews, who persecuted them.

In the late first or early second century, a heathen Greek philosopher named Celsus had written a critical analysis of Jesus, his followers, and the new religion. When Christianity became the state religion of Rome, the church hunted down all copies of Celsus's book and burned them. Nonetheless, we know much of what Celsus said, because in the third century, the church father Origen wrote a rebuttal to Celsus titled *Contra Celsum* (*Against Celsus*). From Origen's rebuttal, which is extant, one may reconstruct much of what Celsus said. There is a lesson here for book burners: It is not enough to burn an offensive book. Make sure to burn the rebuttal, too.

Celsus titled his critique of Christianity *The True Doctrine* or *The True Religion*, an ironic title based on Christianity's claim for itself. Origen, however, missed the irony in the title, and thought that by "the true doctrine" Celsus was boasting of his own belief system. Origen, in rebutting that boast, says no doctrine or religion can be called "true." Then Origen reverses himself by saying, "Christian doctrines are true," thereby validating the irony in Celsus's title.

Origen wrote *Contra Celsum* in eight books, which today would be called eight chapters. I selected those statements by Celsus and the responses by Origen that I considered most important, and they appear in what follows. In Books 1 and 2, Celsus sometimes speaks through the lips of a fictional Jew, perhaps invented to give his book more authority. It is evident that this imaginary fellow is merely a spokesman for Celsus, however, for he criticizes Judaism as enthusiastically as Christianity. Starting with Book 3, we never hear from Celsus's imaginary Jew again, but only Celsus speaking for Celsus.

Celsus in his statements is usually concise and to the point, and I have quoted or paraphrased him, as Origen did. Origen, speaking for himself, however, is usually verbose and often rambling. Sometimes Origen does not make a point or give a rebuttal at all, but goes off on a tangent. I have nonetheless tried to distill Origen, even when tangential. Both writers can be repetitious. I have not deleted all the repetitions, however, because they may reflect those ideas that both men considered most important. My own commentary is preceded by the initials HSR.

THE TRUE DOCTRINE BY CELSUS
Derived from Book 1 of Origen's Contra Celsum

CELSUS: [Christianity's] ethical teachings are commonplace and . . . contain nothing new.

Origen: It is not surprising that the God of all implanted in the souls of all the truths that he taught through the Jewish prophets and Jesus the Savior.

HSR: Origen at the onset affirms that Christianity did not impart anything ethical that mankind did not already possess, an honest but weak beginning.

CELSUS: Christians obtain their power . . . through incantations.

Origen: Christians do not obtain their power through incantations but through the name of Jesus . . . [which] is so powerful against demons that sometimes it is effective even when pronounced by evil men.

HSR: To so empower evil men is not a beneficial thing to do.

CELSUS: Scoundrels [like Jesus] frequently take advantage of the . . . gullible. . . . Some Christians don't even give a reason for what they believe, but use expressions such as, "Don't ask questions! Just believe!". . . And "Wisdom in this life is evil, but foolishness is good."

Origen: Is it better that those who believe without thinking should . . . be helped by their belief . . . or that we should deny them . . . their simple faith until they have had time to devote themselves to the study of whatever is reasonable? . . . Yes, we admit that we Christians teach those who cannot . . . pursue a study of what is reasonable to believe without thinking. . . . [Paul wrote:] "If anyone among you thinks that he is wise in this age, let him become a fool that he may become wise. For the wisdom of this world is folly with God" [1 Cor 3:18–19].

HSR: To "believe without thinking" is neither admirable nor desirable. It is to remain ignorant, which does not benefit the individual or humanity. God nowhere in the Old Testament commands ignorance or teaches that the wisdom of this world is "folly with God." On the contrary. God loves wisdom and extolls it repeatedly:

> And God gave Solomon wisdom and understanding beyond measure . . . so that Solomon's wisdom surpassed the wisdom of all the people of the east. . . . And men came from all peoples to hear the wisdom of Solomon (1 Kings 4:29–34).

> I [Wisdom] speak excellent things. . . . All the words of my mouth are in righteousness. . . . I love those who love me; and those who seek me diligently shall find me. . . . For who-

ever finds me finds life, and finds favor of the Lord [YHVH]. But whoever rejects me injures his own soul; those who hate me love death (Prov 8:1–36).

And those who are wise shall shine like the brightness of the firmament (Dan 12:1–3).

CELSUS: There is an ancient doctrine that has existed from the beginning, which has always been maintained by the wisest of the gentiles [so why bother with the doctrines of Moses and the prophets?]. . . . [Besides] Moses and the prophets wrote much . . . that was slanted in favor of their own doctrine.

Origen: Celsus seems to have said these things . . . to impugn the origin of the Christian religion from the Jews. . . . The writings of Moses have moved many, even those foreign to Jewish culture, to believe . . . that the God who made these laws and gave them to Moses was the Creator of the world.

Celsus regards the Jew who turns to the one God, the Creator of the universe, as inferior to [the gentile] who brings God down to the level . . . of men.

HSR: Origen here praises the Jewish origins of Christianity and belittles those gentiles who have gods that walk among men, apparently not considering Jesus a god who walks among men.

CELSUS: Circumcision . . . originated with the Egyptians [not the Jews].

Origen: Circumcision . . . began with Abraham and was ended by Jesus. . . . Celsus . . . thinks he will more easily prove Christianity as untrue . . . by attacking its origin in Judaism.

HSR: Jesus did not end circumcision, nor any other sacred practice of the Jews. Jesus himself was circumcised and never condemned or revoked it.

CELSUS: It makes no difference by what name one calls the supreme God, whether Zeus, the name used by the Greeks, or the name used by the Indians, or by the Egyptians.

Origen: Is it not absurd to say it is right to call God by the name of Zeus, when Zeus had a father and a mother?

HSR: "Is it not absurd to say it is right to call God by the name" of Jesus, when Jesus "had a father"—whether God or Joseph or someone else—"and a mother," Mary?

CELSUS: Jesus made up the story of his birth from a virgin. He came from a Jewish hick town [in an insignificant nation] and was born of a poor country woman who . . . was driven out by her husband, a carpenter by trade, as she was convicted of adultery . . . and while wandering about in a disgraceful way, she secretly gave birth to Jesus.

Origen: Our Jesus is ridiculed for having come from a Jewish hick town—and not a Greek one—and for not being a member of a famous nation. . . . And yet, he was able to shake the whole human world. . . . Who . . . is not amazed at this man who was able to rise above all the factors that tended to discredit him and to surpass all famous men who ever lived? He accepted his death willingly for the human race. . . . He died to destroy the great devil . . . the ruler of devils. Is it not reasonable that a man who ventured to do such great things for humanity . . . should have had a miraculous birth [from a virgin] rather than a bastard's birth . . . as Celsus thinks . . . through the impure sexual intercourse of adultery, which would have produced a stupid man who would harm mankind by teaching licentiousness, unrighteousness, and other evils?

To the Greeks, who do not believe in the virgin birth of Jesus, I have to say that among the animals there are certain females that have no intercourse. . . . Why, therefore, is it incredible that if God had wished to send some divine teacher, he should have him . . . come into being . . . [without] intercourse? . . . Celsus [speaks like] a vulgar buffoon.

HSR: A "vulgar buffoon"? Celsus is clearly neither vulgar nor a buffoon but shows by his arguments that he is learned and intelligent.

CELSUS: Was the mother of Jesus beautiful? And was it because of her beauty that God had sexual intercourse with her . . . even when she was hated by [her husband] the carpenter, who turned her out of his house?

Origen: How does [Celsus's statement] differ from the vulgar abuse received on street corners? . . . Celsus was very arrogant and boastful when he titled his book *The True Doctrine*, a title used by none of the famous philosophers. Plato says a sensible man will not be confident about obscure questions.

HSR: Origen fails to grasp the irony of Celsus's title. Celsus is referring to Christianity ironically in imitation of Christianity's claim for itself as The True Doctrine or The True Religion.

CELSUS: When Jesus was bathing alongside John [the Baptist], he said he saw what appeared to be a bird fly toward him. What trustworthy witness saw this apparition or heard a voice from heaven adopting him as the son of God?

Origen: To substantiate almost any story, even a true one, as historical fact . . . is one of the most difficult of tasks and in some cases impossible. . . . Achilles had the goddess Thetis as his mother. . . . Aeneas had the goddess Aphrodite [as his mother]. How could anyone substantiate those things? . . . How could anyone prove the historicity of a story like . . . the opening of the heavens . . . and hearing [the voice of God]? . . . [Such] impressions are only in the mind; so there is nothing extraordinary in such things having happened to the prophets when . . . they saw certain marvelous visions or heard utterances of the Lord or saw the heavens open. For I do not imagine that the visible heaven [actually] opened. . . . It was [in their minds] that the heavens opened to Jesus . . . and to John.

HSR: Origen is suggesting that Jesus and John were hallucinating or delusional. Origen thereby negates some of the miracles of Christianity.

CELSUS: Why should Jesus rather than thousands of others be the subject of prophecies?

Origen: [Jesus and only Jesus fulfilled the prophecies about the Messiah:] Concerning his birthplace it was said: "O Bethlehem . . . from you shall come forth . . . one who is to be ruler in Israel" (Mic 5:2). This prophecy would not fit . . . unless it is quite clear that the man was born in Bethlehem.

HSR: The evidence indicates Jesus was born in Nazareth. Even if Jesus were born in Bethlehem, what would that prove when countless others were born in Bethlehem? If, however, Jesus were not born in Bethlehem but in Nazareth, that would prove he was not the Messiah.

CELSUS: If the prophecies possessed by the Jews were so clear, why then, when Jesus came, did the Jews not accept him?

Origen: [Insofar as you object that too many others were born in Bethlehem to make this prophecy specific to Jesus,] a second prophecy is needed which seems to me to refer clearly to Jesus. It was written by Moses: "The scepter shall not depart from Judah, nor the ruler's staff from between his feet, until he comes to whom it belongs" (Gen 49:10). . . . Jesus obviously was the only one [who fit this prophecy]. . . .

HSR: "Obviously"? Who finds this prophecy obvious? Who could believe that Jesus "was the only one" to fit the prophecy?

Origen: [And if you want yet a third prophecy that fits only Jesus, here it is:] Isaiah says the messiah commands prisoners to come forth and those in darkness to appear. And Jesus said to prisoners, "Come forth."

HSR: Origen is not telling the truth. Jesus did not say to prisoners, "Come forth." Jesus never went to a prison; he did not release any prisoners; he did not even visit someone in prison.

Origen: [And if you want yet another prophecy that fits only Jesus:]

> Behold, my servant shall prosper, he shall be exalted and lifted up, and shall be very high. As many were astonished at him—his appearance was so marred, beyond human semblance, and his form beyond that of the sons of men—so shall he startle many nations; . . . he had no form or comeliness that we should look at him, and no beauty that we should desire him. He was despised and rejected by men; a man of sorrows, and acquainted with grief; and as one from whom men hide their faces he was despised, and we esteemed him not. Surely he has borne our griefs and carried our sorrows; yet we esteemed him stricken, smitten by God, and afflicted. But he

was wounded for our transgressions, he was bruised for our iniquities; upon him was the chastisement that made us whole, and with his stripes we are healed. All we like sheep have gone astray; we have turned everyone to his own way; and the Lord has laid on him the iniquity of us all. He was oppressed, and he was afflicted, yet he opened not his mouth; like a lamb that is led to the slaughter, and like a sheep that before its shearers is dumb, so he opened not his mouth. By oppression and judgment he was taken away; and as for his generation, who considered that he was cut off out of the land of the living, stricken for the transgression of my people? (Is 52:13–15; 53:2–8).

I remember once having a discussion with a learned Jew. I cited these prophecies. The Jew said that these prophecies referred to the whole people [of God] in a figure of speech as though of a single person. . . . I made him exceedingly uncomfortable when I cited the words "he was cut off out of the land of the living, stricken for the transgression of my people." If the "people" are the subject of the prophecy, why is this "man" said to have been led to death because of the iniquities of the people of God, if he is not different from the people of God? Who can this be if not Jesus Christ?

HSR: Origen does not deal with that part of Isaiah's prophecy that begins, "Behold, my servant shall prosper," but only the part, which begins, "he was taken away . . . cut off out of the land of the living." Origen interprets this to mean, the "man" [Jesus] was crucified and killed, when in fact the context makes it clear that the "man" [Israel] was isolated from the rest of humanity, a common condition of the Jews. To make Jesus fit Isaiah's prophecy, one has to fragment Isaiah and interpret each fragment with no consideration for the whole.

CELSUS: If Jesus said that every man becomes a son of God . . . what is the difference between Jesus and everyone else?

Origen: Everyone . . . is a son of God. But Jesus is far, far superior to *everyone*.

HSR: So Origen says.

CELSUS: The deeds of Jesus were deeds of a man hated by God; he was a wicked man.

Origen: It is impossible that [Jesus] should be hated by God, since "all things that exist are dear to You God, and You hate nothing that You have created—otherwise, why would You have created it?" (Apocrypha, Wisdom of Solomon, 11:24).

HSR: Origen is saying that God loves everything he created, even evil men, even Jesus. In defending Jesus, Origen besmirches him.

THE TRUE DOCTRINE BY CELSUS
Derived from Book 2 of Origen's *Contra Celsum*

CELSUS: [Jewish believers in Jesus] are deluded. They have left the law of their fathers and have been quite ludicrously deceived.

Origen: There are Jews who believe in Jesus who have not left the law of their fathers.

HSR: Celsus speaks of Jewish believers in Jesus, and Origen confirms their presence even in Origen's day, further evidence that the Jews were not unanimously opposed to Jesus.

CELSUS: Why do you Christians take your origin from Judaism, and then . . . despise what is written in the Law?

Origen: It is true that the beginning of the Christian faith is based on the religion of Moses. . . . It is not true . . . that . . . we "despise what is written in the Law." In fact, we accord it the greatest honor by showing what a depth of wise and mysterious doctrines is contained in it. The Jews, on the other hand, have not looked deeply into their own writings but read them only superficially as stories.

HSR: According to Origen, Christians are wiser than Jews because Christians are able to read the Jewish Scriptures "deeply," that is, allegorically. Allegorical interpretations, however, are in fact falsifications. The allegory merely reflects the allegorist's bias and shows his inability to reconcile the original text with his own belief system.

CELSUS: The doctrine of the resurrection . . . is not new.

Origen: Celsus disparages as stale stuff the doctrine of the resurrection. . . . In reality, all of the doctrines of the Jews living now are myths and trash . . . whereas Christian doctrines are true.

HSR: The doctrine of the resurrection is Jewish—Pharisaic—and antedated Jesus. It is the Jewish doctrine on which Christianity is built. Is the Jewish doctrine of the resurrection among the "myths and trash"?

CELSUS: Jesus kept all the Jewish customs.

Origen: Why does [Jesus' being an observant Jew] support the view that we Christians ought not to believe in him as the son of God? . . . Although we have avoided the mythologies of the Jews, yet we are educated and made wise by a mystical contemplation of their law and prophets.

HSR: Celsus expresses wonderment that Christians believe in Jesus when he was an observant Jew. Origen replies that Jesus' Jewishness presents no difficulties to Christians because they interpret the religion of the Jews "by a mystical contemplation of their law and prophets," by which Origen again means allegory.

CELSUS: Jesus was arrogant and told lies—big lies.

Origen: I challenge anyone to show even a suggestion of a saying uttered by Jesus from arrogance. . . . I challenge anyone to prove what lies he told . . . that Jesus told big lies.

HSR: It is Origen himself in Book 4 who will prove the lies —big lies—that Jesus told: "[It] is sometimes permissible to use deceit and lying. . . . Why then is it unthinkable that something of this sort occurred with [Jesus for] the purpose of bringing salvation? Some people are reformed by certain doctrines that are more false than true." Origen praises that Christianity is built on falsehoods.

CELSUS: Many others of the same ilk as Jesus have appeared to those who wish to be deceived.

Origen: [Name] one!

HSR: In Book 3, Origen himself will name not one but four: Aesculapius, Dionysus, Aristeas, Cleomedes.

CELSUS: Why should the Jews despise the one whose coming they prophesied?

Origen: That is a very foolish question, and I do not think it is reasonable to reply to it. . . . It is obvious that although [the Jews] saw Jesus, they did not know who he was . . . and did not comprehend his divinity. . . . On account of their disbelief . . . the Jews not only will suffer on Judgment Day . . . but have already suffered more than any other people. What nation but the Jews alone has been banished from its own capital and the native place of its ancestral worship?

HSR: Thus Origen begins a very famous and calumnious church teaching: The Jews were banned from Jerusalem for killing Christ.

CELSUS: How could the Jews regard Jesus as God? . . . Jesus did not bring about anything that he professed to do. And when the Jews convicted him, condemned him, and decided that he should be punished, he was caught hiding and escaping [in the Garden of Gethsemane] most disgracefully. Moreover, he was betrayed by those whom he called disciples. Had he been God, he would not have run away, nor been led away under arrest, and least of all, he would not have . . . been deserted and betrayed by friends.

Origen: We Christians charge the Jews with not believing in Jesus as God [even though] he had great power and was a god like the God and Father of the universe. We say that it was to Jesus that the Father gave the command, "Let there be light" . . . and it was Jesus who made everything that the Father commanded him to make. . . . Who else could be capable of fulfilling commands of such magnitude except . . . Jesus?

HSR: Origen states that Jesus was a god as powerful as God because God made Jesus the creator of the universe and commanded Jesus to say, "Let there be light!" Where and when did God make Jesus the creator of the universe? Where and when did Jesus say, "Let there be light!"?

CELSUS: Jesus was betrayed by his own disciples. He neither ruled like a good leader, nor . . . did he inspire in the very men he deceived the admiration . . . that thieves feel toward the king of thieves.

Origen: Aristotle deserted Plato . . . and Aristotle is said to have been Plato's disciple for twenty years . . . whereas Judas did not even spend three years in Jesus' company.

HSR: Origen says that Jesus was just another teacher abandoned by his disciples.

CELSUS: [The disciples] made up the statement that Jesus foretold all that was going to happen to him.

Origen: [Not only did Jesus foretell what was going to happen to him, but] he even foretold what would happen to Christians in later generations. Isn't it wonderful how Jesus predicted: "You will be dragged before governors and kings for my sake" (Mt 10:18)? . . . Is there any doctrine of men besides Christianity that has caused its adherents to be punished?

HSR: "Is there any doctrine of men besides Christianity that has caused its adherents to be punished?" Is this a serious question? If so, the answer is: Multitudinously many.

Origen continues: While Jerusalem was still standing and Jewish worship was going on, Jesus foretold what was going to happen to it by the Romans.

HSR: However, at the annunciation, an angel of the Lord proclaimed that the Father sent Jesus to save the Jews, not to bring about their destruction (Mt 1:21). Are we to conclude that an angel of the Lord is not to be believed?

CELSUS: The disciples recorded things about Jesus so as to make excuses for the events of his life. It is as if someone, while saying that a certain man was righteous, shows him to be immoral, and, while saying that he was holy, shows him to be [most unholy].

Origen: What Celsus is saying [on such matters] is manifestly irrelevant.

HSR: On the contrary, what Celsus has to say is highly relevant. The gospels portray Jesus committing the most immoral and unholy acts—lying and deceiving, name-calling, judging and condemning, vilifying, acting in a violent and destructive manner (overturning tables, whipping peaceful men, wantonly destroying a fig tree)—and then describe him in such a way as to appear righteous and holy. And the church even calls Jesus "Perfect man."

Origen continues: Unbelievers mock at the resurrection of Jesus Christ. We will [remind them of] Armenius's son, who rose from the funeral pyre after twelve days and gave an account of his adventures in Hades. . . . Several others . . . have returned from their tombs. . . . What then is so miraculous if Jesus . . . returned?

HSR: Origen is saying that insofar as others have risen from the dead, there is nothing unique about Jesus having done so. Again, in defending it, Origen is undermining Christianity.

CELSUS: What trustworthy evidence shows that Jesus made predictions [about his death]?

Origen: [Why does Celsus call for such evidence when many besides Jesus predicted their own deaths?] Socrates knew that if he drank the hemlock, he would die. . . . Leonidas, the Spartan General . . . knew that . . . he was about to die . . . at Thermopylae.

HSR: Origen is saying that Jesus' ability to predict his manner of death was not more remarkable than that of Socrates's or Leonidas's, so why should anyone consider Jesus a prophet greater than those men? Again Origin undercuts the uniqueness of Jesus.

CELSUS: [Jesus, whom the Christians call "god"] led his own disciples—men with whom he used to eat and drink—so far astray that they became impious and evil. But a god more than anyone else ought to have done good to all, particularly those who lived with him. . . . Would anyone who had banqueted with a god have become a conspirator against him? And what is even more outrageous, the god himself conspired against those who ate with him by making them traitors and evil.

Origen: Who does not know of men who shared a table with friends and then conspired against them?

HSR: Origen misses the point. Celsus is saying that if Judas had known that Jesus was God, Judas would never have betrayed him. And if Judas had known that Jesus was God and yet want on to betray him, then Jesus being God had to have deliberately made Judas a traitor. That point is validated by the recently discovered *Gospel of Judas*.

CELSUS: If [the things Jesus suffered] had been decreed for him, and if he was punished in obedience to the Father, it is obvious that since he was a god and acted intentionally, that which was done to him was neither painful nor grievous.

Origen: As he intentionally assumed a body . . . not different from any human's, so he assumed with that body its pains and griefs.

HSR: Origen ignores Celsus's objection which is this: If Jesus was fulfilling what the Father had ordained, Jesus ought to have gone to his death resolutely and joyously, bravely accepting the physical pain as other martyrs who went to deaths more painful and more grievous.

CELSUS: Why does . . . Jesus pray that he may avoid . . . death, saying something like, "O Father, if this cup could pass from me"? [Mt 26:39].

Origen: The Savior saw the disasters that would befall the Jewish people and Jerusalem to avenge their acts against him; and it was simply out of his love for the Jews, and not wanting them to suffer what they were going to suffer, that he said, "My Father, if it be possible, let this cup pass from me" (Mt 26:39).

HSR: Origen is saying that Jesus loved his fellow Jews so much and wanted to save them so much that he was willing to forgo the crucifixion on behalf of humanity if only he could come down from the cross not so much to save himself as to spare the Jews punishment! Origen thereby undermines the crux of Christian theology!

CELSUS: Some Christians, as though from a drinking bout, go so far as to oppose themselves and alter the original text of the gospel three or four or more times over, and they change its character to enable them to deny difficulties in the face of criticism.

Origen: I do not know of people who have altered the gospel—except the Marcionites and Valentians and, I think, the Lucanites. Those who alter the gospels . . . do not give cause for any criticism of *real* Christianity.

HSR: Origen himself identifies three groups who adulterated the gospels and then states that adulteration of the gospels has had no impact on Christianity.

CELSUS: The Jewish prophecies could be applied to thousands of others far more plausibly than to Jesus.

Origen: Celsus has put into the mouth of [his imaginary] Jew words that no Jew would ever say. . . . A Jew would set out each prophecy . . . and would reply to the interpretation of the Christians; and although a Jew would not produce a single convincing argument, yet he would try.

HSR: As Origen suggests, a real Jew (not an imaginary one) would "set out each prophecy" and try to produce convincing arguments to show that Jesus could not have been the prophesied Messiah. That is, in fact, what I have done. (See Twenty Prophetic Signs by Which to Recognize the Messiah.)

CELSUS: The prophets say that when the Messiah comes, he will be a great prince . . . not a pestilent fellow like Jesus.

Origen: [Celsus] is just like a Jew! . . . It is consistent with their bitterness to revile Jesus without any plausible argument.

HSR: Origen lost a great opportunity to rebut Celsus. Origen ought to have said Christians do, in fact, believe Jesus was a great prince of Israel. The three wise men, Pontius Pilate, and many of Jesus' followers referred to him as "king of the Jews."

CELSUS: No one gives proof of a god or son of god by the signs and false stories and disreputable evidence [that Christians give]. . . . The sun first shows itself and then goes on to illuminate everything else, and that is what the son of god ought to have done.

Origen: We Christians maintain that Jesus actually did [light up the world like the sun]. For "righteousness arose in his days, and abundance of peace began at his birth" [Ps 72:7–9].

HSR: The psalm (RSV) says: "In his days may righteousness flourish, and peace abound, till the moon be no more." This psalm can hardly be said to describe Jesus; for righteousness did not arise in his day and abundance of peace did not begin at his birth. And even if they had, it was fleeting and did not last "till the moon be no more."

CELSUS: Christians proclaim Jesus to be the son of God; however, they do not give evidence that he was pure and holy, but rather a man who was arrested most disgracefully and crucified.

Origen: Although I have met many Jews who had a reputation for being intelligent, I have not yet met one who believed that Jesus was the son of God.

HSR: Celsus requests evidence that Jesus was "pure and holy." Origen does not give evidence but says rather that the Jews, who have a reputation for intelligence, don't think Jesus was the son of God and don't believe he was pure and holy. Is Origen saying that the Jews aren't really so intelligent after all, or is Origen saying that intelligent people think that Jesus was a fraud?

CELSUS: Those who compiled the [gospel] genealogy arrogantly said that Jesus was descended from the first man [Adam] and from the kings of the Jews.

Origen: [Celsus] does not know how to discuss biblical problems intelligently.

HSR: On the contrary, Celsus demonstrates a keen understanding of biblical problems.

CELSUS: What noble action did Jesus do like God?

Origen: To this day people whom God so wills are cured in Jesus' name.

HSR: To this day people whom God so wills are cured without invoking Jesus' name, and others are not cured in spite of invoking Jesus' name.

CELSUS: [Is it not remarkable that the] one who condemned him [Pontius Pilate] did not suffer?

Origen: It was not so much Pilate who condemned him . . . as the Jewish people. This nation has been condemned by God.

HSR: Has the Jewish nation really been condemned by God? It survives and flourishes. As for the Roman Empire, however, that nation long ago disappeared.

CELSUS: Why . . . didn't Jesus take revenge on those who insulted both him and his Father?

Origen: The same argument can be applied to the Greeks [who believe that Zeus is Father]: . . . Why doesn't Zeus punish those [the Christians] who insulted his deity? If the Greeks answer that, then we Christians will, too.

HSR: Origen is giving as much credibility to Zeus as to God, a remarkable thing for a Christian to do. The Roman Empire had not yet fallen. After the Roman Empire fell, the Greek heathens did say that Rome fell because Zeus took revenge on the Romans for insulting Zeus and the Olympian gods by replacing them with the Christian gods.

CELSUS: Do you Christians . . . criticize the Jews because they do not regard Jesus as God, nor agree with you that he endured sufferings for the benefit of mankind?

Origen: We criticize the Jews . . . because they do not refute the arguments we bring against them that prove Jesus was the Christ, nor furnish a refutation that supports their unbelief.

HSR: Jews did in fact write refutations to show that Jesus was not the Christ, but this was usually done secretly, for it was not safe for them to make these widely known while living in a Christian nation.   The most famous refutation was in the Talmud, but the church did not learn of that until Jewish converts who achieved high station in the church made the church aware of it, whereupon the church began to burn Talmuds, insisting that Jews delete those portions from subsequent editions. In short, the church did not tolerate refutations of Christianity whether from a heathen or Jewish source. Today, no longer having such power, the church ignores refutations or else attacks the writers of such works as being polemicists, slanderers, libelists, or simply "enemies of the church."

Origen continues: We criticize the Jews because . . . they misrepresent Jesus as a vagabond, and they accuse him of being an outcast who roamed about in a body disgracefully unkempt.

HSR: Is this a misrepresentation? Did not Jesus himself say: "Foxes have holes, and birds . . . have nests; but the Son of man has nowhere to lay his head" (Mt 8:20; Lk 9:58)? Did not Jesus say, "Do not concern yourself with [such questions as] . . . "What are we going to wear?" (Mt 6:31). And Jesus' contempt for hand washing was famous (Mt 15:1–20; Mk 7:1–8).

CELSUS: Jesus should never have died [the Jews believed the Messiah would live forever (Jn 12:34)] or if he had to die, at least he should have died nobly, setting an example for martyrs. [But] he did not show himself to be pure but did evil things.

Origen: Let Celsus give a clear proof of a single evil deed done by Jesus.

HSR: This was a nonsensical thing for Origen to have asked because Celsus was long dead. Later, however, Origen himself will give the proof and tell of the evil deeds that Jesus did.

CELSUS: When [the disciples of] Jesus . . . saw that he was being punished and was dying, they did not die with him or for his sake, nor were they persuaded [by his teachings] to despise punishment [and death]. And they even denied that they were disciples. Only now [in current generations] are Christians willing to die for him.

Origen: The sin [of betrayal, denial, and fear of death] was committed when the disciples were still beginners and immature.

HSR: Origen agrees with Celsus that Jesus' disciples acted despicably but attributes that to their immaturity. The implication is that it was only after Jesus' death and with the establishment of the church and its invention of doctrines about Jesus that latter day disciples became mature enough to want to die for him—which is exactly what Celsus had said.

CELSUS: Was it his punishment [execution by crucifixion] that led you to regard this man as the son of God? . . . If so, have not many others been punished at least as disgracefully?

Origen: Celsus behaves likes the lowest class of enemies of Christianity.

HSR: Origen's rebuttal is not only *ad hominem* but also disingenuous. Origen had to have known of the Maccabean martyrs who died nearly two centuries before Jesus. Witnesses to those deaths, which were far more horrible than the death of Jesus, claimed that those deaths took away the sins of the people.

CELSUS: Christians regard Jesus as the son of God because he healed the lame and blind and raised the dead—*so they say*.

Origen: It is *not* fiction . . . not only that which was done by Jesus . . . but also . . . by the disciples, who according to Jesus' promises, have done even greater works than Jesus.

HSR: Origen again negates the uniqueness of Jesus as did Jesus himself: "He who believes in me will also do the works that I do; and greater works than these will he do" (Jn 14:12).

CELSUS: Jesus said in a certain passage: "For false Christs and false prophets will arise and show great signs and wonders" [Mt 24:24].
And in another passage Jesus said: "On that day many will say to me, 'Lord, Lord, did we not prophesy, and cast out demons, and do many wonderful works in your name?' And then I will say to them: 'Depart from me, you evildoers'" [Mt 7:22–23].

Jesus explicitly declared . . . that there will come . . . others, performing miracles of a kind similar to his own, who are evil men and sorcerers. . . . So Jesus . . . convicts himself. . . . Is it not, then, a defective inference to conclude from the same deeds that those done by Jesus are by God whereas the others are done by false christs?

Origen: The divine power of Jesus . . . is suggested by the fact that it was possible for someone to use his name . . . to pretend that he was the Christ, and to appear to perform the same kind of miracles . . . as the true disciples.

HSR: How does Jesus' allowance of the use of his name by deceivers indicate his "divine power"? Doesn't it rather suggest his Satanic power?

Origen continues: Wickedness and trickery would not have gathered together a whole nation [of Christians]!

HSR: A fallacious argument. Majorities are frequently deceived by wickedness and trickery. Consider how the masses may elect charlatans or villains to public office. Ignorance, too, plays a role in mass deception. Consider that the church in Origen's day believed that the earth was at the center of the universe and the sun traveled around it.

CELSUS: How many others have produced wonders like [the resurrection] to convince and exploit through deceit simple minded listeners? The Greeks say that Zamolxis . . . Pythagoras . . . Rhampsinitus . . . Orpheus . . . Protesilaus . . . Heracles . . . and Theseus [were resurrected]. But we must question whether anyone who really died ever rose again . . . or do you Christians think that the stories of those others are merely fables whereas the final act of your tragedy [the crucifixion] is to be regarded as noble and credible?

Origen: No Jew would ever have said this since he believes what is written in the . . . books of Kings about the young boys, one of whom was raised from the dead by Elijah and the other by Elisha (1 Kings 17:21–22; 2 Kings 4:32–35). Jesus' resurrection was even more remarkable . . . because Jesus was resurrected not by a prophet but by his Father in heaven.

HSR: Contrary to Origen's statement, the Old Testament states that Elijah and Elisha raised the dead, not on their own, but through the power of God.

CELSUS: If Jesus really wanted to show the world he had divine power, he ought to have appeared to the very men who treated him so badly and to the man who condemned him [Pilate] and to everyone everywhere.

Origen: It would not have been right for Jesus to appear to the man who condemned him and to those who treated him badly. Perhaps he avoided appearing because he took into consideration the marked limitations of those who could not see him.

HSR: This is nonsense. Had the resurrected Jesus appeared before Pilate and his soldiers, before the High Priest and his cortege, some of them would have been sufficiently impressed to become instant believers. And the new religion would not have met the great resistance it met from the Romans, the Greeks, and the faithful Jews during the first two centuries.

CELSUS: While Jesus lived, he preached openly to everyone and was disbelieved [by most]; but when, after the resurrection, he had established a strong faith, he appeared only to very few and those were already believers.

Origen: Jesus' human characteristics were visible to all, but not his divine characteristics.

HSR: Jesus' divine characteristics were first visible only to devils and demons (Lk 4:41). And Origen will later say that Jesus is the ruler of devils as well as Christians.

CELSUS: All our objections [to Jesus and Christianity] come from the Christian writings themselves, and we need call no further witness; for Christians [by their writings] provide their own refutation.

Origen: Celsus speaks a lot of nonsense about the gospels, but I do not think he has given any evidence that our writings provide their own refutation.

HSR: Celsus has hardly spoken nonsense. If the gospels are objectively criticized and analyzed, I think they do indeed provide their own refutation.

CELSUS: What god that comes among men is disbelieved? Or why is he never recognized by the Jews, the very people who had long been expecting him?

Origen: God is recorded to have been most clearly present with the Hebrews not only by the signs and wonders in Egypt, not only by the way the Jews went through the Red Sea, not only by the pillar of fire and the clouds of light, but also when the Ten Commandments were proclaimed before the whole nation of Jews. . . . And yet, he was disbelieved by the Jews. If they had believed [in the God] whom they had seen and heard, they would not have [proceeded] to make a golden calf. . . . If anyone wants an explanation of the Jews' disbelief in Jesus, [I would say that] it was consistent with their behavior from the beginning.

HSR: This seems like a powerful argument. But it evaporates when one realizes that the Jews, a highly critical and skeptical people, eventually came to believe adamantly and tenaciously in the one God whom they were so slow to accept. But nothing in more than two thousand years has convinced them to believe in Jesus of Nazareth.

CELSUS: Jesus utters threats and empty abuses.

Origen: We find God as revealed through the prophets open to similar accusations. . . . God [threatens] in order to convert men.

HSR: God indeed threatens and abuses, but a man who threatens and abuses is a tyrant, and that does not make him a god.

THE TRUE DOCTRINE BY CELSUS
Derived from Book 3 of Origen's *Contra Celsum*

CELSUS: Christians and Jews quarrel with one another very foolishly. . . . They both believe . . . [the Messiah] was prophesied. . . . They disagree as to whether he has come.

Origen: The Jews are wrong.

CELSUS: Just as a small group of Egyptians in Egypt rebelled against the larger Egyptian community and became the first Jews . . .

Origen: It is the Egyptians who say that about the Jews, and the story is false. The Hebrews who fled from Egypt were a separate people and spoke their own language.

CELSUS: . . . similarly a small group of Jews in Jerusalem in Jesus' day rebelled against the larger Jewish community and became the first Christians.

Origen: This is also a false story. Christians never had a rebellion.

HSR: Celsus's statement about the origin of the Christians is not entirely false. Although the early church did not arise from the Jews through rebellion, it did arise from the Jews through religious conviction. That coincides with the gospels, the book of Acts, and the letters of Paul. One might say that the first Christians did not go to war but were Jewish heretics from the larger Jewish community.

CELSUS: [T]hey [the Jews] suffered . . . through those who followed Jesus and believed him to be the Christ. . . . [A] revolt against the community led to the introduction of new ideas [contrary to those in the Law given by Moses] .

HSR: This is a stunning interpretation for the suffering of the Jews, and one that Origen and the church clearly wanted to suppress. Celsus is saying that the suffering of the Jews—the destruction of the temple, the loss of Jerusalem and their homeland, and their dispersion—occurred because a group of heretical Jews became Christians!

Origen: It is false that some of the Jews rebelled at the time of Jesus against the Jewish community and followed Jesus.

HSR: It is Origen's reply that is false. He is trying to imply that all the of the Jews remained faithful to normative Judaism and all were against Jesus. That conflicts with the gospels, the book of Acts, and the letters of Paul, which report that many Jews rebelled against the larger Jewish community and followed Jesus. That of course supports Celsus. Origen apparently could not deal with the argument that Jewish suffering came about because of the Jews who had become Christians; so he invented a church-pleasing interpretation of history—namely, that all the calamities that befell the Jews came about because all the Jews rejected Jesus.

CELSUS: [Christians] are divided and rent asunder, and each wants to have his own party.

Origen: [A]ny teaching which has had a serious origin, and is beneficial to life, has caused different sects. . . . [S]ince the problems [discussed by philosophers] allow of considerable diversity of opinion, on this account very many sects indeed have come into existence. . . . [Similarly, Christians] interpreted differently the scriptures . . . and sects arose.

HSR: Celsus's statement and Origen's response show that pluralism in early Christianity was widespread. The Roman Catholic Church, however, teaches that Jesus founded that church, which was monolithic until the times of the schisms and the Reformation.

CELSUS: God forbid that I or anyone should do away with the doctrine that the unrighteous will be punished and the righteous deemed worthy of rewards. [It is only because Christian doctrines invoke terrors exceeding all others that people convert.]

Origen: Christian doctrines do not terrorize for the purpose of conversion except our doctrine of hell.

HSR: Origen admits that it is the Christian doctrine of hell that affords Christianity its great power to convert. This great power of conversion is terror not love.

CELSUS: As one approaches Egyptian shrines, one sees magnificent precincts . . . then wonderful temples . . . and [finally] very superstitious and mysterious rites. But when one goes inside [a temple], what does one see? A cat being worshiped or a monkey or a crocodile!

Origen: Are we to think . . . that worshiping Christ crucified is the same as worshiping a dumb beast?

HSR: Celsus does seem to be saying that.

CELSUS: Aesculapius and Dionysus . . . were believed by the Greeks to have become gods. Even though those men performed many noble [and miraculous] deeds on behalf of mankind [Aesculapius could even raise the dead.], I cannot accept the belief that they were gods. They were human.

HSR: Celsus is saying that he doesn't believe that Aesculapius and Dionysus were gods in spite of their wonderful deeds, including Aesculapius's raising the dead, so why should he believe that Jesus was a god.

Origen: The doctrine of immortality was spoken of by the [Greek philosophers] and is in complete agreement with our divine [Christian] teachings. . . . [But] Aesculapius was killed by Zeus with a lightning bolt [because he raised a man from the dead].

HSR: Origen's reply, instead of bolstering Christianity, undermines it: Aesculapius raised the dead. Zeus was so outraged that Zeus killed Aesculapius. By implication, God was so outraged at Jesus for raising the dead, he killed him. Again, Origen is unaware he is undermining Christianity, not defending it.

CELSUS: Aristeas . . . vanished . . . and then reappeared. . . . And Apollo commanded people to regard Aristeas as a god. [But] nobody does.

HSR: Celsus is telling the story of Aristeas, a famous poet who lived in the seventh century BC. Aristeas died suddenly, and his body disappeared. This was considered so miraculous that Apollo commanded the Greeks to worship Aristeas as a god. But none of them do. Similarly, Jesus' body disappeared from the tomb. The Christians consider this a great miracle, but unlike the Greeks in the case of Aristeas, the Christians actually worship Jesus as a god.

Origen: Why do you accuse [Christians] of being mad men because they believe in the miracles of Jesus, whereas you appear to believe such stories about Aristeas?

HSR: Origen again misinterprets Celsus. Celsus states clearly that he doesn't believe the stories about Aristeas, so why should he believe the stories about Jesus.

Origen continues: When we tell stories about Jesus, we give a powerful defense to show that they [actually] happened: We argue that God wanted to establish the doctrine spoken by Jesus. . . . His advent . . . was prophesied . . . so that the whole Jewish nation was hanging on the expectation of [his coming]. . . . And after Jesus' advent, the Jews disputed among themselves—a large number saying that he was the Christ and others saying he was not, and the latter despised him.

HSR: Origen admits that Jesus had a large Jewish following. Earlier, in describing the so-called divine retribution of the fall of Jerusalem, Origen said—and he will repeat it later—that Jesus had no Jewish following whatsoever, that all the Jews opposed him, and as divine retribution, Jerusalem fell. The reason Origen and the church vacillated between *some* of the Jews and *all* of the Jews opposing Jesus is that if only *some* of the Jews opposed Jesus, the destruction of Jerusalem might just as well be attributed to those Jews who became Christians—that is, God was punishing the Jews because of those among them who had become Christians. That indeed is Celsus's argument. But if all the Jews of all time killed Jesus, Christians could reason, and they did, that Jerusalem fell in divine retribution because of the crime of the Jews.

CELSUS: [A man named] Cleomedes . . . climbed into a box, and when people broke into the box, he had vanished. It was a miracle!

Origen: This cannot be compared with the story of Jesus [in the tomb after the crucifixion]. . . . We say the disappearance of Cleomedes was brought about by a demon.

HSR: And the disappearance of Jesus from the tomb? A miracle! The resurrection! As Celsus says, whenever Jesus does something extraordinary, Christians call it a miracle, but when a heathen does exactly the same thing, Christians say it was done by a demon!

CELSUS: The honor [Christians] give to Jesus is no different from that paid to Hadrian's lover [Antinous].

Origen: What is there in common between the noble life of our Jesus and the life of Hadrian's darling? . . . It is through Egyptian magic and spells that Antinous appears to do miracles . . . even after his death. . . . [It is his] demons who have the power . . . to heal. His virtues were invented by [those] who were deceived by a demon. . . . Jesus is very different. . . . The Creator of the universe himself . . . revealed that Jesus was worthy of honor, not only by men . . . but also by demons. . . . To this very day, [men and demons] fear the name of Jesus . . . and accept him in reverence as their lawful ruler.

HSR: Origen is saying that Jesus of Nazareth is not only king of men but also king of demons!

CELSUS: Christians think Jesus is a god even though he was born in a mortal body.

Origen: His mortal body and human soul received the greatest elevation . . . by uniting and intermingling [with God], so that by sharing in divinity, he was transformed into God.

HSR: Who can understand that bit of Christian theology?

CELSUS: The human flesh of Jesus may be compared to gold, silver, and stone [the stuff of which images are made]; but his flesh was more corruptible than those.

Origen: One corruptible thing is not more corruptible than another. . . . Why is it impossible for the flesh of Jesus . . . to change . . . once it lives in the heavenly realms, where it no longer has the properties belonging to [earthly] flesh?

HSR: Origen's suggestion that the flesh of Jesus could become incorruptible in heaven resembles Paul's teaching which the Council of Trent called "foolish." The church maintains that Jesus is in heaven with his corruptible (crucified) flesh.

CELSUS: Christians are able to convince only the foolish, the dishonorable, and the stupid—slaves, women, and little children. . . . Let no one educated, no one wise, no one sensible draw near!

HSR: Celsus is alluding to Jesus' prayer of thanksgiving: "I thank you, Father, Lord of heaven and earth, that you have hidden these things from the wise and understanding" (Mt 11:2; Lk 10:21).

Origen: The gospel wants Christians to be wise, which I can show from the ancient Jewish Scriptures as well as from the Christian writings:

[Jewish Scriptures:] "And God gave Solomon wisdom and understanding beyond measure . . . so that Solomon's wisdom surpassed the wisdom of all the people of the east. . . . For he was wiser than all other men . . . and his fame [spread to] all the nations. . . . And men came from all peoples to hear the wisdom of Solomon, and from all the kings of the earth, who had heard of his wisdom" [1 Kings 4:29–34].

[Christian writings:] The crowds of believers . . . were worthy only of teachings for the masses . . . "but privately to his own disciples Jesus explained everything" [Mk 4:34], honoring those above the masses who were deemed worthy of his wisdom. Paul puts the gift of wisdom first in the list of spiritual gifts given by God [1 Cor 12:8–10].

Let the educated, wise, and sensible come if he wishes, and nonetheless let anyone ignorant, stupid, uneducated, and childish come as well.

HSR: Origen compares the wisdom of Solomon with the wisdom of Jesus. But they are different. Solomon dispensed wisdom openly and freely to all who sought it, and the whole world came to hear of it. Who does not know of the wisdom of Solomon? Jesus' wisdom, however, by Origen's admission, was shared only with the apostles; and to this day, no one knows what that wisdom was.

CELSUS: Judges [in law courts] stop people from lamenting their crimes with piteous cries; for judges don't want their judgment influenced by feelings of mercy, but only by truth. But perhaps your god Jesus does not judge by truth, but rather by flattery.

Origen: What "flattery"?

HSR: Origen ignores the famous deeds of Jesus done out of flattery: Mary's flattery at the wedding of Cana when Jesus did not want to change water into wine (Jn 2:1–9) and the Canaanite woman's flattery when Jesus did not want to heal her daughter (Mt 15:21–28). In both cases, powerful women through flattery got Jesus, who adamantly had refused to do what they wished, to change his mind.

CELSUS: No one can completely change people who sin by nature and habit. . . . It is very hard to completely change human nature.

Origen: It is not true that all men are incapable of a complete change. . . . Those for whom it is very hard to change, we say that the cause lies in their lack of will . . . and determination.

HSR: Today psychologists would agree with Celsus.

CELSUS: The wise turn away from the teachings of Christians, who are led astray and hindered by wisdom.

Origen: [It is true that] Paul said, "God chose the foolish of the world to shame the wise" [1 Cor 1:27].

HSR: Origen agrees with Celsus that wisdom and intelligence interfere with accepting Christianity.

CELSUS: The man who teaches the doctrines of Christianity is like a man who promises to restore health but discourages his patients from seeking [the advice of] expert physicians.

Origen: We Christians discourage those whom we convert from consulting physicians who are philosophers . . . who deny that heaven cares at all for humanity.

HSR: Origen is saying that Christians should be concerned with a physician's philosophical beliefs, not his skill.

CELSUS: Jesus, the teacher of the Christians, says, "I alone will save you."

Origen: Celsus has put words into the mouth of our teacher, "I alone will save you." See what lies Celsus tells about us!

HSR: "Lies"? Did not Jesus say: "He who does not believe [in me] will be condemned" (Mk 16:16); and "No one comes to the Father but by me." (Jn 14:6)?

CELSUS: The Christian teacher Jesus acts like a drunkard who enters a party of drunkards and accuses those who are sober of being drunk.

Origen: No one who is self-controlled and teaches Christian doctrine is drunk.

HSR: This response demonstrates Origen's concrete thinking and inability to grasp a figure of speech, particularly an apt one.

CELSUS: The teacher Jesus, in the company of those with dim vision [the disciples], accuses those with clear vision [the nonbelievers] of being blind.

Origen: We Christians do maintain that those who are ignorant of God and pray . . . before images are blind in the mind.

HSR: At the time of Origen, the church forbade Christians to pray before images. The church eventually would change its position.

CELSUS: Christians insult God by leading the wicked astray with vain hope.

Origen: It is not so much the wicked who are persuaded by the gospel as the unsophisticated and, as the masses say, "the simple minded." Such men try to devote themselves to Christianity out of fear of the threatened punishment [hell]; and they are successfully overcome by gospel-engendered fear of everlasting punishment, terrified by every torture devised by men against them, and by death with its countless agonies. . . . Those who set forth the doctrines of Christianity do not "lead the wicked astray," nor do they "insult God." . . . So let Celsus argue in opposition to the beliefs held by the whole world . . . concerning the immortality of the soul . . . that these doctrines deceive "with vain hope." . . . I accept the judgment of philosophers who affirm the immortality of the soul. We Christians have some ideas in common with them. Another time, I will show that the blessed future life exists only for those who have accepted the religion of Jesus.

HSR: Although Origen says that the whole world believes in the immortality of the soul, he promises to show that heaven exists only for Christians. But he never does. He can't. No one can.

THE TRUE DOCTRINE BY CELSUS
Derived from Book 4 of Origen's *Contra Celsum*

CELSUS: The assertion made by Christians that some God or son of God has come down to the earth as judge of man-kind—the Jews saying that he is yet to come—is most shameful, and no lengthy argument is required to refute it.

Origen: Celsus opposes both Jews and Christians at the same time—the Jews for denying that the Christ has come but hoping that he will do so, and the Christians for affirming that Jesus was the prophesied Christ.

HSR: Celsus defines a major difference between Christians and Jews and disparages both for placing their hope in a messiah who has not come and never will.

CELSUS: God is good and beautiful and happy, and exists in the most beautiful state. If then he comes down to men, he must undergo change—a change from good to bad, from beautiful to shameful, from happiness to misfortune, and from what is most good to what is most evil. [What god] would choose a change like that? . . . It is the nature of an immortal god to remain the same without alteration. Accordingly, it is impossible that God underwent this change.

Either [the Christian] god really does change, as [Christians] say, into a mortal body . . . or he does not change but makes those who see him think he does and leads them astray and tells lies. Deceit and lying are always wrong except as a medicine to heal friends who are either sick or insane.

Origen: Jesus . . . came down to men . . . [but] underwent no "change from good to bad . . . from beautiful to shameful . . . from happiness to misfortune . . . from what is most good to what is most evil." . . . Because of his great love for mankind, God made one special descent [from heaven].

Celsus admits that it is sometimes permissible to use deceit and lying, as in the practice of medicine. Why, then, is it unthinkable that something of this sort occurred with [Jesus for] the purpose of bringing salvation? For some characters are reformed by certain doctrines which are more false than true. . . . [T]here is nothing wrong if the person who *heals sick friends*, healed the human race which was dear to him with such means as one would not use for choice, but to which he was confined by force of circumstances. Since the human race was mad, it had to be cured by methods [of lying and deceit] which [Jesus] saw to be beneficial to lunatics.

HSR: Origen proclaims that Christianity is based on lies and deceit, which is permissible because Jesus used lies and deceit on an insane world for the sake of its salvation!

CELSUS: The Jews say . . . that insofar as life is filled with all manner of evil, it is necessary for God to send someone down so that the wicked may be punished and everything become as pure as it was after the great flood [during Noah's time].

Origen: What is so absurd about that teaching?

HSR: It is "absurd" because immediately after the great flood, evil once more flourished. It is impossible to rid the world of evil, so teachings about a Messiah who will rid the world of evil are indeed absurd.

CELSUS: Christians . . . assert that the son of God has already come on account of the sins of the Jews, but because the Jews punished Jesus by giving him gall to drink [Mt 27:34], they drew down upon themselves the wrath of God.

Origen: One of the facts that show that Jesus was some divine and sacred person is that just on his account such great and fearful calamities have for such a long time befallen the Jews. We will go so far as to say that they will not be restored [to their country or their favored status with God]. For they committed the most impious crime of all when they conspired against the Savior of mankind.

HSR: Celsus says that Christian doctrine changes. At first, it taught that Jesus came to save the Jews because of their sins. Now it teaches that because the Jews sinned when they gave Jesus gall to drink, they drew upon themselves the wrath of God. Which is it? Did Jesus come to save the Jews or to punish them? If to punish them, Jesus cannot be the prophesied Messiah, because the Messiah does not punish. Nonetheless, according to Origen, Jesus proved his divinity by inflicting suffering on the Jews. If "God is love," and if love of enemies is Christian duty, then something is terribly amiss here.

CELSUS: Jews and Christians [may be] compared to a colony of bats or ants coming out of a nest, or frogs holding council around a marsh, or worms assembling in a mound of earth, disagreeing with one another about which is the worst sinner. Each group says: "God shows and proclaims everything only to us . . . pays attention only to us, and sends messengers only to us . . . that we may be with him forever. . . . First in rank is God, and after him comes Man, since he has made us in his image, and all things have been put under us—earth, water, air, and the stars—and all things exist for our benefit. . . ." Christians further say: . . . "God will come or will send his son [again] to consume the wicked, whereas the rest of us will have eternal life." . . . Such assertions would be more tolerable coming from worms and frogs than from Jews and Christians.

Origen: Isn't . . . righteousness . . . of no avail toward preventing a Christian or Jew from becoming a bat? . . . Vices are frequent among people who are neither Jews nor Christians, but vices do not exist among Christians. . . . We are not worms. . . . "No good man is a worm . . . an ant . . . a frog . . . or a bat."

[And by the way] we Christians do not assert that even "the stars" have been put under us.

> HSR: Origen tries to refute Celsus by saying "no good man is a worm," thereby ignoring Jesus, who, on the cross, recited Psalm 22: "My God, my God, why hast thou forsaken me? . . . I am a worm, and no man; scorned by men, and despised by the people. . . . They have pierced my hands and feet . . . they divide my garments among them, and for my raiment they cast lots" (Ps 22:1–18). Finally, Origen loses credibility when he states, "vices do not exist among Christians."

CELSUS: The Jews were runaway slaves who escaped from Egypt. They never did anything important, nor have they ever been of any significance or prominence [and Jesus was one of them].

> Origen: [The Jews] were men who manifested a shadow of the heavenly life upon earth. Among them none was regarded as God other than the supreme God. . . . There were no . . . image makers among them, since the law forbade . . . the making of images which takes hold of unintelligent men and drags the eyes of their soul down from God to earth. . . . Their law courts consisted of the most righteous men . . . surpassing human nature . . . and in order that they might have leisure to hear the divine laws, the days called Sabbaths . . . were instituted. . . . However, as nothing in human nature is permanent, even that society had to be gradually done away with. . . . Providence . . . gave the noble religion of Jesus . . . and overthrew the burnt sacrifices that drag men down from the true conception of God.

> And the Jews were protected by divine power. . . . This protection continued as long as they were still worthy. But . . . under the Romans, because they had committed their greatest sin in killing Jesus, they were entirely abandoned.

HSR: No Christian has ever given a more positive description of the Jews than Origen: "Among them none was regarded as God other than the supreme God." Well, then, how could the Jews regard Jesus as a god? "[As] nothing in human nature is permanent, even Jewish society had to be gradually done away with." I think Origen spoke prematurely. His generalization is nonetheless correct. In that case, will not Christian society "be gradually done away with"?

Origen ridicules the burnt sacrifices of the Jews, but not their blood sacrifices. Why not? Because he considers the crucifixion a blood sacrifice. He says that burnt sacrifices drag men down but he apparently believes blood sacrifices lift men up! Origen ignores that the prophets—and Jesus himself—condemned *all* sacrifice!

CELSUS: The Jews invented a most incredible and crude story that a man [Adam] was formed by the hands of God and given breath, that a woman was formed from his side, that God gave them orders, that a serpent opposed [those orders and gave new ones that] even proved superior to the orders of God . . . [thereby] most impiously making God into a weakling right from the start. . . . The more reasonable of the Jews and Christians are ashamed of these stories and try somehow to allegorize them, but they are incapable of being explained this way, for they are manifestly very stupid fables. . . . They tell of a flood and a prodigious ark holding everything inside it—a fable to tell little children. The allegories that have been [derived and] written from them are far more shameful and preposterous than the [original] fables.

Origen: Although [Celsus] entitled his book *The True Doctrine*, it contains no positive doctrines but just criticizes Jews and Christians.

HSR: Origen at last realizes that Celsus's book is not in praise of ancient Greek truths but is a critique of Christianity, even though he continues to fail to grasp the irony of the title.

CELSUS: The soul is God's work, but the body is not. In fact, there is no difference between the body of a bat, a worm, a frog, or a man. For they are made of the same matter and are equally liable to decay. . . . All the bodies I have mentioned have a single common nature that passes in stages through changes . . . and returns again to what it was.

Origen: [I agree that] even that which is perishable persists through the process of change; for matter, the substance that underlies the perishable quality remains constant, according to the opinion of those who hold that matter is uncreated. . . . But it is not my task now to discuss the nature of the universe when I am replying to the attacks of Celsus.

HSR: Celsus's statement is astute and all the more remarkable considering he wrote it almost two thousand years before modern atomic and genetic discoveries. Origen has the sense to agree with Celsus.

CELSUS: [In spite of Jesus' coming] into the real world, there is no decrease or increase of evil either in the past or the present or the future. Evil . . . is inherent in matter and dwells among mortals. . . . It is inevitable that according to determined cycles, the same things always happened, are now happening, and will [continue to] happen.

Origen: [Consider] flood or drought . . . fertility or famine. . . . [They show] that evil does not always remain constant. Providence . . . cleanses evil by [means of] floods and conflagrations.

No one can know the origin of evil who has not grasped the truth about the Devil. . . . Anyone who intends to understand evil must possess an accurate understanding of demons, and be aware that they are not God's creation. . . . Evil is not caused by God. . . . It is not true that "the matter that dwells among mortals" is responsible for evil.

HSR: Celsus is describing good and evil as extremes of normal variation. His point is that Jesus' coming had no effect on the distribution of good and evil in the world, and couldn't have an effect because they are inherent in nature. Origen misses the point and interprets normal variation as something meaningful, miraculous, and divine.

CELSUS: [Contrary to the teachings of Jews and Christians,] the visible world has not been given to men, but each particular thing comes into existence and then perishes for the sake of the whole, according to the process of change.

Origen: It is a waste of time refuting this.

HSR: "It is a waste of time" only because it is impossible to refute.

CELSUS: God does not take corrective measures on the world like a man who has created something defective and made without skill, when he "purifies" it by a flood or a conflagration. . . . Even if something seems to you to be evil, it is not yet clear whether it really is; for man does not know what is expedient for himself or another or the universe.

Origen: [I might have said the same, but] I wanted to avoid giving anyone an excuse for sinning . . . on the ground that by his sin he would be benefiting the community.

HSR: Origen agrees with Celsus but says he was afraid to admit it lest he encourage sinning. Evidently Origen does not embrace all Christian doctrines.

CELSUS: Everything was made as much for dumb animals as for man.

Origen: Providence primarily cares for mankind. . . . Let Celsus say that the enormous variety of things . . . is not made by Providence, but by some chance meeting of atoms . . . and that no intelligent design caused them to exist. . . . We Christians . . . acknowledge our gratitude to the Creator for the many varieties.

HSR: This debate has essentially not changed in two millennia, and it clearly antedated Darwin.

CELSUS: The day and the night serve people . . . [no] more than they serve ants and flies. . . . If anyone were to call us rulers of the wild animals because we hunt them and feast on them, we would reply by asking why, rather, were we not made for wild animals, since they hunt and eat us. . . . That men . . . live in cities and have a state and positions of authority and leadership proves nothing. For ants and bees have this, too.

Origen: The day and the night do not exist for ants and flies . . . but . . . were made by Providence for mankind. . . . Lions and bears, leopards and boars . . . have been given to us in order to demonstrate our courage. God made the wild animals to be liable to capture through men's intelligence. Celsus does not differentiate between actions done as a result of reason and . . . those that are the product of irrational nature. Bees . . . work [on behalf of men] . . . because men need honey. . . . Man's mind is impelled by reason, whereas the mind [of wild creatures] is impelled by instinct.

If [Celsus] had been a philosopher with any sense of obligation to his fellow-men, he should have avoided destroying Christianity's helpful beliefs, which are held in common . . . with the rest of mankind.

HSR: Celsus thinks like a biologist, whereas Origen thinks like a Christian.

CELSUS: Is there anything . . . more divine than to foreknow and declare the future?

Origen: Foreknowledge of the future is not necessarily divine.

HSR: In Book 6, Origen will change his mind and agree with Celsus, saying, "the proclamation of future events is the mark of divinity."

CELSUS: All things have not been made for man any more than for the lion or the eagle or the dolphin.

Origen: All things have been made for man.

HSR: So there!

CELSUS: God [unlike Jesus] does not become angry with men any more than he becomes angry with monkeys or flies. And God [unlike Jesus,] does not threaten men.

Origen: God does not get angry at monkeys or flies. God [gets angry and] inflicts punishment [only] on men. . . . He threatens them through . . . [Jesus Christ] the Savior . . . so that those who hear his threats may be converted.

HSR: Again Origen admits that Jesus spends an inordinate amount of time issuing threats. The threat of eternal punishment in hell is very powerful—more powerful than any message of love. Threats to induce fear is a tool of the tyrant.

THE TRUE DOCTRINE BY CELSUS
Derived from Book 5 of Origen's *Contra Celsum*

CELSUS: No god or son of god has come to earth or ever will.

Origen: Celsus repeats himself, but it is not necessary for me to do so.

CELSUS: [Regarding the Resurrection:] What sort of human soul would have any further desire for a body that has rotted? . . . That is utterly repulsive, revolting, and impossible. What sort of body, after being entirely decayed, could return to its original state? . . . God cannot do what is shameful, nor does he desire what is contrary to nature. If, out of wickedness, a Christian desires something abominable . . . he ought not to believe that his wish will be granted. . . . As Heraclitus says, "Corpses ought to be thrown away like dung, for they are worse than dung."

Origen: Again Celsus makes fun of the Resurrection. . . . [Paul wrote:] "It is sown in corruption, it is raised in incorruption" [1 Cor 15:42]. . . . There is something secret and mysterious about this doctrine. . . . [Paul] goes on to say: "Lo! I tell you a mystery" [1 Cor 15:51]. The word *mystery* is usually applied to . . . doctrines that are rightly concealed from the masses. Corpses should not be discarded. . . . They are worthy of burial . . . if for no other reason than . . . we not insult the soul that dwelled within.

HSR: Burial does not honor the body, and discarding or burning it does not dishonor it. Nothing that is done to the body insults the soul. Funeral services are performed solely to please the living who believe such ceremonies honor the deceased.

CELSUS: [Jesus of the Jews is] the chorus leader and teacher [of the Christians].

Origen: Our "chorus leader and teacher" came forth from the Jews to control the whole world by the word of his teaching.

HSR: The devil promised Jesus the whole world if only Jesus would worship him. As more and more of the world is converting to Christianity, the implication is that Jesus went on to worship the devil. "To control the whole world" is also a favorite expression of antisemites. The forgery *The Protocols of the Elders of Zion* asserts that the intention of the Jews is to control the whole world.

CELSUS: There is nothing wrong with each nation observing its own laws of worship. Each nation should worship its native and traditional gods.

Origen: Egyptian philosophers . . . would become quite ridiculous if they refused to eat onions in order to observe Egyptian customs. . . . To respect crocodiles as sacred . . . is utterly silly. It is quite insane to respect beasts that have no respect for people, and to treat with honor animals that devour men. And yet, Celsus approves of people who worship and honor crocodiles according to their traditional customs.

HSR: Celsus was making a plea for religious liberty and tolerance. Origen, having the true religion, misses Celsus's point, and justifies Christian intolerance by choosing examples that lend themselves to ridicule.

CELSUS: [Christians ridicule the law of the Jews] but Pindar was right when he said that law is king.

Origen: Christians acknowledge that [Natural] Law is the law of God.

HSR: To prefer Natural Law over Mosaic law or Greek law or Roman law is to prefer the law of the jungle over the law of civilization, however primitive and imperfect.

CELSUS: As if they had some deeper wisdom, the Jews are proud and turn away from the society of others on the ground that others are not on the same level of piety. . . . Jews would certainly not be holier than other people because they are circumcised; for the Egyptians and Colchians did that before the Jews. Nor because they abstain from pigs, for the Egyptians also do this, and in addition abstain from goats, sheep, oxen, and fish. And Pythagoras and his disciples abstain from beans! . . . Nor is it at all likely that the Jews are the favorites of God and are loved more than other people, and as if they had really been assigned some land of the blessed! For we see what sort of people they are and what sort of land it is of which they were thought worthy!

Origen: Celsus accused the Jews of falsely supposing themselves to be the chosen of God, preferred above others. . . . If anyone were to carefully examine Moses' intentions and the society he founded, and were to compare [the Jews] with other nations, he would admire none more.

How admirable that the Jews were taught from childhood . . . to seek God beyond [idols]! And what a splendid thing that, soon after they were born, they were taught about the immortality of the soul . . . and the rewards for people who live good lives! They deserved to be called God's portion because they despised all foretelling of the future by omens and other superstitious things.

It doesn't matter that Celsus doesn't agree. The Jews do possess "some deeper wisdom," not only more than the masses but also more than . . . philosophers; because philosophers . . . bow down before idols . . . whereas even the lowliest Jew looks up only to the supreme God. In this respect at least the Jews are right to be proud to avoid the society of others as polluted and impious. Would that they had not sinned . . . when they conspired against Jesus! . . . Accordingly, we Christians say that although the Jews surely experienced favor with God and were loved more than others, yet this care and grace were transferred to us Christians when Jesus transferred the power of the Jews to those Gentiles who believed in him. That is why, although the Romans have wanted to do everything they could to exterminate the Christians, they have not been successful.

If Celsus wants to imply that there is no difference between Christians and Egyptians who worship . . . the crocodile . . . or the hippopotamus or the dog-faced baboon or the cat, let him!

HSR: When discussing the Jews before the advent of Jesus, Origen exalts them. When discussing the Jews after the advent, Origen denigrates them.

CELSUS: [Christians and Jews tell and believe] fictitious stories and myths.

Origen: If the stories of the Greeks . . . are not to be thought absurd and ridiculous, nor to be "fictitious and mythical," why are those [told and believed by] those who are devoted to God . . . judged unworthy of belief?

HSR: Celsus has already said he thinks the stories of the Greeks are absurd and ridiculous. And it is for that very reason he thinks similar stories about Jesus are equally absurd and ridiculous.

CELSUS: I know very well that some Christians have the same Father as the Jews, but other Christians, not liking the Jewish Father, believe in another Father who is the father of Jesus.

Origen: If [Celsus] thinks it is a charge against Christianity that there are several sects among Christians, on this analogy would it not be considered a charge against philosophy that among the sects of philosophers there is disagreement? . . . . These are the two sects of Ebionites [Christian Jews], the one confessing as we do that Jesus was born of a virgin, the other holding that he was not born in this way but like other men. What criticism is there in this?

HSR: The problem of the "Two Fathers" that Celsus identifies but Origen ignores has never been resolved. All the while Christians say that the Father of the Old Testament is a cruel, punitive, and legalistic god filled with wrath and concerned with justice, they insist there is only one Father. Because Christ is portrayed by the church as loving, gracious, merciful, and forgiving, so too it must be assumed is the New Testament Father of whom Jesus is the Incarnation. The New Testament Father evidently is very different from the Old Testament Father, and yet the church teaches they are the same Father. However loving, gracious, merciful, and forgiving the New Testament Father may be, he is nonetheless the Father who planned and saw to the murder of his own son!

CELSUS: [The different sects of Christians] slander one another with dreadful and unspeakable words of abuse. . . . They utterly detest one another.

Origen: Bitter strife between sects can also be found in philosophy. . . . Christians would never utter "unspeakable words of abuse" about opposing sects.

HSR: Really? Roman Catholics vs. Eastern Orthodox? Catholics vs. Protestants? Catholics plus Protestants vs. Mormons? No "unspeakable words of abuse" between them? Origen again shows he is not credible.

THE TRUE DOCTRINE BY CELSUS
Derived from Book 6 of Origen's *Contra Celsum*

CELSUS: The Greeks [unlike the Christians] . . . refrain from making exalted claims and asserting that such claims were announced by a god or the son of a god. [And the Christians teach] the most stupid and uneducated yokels.

Origen: We Christians say that it is the task of those who teach the true doctrines to help as many people as we can . . . even "the most stupid and uneducated yokels." . . . The disciples of Jesus were uneducated in Greek philosophy.

HSR: Notice that Origen again speaks of Christianity's "true doctrines."

CELSUS: Plato [says] . . . important matters ought to be described in writing or orally . . . at some length for the masses. "What finer thing in life could we do than to describe what is of great benefit to mankind and to bring it . . . to light for all men?" [Plato, Letter 7].

Origen: Jesus . . . is said to have spoken the Word of God to his disciples privately [Mk 4:34]. . . . However, what it is he said has not been recorded. For it did not seem to them that "these matters ought to be described at some length or orally for the masses."

HSR: Plato taught that knowledge of things that benefit mankind must be taught to all mankind. But Origen says that Jesus transmitted whatever special knowledge he had only to his disciples, and Origen believes such things were better kept secret. What good are they if kept secret?

CELSUS: Plato [unlike Jesus or one of his disciples] . . . does not tell incredible tales, nor does he stifle someone who wants to inquire what it is in fact that Jesus professes, nor does he say to everyone at the beginning of his speech: "First, believe that the one of whom I speak is the Son of God!" Plato [unlike Jesus] is not arrogant, nor does he tell lies, nor does he assert that he has discovered something new and has come down from heaven to proclaim it; but he acknowledges the sources from which his doctrines come.

Origen: We Christians believe the Son of God has something more significant to say than Plato's Zeus. The proclamation of future events is the mark of divinity. We most certainly do not say to everyone at the start of our speech what Celsus mockingly attributes to us, "First, believe that the one of whom I speak is the Son of God."

HSR: Christians really don't say that?

CELSUS: Although Jesus was most dishonorably arrested and punished to his utter disgrace, Christians say, "That is all the more reason for believing in him."

Origen: We Christians do not say, "That is all the more reason for believing in him."

HSR: Celsus is saying that Christians take whatever demolishes their faith and twist it into something that supports it. Origen denies it. But denial does not answer the criticism.

CELSUS: Christians proclaim Jesus, whereas others proclaim someone else, and they all have the same glib slogan: "Believe and be saved!"

Origen: Jesus . . . is the only Son of God. . . . [As for the others] because their teaching was not of God, they were all killed.

HSR: And because Jesus' teaching was *of God*, Jesus was *not* killed?

CELSUS: Christians say that the wisdom possessed by men is foolishness with God [1 Cor 3:19]. . . . The reason for this . . . is that Christians aim to convert only the uneducated and stupid. Is it possible that what they are trying to say is something they learned from the Greek philosophers: "Human wisdom is one thing but divine wisdom another"?

Origen: That saying is more ancient than the Greek philosophers. Before them the Jewish prophets spoke of the two kinds of wisdom.

HSR: Celsus is trying to reconcile Paul's statement with that of Greek philosophers. Origen gives the credit not to Greek philosphers but to Jewish prophets.

CELSUS: Jesus' condemnation of the rich—"It is easier for a camel to go through the eye of a needle than for a rich man to enter the kingdom of God" [Mt 19:24]—was manifestly borrowed from Plato.

Origen: What person . . . would not laugh at Celsus . . . when he hears that Jesus, who was born and bred among [ignorant] Jews . . . had read Plato? . . . [Moreover, Jesus] did not mean that poverty without qualification was a blessed state, nor did he mean that wealth without qualification was a blameworthy state. For not even a stupid person would indiscriminately praise the poor when most of them have very bad characters.

[Moreover] the Jewish prophets . . . could not have stolen anything from Plato, for they were earlier than Plato.

HSR: Origen says Jesus did not say that poverty assured heaven, for that would be a stupid thing for Jesus to say when most of the poor are unsavory characters.

CELSUS: Your master, Jesus, and [also] Moses, in whom the Jews believe, give contradictory laws, [so] you Christians try to find another Father instead of the one who is the only Father.

Origen: We spoke at some length about the matter [of the "Two Fathers"] earlier.

HSR: Although Origen did speak earlier about the problem of the "Two Fathers," he did not resolve it, nor has the church. Christians continue to speak, on the one hand, of the angry Old Testament Father, who punishes entire communities by bringing about earthquakes, tidal waves, volcanic eruptions, and other natural catastrophes, and, on the other hand, of the loving New Testament Father who brought about the murder of his only begotten son!

CELSUS: [Christians] make some very blasphemous errors . . . when they invent a Being opposed to God; [the] Devil . . . [or] . . . Satan are the names they give to this Being. . . . These notions are entirely man-made, and it is blasphemy to say that when Almighty God wishes to confer some benefit on humanity, there is a power that opposes him, so he is unable to do it. . . . We must not be deceived [by such blasphemous teachings] . . . but must believe in [God] alone.

Origen: In the Book of Job . . . it is written that the Devil comes to God and asks for power against Job.

HSR: Celsus's point is that Christians by making Satan as powerful as God commit blasphemy against God.   Origen does not refute Celsus.   Instead, he deflects by using the Jewish argument found in the Old Testament book of Job: Satan is not all-powerful; Satan cannot take it upon himself to torment Job but must first obtain God's permission.   This is a very different Satan from the New Testament Satan, who, on his own initiative opposes God, and whom Jesus Christ came to conquer.

CELSUS: Moses and the Hebrew prophets . . . had no idea of the nature of the real world and of mankind, and concocted utter trash.

Origen: It is Celsus . . . who "concocted utter trash," boastfully entitling it *The True Doctrine.*

HSR: Origen defends Judaism because it is the source of Christianity, but he remains obtuse to the irony in the title *The True Doctrine.*

CELSUS: How is it possible that God created evil?

Origen: "Shall we receive good at the hand of God, and shall we not receive evil?" [Job 2:10]. "I am he who creates weal and also woe" [Is 45:7]. "Evil has come down from the Lord" [Mic 1:12].

HSR: Origen gives three Old Testament quotes to show that God created evil, thereby undermining Christianity, which teaches that evil has nothing to do with God but is the exclusive domain of Satan. Realizing this, Origen proceeds to reverse himself:

Origen: We affirm that God did not make evil. . . . Evil . . . is a consequence of God's works . . . just as spiral shavings and sawdust are a consequence of the works of a carpenter. . . . What can be wrong with this doctrine? . . . [God] creates . . . evil to purify and educate those who are unwilling to be educated by reason and sound teaching.

HSR: Origen often gives conflicting views consecutively, but never so blatantly as here where he reverses himself four times: 1. God *did* make evil (according to three prophets). 2. God did *not* make evil (according to Origen speaking for himself). 3. God did *not* make evil *purposefully* but only as a byproduct of making good (according to Origen). 4. God *did* make evil purposefully but in order to purify and educate those who could not be taught in any other way (according to Origen).

CELSUS: God is from nothing. Neither is he attainable by reason. . . . How then can I know God? . . . And how can you show him to me?

Origen: It is true that "God is from nothing." But Jesus shows him to us: "The people who sat [or walked] in darkness [the gentiles] have seen a great light" [Is 9:2; Mt 4:16] . . . which is the God Jesus.

HSR: Celsus says, "God is from nothing," and Origen agrees, "God is from nothing." Celsus asks, "And how can you show

[God] to me?" And Origen says Jesus has shown God to you because Jesus is God. That is standard Christian teaching. Origen, however, does not deal with the statement, "God is from nothing." Christian theology states that Jesus God is not "from nothing" but from the Father, and Jesus Man is not "from nothing" but from the Holy Spirit and the Virgin Mary. Christian theology, therefore, states that Jesus is from one to three sources and not from nothing.

CELSUS: [Christians teach that] because God is . . . hard to see, God thrust his spirit into a human body and sent him down here.

Origen: [Jesus] the Savior said, "God is Spirit, and those who worship him must worship him in spirit and in truth" [Jn 4:24]. By these words, Jesus taught that God must not be worshipped in the flesh. . . . [Therefore,] Jesus is not material . . . [but] an incorporeal being. . . .

HSR: To prove that God is Spirit, Origen here denies the Incarnation.

CELSUS: If a divine spirit were in a body, it must certainly have differed from other bodies in size or beauty. . . . Yet, Jesus' body was . . . little and ugly and undistinguished.

Origen: Admittedly it was written that the body of Jesus was ugly: . . . "He had no form or comeliness that we should look at him, and no beauty that we should desire him" [Is 53:2]. Celsus paid heed to these words . . . but did not pay attention to the psalm where it is said: "Gird your sword, O mighty one, in your beauty and glory" [Ps 45:2–3].

HSR: The psalm is describing a warrior-king preparing for battle. Can that be Jesus? If so, then Jesus is both ugly and beautiful at the same time. Again Origen is comfortable holding two diametrically opposed positions simultaneously.

Origen continues: Neither the gospels nor the apostles give any evidence that Jesus had no form or beauty. . . . And this puts Celsus's criticism of Jesus' [appearance] out of bounds.

HSR: Origen tells us that Isaiah's suffering servant is ugly, whereas the psalm's warrior king is beautiful; the gospels and the Acts of the Apostles do not describe Jesus' physical appearance at all. Origen concludes irrationally that Celsus lied when he said Jesus was ugly.

CELSUS: If God, like Zeus in a [certain] comedy, woke up from a long slumber and wanted to deliver the human race from evil, why did he send Jesus into a tiny corner of the earth [the land of the Jews]? . . . When Zeus woke up, he sent his son Hermes to the Athenians and Spartans, and that makes the audience laugh. Do Christians think it is even funnier for God to have sent his son to the Jews?

Origen: It was quite reasonable [for God to send Jesus to the Jews]—for it was the Jews who had already learned that there was one God . . . and [it was reasonable] that [Jesus would] send forth his light from Judea [the land of the Jews]. . . . [So] I don't see anything "funny" in the son of God being sent to the Jews.

HSR: Origen defends the Jews whenever Celsus attacks them, because Jesus came from the Jews, and the gospels teach that God sent Jesus to the Jews. But Origen himself attacks the Jews whenever their rejection of Jesus is at issue.

THE TRUE DOCTRINE BY CELSUS
Derived from Book 7 of Origen's *Contra Celsum*

CELSUS: It is so typical for a Jewish prophet [like Jesus] to say: "I am God or the son of God or a divine Spirit, and I have come. For the world is coming to an end. And you, O men, are going to perish because of your sins. But I wish to save you. And you shall see me returning again with heavenly power. Blessed is he who worships me, for I will cast everlasting fire upon all the rest. . . . But I will save forever those who believe in me." Having brandished these threats, these [prophetic] Jews go on to add incomprehensible, incoherent, and totally obscure utterances, the meaning of which no intelligent person can discover; for they are meaningless and nonsensical, and give the chance for any fool . . . to take the words in whatever sense he likes.

Origen: Celsus said this out of malice because he wanted to do all in his power to prevent readers of the Jewish prophecies from examining and studying their meaning.

HSR: Origen again misses the point. Celsus is ridiculing Jews like Jesus who prophesy the imminent end of the world. But Celsus does not ridicule the Hebrew prophets, who do not prophesy such things.

CELSUS: If the prophets foretold that Almighty God . . . was going to serve as a slave and be sick and die, would it necessarily follow, just because it was foretold that God would serve as a slave, become sick and die, that by his death people would believe that he was God? But the prophets could not have foretold this. For such a prophecy is evil and impious. So we should not consider whether they did or did not foretell it, but whether such an act of prophecy is worthy of God and is good.

And we should disbelieve what is disgraceful and evil, even if all men predicted it in a state of madness. How, then, is it anything but blasphemy to assert that the things done to Jesus were done to God? If such things were prophesied about the Supreme God, ought we to believe them just because they were prophesied? And even if it was really true that the prophets actually foretold such things about the son of God, it would be impossible to believe them.

Origen: Is Celsus acting from noble motives . . . or . . . a shameless desire to deny by violent language the truth of that which is so obviously true?

[It is true that] the prophecies did not foretell that God would be crucified. . . . [But] they clearly say that the one who suffered human sorrows was a man. And Jesus himself, who knew precisely that it was a man who was to die, said, "But now you seek to kill me, a man who has told you the truth which I heard from God" [Jn 8:40].

HSR: There is nothing "violent" in Celsus's language and nothing "obviously true" in Origen's.

CELSUS: If the prophets foretold that Jesus would be God's son, why had God given the Jews his laws through Moses? . . . For his son, the man from Nazareth, gives contradictory laws. . . . So who is wrong, Moses or Jesus? Or, when the Father sent Jesus, had he forgotten the commandments he had given to Moses? Or, did he change his mind and condemn his own laws and send his messenger Jesus to reveal his complete turnabout?

Origen: Here Celsus, who professes to know everything, has fallen into a very common error. . . . He thinks that in the law and the prophets there is no deeper doctrine beyond that of the literal meaning. . . . The gospel does not lay down laws that contradict the law of God. . . . And neither Moses nor Jesus is "wrong." Nor had the Father "forgotten the commandments that he had given to Moses" when he sent Jesus. Nor did he "change his mind and condemn his own laws, and send his messenger to reveal his complete turnabout."

Christians wish only to correct the law of Moses to conform to the teaching of Jesus. . . . [The law of Moses] does not fit in with the calling of the Gentiles, for they cannot conduct their society according to the literal interpretation of the law of Moses because they are subject to [the law of] Rome. [Moreover] the Providence that long ago gave the law of Moses now has given the gospel of Jesus Christ. Providence did not wish the observances of the Jews to continue; so he destroyed their city and temple. . . . And because it was God who wanted the Gentiles to be helped by the teaching of Jesus Christ, every human design against the Christians has been frustrated.

HSR: Origen, again presenting conflicting ideas simultaneously, says the "gospel does not lay down laws that contradict the law of God" but by the gospel Christians only wish to "correct the law of Moses to conform to the teaching of Jesus" and the law of Rome.

CELSUS: [Christians, who believe in the Incarnation,] say: "How is it possible to have any knowledge [of God] except by sense perception?" That kind of answer is not that of a man with a soul, but wholly of the flesh. . . . If you [Christians would] shut your eyes to the world of the senses and look up with the mind, if you would turn away from the flesh and raise up the eyes of the soul, then and only then will you see God. . . . And if you are looking for an authentic leader, you must flee from deceivers and sorcerers [like Jesus]. . . . You worship a man who is more wretched than a ghost. . . . He is in fact dead.

Origen: Who would not have good reason to laugh at Celsus when he attributes to Christians statements they do not make? . . .

No one who has learned that God is invisible . . . would say, to defend the Incarnation, "How can anyone know God unless they can see him with their own eyes?" . . . Since we affirm that the God of the universe is . . . invisible and incorporeal . . . no man would ever make such a statement. . . . And no Christian would make any statement [in defense of] the "flesh," for he is aware that "those who are in the flesh cannot please God" [Rom 8:8]. Celsus says things about us that have nothing to do with us. . . .

Because of his exceeding love toward mankind, Jesus . . . came down to the level . . . of ordinary men . . . to raise souls from earthly things.

HSR: Origen uses the incarnation to deny the incarnation!

CELSUS: Plato was a more effective teacher [than Jesus] regarding understanding God. [Plato wrote in the *Timaeus*:] "To find the Maker and Father of the universe is difficult, and after finding him, it is impossible to declare him to all men."

Origen: We affirm that human nature is inadequate to seek for God and find him . . . unless it is helped by the God who is the object of the search. He is found by those who . . . admit that they need him and shows himself to those to whom he judges it right to appear. . . . Anyone who understands that Jesus . . . became flesh will come to know the Father and Creator of the universe by looking at the image of the invisible God.

What intelligent person would not laugh at a man who . . . turns his eyes to images and either prays to them or, by means of the sight of these images, offers his prayer to God who is spirit, imagining that [his prayers] must ascend to God from something visible?

HSR: Origen again uses the doctrine of the incarnation to overthrow the doctrine of the incarnation.

CELSUS: I do not say [as Christians do] that those who see are blind, when you [Christians] yourselves are . . . mutilated in your souls and live only for the body, which is a dead thing.

Origen: Celsus and those like him assert that they are wise but exhibit crass stupidity. For after learning in philosophy the great doctrines about God and unintelligible things, they exchanged the glory of the incorruptible God for the likeness of an image of corruptible man. . . . That is why they were forsaken by heaven. . . . "They exchanged the truth about God for a lie and worshiped and served the creature rather than the Creator" [Rom 1:25].

HSR: While attempting to discredit Celsus, Origen demolishes Christianity.

CELSUS: Anaxarchus, who, when cast into a [giant] mortar and while being beaten most violently [with a giant iron pestle], nobly showed contempt for the punishment, saying, "Beat on! Beat the bag you call Anaxarchus, for you are not beating him." . . . This utterance is surely one from a divine spirit. . . . Then, too, consider Epictetus. When his master was twisting his leg, he smiled sweetly, and calmly said, "You are breaking it." And when he had broken it, Epictetus said, "Didn't I tell you that you were breaking it?" What comparable saying did your god utter while he was being punished? . . . You have the presumption . . . to assert that Jesus, a man who lived a most infamous life and died a most miserable death—and a cowardly one, too—was a god.

Origen: [Deceived are] people who seek for God in earthly images and do not look up to the real and supreme God.
Jesus was not led by base cowardice, as some think, when he said, "My Father, if it be possible, let this cup pass from me" [Mt 26:39]. . . . The charge that Jesus "died a most miserable death" could

[equally] be applied to Socrates and to Anaxarchus, whom [Celsus] mentioned a little earlier, and to thousands of others. . . . Jesus . . . gave us "authority to tread upon serpents and scorpions, and over all the power of the enemy; and nothing shall hurt you" (Lk 10:19).

HSR: Celsus says that many men died more violent deaths than Jesus, and many of those, unlike Jesus, went to their deaths nobly; yet no one calls any one of those noble men a god. Origen does not respond to this criticism, probably because it is irrefutable. Instead, Origen responds tangentially by speaking of Jesus' promise to those who believe in him: the ability to tread on poisonous animals and to oppose powerful enemies without coming to harm. Jesus' promise is false and invites disaster. Once more Origen, rather than defending Christianity, undermines it.

CELSUS: [Jesus said:] "But if anyone strikes you on the right cheek, turn to him the other also" (Mt 5:39). That is old stuff and has been better said. . . . Socrates said [in the Crito], "It is never right either to do wrong or to take revenge, or for one who has suffered harm to resist and to requite evil."

Origen: How can anyone find fault with Jews and Christians just because the same doctrines were also set forth by the Greeks?
Christians and Jews avoid . . . images. . . . [I]t is quite impossible both to know God and to pray to images.

HSR: Not "impossible" the church decided.

CELSUS: Christians worship not a god, not even a devil, but a corpse.

Origen: We may leave this matter and move on to others.

HSR: Yes.

THE TRUE DOCTRINE BY CELSUS
Derived from Book 8 of Origen's *Contra Celsum*

CELSUS: If [Christians] worshiped no other God but one, perhaps they would have a valid argument against [polytheism]. But in fact they worship to an extravagant degree this man who appeared recently, and think it is not inconsistent with monotheism if they also worship God's servant Jesus. . . . When they call Jesus son of God, they are not paying the greatest reverence to God but are exalting Jesus excessively. It is not the Christian intention to worship God who is beyond the heavens but rather . . . Jesus, who is the central object of their society. They want to worship only this son of man, whom they put forward as their leader under the pretense that he is Almighty God.

Origen: Some Christians do take the divergent view [that Christ is God] and, because of their rashness, suppose that the Savior is the same as the greatest and supreme God. But I at least do not take this view, since I believe [Jesus when he] said, "The Father [who sent me] is greater than I" [Jn 14:28]. . . . Christians . . . hold that the son is . . . subordinate [to Almighty God]. And we say this because we believe Jesus who said, "The Father [who sent me] is greater than I."

HSR: When Arius said the very things Origen is saying, the church found him guilty of the greatest of heresies. Origen again demolishes the divinity of Jesus.

CELSUS: If, as Christians say, they abstain from feasting with demons, I congratulate them on their wisdom, because they are slowly coming to understand that they are always associating with demons.

Origen: Christians are not ruled by demons but by the supreme God through Jesus Christ who brought us to him. . . . On the other hand, [Jesus considers demons] worthy to govern and to punish the wicked, and perhaps demons were appointed by Jesus, who administers the universe, to rule those who subject themselves to evil.

HSR: Origen is saying that Jesus is the ruler not only of Christians but also of demons. Origen, whose purpose is to refute Celsus and defend Jesus, supports Celsus and undermines Jesus.

CELSUS: Earthly rulers . . . could inflict great harm on those who insulted them. Wouldn't demons of heaven and earth do the same?

Origen: No wise man would want to harm another, but would do all in his power to convert and improve even people who insulted him. . . . Christians conform to the teaching of Jesus, who said: "Love your enemies and pray for those who persecute you, so that you may be sons of your Father who is in heaven" [Mt 5:44–45]. . . . And [long before Jesus] in the words of the prophet [David], "O Lord my God, if I have . . . plundered my enemy without cause, let the enemy pursue me and overtake me, and let him trample my life to the ground, and lay my soul in the dust" [Ps 7:3–5].

HSR: Origen admits that love of enemy is not original with Jesus but is an Old Testament teaching that antedated Jesus.

CELSUS: Christians worship the demon Jesus, who was carried off and crucified . . . and they bind and dedicate themselves to him like an image. . . . Well, they will receive vengeance: "The mills of God grind slowly, but they grind exceedingly small."

Origen: Jesus was not a demon. . . .   Ultimately, when the wicked refuse all remedies, the threatened punishments [the torments of hell] come upon them. . . .   Worth consideration and quoted by Celsus is the reply of the oracle of Apollo at Delphi or of Zeus at Dodona: "The mills of God grind slowly."

HSR: Origen does not deal with Celsus's criticism that in worshiping an incarnate god, Christians worship a demon and an image, and they will eventually be punished for it.   "The mills of God grind slowly."

CELSUS: [How can it be that the Romans] who tortured and punished your god in person suffered nothing for doing so, not even afterward as long as they lived?   What new thing has happened since then which might lead one to believe that he was not a sorcerer but the son of God?

Origen: The city in which the Jewish people thought Jesus worthy of being crucified . . . was not long afterward attacked and besieged so fiercely and for such a long time that it was utterly ruined and made a desert. . . .   This happened on account of the blood of Jesus, which, because of their plot, was poured out upon their land. . . .   This then is the "new thing" that has happened since the time when Jesus suffered.   I refer to the fate of Jerusalem and of all the Jews, and to the sudden birth of the race of Christians which was, so to speak, born in an instant.

HSR: Celsus cannot understand why the Romans, who treated Jesus and his fellow Jews so brutally, flourish instead of being inflicted with God's wrath.   The implication is that there was nothing divine about Jesus.   However, by changing the perpetrators of the crucifixion from the Romans to the Jews, Origen invents what was to become the church's most famous example of divine retribution, not against the Romans but against the Jews.

CELSUS: The Father who sent his son with certain instructions for mankind allowed Jesus to be cruelly treated, his instructions to perish with him, and without ever, during Jesus' whole lifetime, showing the slightest concern. What father was ever so ruthless?

Origen: Jesus delivered God's message [and here it is]: "Truly, truly, I say to you, unless a grain of wheat falls into the earth and dies, it remains alone; but if it dies, it bears much fruit" [Jn 12:24].
And the Father . . . is always caring for the fruits that resulted from the death of the grain of wheat, which are still being produced and will continue to be produced.

HSR: Origen claims to know the message that the Father sent the Son to deliver: John 12:24. That, however, could not have been the message, for it was neither new nor original: "Thy dead shall live, their bodies shall rise. O dwellers in the dust, awake and sing for joy!" (Is 26:19). Moreover, Jesus' analogy in John 12:24 is fallacious. A corpse in the earth is dead, but a seed in the earth is very much alive.

CELSUS: Just as you believe in eternal punishments, so, too, do those devoted to Dionysus. . . . You threaten them with punishment and they threaten you. . . . Both sides make equally strong assertions.

Origen: Anyone who reads both religions with intelligence and with an open mind . . . [will see that] not even the slightest comparison is possible between them.

HSR: Contrary to Origen's assertion, the two religions are comparable and very much alike. Christianity owes as much to the mystery religion of Dionysus as to Judaism.

CELSUS: Christians long for the body and hope that it will rise again in the same form, as if we possessed nothing better or more precious than the body. . . . It is not worthwhile discussing this with Christians. . . . But I will discuss the matter with those who hope they will possess their soul or mind eternally with God . . . and who hold the correct opinion that those who live good lives will be happy, and those who are totally wicked will be afflicted with eternal evil. May this doctrine never be abandoned!

Origen: [Celsus] has often reproached us about the Resurrection. . . . We maintain that the soul . . . is more precious than the body. . . . We long for all that God promises to the righteous. It is in this sense [God's promise] that we long and hope for the resurrection of the righteous.

Even people alien to the Christian faith make many affirmations about the righteous life that are much the same as ours. . . .

Universal [are the] notions of good and evil, righteous and unrighteous. . . . All men should be convinced that if they live good lives, they will come to a better end, but if evil, they will be given over to evil pains and torments. . . . Therefore, Celsus ought not to hate Moses and the Jewish prophets and Jesus [who, along with the heathens, taught the same things].

HSR: Origen again agrees with Celsus that non-Christians also believe in a hereafter and also believe that the reward for good is being with God, and the punishment for evil is separation from God. Celsus wants to know the purpose of the resurrection of the body. Origen does not answer except to say God promised it.

CELSUS: We must never forsake God. . . . In every word and deed . . . let the soul be continually directed toward God. . . . If you happen to be a worshiper of God and someone commands you either to act blasphemously or to say some disgraceful thing [such as expressing a belief in the incarnation], you ought not to put any confidence in him at all. Indeed, you must remain firm in the face of all tortures and endure any death rather than say or even think anything profane about God.

Origen: How I wish . . . all other form of worship would be done away and only that of the Christians prevail! One day it will prevail and be the one and only religion!

HSR: Origen hopes that one day Christianity will prevail over all other religions and become the "one and only" religion.

CELSUS: Christians will surely not say that if the Romans were . . . to neglect their customary honors to the gods and men and were to call upon your Most High, or whatever name you prefer, he would come down and fight on their side, and they would have no need for any other defense.

Origen: Celsus raises the question of what would happen if the Romans were to become . . . Christians. . . . Imagine! Not as now, just a few, but the whole Roman Empire! . . . If, as Celsus suggests, all the Romans converted and prayed, they would be superior to their enemies, and would have no need to fight wars at all, since they would be protected by divine power.

HSR: As Origen hoped and prophesied, the Roman Empire did convert to Christianity. But that conversion, contrary to Origen's prophecy, did not spare the empire from war, nor protect it by divine power. Shortly after converting to Christianity, the Roman Empire was destroyed and came to an end.

6. JESUS OF NAZARETH

THE JEW

JESUS OF NAZARETH, THE JEW

By the fourth century, Jesus of Nazareth, a poor Jew from one of the poorest provinces in the Roman Empire, had become the most influential man who ever lived. Even more, he had become the empire's God.

Ironically, Jesus observed and practiced Judaism his entire life. He was not a Christian and did not teach Christianity. He worshipped neither himself nor the Trinity. He was a monotheist and worshipped only YHVH. He was a Jew. The woman of Samaria said to Jesus:

How is it that you, a Jew, ask a drink of me? (Jn 4:9).

The Hebrew Scriptures proclaim:

Hear O Israel: the Lord [YHVH] is our God; the Lord [YHVH] is one (Deut 6:4).

Jesus proclaimed:

Hear O Israel: the Lord [YHVH] our God, the Lord [YHVH] is one (Mk 12:29).

The Hebrew Scriptures command:

You shall serve the Lord [YHVH] your God (Ex 23:25).

Jesus said:

> *Scripture says,* **You shall worship the Lord your God [YHVH]**—[and then he added]—*and him only shall you serve* (Mt 4:10).

Jesus did not renounce the Covenant between his people and God, which the church calls the "Old" Covenant, as if it has been revoked and replaced by a "New" Covenant. Jesus, as the sign of that Covenant, was circumcised when he was eight days old; he never decried his own circumcision or circumcision in general. Jesus celebrated the seventh day, Saturday, the Sabbath Day, not the first day, Sunday, the "Lord's Day." Jesus loved the Law or the Torah and repeatedly said it could not be revoked; he went to synagogue and Temple, not church. Jesus observed Hanukah, the Festival of Dedication (Jn 10:22), not Christmas, and he celebrated Passover (Mt 26:18; Mk 14:14; Lk 22:8, 22:11), not Easter.

Jesus preached the perpetuity of the Law of Moses in its entirety (Mt 5:18), and not only the Ten Commandments. He taught what he considered the two greatest commandments, and they were not among the Ten Commandments (Mk 12:28–31) but were among the over six hundred Hebrew commandments the church rejects. He observed the minutest details of the Law, including the ritual one must follow after cleansing a leper (Mt 8:4; Lk 5:14) and the tithing of herbs (Mt 23:23; Lk 11:42). In spite of his disputes with the Pharisees, Jesus called them the authentic interpreters of the Law and commanded his disciples to follow their teachings (Mt 23:1–3).

The apostles, in following Jesus, did not abandon Judaism and the Temple. The gospel according to Luke concludes: **And the apostles returned to Jerusalem with great joy and were continually in the Temple praising God** (Lk 24:52–53).

The book of Acts states: **Day after day, the apostles all went regularly to the Temple** (Acts 2:16).

In praying for my conversion, the church wants me to exchange the religion *of* Jesus for the religion *about* Jesus.

JESUS AND THE HEBREW SCRIPTURES

The church refers to the Hebrew Scriptures as the "Old Testament" as if it were something worn out, discarded, and replaced by the New Testament. But Jesus did not call the Hebrew Scriptures the "Old Testament," and he never once mentioned the "New Testament." He called the Hebrew Scriptures *scriptures* (e.g., Mt 21:42) or *scripture* (e.g., Mk 12:10), and for him there were no others and never would be. Jesus considered the Hebrew Scriptures real, essential, and vital, and at the times of his deepest distress, he quoted them:

Scripture:

> **You shall not put the Lord [YHVH] your God to the test** (Deut 6:16).

Jesus said it this way:

> *It is written,* **You shall not tempt the Lord [YHVH] your God** (Mt 4:7).

Scripture:

> **You shall serve the Lord [YHVH] your god** (Deut 6:13).

Jesus said it more emphatically:

> *It is written,* **You shall worship the Lord [YHVH] your God,** *and him only shall you serve* (Mt 4:10; Lk 4:8).

Scripture:

> **Man does not live by bread alone, but . . . by everything that proceeds out of the mouth of the Lord [YHVH]** (Deut 8:3).

Jesus said it thus:

> *It is written,* **Man shall not live by bread alone, but by every word that proceeds from the mouth of God** (Mt 4:4).

JESUS' PROMISE TO THE JEWS

Jesus did not teach the Jews that he had come to replace Judaism with a new religion. He promised the Jews a high place in the Kingdom of Heaven, while all who teach laying aside the Law, he promised the lowest place.

> *Whoever then relaxes one of the least of these commandments and teaches men so, shall be called least in the kingdom of heaven; but he who does them and teaches them shall be called great in the kingdom of heaven* (Mt 5:19).

In trying to convert me, the church wants me to forfeit a high place in heaven and exchange it for a low place reserved for the church.

HEBREW SCRIPTURAL COMMANDMENTS
Scripture:

> **If you obey the commandments of the Lord [YHVH]
> your God, which I command you this day, by loving
> the Lord [YHVH] your God, by walking in his ways,
> and by keeping his commandments . . . then you
> shall live** (Deut 30:16).

Jesus:

> *If you would enter life, keep the commandments*
> (Mt 19:17).

Jesus was speaking not only of the Ten Commandments but of
all of them. We know this because Jesus taught (Mk 12:28–
31) that the two greatest commandments were not even among
the Ten Commandments:

> **And one of the scribes . . . asked Jesus, "Which
> commandment is first of all?" Jesus answered,**
>   *The first is,* **"Hear O Israel: The Lord [YHVH] is
> our God, the Lord [YHVH] is one"** [Deut 6:4].
>   *The second is this,* **"You shall love your neighbor as
> yourself"** [Lev 19:18]. *There is no other command-
> ment greater than these* (Mk 12:28–31).

The church ignores the first commandment and teaches that the
second was original with Jesus!

JESUS AND THE PHARISEES
The Law consisted of two parts: the Written Law, or Scrip-
tures; and the Oral Law, or the traditions and interpretations of
Scriptures by the Pharisees. In the second century AD, the

Oral Law was written down and codified as the book called the *Mishnah*, which was to become the first book of a larger corpus of books, written during the middle ages, called the *Talmud*.

Jesus did not dispute Scriptures with the Pharisees. It was a few matters of the Oral Law on which they disagreed; for example, the Pharisees allowed divorce and required hand washing, whereas Jesus disallowed divorce and scorned hand washing. The church, however, does not make the distinction between Written and Oral Law, but speaks of both together as "Old Law." The church also teaches that, apart from the Ten Commandments, Jesus revoked the "Old Law." But as we have seen, that is not so. Jesus did not criticize the Old Law, let alone revoke it. To revoke it would be to abrogate the word of the Father, but Jesus only wanted to do the will of the Father. He insisted on observing all six hundred and thirteen commandments, even the least of them (Mt 5:19).

The church despises the Pharisees and consequently so do the faithful. And yet, almost every important teaching of Jesus of Nazareth, he adopted from the Pharisees. Yes, there were Pharisaic traditions with which Jesus disagreed, but he did not abolish those traditions any more than he abrogated the Old Law, contrary to the teachings of the church.

Here are examples of Jesus' disagreements with the Pharisees. It is important to observe that Jesus might just as well have been speaking to the church:

> *You abandon the commandments of God, but hold fast to the traditions of men* (Mk 7:8).

> *You have a fine way of rejecting the commandments of God in order to keep your traditions* (Mk 7:9).

Nonetheless, Jesus commanded his disciples to obey the Pharisees, even when he disagreed with them:

> **The scribes and the Pharisees sit on Moses' seat; so practice and observe whatever they tell you** (Mt 23:2–3).

DISAGREEMENT WITH THE PHARISEES

The Pharisees considered themselves authoritative on matters of the Law but not infallible. Disagreement among Jews was not forbidden but encouraged and at times even required. The Pharisees realized that interpretation was subject to human fallibility, so they typically gave the minority opinion as well as the majority:

> Why do they record the opinions of Rabbi Shammai and Rabbi Hillel when their opinions did not prevail? In order to teach future generations that a man should not persist in his opinion, for even the fathers of the world [the Pharisees, who were the early Rabbis] did not have all their opinions prevail (*The Mishnah*, Eduyot 1:4).

The Council of Pharisees even taught that it was the responsibility of a man who had confidence in the correctness of his interpretation to rely on himself and not on the Council:

> If a Council of Pharisees made a rule contrary to any of the commandments of God . . . and if an individual proceeded and acted in error as a result of this rule . . . he is not to be blamed because he relied on the ruling of the Council. But if a Council of Pharisees ruled erroneously and a member of the Council knew that they had erred, or a disciple who was capable of deciding matters of Law knew that they had erred, and still went ahead

> and acted in accordance with the ruling . . . such a one
> is blameworthy, since he did not have to depend on the
> Council's ruling. This is the general rule: Anyone who
> can rely on himself must be blamed [when he does not
> do what he knows to be right], but anyone who must
> rely on the Council is exempt from blame (*The
> Mishnah*, Horayot 1:1).

This was a revolutionary idea in antiquity, and remains so to
this day. It is the only ancient teaching to make disobedience a
requirement and a virtue. Therefore, it was not disagreement
with the Pharisees on ethical or moral matters that brought Jesus of Nazareth into disfavor with them. It was Jesus' high-
handedness, provocations, and invectives. It was, in short, his
ungodly behavior.

JESUS' PROVOCATIVE QUESTIONS ABOUT THE SABBATH

Jesus posed two provocative rhetorical questions to the
Pharisees. The first was:

> *Is it lawful on the Sabbath to do good or to do harm?*
> (Mk 3:4; Lk 6:9).

Jesus knew the answer. Everyone knows the answer. Common sense, not law, expects one to do good and not to do harm
on any day of the week, let alone the Sabbath.

The second question was:

> *Is it lawful on the Sabbath . . . to save life or to kill?*
> (Mk 3:4).

Again Jesus knew the answer. Again everyone knows it.
Again common sense expects one to save a life and not to kill

on any day of the week, let alone the Sabbath. However, the church taught that by asking these questions and by doing good deeds and healing on the Sabbath, Jesus revoked the Sabbath!

It is important to observe that Jesus did not save lives on the Sabbath. He never saved someone from choking or bleeding to death. Instead, Jesus chose to heal long-standing chronic illness on the Sabbath. The Pharisees had ruled that a healer ought to discriminate between emergencies and chronic illness, but they did not enforce the rule because of the possibility that any illness might be life threatening:

> If a man has a sore throat, medicine may be adminis-
> tered on the Sabbath since it is unknown whether his
> life is in danger or not. And whenever there is any
> doubt whether life is in danger, such concern overrides
> anything concerning the Sabbath (*The Mishnah*,
> Yoma 8:6).

In repeatedly performing cures of chronic illness rather than emergency interventions on the Sabbath, Jesus was acting in a provocative and highhanded way. What Christian doctor would leave his Sunday dinner to heal lifelong lameness? That kind of illness could just as well be healed on any day of the week. If a Christian doctor actually left his Sunday dinner to cure a chronic illness, would anyone consider him noble? On the contrary. Most people would consider such a man a show-off, trying to impress the mob. Jesus himself preached the contemptibility of showing off: *They do all their deeds to be seen by men* (Mt 23:5).

In addition to being a healer, Jesus was a carpenter. Carpentry was a trade and therefore a kind of work forbidden on the Sabbath. Significantly, Jesus did not practice carpentry on the Sabbath. He did not build a table or a chair or a cabinet. He did not do so because he did not wish to break the Sabbath.

John the evangelist lied when he said, **And this was why the Jews persecuted Jesus, because he worked on the Sabbath** (Jn 5:16). Jesus did not work on the Sabbath. Healing was permitted on the Sabbath; carpentry was not.

Apart from healing, what else did Jesus do on the Sabbath? He preached. Like healing, preaching on the Sabbath was not considered work and not prohibited. Preaching on the Sabbath was what preachers traditionally did. The Pharisees preached on the Sabbath, and the descendants of the Pharisees, the rabbis, do it still. John, himself a Jew, had to have been aware that Jews would know he was lying, but at the time John was writing, he no longer cared what the Jews thought. John was writing for Gentiles who were ignorant of Jewish law. So John was able to deceive his audience.

By healing chronic illness on the Sabbath, Jesus did not break the Sabbath, but he did behave in a highly provocative and high-handed manner. The word of God says:

> **If a man does anything highhandedly . . . that man reviled the Lord [YHVH], and that person shall be cut off from his people. For he despised the word of The Lord [YHVH], and has broken the commandment, and he shall be completely cut off, and his iniquity shall be upon him** (Num 15:30–31).

Another example of Jesus behaving highhandedly:

> **Now [Jesus] was teaching in one of the synagogues on the Sabbath. And there was a woman who had a spirit of infirmity for eighteen years. She was bent over and could not fully straighten herself. And when Jesus saw her, he called her and said to her, _Woman! You are freed from your infirmity!_ And he laid his hands upon her, and immediately she was made straight, and she praised God. But the ruler**

> **of the synagogue, indignant that Jesus had healed on the Sabbath, said to the people, "There are six days on which work ought to be done. Come on those days, and be healed, not on the Sabbath day." Then [Jesus] answered him,** *Hypocrites! Does not each of you untie his ox or ass from the manger, and lead it away to water it? And ought not this woman, a daughter of Abraham whom Satan bound for eighteen years, be loosed from this bond on the Sabbath day?* (Lk 13:10–17).

Choosing the Sabbath to heal an eighteen-year-old infirmity is neither noble nor loving. Although the leader of the synagogue made a reasonable request, Jesus denounced him and became verbally abusive. The object of his abuse was not only the leader but the entire congregation. Name-calling or shouting invectives is never appropriate, particularly when Jesus himself taught that name-calling is deserving of death and will be rewarded with everlasting hell.

Moreover, Jesus reveals how superstitious he is by teaching that disease is punishment for sins and is bondage to Satan. Finally, what did the watering of domestic animals, a daily necessity even on the Sabbath, have to do with curing an illness that was eighteen years old?

Jesus behaved in such a highhanded and provocative manner that the leader of the synagogue might well have suggested excommunication. But he didn't, and Jesus departed in peace. The tone of the gospel, however, is so hateful toward the leader and the congregation that it may be difficult for a reader to realize how reasonable was the leader, and how volatile was Jesus. And the church teaches that the incident shows that Jesus revoked the Sabbath!

DINNER WITH THE PHARISEES
AND THE CONFLICT OVER HAND WASHING

The Pharisees often invited Jesus to dinner, and he accepted willingly:

> **One of the Pharisees asked [Jesus] to eat with him, and he went into the Pharisee's house, and sat at table** (Lk 7:36).

> **While he was speaking, a Pharisee asked him to dine with him; so he went in and sat at table** (Lk 11:37).

> **One sabbath . . . he went to dine at the house of a ruler who belonged to the Pharisees** (Lk 14:1).

Once seated, however, a conflict arose:

> **While [Jesus] was speaking, a Pharisee invited him to dinner; so he went in and sat down at table. The Pharisee was amazed to see that he did not first wash before dinner. And the Lord said to him,** *Now you Pharisees wash the outside of the cup and the dish, but inside you are full of extortion and wickedness. You fools!* (Lk 11:37–40).

Word got around that Jesus and his disciples did not wash their hands before dinner, and the Pharisees questioned Jesus on the subject:

> **Then Pharisees and scribes came to Jesus from Jerusalem and said, "Why do your disciples transgress the tradition . . . [and] not wash their hands when they eat." He answered them,** *And why do you transgress the commandment of God for the sake of your tradition? . . . You hypocrites! . . .* **And he called the people . . . and said to them,** *Hear and Under-*

stand: not what goes into the mouth defiles a man,
but what comes of the mouth, this defiles a man
(Mt 15:1–11).

Then the disciples came and . . . Peter said to him,
"Explain the parable to us." And [Jesus] said, *Do*
you not see that whatever goes into the mouth passes
into the stomach, and is evacuated. But what comes
out of the mouth proceeds from the heart, and this
defiles a man. For out of the heart come evil
thoughts. . . . These are what defile a man; but to eat
with unwashed hands does not defile a man
(Mt 15:12–20).

The Jewish custom of washing hands had no basis in knowledge of public health. It was merely a Pharisaic tradition, a
tradition that Jesus did not like. His reason was that washing
the hands before eating did not wash the heart. Evil words
defiled a man; but eating without washing hands did not.

Although clean hands as well as clean dishes, do not assure
righteousness, neither do dirty hands. Dirty hands do, however, spread disease. The Pharisees did not know that; that was
not discovered until the 19th century. But if Jesus had been
sent by God—if Jesus were God!—he surely would have
known that. But he didn't. Instead Jesus made a statement
that appeared to carry a noble sentiment, but did not improve
mankind's spiritual health, and had a disastrous effect upon the
public health. During the Middle Ages, when great popula-
tions of Europe were decimated by plagues and epidemics,
more Jews than Christians seemed to survive. The church accused the Jews of having made a pact with Satan. But the
greater survival rate of the Jews had nothing to do with Satan.
If it was real, it probably was associated with the Pharisaic tradition of frequent hand washing.

Jewish physicians enjoyed an extraordinary reputation during the Middle Ages, probably because, with no more scientific knowledge than Christian physicians, they washed their hands between patients. Resistance to hand washing among Christian physicians continues to this day. To acquiesce would be to acknowledge that the Pharisees were right and Jesus was wrong.

GUESTS TO BE INVITED TO A DINNER PARTY AND TURNING THE OTHER CHEEK

Jesus taught which guests a host should invite to a dinner party:

> *When you give a dinner or a banquet, do not invite friends, relatives, or rich neighbors lest they also invite you in return and you be repaid. When you give a feast, invite the poor, the maimed, the lame, and the blind, and you will be blessed because they cannot repay you. You will be repaid at the resurrection of the just* (Lk 14:12–14).

Jesus probably based that advice partly in self-interest and partly on the Pharisees' extraordinarily generous treatment of him. The Pharisees continued to invite Jesus to dinner, even though they knew in advance that he would not wash his hands and that he would insult them. It was the Pharisees who turned the other cheek, a teaching they learned—and Jesus probably learned it there, too—from the "Old Law": **Give your cheek to the smiter and take his insults** (Lam 3:27–30).

THE PREACHER AND TEACHER

JESUS OF NAZARETH, PREACHER AND TEACHER

John the Baptist went about preaching: **Repent for the Kingdom of heaven is at hand!** (Mt 3:6). Jesus of Nazareth preached the same message: *Repent for the Kingdom of heaven is at hand!* (Mt 4:17). Today on street corners in many cities of the world, people are still preaching that message.

Jesus told the apostles that preaching was his purpose in life:

> *Let us move on to the next town so that I can preach there, too, because that is the reason I came out* (Mk 1:38–39).

That is the reason I came out. If that is the reason, when did it occur to Jesus that he was more than a preacher?

ENJOYMENT OF LIFE

The Hebrew Scriptures teach joy and love of life, but Jesus taught despair and hatred of life.

Hebrew Scriptures:

> **I have set before you life and death . . . choose life, that you and your descendants may live, loving the Lord [YHVH] your God. . . . For that means life to you and length of days** (Deut 30:4–20).

> **I know that there is nothing better for men than to be happy, and to enjoy themselves all the days of their lives. That, too, is God's gift to man** (Eccles 3:10–13).

> **I command enjoyment; for man has no better thing under the sun that to eat and drink and enjoy himself** (Eccles 8:15).

> **Go eat your bread with enjoyment and drink your wine with a merry heart.   For God approves it!** (Eccles 9:7–8).

Jesus:

> *Woe unto you with full stomachs now, for you shall hunger.   Woe unto you that laugh, for you shall mourn and weep* (Lk 6:17–25).

> *He who loves his life loses it, and he who hates his life in this world will keep it for eternal life* (Jn 12:25).

Jesus did not enjoy life. He was joyless, "a man of sorrows," who never laughed or danced or sang—except as he is depicted in Broadway musicals.

LOVE YOUR NEIGHBOR BUT HATE YOURSELF, YOUR FAMILY, AND THE WORLD

Although Jesus of Nazareth preached love, he rarely practiced it, whereas he also preached hate and often practiced that. Jesus preached mercy and forgiveness, but he often was spiteful and pitiless.

At first Jesus taught the importance of love. He called **Love your neighbor as yourself** (Lev 19:18) one of the two greatest commandments of the Hebrew Scriptures (Mt 19:19; 22:39; Mk 12:31; 12:33; Lk 10:29). He gave a variant of that commandment to his friends and called it a "new" commandment: *A new commandment I give to you, that you love one another; even as I have loved you* (Jn 13:34). There was nothing "new" about it. Friends normally love their friends. The very word *friend* in Greek and Latin is derived from the word *love*.

Despite his early preaching on love, Jesus changed his mind. Hatred became an absolute requirement for being a disciple:

> *If anyone comes to me and does not hate his own father and mother and wife and children and brothers and sisters—yes, and even his own life!—he cannot be my disciple* (Mt 14:26–33; Lk 14:26).

A man wanting to become a disciple made only one request, that Jesus allow him enough time to bury his father. Jesus denied the request and said contemptuously, *Leave the dead to bury their own dead* (Lk 9:60). Another man wanting to become a disciple requested that Jesus allow him just enough time to say good-bye to his family. Jesus denied the request:

> **A man wanted to become one of Jesus' disciples and said, "I will follow you, Lord. But first, let me go home to say good-bye to my family." Jesus replied,** *No man who says he wants to be a disciple of mine and looks back is fit for the Kingdom of God* (Lk 9:61–62).

God loves the world:

> **For God so loved the world that he gave his only son** (Jn 3:16).

But Jesus hated the world:

> *I have come to set fire to the earth and how I wish it were already in flames!* (Lk 12:49).

John confirming Jesus wrote:

> **If anyone loves the world, love for the Father is not in him** (1 Jn 2:15).

Jesus taught that self-hatred was an essential requirement to obtain eternal life:

> *The man who loves himself is lost, but he who hates himself in this world will be kept safe for eternal life* (Jn 12:25).

"JESUS LOVES YOU"

Those who would convert me frequently say, "Jesus loves you." Jesus doesn't love me. Jesus hardly loves anyone:

> *If anyone will not receive you or listen to your words, shake off the dust from your feet as you leave that house or that town. Truly I say unto you that on Judgment Day, Sodom and Gomorra shall receive a lighter sentence than that town* (Mt 10:12–15).

> *Woe to you, scribes and Pharisees, hypocrites! . . . Woe to you, blind guides! . . . Blind fools! . . . Blind men! . . . Serpents. Brood of vipers. How are you to escape being sentenced in hell!* (Mt 23).

> *You Pharisees! . . . You fools!* **In reply to this, one of the lawyers said, "Master, when you say things like this, you insult us, too."** *Yes, you lawyers! It is no better for you!* (Lk 11:39–48).

> *But as for these enemies of mine who did not want me to be their king, bring them here and slay them before me* (Lk 19:27).

Jesus *loves* me?

THREATS

Jesus issued threats. Threats incite fear. And fear is the very opposite of love. Threats are designed to gain absolute control and undivided loyalty. They are among the principal weapons of the tyrant. Jesus threatened:

> *No one comes to the Father but by me* (Jn 14:6).

> *He who does not believe will be condemned* (Mk 16:16).

TO LOVE OR TO HATE ENEMIES

Jesus said:

> *You have heard that it was said you shall love your neighbor and hate your enemy. But I say to you, Love your enemies* (Mt 5:43–44).

Jesus' source for "love your neighbor" was the Old Testament :

> **Love your neighbor** (Lev 19:18).

And Jesus' source for "love your enemies" was also the Old Testament:

> **When the King of Israel was face to face with his Syrian enemies, he said to Elisha the prophet, "Father, shall I slay them? Shall I slay them?" And Elisha answered, "You shall not slay them. Would you slay those whom you have taken captive with your sword and with your bow? Set bread and water before them that they may eat and drink and then let them return to their own king." So the King of Israel prepared for his enemies a great feast. And**

when they had eaten and drunk, he sent them away to return to their master (2 Kings 67:21–23).

Do not say, "I will repay evil with evil" (Prov 20:22).

Do not rejoice when your enemy falls (Prov 24:17).

If your enemy is hungry, give him bread to eat. And if he is thirsty, give him water to drink (Prov 25:21).

What then was Jesus' source for "hate your enemy"? Jesus taught:

And if anyone will not receive you . . . . it shall be more tolerable on the day of judgment for the land of Sodom and Gomorah than for that town (Mt 10:14–15; cf. Lk 10:10–12).

And you, Capernaum, will you be exalted to heaven? You shall be brought down to Hades (Mt 11:23).

Woe to you, scribes and Pharisees, hypocrites! . . . You serpents, you brood of vipers, how are you to escape being sentenced to hell? (Mt 23:29–33).

He who does not believe will be condemned (Mk 16:16).

But as for these enemies of mine who did not want me to be their king, bring them here and slay them before me (Lk 19:27).

There is no better example of "hate your enemy" in the entire bible than that. When Jesus preached, *You have heard that it was said . . . hate your enemy*, his source was none other than himself!

LOVE, MERCY, FORGIVENESS

The church speaks as if Jesus invented love, mercy, and forgiveness, but he learned all three of those attributes of grace from the "Old Law":

> The Lord [YHVH] our God is merciful and gracious, long suffering and abundant in goodness and truth, keeping mercy unto the thousandth generation, forgiving iniquity and transgression and sin (Ex 34:6–7).

> The Lord [YHVH] your God is a merciful God (Deut 4:31).

> O Lord [YHVH] God of Israel . . . Hear the prayers of your servant and your people Israel. . . . And when you hear, forgive. . . (1 Kings 8:23–43).

> Lord [YHVH]. . . . You have forgiven the guilt of your people and put away all their sins (Ps 85:1–3).

> As a father shows compassion on his children,
> so the Lord [YHVH] is compassionate
> to those who revere him.
> for he knows what we are made of.
> He remembers that we are dust.
> As for man, his days are like grass.
> He is like a flower in the field.
> The wind passes over it, and it is gone.
> And the very earth that sustained it
> does not remember where it grew.
> But the steadfast love of the Lord [YHVH]
> is from everlasting to everlasting (Ps 103:13–17).

> If you, O Lord [YHVH], should mark iniquities,
> Lord [YHVH], who could stand? (Ps 130:3).

Thus says the Lord [YHVH], though your sins be as scarlet, they shall become as white as snow (Is 1:18).

O Israel. . . .
I have swept away your transgressions like a cloud and your sins like mist.
Return to me for I have redeemed you (Is 44:22).

Thus says the Lord [YHVH],
Let the wicked forsake his ways, and his schemes.
Let him return to the Lord [YHVH]
that he may have mercy on him
and to our God for he will abundantly pardon him
(Is 55:6–7).

Come back to me, apostate Israel, says YHVH.
I will no longer look on you in anger,
for my love is unfailing. . . .
I will not be angry forever. . . .
Come back to me, apostate children (Jer 3:11–14).

Have I any desire, says the Lord God,
for the death of a wicked man?
Would I not rather that he mend his ways and live?
(Ezek 18:21–23).

What does the Lord [YHVH] require of you
but to do justice and to love kindness
and to walk humbly with your God? (Mic 6:8).

Jesus learned forgiveness also from the Pharisees:

> **For transgressions between man and God, the Day of Atonement effects atonement; but for transgressions between a man and his fellow man, the Day of Atonement effects atonement only if he has reconciled with his fellow man** (*The Mishnah*, Yoma 8:9).

Jesus said it this way:

> *If, while bringing your gift to the altar, you suddenly remember that your brother has a grievance against you, leave your gift by the altar. First go and make peace with your brother, and then come back and offer your gift* (Mt 5:23–24).

FORGIVENESS OF ADULTERY

The Jews of Jesus' time must have considered Mary an adulteress, but the gospels do not mention it. Although one of the Ten Commandments is **Thou shall not commit adultery**, Hosea speaking for God said: **I shall not punish your daughters for playing harlots, nor your sons' wives for their adultery** (Hos 4:14). For the famous but spurious story of Jesus forgiving the adulteress, see the Novation Heresy, pp. 461–2.

THE "SACRAMENT" OF MARRIAGE

The church teaches that Jesus instituted the "sacrament" of marriage, but Jesus disdained marriage, and discouraged it for anyone wanting eternal life:

> *The people of this age marry, but those accounted worthy to attain the new age and the resurrection from the dead do not marry* (Lk 20:34).

Jesus did not institute the sacrament of marriage. Jesus instituted the sacrament of the single life.

"THE HOLY FAMILY"

The church calls Jesus' family "the Holy Family" and adores it, but Jesus did not call his family "holy" or adore it.

The so-called holy family was highly dysfunctional. Jesus lived at home until his early thirties, and expressed no interest in women during that time. While living at home, Jesus practiced carpentry, his father's trade, but there is no indication of a warm relationship between the father and son. Jesus said, ***And call no man your father on earth, for you have one father who is in heaven*** (Mt 23:9). Mary and Joseph also had a distant relationship. No words of tenderness are exchanged between them. Joseph disappears long before the crucifixion, and no one knows what happened to him—or cares. He is not missed by Jesus or Mary, the church, or anyone else.

Jesus' interactions with his mother were universally hostile; he did not have a kind word to say to her or about her. At the wedding of Cana, Jesus called Mary not *Mother* or *Mama* or even *Mary*. He called her, ***Woman!*** (Jn 2:4).

And what did Jesus' family think of him?

> **Even Jesus' brothers did not believe in him** (Jn 7:2–5).

> **When his friends heard it they went out to seize him, for they said, "He is beside himself"** (Mk 3:21).

"He is beside himself" is the RSV translation, but it is an understatement. The Greek is: ἐξέστη (*He is out of his mind*). The Latin is: ***in furorem versus est*** (*He is raving mad*).

JESUS AND LUST

Jesus of Nazareth disallowed our most basic needs and feelings. He taught that the man with lust in his heart was as evil as the man who commits adultery and would be similarly punished. Jesus gave the preventive: If lust arises from seeing a beautiful woman, then blind oneself. If lust provokes one to masturbate, then cut off the hand or testicles. It was better to lose an eye or a hand or the testicles than to go to hell:

> *You have heard . . . Thou shalt not commit adultery, but I say to you that anyone who even looks at a woman with lust in his eyes has already committed adultery with her in his heart. If your right eye makes you sin, pluck out your eye and throw it away! It is better to lose only one part of your body than that your entire body be thrown into hell! If your right hand makes you sin, cut it off, and throw it away! It is better to lose only one part of your body than that your entire body go to hell* (Mt 5:27–30).

> *[T]here are eunuchs who have made themselves eunuchs for the sake of the kingdom of heaven. He who is able to receive this, let him receive it* (Mt 19:10–12).

Jesus did not blind himself, nor cut off a hand. Did he make himself a eunuch for the Kingdom of Heaven? The gospels do not say. But neither do they say that Jesus advocated virginity or continence. Nonetheless, in 1965, Pope Paul VI, decreed:

> Perfect and perpetual continence for the sake of the Kingdom of Heaven was recommended by Christ. . . .
> By preserving virginity or celibacy for the sake of the Kingdom of Heaven (Mt 19:12), priests are consecrated in a new and excellent way to Christ. They more readily cling to him . . . espousing one husband . . . presenting themselves as a chaste virgin to Christ (2 Cor 11:2) (*Presbyterorum Ordinis* [On the Ministry and Life of Priests]).

Think of all those virgin priests clinging to their husband, Jesus Christ!

JESUS AND ANGER

Jesus taught that anger was a sin of the same magnitude as murder and would be similarly punished:

> *You have heard. . . .* **"You shall not kill; and whoever kills shall be liable to judgment."** *. . . but I say to you that anyone who is angry with his brother must be brought to judgment* (Mt 5:21–22).

And yet, Jesus had violent outbursts of anger:

> **Jesus went up to Jerusalem. In the temple he found . . . the money-changers at their business. And making a whip of cords, he drove them all . . . out of the temple; and he poured out the coins . . . and overturned their tables. And he told those who sold the pigeons,** *Take these things away; you shall not make my Father's house a house of trade* (Jn 2:13–16).

NAME-CALLING: "FOOLS"

Jesus decried insults, particularly invectives or name-calling. He specifically warned that anyone who called another "Fool!" would go to hell:

> *If a man insults his brother, he must answer for it in a court of law; but whoever says "You fool!" must answer for it in hell fire* (Mt 5:22).
>
> *I tell you that on Judgment Day men will be held accountable for every careless word they uttered. By your words you will be justified and by your words you will be damned* (Mt 12:36).

By his own teaching, Jesus condemned himself to hell:

> *But woe to you, scribes and Pharisees, hypocrites! . . .*
> *Woe to you, scribes and Pharisees, hypocrites! . . .*
> *Woe to you, blind guides . . . blind fools! . . . blind*
> *men! . . . Woe to you, scribes and Pharisees, hypo-*
> *crites! . . . You blind guides! . . . Woe to you, scribes*
> *and Pharisees, hypocrites! . . . Woe to you, . . . scribes*
> *and Pharisees, hypocrites! . . . Woe to you, scribes*
> *and Pharisees, hypocrites! You serpents, you brood of*
> *vipers, how are you going to escape being sentenced to*
> *hell?* (Mt 23:13–33).

> *Now you Pharisees wash the outside of the cup and*
> *the dish, but inside you are full of extortion and wick-*
> *edness. You fools!* (Lk 11:37–40).

NAME-CALLING: "DOGS"

Jesus reserved a particularly insulting invective for the gentiles. He called them "dogs!"

> *It is not right to take bread for the Children [of Israel]*
> *and throw it to the dogs!* (Mt 15:23–26).

If the King of the Jews calls the gentiles "dogs," what must the "dogs" think of themselves—and of him? That surely is a source of Christian antisemitism.

Jesus taught his disciples: *Go not into the way of the gentiles* (Mt 10:5). What was it about the gentiles that Jesus disliked? He probably was offended by their disdain of the Law, especially the Sabbath, circumcision, and the dietary laws. But there had to have been more about the gentiles that upset him. Most of the Jews of Judea during the Roman occupation were poor, whereas the Romans were rich. Jesus had to have seen domestic slaves of the Romans at the market place selecting for their masters the choicest fish, poultry, lamb, wine, and produce, and choosing the finest fabrics for clothing. Jesus was contemptuous of that, for he said:

> ***Do not concern yourself with, "What are we going to eat?" or "What are we going to drink?" or "What are we going to wear?" These are the kinds of things that concern the gentiles*** (Mt 6:31–33).

Despite Jesus' contempt of the "dogs," they could win him over by flattery. Take the case of the Canaanite woman who wanted Jesus to cure her daughter. At first Jesus refused even to talk to her. After much imploring on her part, Jesus explained that he was sent only to the children of Israel who sit at the Master's table and eat the Master's bread. The Master cannot waste his time on the "dogs":

> **A Canaanite woman . . . came shouting. "Sir, have pity on me, son of David. My daughter is tormented by a devil!" But Jesus did not say even one word to her in reply. His disciples came and begged him, "Send her away! See how she comes shouting after us!" And Jesus said to her, *I was sent to the lost sheep of Israel, and only to them.* But the woman fell at his feet and implored him, "Help me, sir!" To this Jesus replied, *It is not right to take bread for the children and throw it to the dogs!* (Mt 15:23–26).**

At this point, the Canaanite woman gives Jesus a disarming answer. She points out that no matter how carefully the children eat their bread, a few crumbs always fall from the table to the floor, where the dogs may eat them:

> **"Yes, Lord, yet even the dogs eat the crumbs that fall from their master's table"** (Mt 15:27).

Jesus melts:

> **Then Jesus answered her,** *O woman, great is your*
> *faith! Be it done for you as you desire!* **And her**
> **daughter was healed instantly** (Mt 15:21–28; cf.
> Mk 7:26–29).

DEMONIZATION

To demonize people is name-calling of the worst sort. Yet
on one occasion Jesus became so angry at a group of Jews he
called them *sons of Satan* (Jn 8:44). On another occasion Jesus became so angry at Peter, he called him *Satan* (Mt 16:22).
By such words, Jesus condemned himself. It is worth noting
that the church believes Jesus when he calls Jews "sons of Satan" but pays no attention when he calls Peter "Satan." Is that
fair?

GOD WILL PROVIDE

Jesus taught that men had no need to plant, raise crops, and
harvest; sheer sheep; or provide shelter for themselves; for
God would provide the necessities of life:

> *Consider the ravens. They neither sow nor reap.*
> *They have neither silo nor barn. Yet God feeds them.*
> *You are worth far more than the birds* (Lk 12:24–25).

> *And why are you anxious about clothing? Consider*
> *the lilies of the field, how they grow; they neither toil*
> *nor spin* (Mt 6:28; Lk 12:27).

That advice is not only completely unrealistic but also conflicts
with the Old Testament story of Joseph in Egypt. The moral of
that story was that if one stores up during a time of plenty,

there will be adequate provisions during a time of famine. "God helps those who help themselves" goes the adage. Jesus taught the opposite: Why bother when God will provide for you? In short, Jesus taught, Be a bum!

ON BOTANY

Jesus had no understanding of science, specifically botany. He did not understand that a seed was a living thing. He thought when a seed was planted, it died; that it returned to life after being in the earth for several days, whereupon it sprouted and bore a new plant that went on to flower and fruit. Jesus made an analogy between the sprouting of a "dead" seed and the resurrection of a corpse:

> ***Truly, truly, I say to you, unless a kernel of corn falls into the earth and dies, it remains alone; but if it dies, it bears much fruit*** (Jn 12:24).

With no understanding of simple botany would Jesus have any understanding of the universe? Would he have understood genetics, physics, or chemistry? Big Bang? $E = mc^2$? The expanding universe? Quantum mechanics? The uncertainty principal? Would Jesus have understood the calculus or probability theory? Copernican and Galilean astronomy? There is no evidence that Jesus thought any differently about the world from the ordinary Jews of his day—that the earth was flat, that the sun traveled around the earth, that the earth was the center of the universe, and the universe was about 3,700 years old. How in the world can Jesus be God?

THE GOLDEN RULE

Jesus gave what the church calls "the golden rule":

> ***And as you wish that men would do to you, do so to them*** (Lk 6:31).

This is a variant of:

> **Love your neighbor as yourself** (Lev 19:18).

Jesus called this commandment one of the two greatest commandments:

> **Love (ἀγάπη) [*agape*] your neighbor as yourself** (Mt 19:19; 22:39; Mk 12:31; 12:33; Lk 10:29).

However, the golden rule is not as "golden" as it sounds. Cynics have suggested that it was used to justify the sexual orgies and licentiousness of early Christians, vividly described in the heathen and patristic literature, and that it remains the rule for those who engage in sexual promiscuity and molestation of children. Peter wryly observed:

> **[L]ove (ἀγάπη) [*agape*] covers a multitude of sins** (1 Pet 4:8).

Paul came closer to defining a golden rule:

> **Love (ἀγάπη) [*agape*] does no wrong to a neighbor** (Rom 13:10).

This is similar to the version of Hillel, the rabbi who lived around the same time as Jesus:

> That which is hateful to you, do not do to your fellow
> (*Babylonian Talmud*, Shabbat 31a).

Hippocrates applied a similar precept in his "Oath of a Physician" to the relationship of a physician to his patient: "I will use treatment to help the sick according to my ability and judgment, but never with a view to injury and wrong-doing" and "Into whatsoever houses I enter, I will enter to help the sick, and I will abstain from all intentional wrong-doing and harm" (translation by W. H. S. Jones, *Hippocrates*, Loeb Classical Library, vol. 1, Harvard University Press, Cambridge, MA, AD 1923). Hippocrates's precept is usually stated simply as, "Do no harm." To make the precept universal, it needs to apply to everyone's responsibility to neighbors and strangers. "Do no harm" is the most love one can realistically give to—or expect from—a neighbor or a stranger.

PARABLES

The apostles were puzzled by Jesus' parables, so they asked him to clarify them. His answer surely astonished them, for it is astonishing still. Jesus said that the purpose of his parables was not to teach, but to mislead nonbelievers so they will not repent, will not be forgiven, and will not go to heaven! In short, the purpose of Jesus' parables was to ensure that nonbelievers go to hell!

> *To you has been given the secret of the Kingdom of*
> *God. But for outsiders, everything is in parables so*
> *that they may look but not see, so that they may hear*
> *but not understand, in order that they may not repent*
> *and be forgiven* (Mk 4:11–12).
>
> *You have been given the secrets of the Kingdom of*
> *God, but everyone else has only parables so that they*

> *may look but not see, hear but not understand*
> (Lk 8:9–10).

> *I came into the world that those who do not see may
> see, and those who see may become blind* (Jn 9:39).

The disciples remained puzzled:

> **Some of Jesus' disciples said to one another, "What
> does he mean?"** (Jn 16:17).

> **No one [of the disciples] at table understood what
> Jesus meant** (Jn 12:28).

Jesus responded:

> *You don't understand this parable? Then how will
> you ever understand any parable!* (Mk 4:13).

> **His disciples asked him about the parable. And he
> said to them, *"Then are you also without understand-
> ing?"*** (Mk 7:17–18).

> *Why don't you understand me?* (Jn 8:43).

Indeed.

MIRACLES

MIRACLES

Jesus began his ministry as a preacher, and the earliest gospel was a collection of Jesus' sayings, among which were denouncements of miracles. Jesus wanted people to believe in God without miracles, which he considered the evil work of false christs and false prophets:

> *False christs and false prophets will arise and show great signs and do miracles, so as to lead astray, if that is possible, even the elect. Lo! I have warned you!* (Mt 24:24–25).

The gentiles, however, would not believe in Jesus without miracles. So miracles were invented to please them. The gentiles did not have an expectation of eternal peace on earth, and so they would not notice that the greatest of miracles—the one the Jews expected most—was missing from Jesus' roster.

The Roman historian Tacitus reported the miracles performed by the Emperor Vespasian:

> Many marvels occurred to mark the favour of heaven . . . toward him [Vespasian]. . . . [A blind man] threw himself before Vespasian's knees, praying him with groans to cure his blindness . . . and he besought the emperor to deign to moisten his cheeks and eyes with his spittle. Another [man] whose hand was useless . . . begged Caesar to step and trample on it. Vespasian at first ridiculed these appeals. . . ; then, when the [two] men persisted. . . . [he relented]. Such perhaps was the wish of the gods, and it might be that the emperor had been chosen for this divine service; in any case, if a cure were obtained, the glory would be Caesar's. . . . So Vespasian, believing his good fortune was capable

> of anything and that nothing was any longer incredible,
> with a smiling countenance, and amid intense excite-
> ment on the part of the bystanders, did as he was asked
> to do. The hand was instantly restored to use, and the
> day again shone for the blind man. Both facts are told
> by eye-witnesses even now when falsehood brings no
> reward (Tacitus, *Histories*, 4:81, pp. 158–161).

Those who believed that the Roman Emperor performed such miracles expected no less from the new Jewish God.

Some of Jesus' miracles are tawdry, such as turning water into wine (Jn 2:1–11) and retrieving a silver coin from a fish's mouth (Mt 17:27). Some are wanton and cruel, such as commanding demons to enter a herd of swine and then commanding the swine to run off a cliff (Mt 8:30–32; Mk 5:11–13; Lk 8:32–33), or destroying a fig tree because it was not bearing figs out of season (Mk 11:12–21).

Turning water into wine was one of Jesus' most famous miracles (Jn 2:1–11). Jesus and his mother are invited to a wedding in the town of Cana, and during the banquet the wine runs out. Mary tells Jesus to turn water into wine. He becomes angry at her and tells her to mind her own business. But Mary's power over her son triumphs, and Jesus obeys. The church considers this a great miracle, but how was humanity served by it? It resembles a magician's trick. What did that incident show other than how powerful Mary was and how weak her son was by comparison? And, perhaps, how much Mary enjoyed wine? The Messiah was expected to inaugurate peace on earth, not do a cheap stunt to satisfy his powerful mother.

Of all Jesus' miracles, the miracle of the fig tree best illustrates how spiteful and violent Jesus could be:

> **And seeing in the distance a fig tree in leaf, he went
> to see if he could find anything on it. When he came**

> **to it, he found nothing but leaves, for it was not the season for figs. And he said to it,** *May no one ever eat fruit from you again. . . .* **[Next] morning, [the apostles] saw the fig tree withered away to its roots. And Peter said to him, "Master, look! The fig tree which you cursed has withered"** (Mk 11:12–21).

Why didn't Jesus command the fig tree to bear figs instead of cursing and destroying it? Making a tree bear fruit out of season would have been truly miraculous. Anyone can destroy a tree.

Among Jesus' so-called lofty miracles was feeding a huge crowd with a few loaves and fishes. This was based on a similar miracle performed by the prophet Elisha (2 Kings 4:38–44). But what good was it to provide one good meal for the poor, when afterward they returned to their hunger and abject misery? Jesus taught that we must resign ourselves to the plight of the poor, and let God provide for them, even as he provides for the birds and wildflowers. But the Messiah was expected to bring an end to human misery forever.

Jesus told people to perform a miracle so great that not even he attempted it:

> *I tell you, if anyone says to this mountain,* **"Be lifted up from your place and hurled into the sea"** *and has no inward doubts but believes that what he says will happen, it will happen!"* (Mk 11:23–24).

Leveling mountains was one of the signs of the Messiah (Is 40:4; Lk 3:5). Why didn't Jesus hurl a mountain into the sea? Perhaps he didn't have enough faith.

Not bringing peace on earth and not hurling a mountain into the sea resulted by default in the raising of Lazarus from the dead becoming Jesus' most famous miracle:

> **After Lazarus was dead, Martha said to Jesus,**
> **"Lord, if you had been here, my brother would not**
> **have died." . . . Then Mary said, "O Lord, if you**
> **had been here, my brother would not have died"**
> (Jn 11:21–32).

Curing a sick man is not nearly so impressive as raising a dead
one. So Jesus allowed Lazarus to die in order to resurrect him
so that the son of God may be glorified (Jn 11:4). The Jews
were not impressed. Others had raised the dead before Jesus
and still others would do so after him.

Before Jesus, Elijah had raised the dead:

> **The son of the woman of the house [in which Elijah**
> **lived] became ill; and his illness was grave, and he**
> **stopped breathing. . . . And Elijah said to the**
> **woman, "Give me your son." And Elijah took the**
> **boy from her breast and carried the boy upstairs**
> **into his own bedroom and laid him on his own bed.**
> **And Elijah cried to the Lord, "O Lord my God, hast**
> **thou brought disaster upon the widow in whose**
> **house I am living by slaying her son?" Then Elijah**
> **stretched himself upon the child three times and**
> **cried to the Lord, "O Lord my God, let this child's**
> **soul come into him again." And the Lord heard Eli-**
> **jah's voice, and the soul of the child reentered him,**
> **and he came back to life** (1 Kings 17:17–22).

Before Jesus, Elisha, the disciple of Elijah, had also raised the
dead:

> **When Elisha entered the house, there was the boy,**
> **dead on the bed where he had been laid. Elisha**
> **went into the room, shut the door, and prayed to the**
> **Lord. Then, getting on the bed, he lay upon the**
> **child, putting his mouth to the child's mouth, his**

eyes to his eyes, his hands to his hands, and as he pressed upon him, the child's body grew warm. . . . and the boy opened his eyes (2 Kings 4:32–36).

After Jesus, Peter and Paul raised the dead:

There was at Joppa a disciple named Tabitha. . . . She fell sick and died. . . . Peter knelt and prayed, then turning to the corpse, he said, "Tabitha, rise!" And she opened her eyes (Acts 9:36–40).

And a young man . . . was sitting in the window. He sank into a deep sleep as Paul talked still longer; and . . . he fell down from the third story and was taken up dead. But Paul went down and bent over him, and embracing him said [to the watching crowd], "Do not be alarmed for his life is in him.". . . And they took the lad away alive (Acts 20:9–12).

The Greeks were impressed. Had the Jews been impressed, they would have attributed the miracle not to Paul but to God because the Jews attributed all miracles to God: After Jesus cured the paralyzed man, **the people were filled with awe at the sight, and praised God for granting such authority to men** (Mt 9:6–8). Regarding Jesus' own resurrection, Peter said, **God resurrected Jesus** (Acts 2:32).

It is important to note that Jesus said he raised Lazarus from the dead for the glory (Jn 11:4). Others who raised the dead made no such statement regarding their motivation. Was Jesus simply more honest than they? If so, was Jesus teaching that acts of kindness are not done altruistically but for the glory?

EXORCISM

The most futile of Jesus' miracles was exorcism. Jesus, knowing its futility, taught against exorcism, but no one paid attention, particularly when Jesus himself did not give up performing them. The problem with exorcism, according to Jesus, was that it succeeded only temporarily; in the end, it made matters worse, for the exorcised demon returned, bringing back with it seven more demons!

> *When an unclean spirit has gone out of a man, it passes about the desert seeking rest, but finds none. Then it says, "I will return to the house from which I came." And when it comes home, it finds it empty, swept clean and put in order. Then it goes and brings back with him seven other spirits more evil than himself, and they all enter and live there; and the final state of that man becomes worse than before* (Mt 12:43–45; Lk 11:24–26).

COMMANDING SECRECY

Jesus commanded those he cured before great throngs of people to keep the miracle a secret, which is quintessential false humility and hypocrisy, for public events cannot be kept secret:

> Jesus was followed by a great crowd. Once a leper approached him. . . . Jesus stretched out his hand, touched him, and said, . . . *Be clean!* And the man's leprosy was cured instantly. Then Jesus said to him, *Be sure to tell no one* (Mt 8:1–4).

> Jesus had many followers and he cured all who were ill; and he gave strict instructions that it was not to be made known (Mt 12:15–16).

> [The] president of the local synagogue . . . begged [Jesus] to come to his home because his only daughter . . . was dying. Jesus could hardly breathe for the crowds. . . . Even as the president was speaking, another man came to him with the message, "Your daughter is dead. Do not trouble Rabbi Jesus any further." But Jesus overheard and interjected, *Do not be afraid, but show faith, and she will be well.* . . . Jesus took the child's hand in his own and said, *Wake up, my child!* Her spirit returned to her, she got out of bed, and Jesus told them to give her a bite to eat. Her parents were astonished, but Jesus forbade them to tell anyone (Lk 8:38–56).

> Jesus forbade them to tell anyone. And the more he forbade them, the more they proclaimed it! (Mk 7:32–36).

PROCLAIMING LIBERTY

Jesus did many miracles, none of which benefited humanity. The Messiah was expected to bring peace on earth. And the Messiah was expected to proclaim liberty and set political prisoners free:

> The spirit of the Lord [YHVH] God is upon me, because the Lord [YHVH] has anointed me to bring good tidings . . . to proclaim liberty to the captives, and the opening of prison doors to those held captive (Is 61:1).

Jesus did not proclaim liberty, nor open a single prison door.

John the Baptist was arrested and imprisoned. Desperate, John sent Jesus a message asking whether Jesus was the Messiah who was expected to proclaim liberty and set political prisoners free. Here is Jesus' response:

> **Now when John heard in prison about the deeds of the Christ [the blind are made to see, the lame to walk, lepers are cleansed, the deaf hear, the dead are resurrected, the poor hear good news preached], he sent word by [his] disciples and said to him, "Are you he who is to come, or shall we look for another?" And Jesus answered,** *Go and tell John. . . : the blind receive their sight and the lame walk, lepers are cleansed and the deaf heard, and the dead are raised up, and the poor have good news preached to them* (Mt 11:2–6).

Jesus ignores John's urgent question and speaks about miracles irrelevant to John. Why? Because it is easier to raise the dead than to open a prison door!

> **Now when he [Jesus] heard that John had been arrested, he withdrew into Galilee** (Mt 4:12; cf. Mk 1:14).

Galilee was in the opposite direction from John's prison. Why did Jesus abandon John, particularly when Jesus considered him the greatest man alive, greater than himself, and equal to the prophet Elijah? Was it not because Jesus was so ashamed of not being able to set John free that Jesus ran as far from John as possible? Jesus lacked the courage to visit John in prison, even though he taught that not visiting someone in prison was a sin so grave its reward was the fires of hell:

> *When the Son of man comes in his glory . . . then he will sit on his glorious throne. . . . Then the King will say to those at his right hand [the righteous], "Come, O blessed of my Father, inherit the kingdom. . . . I was in prison and you came to me." Then the righteous will answer him, "Lord . . . when did we see thee . . . in prison and visit thee?" And the King will*

answer them, "Truly, I say to you, as you did it to one of the least of these my brothers you did it to me."

Then [the Son of man] will say to those at his left hand [evil men], Depart from me, you cursed, into the eternal fire prepared for the devil and his angels; for I *was . . . in prison and you did not visit me.* **Then they also will answer, "Lord, when did we see thee . . . in prison, and did not minister to thee?"** *Then he will answer them, Truly I say to you, as you did it not to one of the least of these, you did it not to me. And they will go away into eternal punishment*
(Mt 25:31–46).

By not proclaiming liberty and by not setting John free, Jesus showed John that Jesus was not the Messiah. By not visiting John in prison, Jesus, according to his own teachings, was going to hell.

HOW JESUS COULD HAVE BENEFITED HUMANITY

Jesus' miracles had no lasting effect. They did not benefit mankind or alleviate human misery. Most of the miracles were performed on individuals. None were performed on the community of Israel or on all of humanity. Jesus did them not for altruistic reasons but for self-promotion and glorification. He did them for show.

Jesus could have alleviated human misery without doing a single miracle, simply by commanding the people to wash their hands and by not negating this tradition of the Jews. Teaching that alone would have saved countless lives by minimizing the transmission of communicable diseases.

WAS JESUS THE MESSIAH?

PROPHECIES AND SIGNS

At the time of Jesus of Nazareth, most Jews expected the coming of the Messiah. Such expectations were based principally on signs contained in the ancient prophecies concerning an end to war and the revelation of the glory of the Lord [YHVH] and his kingdom on earth:

> **Men shall beat their swords into plowshares,**
> **and their spears into pruning hooks.**
> **Nation shall not lift up sword against nation,**
> **neither shall they learn war anymore**
> (Is 2:4; Mic 4:3).

> **And the glory of the Lord [YHVH] shall be revealed**
> **and all mankind shall see it together** (Is 40:5).

Jesus at first scoffed at such signs, even as he was beginning to think of himself as the expected Messiah:

> *An evil and adulterous generation seeks for a sign*
> (Mt 12:39; 16:4; cf. Lk 11:29).

> [T]he disciples came to [Jesus] privately, saying, "Tell us . . . what will be the sign of your coming and of the close of the age?" And Jesus answered them, *Take heed that no one leads you astray. For many will come . . . saying, "I am the Christ," and they will lead many astray. . . . And many false prophets will arise and lead many astray. . . . [I]f anyone says to you, "Lo, here is the Christ!" or "There he is!" do not believe it. For false Christs and false prophets will arise and show great signs and wonders, so as to lead astray, if possible, even the elect* (Mt 24:3–24).

[The] Pharisees came and began to argue with Jesus, seeking from him a sign from heaven. . . . And he sighed deeply in his spirit and said, *Why does this generation seek a sign? Truly I say to you, no sign shall be given to this generation* (Mk 8:11–12).

Being asked by the Pharisees when the kingdom of God was coming, [Jesus] answered them, *The kingdom of God is not coming with signs* (Lk 17:20).

The Jews were expecting in the Messiah a herald on the mountain top announcing the good news (gospel) of the arrival of God's kingdom with eternal peace on earth. They were not expecting a messiah who would suffer and die, then rise again, or a messiah who would save them from their sins, or a messiah who was the only begotten son of God, or a messiah who was the incarnation of God.

TWENTY PROPHETIC SIGNS
BY WHICH TO RECOGNIZE THE MESSIAH

At least twenty prophecies or signs described in Hebrew Scriptures identified the Messiah:

1. MESSENGER OF THE GOOD NEWS—
THE GOSPEL OF PEACE ON EARTH

First and foremost, the Messiah will be the messenger of the good news (gospel) of everlasting peace on earth:

Men shall beat their swords into plowshares,
and their spears into pruning hooks.
Nation shall not lift up sword against nation,
neither shall they learn war anymore
(Is 2:4; Mic 4:3).

Thus says the Lord [YHVH]: I will abolish the bow, the sword, and war from the land; and I will make you go to sleep at night in safety (Hos 2:18).

[A]nd he shall be a man of peace (Mic 5:5).

Speak ye tenderly to Jerusalem. And cry unto her that her warfare is over (Is 40:1–2).

O thou that tellest good tidings [the gospel]
to Zion,
Get thee up into the high mountain;
O thou that tellest good tidings to Jerusalem,
Lift up thy voice with strength;
Lift it up, be not afraid;
Say unto the cities of Judah:
Behold your God! (Is 40:9–10).

How beautiful upon the mountains
are the feet of him
   who brings good tidings [the gospel],
who publishes peace,
who brings good tidings of good,
who publishes salvation,
who says to Zion, "Your God reigns!"
Hark! Your watchmen lift up their voice,
together they sing for joy,
for eye to eye they see
the return of the Lord [YHVH] to Zion!
Break forth together into singing (Is 52:7–10).

Behold, on the mountains the feet of him who brings good tidings, who proclaims peace! (Nah 1:15).

And he shall reconcile fathers to their children and children to their fathers (Mal 4:5).

But Jesus announced something different.   Jesus preached the contrary; he was not messianic but anti-messianic:

> *Do not think that I have come to bring peace on earth; I have not come to bring peace, but a sword.   For I have   come   to   set   a   man   against   his   father . . .* (Mt 10:34–5).

> *Do you think that I have come to give peace on earth? No, I tell tell you but rather division; for henceforth in one house there will be . . . divided . . . father against son, son against father . . . .* (Lk 12:51).

> *Nation will rise against nation* (Mt 24:7; Mk 13:8; Lk 21:10).

> *I have come to set fire to the earth and how I wish it were already in flames! . . .   Do you suppose I came to establish peace on earth?   No, indeed!   I have come to bring division!* (Lk 12:49).

2.   PEACE ON EARTH BEGINS WITH PEACE IN THE HOME

Peace on earth begins with peace in the home.   Should, however, a false messiah come who does not inaugurate peace in the home, and should the people believe that man is the Messiah, then God will utterly destroy the land:

> **And he shall reconcile fathers to their children and children to their fathers.   Otherwise, I shall come and smite the land with utter destruction** (Mal 4:5–6).

Jesus taught:

> *I have come to set a man against his father, a daughter against her mother, and a daughter-in-law against her mother-in-law. A man's enemies will be his own kindred* (Mt 10:34–36).

> *Henceforth in one house there will be five divided, three against two, two against three. Divided! Father against son, son against father, mother against daughter, daughter against mother, mother-in-law against daughter-in-law, daughter-in-law against mother-in-law* (Lk 12:49).

> *If anyone does not hate his own father and mother . . . he cannot be my disciple!* (Lk 14:26).

Accepting Malachi's prophecy, one could reasonably conclude that the utter destruction of the land of Judea came about because of the many Jews who believed in Jesus, not because of the many who rejected him.

3. WOLF AND LAMB DWELL IN PEACE

When the Messiah comes, the wolf will lie down with the lamb with no thought of devouring it. Indeed, all wild animals will become so tame that children will lead them on leashes just as they lead dogs and horses:

> **The wolf shall dwell with the lamb, and the leopard shall lie down with the kid, and the calf—even a fat calf—and the lion shall dwell together. And a little child shall lead them** (Is 11:6).

Those things did not happen with the coming of Jesus. It is apparently easier to raise the dead than to make wolves lose interest in eating lambs.

4. JUSTICE AND RIGHTEOUSNESS
The Messiah will not only inaugurate everlasting peace, but also everlasting justice and righteousness:

> **And there shall be peace everlasting . . . with justice and righteousness forever and ever** (Is 9:6–7).

> **Behold my servant, whom I uphold,**
> **my chosen, in whom my soul delights;**
> **I have put my Spirit upon him,**
> **he will bring forth justice to the nations** (Is 42:1).

Jesus had nothing to do with justice, and little to do with righteousness.

5. PROCLAIMING LIBERTY
When the Messiah comes, political prisoners will be set free:

> **The Lord [YHVH] has anointed me to bring good tidings [good news] to the afflicted . . . to proclaim liberty to captives, and the opening of the prison to those held captive** (Is 61:1).

Jesus did not proclaim liberty. He did not open a single prison door, and refused even to visit John the Baptist in prison.

6. A GREAT PRINCE OF ISRAEL
The Messiah will be a great prince of Israel:

>**A star shall come forth out of Jacob, and a scepter shall rise up out of Israel** (Num 24:17).

That is one prophecy stated two ways, each using metonymy as the figure of speech and both indicating the coming of a king of Israel. *Star* stands for a splendid person (similar to movie star), and *scepter* stands for a king.

Jesus of Nazareth fulfilled this prophecy for those who considered him"King of the Jews."

7. BORN IN BETHLEHEM
The Messiah will be born in Bethlehem:

>**And you, Bethlehem . . . out of you shall come forth a ruler for Israel. . . . and he shall be a man of peace** (Mic 5:2–5).

To judge by his name, Jesus of Nazareth's hometown was not Bethlehem but Nazareth, but there were no prophecies concerning Nazareth. Nathanael, while considering whether to become an apostle learned that Jesus' hometown was Nazareth, not Bethlehem, asked:

>**Can anything good come out of Nazareth?** (Jn 1:46).

Others asked:

>**Has not the scriptures said that the Christ . . . comes from Bethlehem. . . ?** (Jn 7:40–42).

Being born in Bethlehem would not prove that one was the Messiah, but not being born there would prove one was not the Messiah. So church redactors changed Jesus' hometown from Nazareth to Bethlehem. In spite of the evidence supporting Nazareth as Jesus' hometown, let us assume Jesus of Nazareth was born in Bethlehem, in which case he would fulfill this prophecy. But what of the second part of the prophecy? Was Jesus a man of peace? From the messianic point of view, this has already been discussed in item 1. Jesus and peace from a non-messianic point of view is discussed later.

8. UNIQUE NAMES
The Messiah will have unique names:

> **The Lord [YHVH] himself will give you a sign. Behold, a young woman** [The church says "virgin"] **shall conceive and bear a son, and shall call his name Immanuel** [which means "God With Us"] (Is 7:14).

> **[A]nd his name shall be called Pele-yoez-el-gibbor-Avi-ad-sar-shalom** [which means "A wonderful counselor is Almighty God, the Everlasting Father, the Prince of Peace"] (Is 9:6).

> **And this is the name by which he will be called: YHVH-tseed-kaynu** ["The Lord [YHVH] is Our Righteousness"] (Jer 23:6).

It is highly significant that there is no prophecy for the name Jesus. In the gospels, the name Jesus was assigned by an angel (Mt 1:21; Lk 1:30–31), who did not explain why he rejected the three names given by God. Why would God, who had expressly given unique names to the Messiah so that everyone would immediately recognize him, change his mind and assign a name so ordinary no Jew could recognize him? Matthew gives the following nonsensical explanation:

> **An angel of the Lord appeared to [Joseph] in a dream saying, . . . "You shall call his name Jesus, for he will save his people from their sins." All this took place to fulfill what the Lord had spoken by the prophet: Behold, a virgin shall conceive and bear a son, and his name shall be called Emmanuel [or Immanuel], which means God with us** (Mt 1:20–23).

The angel, to make sense, ought to have said, "Name the child Emmanuel, which means 'God with us.'" Instead the angel said, "You shall call his name Jesus for he will save his people from their sins." The name Jesus, however, does not mean "save his people from their sins." The name Jesus means "YHVH is our savior." That explains why Jesus was the commonest name of Jews at the time of Jesus of Nazareth. The name Jesus, unlike the messianic names given by God, was not unique as the angel implied, but, on the contrary, was highly ordinary.

Jesuses in the New Testament are:
>Jesus of Nazareth.
>Jesus ben Sirach, author of the Book of Ecclesiasticus.
>Jesus bar Abbas, the criminal to whom, the gospels report, Pontius Pilate granted amnesty at the same time he condemned Jesus of Nazareth.
>Jesus "who is called Justus" (Col 4:10–12).

Jesuses mentioned by Josephus include:
>Jesus, the high priest who changed his name to Jason.
>Jesus, son of Saul.
>Jesus Abiezer.
>Jesus, son of the high priest Jozadak.
>Jesus, son of Joiada.

Jesus, the high priest, son of Simon.
Jesus, the high priest, son of Phabes.
Jesus, the high priest, son of See.
Jesus, son of Damnaeus.
Jesus, son of Gamallel.
Jesus, son of Gamalas [not to be confused with
      Gamallel].
Jesus, son of Sapphias.
Jesus, son of Sapphas [not to be confused with
      Sapphias].
Jesus, the bandit chief.
Jesus, the Galilean army commander.
Jesus, the zealot.
Jesus, brother of Chares and kinsman of Justus of
      Tiberias.
Jesus, son of Aramas.
Jesus, son of Naue.
Jesus, son of Tebuthi.
Jesus, the peasant son of Ananias.

Clearly the name Jesus does not make a man the Messiah.

9. OF DAVID'S LINEAGE
The Messiah will be of David's lineage:

> **The Lord [YHVH] said to David, "When your days
> are over, and you join your fathers in the grave, I
> will raise up your son after you, the seed of your
> body, and I will establish his kingdom. He shall
> build a House for my Name. And I will establish the
> throne of his kingdom forever. I will be his father
> and he shall be my son"** (2 Sam 7:12–13).

God is telling David that his son Solomon will build the Temple, that Solomon will be a son of God, and that Solomon's kingdom will last forever. God says nothing about the Messiah being descended from David. Nonetheless, the rabbis in Jesus' day maintained that the Messiah would be descended from David. Jesus of Nazareth was puzzled by that and asked:

> **How can the rabbis maintain that the Messiah is the son of David?** (Mk 12:36–37; cf. Mt 22:41–46).

Nonetheless, gospel redactors went on to prove that Jesus was a descendent of David. Matthew traces Jesus to David and then from David to Abraham (Mt 1:1–16). Luke traces Jesus to David, from David to Abraham, and then all the way to Adam, whom Luke calls significantly **the son of God** (Lk 3:38). Paul, like Jesus, rejected the genealogies:

> **Give no credence to . . . the endless genealogies** (1 Tim 1:4).

From the theological point of view, if Jesus was the only begotten son of God, as the church maintains, what need was there for genealogies? Is anything necessary beyond the miraculous and unique genealogy of Son of God, especially *only begotten Son of God*?

Let us return to the prophecy in 2 Samuel that began this item, "Of David's Lineage." The church ends that prophecy with the line: **I will be his father and he shall be my son** (2 Sam 7:12–13) and insists that can refer only to Jesus, whereas the context indicates it can only refer to Solomon. To decide the case, one only has to read the line that follows: **When [this son of mine] commits iniquity, I will punish him as any father would, and not spare the rod!** (2 Sam 7:14). The Father intends to punish the son for his iniquity! If Jesus is the son, as the church maintains, then Jesus was crucified as punishment for his own iniquity, not to take away the sins of the world.

10. RIDING ON AN ASS

Zechariah prophesies that after victoriously accomplishing everything expected with the coming of the Messiah, the Messiah will enter Jerusalem triumphantly but humbly riding on an ass:

> **Shout, O daughter of Jerusalem! Lo, your king comes to you triumphant and victorious, humbly riding on an ass, on the colt of an ass** (Zech 9:9).

The church ends Zechariah's prophecy there, and asserts that Jesus' entering Jerusalem riding on an ass proves that Jesus was the Messiah. What makes Zechariah's prophecy important, however, is not so much the Messiah's riding on an ass—countless people have done that—as what follows, which the church omits:

> **That will be the end of war chariots going forth from Ephraim [Israel] and war horses from Jerusalem. And that will be the end of the warrior's bows** (Zech 9:9–10).

First the Messiah announces an end to war; then, when peace comes to the earth, he enters Jerusalem riding on an ass. Jesus won the trophy without accomplishing the task!

11. PRECEDED BY ELIJAH

The Messiah will be preceded by Elijah the prophet:

> **Behold, I will send you the prophet Elijah before the
> coming of the great and terrible day of the Lord**
> (Mal 4:5–6).

Jesus, knowing that Elijah had not come, asks his followers to
make an allowance and let John the Baptist take the place of
Elijah so that Jesus can fulfill the prophecy:

> *For all the prophets and the Law prophesied until
> John [the Baptist]; and if you are willing to accept it,
> he is Elijah who is to come* (Mt 11:14).

And Luke has an angel say that John the Baptist will come **in
the spirit and power of Elijah** (Lk 1:17). John was a good
man, but he was no Elijah.

12. AN END TO VIPERS AND POISONS

When the Messiah comes, babies will be able to play with
vipers, for they will no longer strike and their venom will no
longer be poisonous:

> **The suckling child shall play over the hole of the
> asp, and the weaned child shall put his hand in the
> adder's den. They shall not strike or kill** (Is 11:8–9).

Jesus taught that believers in him would be protected not only
from poisonous snakes but from any kind of poison:

> *And these signs will accompany those who believe in
> me: . . . they will handle venomous snakes, and if
> they drink poison, it will not hurt them* (Mk 16:17–18).

Jesus was not telling the truth, and it would be foolish for his followers to believe him and try this.

13. MOUNTAINS SINK, VALLEYS RISE

The prophets saw geological wrinkles as defects that needed correction. So they prophesied that when the Messiah comes, mountains will sink and valleys will rise, and the earth will become one great smooth and wrinkle-free plain:

> **Every valley shall be lifted up,**
> **and every mountain and hill be made low;**
> **the uneven ground shall become level,**
> **and the rough places a plain** (Is 40:4–5).

John the Baptist, expecting that Jesus of Nazareth would fulfill that nonsensical prophecy, shouted this version:

> **Every valley shall be filled, and every mountain and**
> **hill shall be brought low, and the crooked shall be**
> **made straight, and the rough ways shall be made**
> **smooth** (Lk 3:5–6).

Jesus did not bring down mountains nor raise up valleys.

14. THE DISABLED BECOME ABLE-BODIED; THE DESERTS GUSH WATER

When the Messiah comes, all the disabled will become able-bodied, and the deserts will gush water:

> **The eyes of the blind shall be opened,**
> **and the ears of the deaf unstopped;**
> **then shall the lame man leap like a hart,**
> **and the tongue of dumb sing for joy.**

> **Waters shall break forth in the wilderness**
> **and streams in the desert;**
> **burning sand will become a pool,**
> **and parched ground, springs of water** (Is 35:5–7).

The Messiah will bring an end to blindness, deafness, lameness, muteness, etc. Jesus of Nazareth, the gospel redactors say, cured a few people. But Isaiah was speaking of curing them all and bringing disabilities to an end forever. As for bringing water to the desert, Jesus did not attempt it!

15. DESERTS BLOOM
When the Messiah comes:

> **The desert shall rejoice and bloom** (Is 35:1).

Jesus did not make the desert bloom.

16. AN END TO PAIN AND SUFFERING
When the Messiah comes, there will be no more pain, suffering, or destruction:

> **There shall be no hurt or destruction in all my holy mountain** (Is 11:9).

Jesus did not end pain, suffering, destruction.

17. GENERALIZED RESURRECTION
When the Messiah comes, every righteous person who ever lived will rise from the dead in the generalized resurrection:

> **The dead shall live! Their bodies shall rise!**

O dwellers in the dust, awake and sing! (Is 26:19).

And many of those who sleep in the dust of the earth shall awake, some to everlasting life, and some to shame and everlasting contempt (Dan 12:1–3).

Thus says the Lord God: Behold, I will open your graves, and raise you from your graves (Ezek 37:12).

The dead shall live! Their bodies shall rise!
O dwellers in the dust, awake and sing! (Is 26:19).

The Messiah was not expected to die and undergo his own resurrection. The Messiah was expected to bring about the generalized resurrection of all the righteous who had ever lived. Jesus did not do that.

18. WHOLE WORLD AS WITNESS

When the Messiah comes, the whole world will witness it:

And the glory of the Lord shall be revealed, and all mankind shall see it together (Is 40:5).

With the coming of Jesus, a few believers saw something, but mankind as a whole saw nothing.

19. ANNOUNCING THE KINGDOM OF GOD

When the Messiah comes, he will announce the inauguration of the Kingdom of God on earth forever and ever:

O herald of good news [the gospel] to Zion,
lift up your voice with strength!
O herald of good news [the gospel] to Jerusalem,

> **lift up your voice! Fear not!**
> **Say to the cities of Judah,**
> **"Behold your God!**
> **Behold the Lord [YHVH] our God comes with might**
> **and his arm rules for him"** (Is 40:9–11).
>
> **And the government shall be upon his shoulder. . . .**
> **and there shall be peace everlasting . . . with justice**
> **and righteousness forever and ever** (Is 9:6–7).

Over and over again the prophets shout of peace everlasting
with justice and righteousness. Jesus did not inaugurate these
things.

20. THE UNIVERSAL THANKSGIVING

When the Messiah fulfills the prophecies, the peoples of the
earth will praise the Lord [YHVH]:

> **And the nations shall come toward your light and**
> **their kings to your sunrise. Lift up your eyes and**
> **look all around: they come together, all of them, and**
> **come to you. . . . They shall bring gold and frankin-**
> **cense, and shall proclaim the praise of the Lord**
> **[YHVH]** (Is 60:1–6).

Instead of all the nations coming towards God's sunrise praising God in thanksgiving, three wise men followed a star to
Bethlehem one night, bringing gold and frankincense and
myrrh.

DID JESUS FULFILL THE CRITERIA
FOR THE MESSIAH?

Above are listed twenty signs or prophecies concerning the coming of the Messiah. Others could probably cite more. Jesus of Nazareth fulfilled none. The church believes he fulfilled three: he was born in Bethlehem (that is doubtful); he was "King of the Jews" (that is debatable); and he entered Jerusalem riding on an ass (yes, he did do that—before achieving all that the Messiah was to achieve; Jesus took the prize without winning the contest, let alone entering it!). Even if we were to allow those three signs, a score of three out of twenty, or fifteen percent, is a failing grade by any standard. That best explains why Jesus scorned signs.

JESUS' PEACE

The Messiah first and foremost was to announce everlasting world peace. Unable to give the everlasting peace of the Messiah and knowing his anti-messianic messages would disqualify him as the Messiah, Jesus began to speak, not of messianic peace, but of a different kind of peace, an incomprehensible and vague kind of peace, a peace that anyone was capable of giving:

> *Peace I leave with you, my own peace I give you, not as the world gives do I give you* (Jn 4:27).

> *[I]n me you may have peace. In the world you have tribulation; but be of good cheer, I have overcome the world* (Jn 16:33).

> **Jesus . . . said to [the disciples],** *Peace be with you. . .* **Jesus said to them again,** *Peace be with you. . . .* **Jesus . . . said,** *Peace be with you* (Jn 20:19–26).

Not once but three times Jesus said, *Peace be with you.* Did he think by repetition of this ordinary middle eastern greeting or farewell that he could negate all the hateful and destructive anti-messianic pronouncements he had made?

PROPHECIES THAT PROVE JESUS WAS NOT THE MESSIAH

The prophets had warned of Jesus' kind of peace:

> **I give to Jerusalem a herald of the good news [the gospel].**
> **But when I look there is no one. . . .**
> **Behold, they are all a delusion!**
> **Their works are nothing!** (Is 41:27–28).

> **They have healed the wound of my people lightly, saying, "Peace, peace," when there is no peace** (Jer 6:14; 8:11).

> **We looked for peace, but no good came; for a time of healing, but behold, terror** (Jer 8:15; 14:19).

"BLIND GUIDES, BLIND FOOLS, BLIND MEN"

Jesus of Nazareth, in a curse on the Pharisees, exclaimed:

> *Woe to you, scribes and Pharisees, hypocrites! . . . Woe to you, blind guides . . . blind fools! . . . blind men! . . . Woe to you, scribes and Phariseess! . . . You blind guides! . . . Woe to you, scribes and Pharisees, hypocrites! . . . You serpents, you brood of vipers, how are you going to escape being sentenced to hell?* (Mt 23:16–33).

There is no trace of sweet Jesus here. No trace of the mild and meek Jesus of forgiveness and mercy. No sign of "amazing grace."

Jesus is directing his curse at the Scribes and the Pharisees, but elsewhere he extended it to the Jews who did not believe in him. Later the church extended the curse collectively to all the Jews of all time. The church taught that the Jews are "blind," by which it meant stupid or undiscerning. Can it be that this highly discerning and intelligent people, who, alone of all the peoples on the earth, were able to see the invisible God of Abraham, Isaac, and Jacob, were unable to see the incarnate and visible God Christians call Jesus Christ?

The church, understandably unwilling to call the non-believing Jews discerning or intelligent, called them by the pejorative relatives of those words—*clever*, *calculating*, *cunning*, *conniving*, *crafty*. It was not the Enlightenment that overturned that caricature. It took the Nobel Prize to do that. Although the Jews comprise far less than one percent of the world's population, they have won more prizes than any other group. Can it be that this people with such clear vision on all subjects are blind in one area only—in their inability to see Jesus of Nazareth as the Messiah?

JESUS' PROMISE

Jesus made a promise that anyone can make—giving life everlasting to those who believed in him. But the Messiah was not expected to make promises. The Messiah was expected to deliver!

UNFULFILLED GOSPEL PROPHECIES

Jesus not only did not fulfill most of the prophecies of the Hebrew Scriptures, but also he did not fulfill some of the prophecies of the gospels:

> **Zechariah was filled with the Holy Spirit, and prophesied, saying, Blessed be the Lord God of Israel. . . . that we should be saved from our enemies, and from the hand of all who hate us . . . [and] that we . . . might serve [God] without fear . . . all the days of our life. . . . [and] give light to those who sit in darkness** (Lk 1:67–79).

Zechariah prophesied that with the coming of the Messiah, the Jews would be saved from their enemies and would be able to serve God without fear.   Zechariah was reaffirming the prophecies of Isaiah and Micah (Is 2:4; Mic 4:3). Jesus did not fulfill Zechariah's prophecy. On the contrary, with Jesus' coming, the Jews were delivered into the hands of their enemies and could serve God only in continual fear.

Here is another unfulfilled gospel prophecy:

> **Now there was a man in Jerusalem, whose name was Simeon. . . . And inspired by the [Holy] Spirit . . . he took [the baby Jesus] up in his arms and blessed God and said, "[M]ine eyes have seen . . . a light for revelation to the Gentiles, and for glory to thy people Israel** (Lk 2:25–32).

Simeon prophesied that Jesus would be a light to the Gentiles and bring glory to God's people Israel.   Jesus may have brought light to the Gentiles, but he did not bring glory to Israel.

THE MESSIAH WHO WENT AWAY

Hebrew scriptures had no prophecy of a Messiah who was to go away. And so, on learning that Jesus intended to leave the earth and go to heaven, some Jews were puzzled:

> **A crowd of Jews said to Jesus, "We have read in the Law that the Christ remains forever. How can you say that the Son of man must be lifted up?"** (Jn 12:34).

Jesus did not answer. Instead, he added to their puzzlement by giving an obscure utterance:

> *The light is with you for a little longer. Walk while you have the light, lest the darkness overtake you; he who walks in the darkness does not know where he goes. While you have the light, believe in the light, that you may become sons of light* (Jn 12:35–36).

IMMINENT SECOND COMING

Jesus taught that he had accomplished all that the Father had meant him to accomplish. He said nothing about a Second Coming:

> *The time is fulfilled, and the Kingdom of God is at hand* (Mk 1:14).

> *I glorified thee on earth, having accomplished the work which thou gavest me to do* (Jn 17:4).

Peter confirmed that the Christ had finished his work at the end of time. Peter did not say Christ was returning a second time to do unfinished business:

> **[Christ] . . . was made manifest at the end of times**
> (1 Pet 1:20).

Paul, realizing that Jesus had not accomplished what the Christ was meant to accomplish, wrote of the second coming, which, he said, was imminent:

> **Christ . . . will appear a second time** (Heb 9:28).

> **The Lord is coming soon** (Phil 3:20).

> **The appointed time is almost here. . . . [T]he present shape of the world is passing away** (1 Cor 7:29).

Jesus, however, did not come a second time, and the present shape of the world did not pass away. So Paul gave up hope of a second coming, and began to write that man's hope lay not in a second coming but beyond the grave. That was old stuff, the stuff of the Greek philosophers and the Hebrew prophets. In the meantime, believers wait . . . and wait . . . and wait. . . .

THE THIRD COMING

The church speaks of Jesus' second coming, but he already had a second coming. At his first coming, he lived and died, accomplishing almost nothing expected of the Messiah. At his second coming, he was resurrected, reappeared to his apostles, and ascended to heaven, again accomplishing almost nothing expected of the Messiah. If he were to come again, it would be his third coming. How many times must Jesus come to accomplish what the Messiah was expected to accomplish at his first coming?

MATTHEW'S GENERALIZED RESURRECTION

Jesus did not bring about the generalized resurrection, one of the great miracles expected at the coming of the Messiah. Strangely, however, in Matthew's gospel the generalized resurrection begins (Mt 27:51–54). Graves and tombs open, and the righteous dead rise. This had to have been the greatest miracle of all time! Matthew said the start of the generalized resurrection had witnesses—a Roman centurion, a few Roman guards, and many women watching at a distance. Curiously, however, these witnesses did not report this marvelous event to anyone.

And what of the newly risen dead themselves? Surely they went home. Weren't their families, friends, and neighbors astonished? Didn't someone run and tell the Pharisees and Pontius Pilate? On the contrary, everyone who witnessed or participated in Matthew's generalized resurrection remained silent. How can that be? Everyone spoke of Jesus' miraculous cures even though Jesus commanded them to keep silent, but no one told Matthew's resurrected righteous to remain silent. And yet, they did not speak of it. No one speaks of it to this day, least of all the church. Why? Because some miracles are so incredible that even the most gullible do not believe in them!

Curiously, too, Matthew's generalized resurrection aborts as quickly as it began. Why? We can only guess. Matthew knew that the generalized resurrection was an essential miracle accompanying the Messiah. So Matthew must have thought if Jesus was really the Messiah, Matthew could confidently describe the beginnings of a fictitious generalized resurrection, so certain was he that Jesus would shortly bring about the real thing. But Jesus did not.

The church cannot talk of such things. If the church were to admit that Matthew's generalized resurrection was a hoax, what would people say of his gospel? And so the church ignores Matthew's account and teaches that the generalized resurrection will occur at the Second Coming. But will it? Can it? The earth is already overpopulated. How will it accommodate all the corpses of the righteous from time immemorial rising together? We would be packed together like sardines in a can. Realizing that, Christian fundamentalists have invented a new concept—the Rapture. The Rapture enables an overpopulated earth to discharge its great load of believers into the sky. And the nuclear apocalypse that follows the Rapture will annihilate the nonbelievers. The fundamentalists fully expect the fulfillment of Jesus' hateful wish:

> *I have come to set fire to the earth and how I wish it were already in flames!* (Lk 12:49).

GOD NEVER CALLED JESUS *MY* CHRIST

If Jesus of Nazareth was God's Christ, why is it that God never called Jesus *my* Christ when God called others by that title?

The Hebrew word **משיח** (*mah-she-ahckh,* singular; *mah-she-ckhai,* plural) may be translated by three English words—all perfect synonyms identical in meaning—*messiah, christ,* or *anointed.* In antiquity, the translation of choice into ancient Greek and Latin was *christ.* But in modern English, the translation of choice varies depending on the person to whom the word refers. When it refers to Jesus, the word selected is usually Christ or Messiah but rarely Anointed and in all cases with a capital C or M or A. When the word refers to someone other than Jesus, the word selected is invariably *anointed* and with a lower case *a.* This is a Christian convention reflecting a Christian bias. No matter how one translates the word, however, God shows his intimacy with that person by calling him not simply christ or messiah or anointed, but *my* christ or *my* messiah or *my* anointed. The following example illustrates this:

Psalm 105:15: **Touch not my anointed ones.**

The ancient Greek (Septuagint) **χριστῶν μου** (*christon mou*) was translated into ancient Latin (Vulgate) as *christos meos*, and then into English (King James and RSV) as "*my* anointed ones."

It is of the highest significance that although God calls the Jews or their patriarchs or prophets or kings *my* anointed ones, *my* messiahs, or *my* christs, God never calls Jesus of Nazareth *my* Messiah, *my* Christ, or *my* Anointed. Why—if he really was? The book of Acts describes an occasion when disciples pray to God, and in their prayer, they quote a Psalm of David in which the title *his* Anointed appears. The disciples take it upon themselves to say that the title refers to Jesus:

> **[The disciples] lifted their voices together to God and said, "Sovereign Lord. . . .**
>> **'Why did the Gentiles rage,**
>> **and the peoples imagine vain things?**
>> **The kings of the earth set themselves in array,**
>> **and the rulers were gathered together,**
>> **against the Lord**
>> **and against his Anointed'** [Ps 2:1–2]—
> **for truly in this city there were gathered together, against thy holy servant Jesus, whom thou did anoint, both Herod and Pontius Pilate, with the Gentiles and the people of Israel, to do whatever thy hand and thy plan had predestined to take place"** (Acts 4:24–28).

Although the Psalm does not tell us to whom *his* Anointed refers—the context suggests David—nevertheless, the disciples took a leap of faith and made it refer to Jesus. But God never calls Jesus *my* Anointed. God surely would have called Jesus *my* Anointed if Jesus had been *his* Anointed.

THE ADVOCATE AND THE SPIRIT OF TRUTH

Just before the risen Christ ascended into heaven, he said to his disciples: *It is to your advantage that I go away* (Jn 16:7). That was a strange thing to say because the promised Messiah was not expected to go away. Why was it to the disciples' advantage that Jesus go away? Jesus says:

> *If I do not go away, the Advocate will not come to you. But if I go, I will send him to you* (Jn 16:7).

Why is it more important for the Advocate to come than for Jesus to stay? And who is the Advocate? Jesus does not say. Instead, he makes another obscure statement:

> *There is still much that I could say to you, but the burden would be too great for you now. When the Spirit of truth comes, he will guide you into the whole truth* (Jn 16:12–13).

Who is the Spirit of truth? As with the Advocate, Jesus does not say. Why does Jesus take such care to speak of the Advocate and the Spirit of truth as if they were two different persons? The church says that the Advocate and the Spirit of truth are none other than the Holy Spirit! But why would Jesus invent new names for the Holy Spirit? What is one to make of this? Here are suggestions:

Jesus realized that he had not shown himself to be the Messiah, and moreover that he had created more problems than he had solved. As a result, it was time for him to go, and time for the Advocate and the Spirit of truth to come, the Advocate to defend Jesus, the Spirit of truth to explain everything that Jesus wasn't able to explain himself. Jesus was saying that he needed help to extricate himself from the mess he had created. So Jesus went away. But the Advocate did not come to defend him. Neither did the Spirit of truth come to explain things on his behalf.   And neither did the Holy Spirit, although the church seemed to think it did.

We are left with unanswered questions.   Would the Messiah need anyone to defend him or explain his words, his deeds, his purpose?   Would the Messiah say, *I have yet many things to say to you, but you cannot hear them now* (Jn 16:12)?   Did Jesus really believe he was the Son of God?   I think not.   If he did, why did he say, *No one knows who the Son is but the Father* (Lk 10:22)?

SIGNS, REVELATION, AND EVIDENCE

The Greeks believed they could understand the world through reason alone.   Evidence was not important to them. Reason without evidence, however, permits multiple philosophical systems to arise, none of which can be tested.   As a result, Socrates, perhaps the greatest of the Greek philosophers, concluded that there was no way of knowing anything, and that was the beginning of wisdom.   That is the "last analysis" of a thought system based entirely on reason without evidence.

The Jews, on the other hand, believed that reason was necessary but insufficient to arrive at wisdom.   Evidence was also necessary.   They called religious evidence "revelation."   In revelation, God revealed himself not to one or two or a few witnesses but to the entire nation of Jews.   Because the Jews were too primitive to have knowledge of statistical sampling and testing, something of cosmic proportions had to be demonstrated to the entire community before they would believe it. Thus, when God delivered the Ten Commandments to Moses at Mt. Sinai, all Israel were witnesses.   Moses summoned Israel, and stated:

> The Lord [YHVH] our God made a covenant with us in Horeb. Not with our fathers did the Lord make this covenant, but with us, who are all of us here alive this day. The Lord [YHVH] spoke with you face to face at the mountain, out of the midst of the fire (Deut 5:1–4).

> The Lord [YHVH] spoke to all your assembly at the mountain out of the midst of the fire . . . with a loud voice; and he added no more. . . . And when you heard the voice . . . you came near to me, all the heads of your tribes, and your elders; and you said, "Behold, the Lord [YHVH] our God has shown us his glory and greatness, and we have heard his voice out of the midst of the fire" (Deut 5:22–24).

When God freed the Jews from their slavery in Egypt, God said to all of them: **You have seen what I did to the Egyptians, and how I bore you on eagles' wings and brought you to myself** (Ex 19:3–4). And the five books of Moses which comprise the first five books of the Christian bible [!] conclude with these words:

> And there has not arisen a prophet the likes of Moses in all of Israel, whom the Lord [YHVH] knew face to face, none like him for all the signs and wonders which the Lord [YHVH] sent him to do in the land of Egypt, before Pharaoh and all his servants and all his land, and for all the mighty power and all the great and terrible deeds which Moses did in the sight of all Israel (Deut 34:10–12).

Jesus of Nazareth, however, did nothing in the sight of all Israel, but only before a crowd of witnesses or just a few witnesses or even only one witness. The New Testament is told by very few witnesses none of whom speak of revelation to the whole community. Peter commented on this defensively:

> **God raised [Jesus] on the the third day and made him manifest, not to all the people** [as he did in the case of Moses]**, but to us who were chosen by God to be witnesses** (Acts 10:39–41).

The Pharisees expected that when the Messiah came, God was going to reveal himself not only in the sight of all Israel, but in the sight of the whole world. Isaiah proclaimed:

> **And the glory of the Lord shall be revealed, and all flesh shall see it together** (Is 40:5).

THE SIGN OF JONAH

Jesus called signs evil, characteristic of false Christs and false prophets (Mt 24:24–25). And he taught that those who wanted signs, no less than those who gave them, were evil. Nonetheless, Jesus eventually relented and said that he would give one sign—one sign only—the sign of Jonah:

> *[S]ome of the scribes and Pharisees said to him, "Teacher, we wish to see a sign from you." But he answered them, An evil and adulterous generation seeks for a sign; but no sign shall be given to it except the sign of the prophet Jonah. For as Jonah was three days and three nights in the belly of the whale, so will the Son of man be three days and three nights in the heart of the earth* (Mt 12:38–40).

Jesus tells exactly how long Jonah was in the whale:

Jonah was in the belly of the great fish for three days and three nights (Jon 1:17).

Because the sign of Jonah was going to be Jesus' one and only sign, everyone expected him to get it right. But he didn't. He promised to be in the earth for three days and three nights, the same amount of time that Jonah spent in the belly of the great fish. Jesus was buried on Friday afternoon. So if Jesus were in the earth for three days and three nights, then he should rise on Monday afternoon. On three different occasions, Jesus confirmed that (Mk 8:31, 9:31, 10:34). But instead of Monday afternoon, his empty tomb was discovered on Sunday morning! Jesus miscalculated—or someone did—and his body disappeared one day early. What was to be done about that? The redactors went to work. Jesus' prophecy was negated, and "three days" was changed to "on the third day" which was Sunday. And redactors made that change five times!

> **and on the third day he will rise** (Lk 18:33; cf. Mt 16:21; 17:23; 20:19; Lk 9:22).

But "third day" would not satisfy Jesus' sign of Jonah because three days and on the third day are not the same. The redactors went back to work. And Jesus, negating the sign of Jonah, said:

> **[B]ehold, something greater than Jonah is here** (Mt 12:41–42).

MORE SIGNS

After emphatically stating that he was not going to give any signs, and after stating that he would give one sign only, the sign of Jonah, and after not fulfilling that sign and consequently discrediting it, Jesus went on to give a multitude of signs of remarkable variety. Here are a few: Jesus fed a large crowd with a few loaves and fishes, he cured several sick people, raised Lazarus from the dead, turned water into wine, enabled a disciple to find a coin in a fish's mouth, drove a herd of possessed swine over a cliff, and destroyed a fig tree because it was not bearing figs out of season.

Many of the signs he did secretly, but many others he did publicly with great crowds witnessing them. Even so, he commanded the crowds not to bear witness to the signs, but to keep them secret. But of course the witnesses went on to talk about them.

John the evangelist says, **Though he had done so many signs before them, yet they did not believe in him** (Jn 12:37). They did not believe in him! Astounding! They did not believe in him because either he did not do them or else none of them had anything to do with inaugurating peace on earth, delivering justice to the Gentiles, proclaiming liberty, or bringing an end to pain and suffering.

UNSPECIFIED SIGNS

Jesus was on a roll. Once he started giving signs he got carried away, doing more and more signs, countless signs, endless signs, most unspecified:

> **Now when he was in Jerusalem at the Passover feast, many believed in his name when they saw the signs which he did** (Jn 2:23).

> [Nicodemus, a Pharisee and a leader of the Jews said to Jesus,] **"Rabbi, we know that you are a teacher come from God; for no one can do these signs that you do, unless God is with him"** (Jn 3:2).

Now Jesus did many other signs in the presence of the disciples . . . that you may believe that Jesus is the Christ (Jn 20:30).

But there are also many other things which Jesus did; were every one of them to be written, I suppose that the world itself could not contain the books that would be written (Jn 21:25).

THE DISCIPLES AND SIGNS

Jesus told his disciples they, too, would do signs:

And these signs will accompany those who believe . . . they will cast out demons; they will speak in new tongues; they will pick up serpents, and if they drink any deadly thing, it will not hurt them (Mk 16:17–18).

CHASTISING THOSE WHO IGNORE SIGNS

First Jesus called those who wanted signs "evil" (Mt 12:39; Lk 11:29), but then he called those those who ignored signs "hypocrites":

When you see clouds gathering in the west, you say immediately, "It is going to rain." And rain it does. And when you feel the south wind, you say, "We are in for a heat wave." And so it comes. What hypocrites you are! You know how to forecast the weather. How come you cannot recognize this fateful hour? (Lk 12:54–56).

SATAN'S PROMISE

Satan promised Jesus the world if only Jesus would worship him:

> **The devil took [Jesus] to a very high mountain, and showed him all the kingdoms of the world . . . and he said to him, "All these I will give you, if you will fall down and worship me"** (Mt 4:8–9).

> **And the devil took him up and showed him all the kingdoms of the world . . . and said, "If you will worship me, this shall be all yours." . . . And when the devil had ended every temptation, he left him until an opportune time** (Lk 4:5–13).

Jesus did not succumb to the devil in the desert. So the devil departed fully confident that he had achieved something, but it would not bear fruit **until an opportune time**. When did the opportune time arise? The gospels do not say. But it did occur. For in time demons and devils recognized and worshiped Jesus as the Christ. They were first:

> **And they went into Capernaum. . . . And immediately there was in their synagogue a man with an unclean spirit; and he cried out, "What have you to do with us, Jesus of Nazareth? Have you come to destroy us? I know who you are, the Holy One of God." But Jesus rebuked him, saying, *"Be silent, and come out of him!"*** (Mk 1:21–25; cf. Lk 4:31–35).

> **And [Jesus] cast out many demons; and he would not permit the demons to speak, because they knew him** (Mk 1:32–34).

> **And whenever the unclean spirits beheld him, they fell down before him and cried out, "You are the Son of God." And he strictly ordered them not to make him known** (Mk 3:11–12).

> **And demons also came out of many, crying, "You are the Son of God." But he rebuked them, and would not allow them to speak, because they knew that he was the Christ** (Lk 4:41–2).

Jesus, not content to be recognized by demons and devils, asked the apostles, *But who do you say that I am?* Peter answered, **You are the Christ** (Mk 8:29). Peter was the first of the apostles to acknowledge Jesus as the Christ. Shortly afterward, Jesus called Peter *Satan* (Mk 9:33). What is the significance of *that* demonization?

"HOW CAN SATAN CAST OUT SATAN?"

Jesus asked: *How can Satan cast out Satan?* (Mk 3:23). That is not the rhetorical question that Jesus implied it was, with the expected answer "Satan cannot cast out Satan!" Satan can indeed cast out Satan, when Satan casts out Satan for the purpose of deception. Jesus cast out Satan as we have just seen. And Jesus taught, *The devil has nothing to do with the truth* (Jn 8:44).

GOD NEVER PROMISED A MESSIAH

God never promised a Messiah. God never said I am going to send a Messiah to perfect the imperfect world I made. Isaiah and other prophets allude to a Messiah, but God does not. The snake was already present in paradise at the beginning, and God did not exclude the snake when he called the works of creation **good**. By means of the great flood, God demonstrated to mankind the impossibility of ridding the world of evil, for immediately after the flood, evil reappeared. So John made a great theological blunder when he wrote:

The reason the son of God appeared was to destroy the works of the devil (1 Jn 3:8). That is contrary to the will of God.

Those who wait for the Messiah wait in vain. If men want a world of peace and good will with evil controlled, they have to make it themselves. Men who invoke the Messiah to obliterate a so-called evil or imperfect world are arrogant. Isaiah got it right when he said:

> **Does the pot argue with the potter, or the clay with the hand that shapes it? Will the clay ask, "What are you making?" or say, "Your pot is defective." Woe to him who says to a father, "What kind of child are you making?" or to a pregnant woman, "What do you think you're getting for your labor?" Thus says the Lord [YHVH], the Holy One of Israel and its Maker, "How dare you tell me what kind of children to make! How dare you criticize me and my handiwork!"** (Is 45:9–11).

Job also got it right when he said:

> **Shall we receive good at the hand of God, and shall we not receive evil?** (Job 2:10).

JEWS WHO DID NOT BELIEVE IN THE COMING OF THE MESSIAH

A belief in the Messiah was not essential to being a Jew at the time when Jesus of Nazareth lived. The Sadducees did not believe in the Messiah, and the high priest was a Sadducee. So how could the high priest be expected to receive Jesus or anyone else as the Messiah? To him, anyone who claimed to be the Messiah was a pretender to the title, a charlatan.

It was the Pharisees, the predecessors of the rabbis, who developed the concept of the Messiah. But even among the Pharisees and rabbis were those who did not believe in the coming of the Messiah. Rabbi John (Yochanan), a friend of the great Rabbi Akiba, joked, "Akiba, men will grow grass on their faces before the Messiah comes" (Palestinian Talmud, Ta'anit, 4:5).

THE PROBLEM OF EVIL AND THE MESSIAH

Philosophers speak endlessly of the problem of evil, and so does the church. The church speaks of evil as something that Satan, not God, created. The church in effect has invented a god of good, the Trinity, and a god of evil, Satan, each god equally powerful and constantly at war with each other. The church denies, however, that Satan is a god. If Satan is not a god equal with Trinity, then what is he? A fallen angel? How could a fallen angel be as powerful as Almighty God?

In the garden of Eden, before Adam and Eve even thought of eating the forbidden fruit, God had placed evil there in the form of a serpent. So evil had nothing to do with Adam and Eve. Apparently God did not want man to know that he had created evil because he realized that man would have a hard time understanding it. That is why he forbade Adam from eating the fruit that would enable him to recognize evil.

Why would a good God create evil? That is another great question of the ages. Isn't the answer so that men might be challenged? Paradise without challenge is boring. Solving problems keeps man productive, occupied, and gives meaning to life. Looking for cures for cancer, drought, flood, and war prevent man from getting bored in paradise. And if God deliberately created a world with evil so that man might be challenged, the notion of his sending a Messiah is false. So the idea that Jesus of Nazareth or anyone else is the Christ is false.

And messianic prophecies are false. Such prophecies say in effect that the world that God created contained errors, including evil, and God was planning to rectify those errors by sending the Messiah. Aren't people who teach that presumptuous? Don't they insult God?

The prophet Isaiah wrote unsurpassably beautiful poetry and was a supreme idealist who could not believe that a benevolent, just, loving, and merciful God could create a world full of injustice, hatred, and cruelty, a world with war, poverty, disease, disasters, poisonous beasts, pain, sorrow, misery, and death. Isaiah, for all his idealism and magnificent poetry, was in the end just another false prophet. Wolves will never cease being predators of lambs. Babies will never be able to play with cobras or rattlesnakes. Children will never lead lions and tigers on leashes. And the world will never cease from having tyrants who intimidate, oppress, exploit and otherwise harm people. Evil cannot be extinguished. It is part of creation. And God said it is "good." Evil can only be controlled.

REDEEMER AND SAVIOR

THINGS GOD SAID ABOUT SAVIOR AND REDEEMER
Here are things God said about the Savior and Redeemer:

> **I alone am the Lord [YHVH]; and beside me there is no Savior** (Is 43:11).

> **Thus says the Lord [YHVH], the King of Israel and his Redeemer, the Lord of hosts; "I am the first and I am the last; besides me there is no god"** (Is 44:6).

> **I, the Lord [YHVH], am your Savior and your Redeemer** (Is 60:16).

> **Although I say to the wicked, "You shall surely die,"**
> **yet if he turns from his evil ways and does what is**
> **lawful and right . . . he shall surely live, he shall not**
> **die! None of the sins that he has committed shall be**
> **remembered against him!** (Ezek 33:10–16).

> **I am the Lord [YHVH] your God. . . . You know no**
> **God but me, and beside me there is no Savior**
> (Hos 13:4).

Matthew says that an angel of God told Mary to name her baby Jesus, **for he will save his people from their sins** (Mt 1:21). That instruction implies that the name Jesus means savior, but it doesn't. The name Jesus means YHVH is savior. Does God's angel make mistakes? Moreover, Jesus did not save his people [the Jews] from their sins, did he? If he did, then why did the church go on to teach that the Jews were damned for killing Jesus and rejecting him?

Regarding the title redeemer, the angel was silent. Significantly, no one in the entire New Testament calls Jesus "redeemer." Only the church calls Jesus "Redeemer." Redeemer, however, like Savior, is a title reserved exclusively for YHVH.

THINGS GOD NEVER SAID

There are things the church or Jesus says about Jesus that God never said about him:

God never said, "Behold, Jesus of Nazareth, my Messiah! my Christ!"

God never said, "Jesus is my only begotten son!"

God never said, "Jesus is the Way and the Truth and the Life!"

God never said, "No one comes to me except through Jesus!"

God never said, "Jesus is a member of the Trinity of which I am only one person of three and Jesus is another person equal with me and of the same substance!"

God never said, "I have relinquished my role as Savior and Redeemer and given those titles to my son, to Jesus!"

MARTYRDOM, SACRIFICE, AND REDEMPTION

In the days of Judah Maccabee, almost two centuries before Jesus lived, there were Jews who believed that martyrs redeemed the sins of their people and that the righteous dead would be resurrected. The church patterned its own teachings on those beliefs. When the old priest Eleazar was being tortured to death, he said:

> The King of the Universe shall raise us up, who have died for his Laws, unto everlasting life (2 Macc 7:9).

> It is good, on being put to death by men, to look for hope from God to be raised up again by him; as for you, you shall have no resurrection to life (2 Macc 7:14).

> Let my blood be a sacrifice to take away the sins of the people, and take my life to redeem theirs (4 Macc 6:27–29).

When the famous mother and her seven sons were martyred, the author of Four Maccabees wrote the following about their martyrdom:

> The nation was purified; the martyrs have become . . . a substitute, dying for the sins of the people (4 Macc 176:20–22).

The death of Jesus of Nazareth was just another in a long line of martyrdoms that many Jews thought redeemed the sins of the people. The Hebrew Scriptures, however, repeatedly teach that each person has to redeem his own sins, and that no person's death can take away another's sins:

> **[E]very man shall be put to death for his own sin** (Deut 24:16).

> **No man can by any means redeem his brother** (Ps 49:8).

> **[E]veryone shall die for his own sin** (Jer 31:30; 2 Kings 14:6; 2 Chron 25:4).

The martyrdom of Eleazar, the mother and her seven sons, and Jesus of Nazareth were meaningless deaths carried out by brutal murderers. The notion that martyrdom or self-sacrifice brings redemption is rationalization—an attempt to give meaning to the meaningless and to show that the death of innocents was not in vain, when in fact such deaths were in vain. Human sacrifice is never acceptable to God. How then could Jesus be a suitable victim for sacrifice, an acceptable offering to God? Most important of all, God did not even want sacrifice:

> **I desire mercy, not sacrifice** (Hos 6:5).

> **The sacrifice acceptable to God is a broken spirit, a broken and contrite heart** (Ps 51:17).

> **Bring me no sacrifices! They are in vain!** (Is 1:13).

Sacrifices were a barbaric practice of primitive man. There was nothing sacred about them. And they did not take away sins.

SON OF MAN

WAS JESUS SON OF MAN?

A crowd of Jews asked Jesus, **"Who is this Son of man?"** (Jn 12:34). Jesus did not answer. Elsewhere in the gospels, Jesus sometimes implied that Son of man referred to someone other than himself; at other times he implied it referred only to him. As on so many subjects, Jesus was not clear. The church, however, went on to say that Jesus alone was Son of man. But was he?

Son of man, as it is used in the Hebrew Scriptures, usually means a very ordinary man:

> **[W]hat is man that you are mindful of him and the son of man that you care for him? Yet you have made him a little less than God and do crown him with glory and honor. You have given him dominion over the works of your hands** (Ps 8:4–6).

The psalmist marvels that man or the son of man is a little less than God. The psalmist is speaking of all people in which case being a little less than God is a great honor bestowed upon people (as compared, for example, to the other creatures, which receive no such honor). However, if the psalmist is not speaking of people in general, but is speaking specifically and only of Jesus of Nazareth, then the psalmist gives another proof text that Jesus was not God but inferior to God, being "a little less" than God.

The book of Daniel gives the title son of man a special meaning. Daniel lived at a time when apocalyptic ideas were beginning to appear—about the second century BC. He prophesied that a time would come when God would select out of the myriad ordinary sons of men a special son of man,

whom God would exalt, give everlasting glory, and appoint to
rule the world:

> **I saw in the night visions, and—behold!—with the**
> **clouds of heaven there came one like a son of man.**
> **And he came to the Ancient of Days and was pre-**
> **sented before him. And to him was given dominion**
> **and glory and kingdom, that all peoples, nations,**
> **and languages should serve him. His dominion is an**
> **everlasting dominion which shall not pass away and**
> **his kingdom is one, and it shall not be destroyed**
> (Dan 7:13–14).

It is important to note that Daniel does not say that the son of
man (by convention, Daniel's special Son of man is usually
capitalized to distinguish him from ordinary sons of men, and
henceforth I shall follow that convention) and the Messiah are
one and the same man. They were two different men, each
with a different mission, the Messiah a *herald* announcing the
coming of God's reign of eternal peace on earth, Son of man
an eternal *ruler*, God's representative on earth, to reign over
the Kingdom of God.

The Book of Enoch, composed around the same time as the
the Book of Daniel, developed Daniel's concept of Son of
man. The early church greatly admired the Book of Enoch—Jude in the first century, Barnabas and Athenagoras in the
second, and Clement of Alexandria, Irenaeus, and Tertullian in
the third. It was so greatly admired that it was incorporated
into the early canon of the New Testament. The Book of
Enoch spoke of Enoch as Son of man.

But in the fifth century, the church, having decided that Jesus of Nazareth was the one and only Son of man, expunged
the Book of Enoch from the New Testament under express orders from the church fathers Hilary, Jerome, and Augustine.

All copies of the Book of Enoch were burned. Thus did Jesus become the one and only Son of man.

The Book of Enoch was destroyed for reasons other than Enoch's being the competitor to the title that now belonged exclusively to Jesus. Those reasons, however, did not become evident until the nineteenth century, when an ancient copy of the Book of Enoch was discovered in Abyssinia. That discovery generated so much excitement that Protestant scholars have been studying the Book of Enoch ever since.

The scholars were surprised to discover that the gospels at times ascribed to Jesus the same words, ideas, miraculous deeds, and diction that the Book of Enoch ascribed to Enoch. For example, Enoch says, "the Son of man shall sit on his glorious throne" (1 Enoch 62:5). Jesus says, *the Son of man shall sit on his glorious throne* (Mt 19:28). Enoch makes a descent into hell and then returns to earth, and so does Jesus. Enoch uses the word "Woe" to begin a curse, and so does Jesus. But Enoch and Jesus curse different things. Enoch curses evil-doers, whereas Jesus curses the world and its temptations, those who are intelligent and wise, those who are rich, who enjoy life, and are admired by others:

Enoch:

> Woe to those . . . for transgressing the wise. . . .
> Woe to those who . . . transgress the eternal Torah
> [the first five books of the Bible, but here meaning the Mosaic Law]. . . .
> Woe to you who spread evil to your neighbors. . . .
> Woe to [those] who reject the . . . eternal heritage of their fathers (Enoch 94:6–7; 103:4–7).

Jesus:

> *Woe to the world for temptations to sin!* (Mt 18:7).
>
> *Woe to you, scribes and Pharisees, hypocrites! . . .*
> *Woe to you blind guides! . . . Blind fools! . . .*
> *Woe to you scribes and Pharisees, hypocrites! . . .*
> *Serpents! Brood of vipers! . . . You fools!* (Mt 23).
>
> *Woe to you that are rich. . . .*
> *Woe to you that are full now. . . .*
> *Woe to you that laugh now. . . .*
> *Woe to you, when all men speak well of you* (Lk 6:24–26).

Although Enoch repeatedly praises righteousness, Jesus hardly speaks of it. Enoch:

> This is the Son of man who has righteousness, with whom dwells righteousness, and who reveals all the treasures hidden because God has chosen him (Enoch 46:3).
>
> This is the Son of man who is born unto righteousness. . . . He proclaims unto you peace in the name of the world to come. . . . And all shall walk in his ways since righteousness never forsakes him. . . (Enoch 71:14–16).

Enoch proclaims that on Judgment Day, those who did evil to the Jews—forced them to convert (to a heathen religion), turned them away from the Law, and otherwise harmed them—shall be destroyed, along with their images and houses of worship, and they will be cast into the fires of hell and their souls will perish into oblivion (Enoch 91:7–9). Jesus, however, condemns to the eternal fires of hell not those who do evil to the Jews or anyone else, but those who do not believe in him. Enoch's punishment is merciful oblivion, whereas Jesus' punishment is the cruel, pitiless, and endless torture of eternal hellfire.

When the church discovered that Enoch condemned the very acts the church was engaging in, the Book of Enoch had to be destroyed, for Enoch in effect was condemning the church!

Some Jews in the gospel asked Jesus, **Who is this 'Son of man'?** Jesus did not answer.

PROPHET

WAS JESUS A PROPHET?

Matthew says that many Jews considered Jesus a prophet:

> **[The] multitudes . . . held Jesus to be a prophet** (Mt 21:46).

The Hebrew Scriptures tell how to distinguish a true prophet from a false one:

> **When a prophet speaks in the name of the Lord [YHVH], if the word does not come to pass or come true, that is a word which the Lord [YHVH] has not spoken, the prophet has spoken presumptuously** (Deut 18:21–22).

Jesus said it succinctly:

> *Beware of false prophets. . . . You will know them by their fruits* (Mt 7:15–16).

The Hebrew Scriptures prescribe the punishment for a false prophet:

> **The prophet who presumes to speak a word in my name which I have not commanded him to speak . . . that same prophet shall die** (Deut 18:20).

Did Jesus speak words that God had not commanded him to speak? Jesus prophesied:

> *I tell you this: the present generation will live to see it all* (Mt 24:34).

> *The time is fulfilled, and the Kingdom of God is at hand* (Mk 1:14).

> *There are some standing here who will not taste death before they see the Kingdom of God* (Mk 9:1; Lk 9:27).

But the time was not fulfilled; the Kingdom of God did not come; and Jesus' generation did not live "to see it all." More than two thousand years have passed, and still nothing has happened.

Jesus prophesied:

> **When Jesus came in sight of Jerusalem, he wept over it and said. . . .** *For a time will come upon you when your enemies . . . will bring you to the ground . . . and not leave you one stone standing on another* (Lk 19:42–45).

Today in Jerusalem, the western and southern walls of the Temple precincts still stand "one stone standing on another."

There are scholars who say that when Jesus rails against the Jews, he does so in a "purifying" sense like the Hebrew prophets. But that is not so. Jesus does not rail; he rants and he raves. He is insulting, pitiless, and spiteful. And, unlike the Hebrew prophets, Jesus does not end his harangue on a note of love and reconciliation:

> ***Woe to you, scribes and Pharisees, hypocrites!* . . .**
> ***Woe to you blind guides!* . . . *Blind fools!* . . .**
> ***Woe to you scribes and Pharisees, hypocrites!* . . .**
> ***Serpents! Brood of vipers! You Pharisees!* . . .**
> ***You fools!*** (Mt 23).

There is nothing "purifying" in this condemnation, and not a trace of love. Compare the prophet Isaiah at his harshest:

> **Ah, sinful nation, people laden with iniquity, off-spring of evildoers, children given to corruption. They have forsaken the Lord [YHVH], they have spurned the Holy One of Israel, and they are utterly estranged** (Is 1:4).

But Isaiah concludes:

> **Come now, let us reason together, says the Lord [YHVH]. Though your sins are like scarlet, they shall be white as snow** (Is 1:18).

SON OF GOD

THE MANY SONS OF GOD

The church teaches that Jesus is the only son of God and that God is the only Father of Jesus. But Luke calls Adam **the son of God** (Lk 3:38). And all of Adam's early descendants are also called sons of God:

> **When men began to multiply on the face of the earth, and daughters were born to them, the sons of God saw that the daughters of men were fair, and took to wife such of them as they chose** (Gen 6:1–2).

Beginning with Abraham, God called the Jews "sons of God":

> **You are the sons of the Lord [YHVH] your God** (Deut 14:1).

David, on being anointed King of Israel, said he was a "begotten" son of God:

> **I will tell of the decree of the Lord [YHVH]. He said to me, "You are my son. Today I have begotten you"** (Ps 2:7).

The prophets said:

> **The Lord [YHVH] has spoken: Sons have I reared and brought up** (Is 1:2).

> **I thought how I would place you among my sons. . . . And I thought how you would call me "My Father"** (Jer 3:19).

> **You are the sons of the living God** (Hos 1:10).

> **When Israel was a child, I loved him; and out of Egypt I called my son. . . .** (Hos 11:1).

Israel shouts joyfully:

> **You, O Lord [YHVH], are our Father** (Is 63:16; cf. 64:8).

The responsive refrain "You are my son! You are our Father!" appears repeatedly throughout the Hebrew Scriptures.

"OUR FATHER"

Jesus made no unique claim to God as Father. On saying good-bye to the disciples, Jesus said:

> *I am ascending to my Father and your Father* (Jn 20:17).

Jesus taught his disciples to pray, *Our Father who art in heaven* (Mt 6:9). He did not teach them to pray, "Father of Jesus, who art in heaven." And Jesus said:

> *Call no man your father on earth, for you have one Father, and he is in heaven* (Mt 23:9).

> *Forgive . . . so that your Father who is in heaven also may forgive you* (Mk 11:25).

Jesus spoke of many sons of God:

> *Blessed are the peacemakers, for they shall be called sons of God* (Mt 5:9).

> *Love your enemies and pray for those who persecute you so that you may be a son of your Father who is in heaven* (Mt 5:44).

> *Those considered worthy . . . are sons of God* (Lk 20:35).

Jesus' disciples also spoke of many sons of God. Paul wrote:

> **For all who are led by the Spirit of God are sons of God** (Rom 8:14).

> **When we cry, "Abba! Father!" it is the Spirit itself bearing witness with our spirit that we are children of God** (Rom 8:17).

John wrote:

> **See what love the Father has given to us, that we should be called the children of God** (1 Jn 3:1).

> **Whoever loves is the child of God** (1 Jn 4:7).

DAUGHTER OF GOD

> **God created man in his own image, in the image of God he created him; male and female he created them** (Gen 1:27).

Insofar as God is male and female, if Jesus of Nazareth is the incarnation of God, then Jesus ought to be not only the Son of God but also the Daughter of God. But he wasn't. Jesus was male.

"YOU ARE MY SON, TODAY I HAVE BEGOTTEN YOU"

When David as an adult was anointed King of Israel, he said God blessed him with the following words: **You are my son, today I have begotten you** (Ps 2:7). The word *begotten* literally means conceived by egg and sperm. From David's context, however, that word is clearly metaphorical, and the metaphor means *anointed*, chosen by God for a high purpose; it is not literal, not egg and sperm. That David would use a sexual metaphor at this momentous occasion in his life was so consistent with David that the psalm has never been a source of difficulty for scholars or ordinary readers. On the contrary. After David's anointment, all Jewish kings and high priests were anointed with the recitation of those very words. As a result, God had many "begotten" sons, all begotten as adults by anointment.

Significantly, and in contrast, Jesus of Nazareth, although considered by the church both "King of the Jews" and high priest who sacrificed himself on the altar of the cross, was not anointed by God in any of the four gospels with the words, **You are my son, today I have begotten you.** Aware of this great deficiency, church redactors during or after the fourth century took Paul's letter to the Hebrews, already a well-known forgery, and added the following words implying that God said them only to Jesus:

> **"Thou art my Son, today I have begotten thee"** (Heb 1:5).

> **Christ did not exalt himself to be made a high priest, but was appointed by him who said to him, You are my son, today I have begotten you** (Heb 5:5).

It is important to note that the forgers of the letter to the Hebrews held back and did not say Christ was *anointed* by God but rather he was *appointed* by him. And even though God purportedly said this when Jesus was an adult, just as God had said it in the case of David, the church nonetheless taught that Jesus was not just another metaphorical begotten son of God, but was truly and literally the one and only begotten son of God, conceived by Mary through the Holy Spirit. By teaching that, the church committed the gravest of blunders. Camels, sheep, dogs, pigs, and other animals beget; heathen gods beget;

and men beget. But God does not beget, neither on his own nor through the Holy Spirit, except metaphorically through anointment of special men. God *creates* like a craftsman (Gen 2:7; Is 64:8).

THE FATHER "BEGOT" JESUS BUT "CREATED" THE REST OF US

The church father Ambrose in the second century was the first to teach that Jesus of Nazareth was literally the only "begotten" Son of God. Ambrose wrote:

> Pray the 'Our Father'. . . but do not claim any special privilege. . . . The Father begot Christ but he created us (*De Sacramentis*, v. 4).

If the Holy Spirit impregnated Mary without sexual intercourse, the Spirit nonetheless had to have delivered divine sperm to her. In Luke's gospel, an angel prepares Mary for that forthcoming impregnation:

> **The Holy Spirit will come upon you, and the power of the Most High will overshadow you** (Lk 1:35).

But the Holy Spirit does not cast shadows. No spirit casts shadows. Men cast shadows. So Luke got it half right. Mary was indeed overshadowed, and Jesus was indeed begotten. But not by the Most High and not by the Holy Spirit.

WAS JESUS CONCEIVED WITH DIVINE SEMEN?

The church teaches that Jesus of Nazareth was not begotten by human semen. The implication is that Jesus was begotten by divine semen, although without sexual intercourse.

Jesus could not have been conceived without semen, for then he would have received only his mother Mary's X chromosomes, in which case he would have been a girl. Only with semen could Jesus have received the Y chromosome necessary to make a boy.

THE GREEK MYSTERY RELIGION OF THE SON OF GOD

Son of God meant one thing to the Jews, another to the Greeks. To the Jews, son of God meant a Jew, any Jew. To the Greeks, son of God meant Dionysus, son of God, son of Zeus. The name Dionysus itself means son of God. The mother of Dionysus was a mortal woman named Semele.

Dionysus was the god of the grape, of the grape vine, and of wine. To be productive of fruit, the grape vine has to be severely pruned each year. According to the myth, Dionysus suffered so greatly during pruning that he died. But each spring, he miraculously came back to life. The Greeks called the budding of the "dead" vine the resurrection. And Dionysus, they called, the resurrected god.

During the mysteries and sacraments devoted to Dionysus, celebrants drank his wine, which they believed was his blood. Those who imbibed could feel Dionysus coursing through their bodies and giving them a sense of warmth and well-being. All fear was conquered, and worshipers were transported by joy, love, and freedom. Through this divine union with the god, celebrants became divine themselves.

The festival in honor of Dionysus's resurrection was celebrated every spring. People felt about Dionysus as about no other, and he became the most important god of Greece. Those who worshiped Dionysus believed that through his death and resurrection their own souls lived forever. Cicero, a believer, wrote, "Nothing is higher than these mysteries. . . . They have not only shown us the way to live joyfully, but they have taught us how to die with a better hope" (Edith Hamilton, *Mythology*, New York: The New American Library, A Mentor Book, 1940, 1961, pp. 47–62).

To become Christians, the celebrants of the mysteries merely had to exchange Dionysus for Jesus. But the Greeks had to be persuaded that the trade was worthwhile. And so John the evangelist had Jesus say: ***I am the true vine and my Father is the gardener*** (Jn 15:1), the implication being that Dionysus was the false vine and his father, Zeus did not tend him or care about him, whereas Jesus was the true vine and his Father tends him and cares deeply about him.

GODS HAVE INTERCOURSE WITH MORTAL WOMEN

In Greek and Roman mythology, the immortal gods had intercourse with mortal women. The most famous example is Zeus, Father of Gods and men, who had intercourse with Semele, a mortal woman whom he loved; from that union came the God Dionysus, who is of great importance in the history of Christianity.

Josephus, the historian of the first century, reports the following historical incident between a fraudulent god and a mortal woman:

> There lived in Rome a woman by the name of Paulina, who enjoyed a wonderful reputation because of the virtuous life she led. She was both very rich and very beautiful, and at that age when women are most attractive. She was married to a man named Saturninus, who, in every way, equaled her in excellence of character.
>
> Mundus, a young man high in government, fell in love with Paulina. He confided this to his servant-

woman Ida, who devised a scheme to help him achieve his goal. Ida went to the priests of the goddess Isis and bribed them to entrap the virtuous woman.

The eldest of the priests went immediately to Paulina and told her that he was sent by the god Anubis who had fallen in love with her and wanted her to come to him. She received the message kindly and valued herself greatly because of this condescension of the god. And she told her husband. He agreed to her acceptance of the offer, completely satisfied with the chastity of his wife.

Accordingly, she went to the temple of the god Anubis and dined there. And when it was the hour to retire, the priest shut the temple doors, and in the holy of holies, the lights were extinguished. Then Mundus came. And Paulina was at his service all night long, believing he was the god. In the early hours of the morning, Paulina went to her husband, and told him how the god had come to her. Even among her friends, she spoke openly of this favor of the god, and how greatly she valued it (Paraphrased after Josephus, *Jewish Antiquities* 18:66–80).

HORUS AND JESUS

Jesus of Nazareth had a striking resemblance not only to the Greek god Dionysus, but also to the the Egyptian god Horus.

Horus was the "only begotten son" of the God Osiris. He was born of a virgin, although some doubted it. His mother's name was Isis or Meri. To Meri came an annunciation by an angel. His foster father's name was Seb (Joseph), who was of royal descent.

Horus was born humbly in a cave at the time of the winter solstice. His birth was heralded by a star, and was announced by angels to shepherds. He was baptized in the river Eridanus by a man named Anup the Baptizer. He was tempted by Set (Satan), but resisted. He surrounded himself with disciples.

Horus walked on water, cast out demons, and healed the blind. He raised Osiris from the dead. His most famous address was called the "Sermon on the Mount."

Horus died by crucifixion, accompanied by two thieves, and was buried in a tomb. He descended into hell, was resurrected after three days, and was transfigured on a mountain.

Horus was regarded as Savior, but was more often called Krst, or the Anointed one. He was also called the Good Shepherd, the Lamb of God, the Bread of Life, the Son of man, and the Word. His zodiac sign was the fish.

ASPIRING TO GODHEAD

The Hebrews taught that aspiring to godhead was a grave sin. The prophet Isaiah spoke of the King of Babylon's aspirations for godhead as a warning to all:

> **How you are fallen from heaven, O Morning Star, Son of the Dawn! How you are cut down to the ground. . . . You said in your heart: "I will ascend to heaven, above the stars of God will I exalt my throne. . . . I will make myself like the Most High." But you are brought down to the nether world, to the depths of the Pit** (Is 14:12–15).

The church "solved" the problem of men aspiring to godhead by inverting it and having God humble himself and condescend to become man. The church father Athanasius wrote: "God became man so that men might become gods." And the church father Augustine wrote: "To make men gods, God was made man." Whether man ascends to godhead or gods descend to manhood, the end result is the same. But God does not condescend to become a man simply because men wish it to be so. Jesus, a Jew who believed what the Jews believed and not what the gentile church later taught, said: *God is spirit, and those who worship him must worship in spirit and truth* (Jn 4:24).

ONLY BEGOTTEN SON OF GOD

If Jesus of Nazareth was truly the only begotten son of God, then the God who begat Jesus could not have been YHVH. Perhaps it was Zeus, king of gods and men, or Ares, god of war.

"MY BELOVED SON"

Who called Jesus "my beloved Son"?

> **And when Jesus was baptized, he went up immediately from the water, and behold, the heavens were opened and [Jesus] saw the Spirit of God descending like a dove, and alighting on him; and lo, a voice from heaven, saying, "This is my beloved Son with whom I am well pleased." Then Jesus was led up by the Spirit into the wilderness to be tempted by the devil** (Mt 3:16–17; 4–1).

This verse is a cascade of non sequiturs. The heavens opened and the Spirit of God descended on Jesus like a dove. What does "like a dove" mean? Then came "a voice from heaven." Why from heaven rather than from the Spirit of God who descended from heaven and lighted on Jesus? Whose voice was it? Then the Spirit led Jesus into the wilderness so that he could be tempted by Satan. Why? Redactors of Matthew tried again:

> [Jesus] was still speaking, when lo, a bright cloud overshadowed him, and a voice from the cloud said, "This is my beloved Son, with whom I am well pleased; listen to him." When the disciples heard this, they fell on their faces, and were filled with awe. . . . And when they lifted up their eyes, they saw no one but Jesus only (Mt 17:5–8).

This time there is no "Spirit of God descending like a dove." Instead of coming from heaven, a voice comes from a cloud. But again, whose voice was it?

Mark tells the story this way:

> Jesus . . . was baptized by John. . . . And when he came up out of the water, immediately he saw the heavens open and the Spirit descending upon him like a dove; and a voice came from heaven, "Thou art my beloved Son; with thee I am well pleased." The Spirit immediately drove him out into the wilderness. And he was in the wilderness forty days, tempted by Satan (Mk 1:11–13).

Again the Spirit descended upon Jesus "like a dove." And again a voice comes from heaven. Again we do not know whose voice it was. Again the Spirit immediately drives Jesus into the wilderness to be tempted by the devil.

Luke tells the story this way:

> Now when all the people were baptized, and when Jesus also had been baptized and was praying, the heaven was opened, and the Holy Spirit descended upon him in bodily form as a dove and a voice came from heaven, "Thou art my beloved Son; with thee I am well pleased" (Lk 3:22).

Luke, deriving his version from the others, takes it upon himself to clarify Matthew and Mark, just as he clarified Matthew's version of the Sermon on the Mount: Luke does not speak of the "Spirit" or the "Spirit of God" that descended on Jesus. Luke tells us plainly it was the "Holy Spirit"; the Holy Spirit descended "in bodily form as a dove." A real dove, at last! A dove—the Incarnation of the Holy Spirit! Curiously the church doesn't speak of *that* Incarnation. But again the voice comes from heaven, not from the Holy Spirit. But Luke like the others does not answer the critical question: Whose voice was speaking from heaven? Gabriel? A heavenly host?

John, who never loses an opportunity to proclaim Jesus as the Son of God, ignores the story altogether, perhaps because even John found it incredible.

Significantly, none of the evangelists says that the voice from heaven was God's.

WHO IS THE SON OF GOD?

Who is the Son of God, the only begotten Son of God? Even Jesus, after all is said and done, said he did not know: *No one knows who the Son is but the Father* (Lk 10:22).

PERFECT MAN

PERFECT MAN

At the Council of Chalcedon in 451, the church declared that Jesus of Nazareth, was "Perfect man," that is, man free from sin. However, Jesus did not consider himself free from sin:

> *Why do you call me good? No one is good but God alone* (Mk 10:18).

THE RICH AND THE POOR

A perfect man speaks clearly, but Jesus often did not. He frequently sent mixed messages. Consider the case of the rich and the poor. At first Jesus seemed to favor the poor and condemn the rich:

> **And behold, one [young man] came up to him, saying, "Teacher, what good deed must I do, to have eternal life?" And [Jesus] said to him. . . . "If you would enter [eternal] life, keep the commandments." . . . The young man said to him, "All these I have observed, what do I still lack?" Jesus said to him, "If you would be perfect, go, sell what you possess and give to the poor, and you will have treasure in heaven; and come, follow me." When the young man heard this, he went away sorrowful; for he had great possessions.**
>
> **And Jesus said to his disciples, "Truly, I say to you, it will be hard for a rich man to enter the kingdom of heaven. Again I tell you, it is easier for a camel to go through the eye of a needle than for a rich man to enter the kingdom of God."** (Mt 19:16–26; cf. Mk 10:21–27; cf. Lk 18:22–28).

The young man of this story chose to stay rich. And so, too, does the Pope and the Vatican. Perhaps they think giving away all their treasure to the poor is a futile gesture because it would not alleviate poverty. Jesus taught:

> ***The poor you have with you always*** (Mt 26:11; Mk 14:7; cf. Jn 12:8).

Jesus dismissed hunger, starvation, and exposure as irremediable:

Do not be anxious saying, What shall we eat?" (Mt 6:31–32).

Do not be anxious about your life, what you shall eat, nor about your body, what you shall wear. For life is more than food and the body more than clothing. Consider the ravens; they neither sow nor reap . . . and yet God feeds them (Lk 12:22–24).

Consider the lilies of the field . . . they neither toil nor spin (Mt 6:28; Lk 12:27).

In reality, during harsh winters, God does not provide for the birds, and many birds, along with many poor, die of exposure and starvation. Jesus consoled the poor thus:

Blessed are the poor, for yours is the Kingdom of God (Lk 6:20).

As for the rich, Jesus changed his mind about them, and even favored them over the poor. He took particular delight in capitalists, although they were not called by that name in his day. He loved anyone who invested and made a profitable return. Jesus told the following story: A rich man, who had three servants, was planning to take a trip. He entrusted five bags of gold to the first servant, two bags to the second, and one bag to the third. The first and second invested the gold, but the third buried his for safekeeping. When the master returned, the first servant's investment of five bags had yielded ten. The second's two bags yielded four. But the third servant could only bring forth the original bag. The master was pleased with the first two servants but displeased with the third. He ordered him to turn over his bag, cursed him, killed him, and sent him to hell! The moral of the story:

> *For to everyone who has will more be given, and he will have in abundance; but from him who has not, even what he has will be taken away* (Mt 25:29; cf. Lk 19:12–26).

Jesus is the very model of what antisemites call a "money grubbing Jew." Was he "Perfect man"?

SERMONS ON MOUNTAIN AND PLAIN

Jesus' Sermon on the Mount is famous. Its blessings put Jesus in a highly favorable light, even though some of the blessings are unrealistic or unintelligible:

> **[Jesus] went up on the mountain, and when he sat down his disciples came to him. And he opened his mouth and taught them, saying:**
>
> *Blessed are the poor in spirit, for theirs is the kingdom of heaven.*
>
> *Blessed are those who mourn, for they shall be comforted.*
>
> *Blessed are the meek, for they shall inherit the earth.*
>
> *Blessed are those who hunger and thirst for righteousness, for they shall be satisfied.*
>
> *Blessed are the merciful, for they shall obtain mercy.*
>
> *Blessed are the pure in heart, for they shall see God.*
>
> *Blessed are the peacemakers, for they shall be called sons of God.*
>
> *Blessed are those who are persecuted for righteousness' sake, for theirs is the kingdom of heaven.*
>
> *Blessed are you when men revile you and persecute you and utter all kinds of evil against you falsely on my account* (Mt 5:1–11).

The problems with the blessings:

- The phrase "poor in spirit" is obscure. It does not mean the poor, and it cannot mean those who are deficient in spirituality.
- Jesus does not comfort mourners. Quite the contrary. To mourners, Jesus said, most discomfortingly, **Leave the dead to bury their own dead** (Mt 8:22; Lk 9:60). But even if Jesus had comforted mourners, there is nothing original in that act of ordinary kindness.
- It is not true that the meek shall inherit the earth. That is wishful thinking and contrary to natural selection and survival of the fittest, laws presumably laid down by God.
- Jesus does not promise to satisfy those who are hungry, but "those who hunger and thirst for righteousness." Jesus does not say just how that kind of hunger will be satisfied.
- Jesus does not say under what circumstances "the merciful . . . shall obtain mercy." In heaven?
- If all men are sinners, who are the "pure in heart"?
- Jesus does not say in what way persecuted believers are blessed.

According to Luke, when Jesus came down from the mountain, he went on to deliver a Sermon on the Plain, whereupon the first thing Jesus did was to clarify some of the problems (identified above) in Matthew's Sermon on the Mount:

> **And [Jesus] came down [from the mountain] . . . and stood on the plain with a great crowd of disciples and a great multitude. . . . And he lifted up his eyes on his disciples, and said:**
>
> **Blessed are you poor, for yours is the kingdom of God. Blessed are you that hunger now, for you shall be satisfied.**

> *Blessed are you that weep now, for you shall laugh.*
> *Blessed are you when men hate you . . . on account of*
> *the Son of man! Rejoice . . . your reward is great in*
> *heaven* (Lk 6:17–23).

On the plain, Jesus blesses not the "poor in spirit" but the "poor."

On the plain, Jesus blesses not "those who hunger . . . for righteousness," but those who are hungry. Jesus, however, does not explain how he intends to satisfy world hunger.

On the plain, Jesus addresses not only mourners, but all who weep, telling them that they will eventually laugh. That is hardly an original idea (see Psalm 30:5), but at least it is comforting.

On the plain, Jesus explains in what way hated believers are blessed: they shall inherit heaven.

Luke in the Sermon on the Plain thereby solves the difficulties in the blessings in Matthew that lend themselves to solution, and deletes those that are incomprehensible or untrue. The omitted blessings are: "the meek . . . shall inherit the earth"; "the merciful . . . shall obtain mercy"; "the pure in heart . . . shall see God."

Then Jesus takes the listener by surprise, turning from blessing to cursing:

> *But woe to you that are rich, for you have received*
> *   your consolation [reward].*
> *Woe to you that are full now, for you shall hunger.*
> *Woe to you that laugh now, for you shall mourn and*
> *   weep* (Lk 6:17–25).
> *Woe to you, when all men speak well of you. . .*
> (Lk 24–26).

These curses clearly reveal a different Jesus, one who is a spiteful and hateful.

VOLATILE AND UNCONTROLLABLE RAGE

Jesus had a volatile temper that could go rapidly from anger to uncontrollable and violent rage. Take the case of Jesus and the money changers in the temple precincts. At first Jesus grew angry at them. Even anger was inappropriate because they had every right to be there, for their job was making change or converting currency for foreigners making pilgrimage to Jerusalem who wished to buy pigeons or other sacrificial animals for temple sacrifice. Their stalls were not located within the Temple itself as the gospels say, but in the courtyards outside. After giving the money changers a severe tongue lashing, Jesus overturned their counting tables, savagely whipped them, and finally drove them from the Temple precincts. Sweet Jesus? Gentle Jesus?

Or take the case of Jesus and the fig tree. It bore no fruit, not being the season for figs. But Jesus wanted figs. Not getting what he wanted when he wanted it, Jesus cursed and destroyed the tree.

IMPERFECT AND SINNER FROM BIRTH

According to Luke's gospel, Jesus was stained with sin at his birth and so was his mother who gave birth to him:

> **And at the end of eight days, when he was circumcised, he was called Jesus. . . . And when the time came for [mother and child's] purification according to the law of Moses, they brought [the baby Jesus] up to Jerusalem to present him to the Lord . . . and to offer a sacrifice according to what is said in the law of the Lord** (Lk 2:21–24).

BAPTISM

The church teaches that baptism removes original sin. But Jesus did not teach that. Jesus never did teach the purpose of baptism.

Jesus was baptized by John the baptist, but it is not clear why. The church teaches: "[By his baptism, Jesus] allows himself to be numbered among sinners" (*Catechism of the Catholic Church*, p. 136). The church is saying that Jesus wanted to be considered no different from ordinary men born with original sin. In short, Jesus was pretending to be one of the guys. If that is so, that would be another example of Jesus' deceit, in which case, as a sinner, Jesus was in need of baptism.

MIXED MESSAGES ON JUDGMENT

Jesus was not perfect. He frequently sent mixed messages. Take the case of passing judgment:

> *Judge not that you be not judged* (Mt 7:1).

That statement is famous. Others are similar:

> *I judge no one* (Jn 8:15).

> *I did not come to judge the world* (Jn 12:47).

But Jesus reverses himself:

> *The Father judges no one but has given all judgment to the Son* (Jn 5:22).

> *Even if I do judge, my judgment is true* (Jn 8:15–16).

> *For judgment I came into this world* (Jn 9:39).

MORE MIXED MESSAGES

Jesus sent other mixed messages (statement A conflicts with statement B):

A: *Jesus gave them strict orders not to tell anyone* (Mk 8:29–30).

B: *I have spoken openly to everyone. . . . I have said nothing in secret* (Jn 18:20).

A: *If I testify on my own behalf, that testimony is not valid* (Jn 5:31).

B: *My testimony is valid even though I do bear witness about myself* (Jn 8:14).

A: *He who is not with me is against me* (Mt 12:30).

B: *He that is not against you is for you* (Lk 9:50).

A: *Do not condemn and you will not be condemned* (Lk 6:37).

B: *Woe to you, scribes and Pharisees, hypocrites! . . . Blind fools! . . . Blind men! . . . Serpents. Brood of vipers. How are you to escape being sentenced in hell!* (Mt 23).

A: *If you forgive others the wrongs they have done, the heavenly Father will likewise forgive you. But if you do not forgive others, then the wrongs that you have done will not be forgiven by your Father* (Mt 6:14–15).

B: *But if you retain the sins of any, they are retained* (Jn 20:22–23).

A: *Love your neighbor as yourself* (Mt 19:19; 22:39; Mk 12:31).

B: *The man who loves himself is lost, but he who hates himself in this world will be kept safe for eternal life* (Jn 12:25).

A: *He who believes in the son has eternal life* (Jn 3:36).

B: *Anyone who speaks a word against the Son of man will receive forgiveness* (Lk 12:10).

A: *For all who take the sword will perish by the sword* (Mt 26:52).

B: *Do not think that I have come to bring peace on earth. I have not come to bring peace, but the sword* (Mt 10:34–36).

EXTRAORDINARY HEALERS

Jesus taught his followers that in his name they would cure the sick:

> *In my name . . . [followers] will lay their hands on the sick, and they will recover* (Mk 16:17–18).

Sometimes they recovered and sometimes they didn't. If the disciples of Jesus were to become such extraordinary healers, why during the Middle Ages, did emperors, kings, and even popes choose for their personal physicians not Jesus' disciples but Jews?

HEAVY BURDENS

Jesus castigated the Pharisees for placing *heavy burdens on men's shoulders, but they will not raise a finger to lift a load themselves* (Mt 23:4–5). And yet Jesus placed even heavier burdens on men's shoulders than the Pharisees:

- Jesus taught that lust was as sinful as committing adultery and would be similarly punished by the fires of hell.
- Jesus taught that getting angry was as sinful as committing murder and would be similarly punished by the fires of hell.
- Jesus taught that disease was punishment for sins; if one wanted to be cured, one had to be forgiven and cease sinning. After curing a paralyzed man, Jesus commanded: *See, you are well! Sin no more in order that nothing worse befall you!* (Jn 5:14). That is superstitious nonsense. Illness is part of nature, and has nothing to do with sins. Hippocrates, the Father of Medicine, who lived five centuries before Jesus, taught that, liberating mankind from an evil superstition. Jesus reintroduced the superstition, and the church continues to teach it: "[I]llness is mysteriously linked to sin and evil" (*Catechism of the Catholic Church*, p. 375).
- Jesus commanded: *Be perfect even as your heavenly Father is perfect* (Mt 5:48). No human being can be perfect, and striving for perfection is futile. The frustration at not achieving perfection may lead to depression, even suicide. Jesus was cruel to give people that impossible commandment, with dire consequences.
- Jesus commanded: *Raise the dead* (Mt 10:8). What was the purpose in giving people that impossible commandment?

Jesus placed far heavier burdens on men's shoulders than the Pharisees ever did. Jesus did not lighten their load, but increased it.

ASKING QUESTIONS

Jesus frequently became angry when people asked him questions. He seemed to think that the purpose of their question was not to clarify or gain understanding but to express doubt in him, to question him. He would lash out at the questioner, attack, insult, and curse him. His disciples were well aware of that behavior and were afraid of it, and so they tried not to ask him questions: **The disciples did not understand his saying, but they were afraid to ask him** (Mk 9:32).

NOT PRACTICING WHAT HE PREACHED

Jesus was disdainful of those who did not practice what they preached:

> *Practice and observe whatever [the scribes and Pharisees] tell you, but not what they do; for they preach, but do not practice* (Mt 23:3).

And yet, Jesus himself did not practice what he preached. He preached love of enemy, but he frequently cursed his enemy.

Jesus condemned those who made a show of religion:

> *Be careful not to make a show of your religion before men. For if you do, no reward awaits you in your Father's house in heaven* (Mt 6:1).

And yet, Jesus made a show of religion: He could have saved a sick Lazarus from dying, but Jesus said it was better to let Lazarus die and raise him from the dead because raising a dead man brought glory. Raising the dead would impress even God, which was important *so that the Son of God may be glorified* (Jn 1:1–4).

TELLING LIES
Jesus was not perfect. He told lies, and he was deceitful:

> **Now the Jews' feast of Tabernacles was at hand. So his brothers said to him, "Leave here and go to Judea, that your disciples may see the works you are doing. For no man works in secret if he seeks to be known openly. If you do these things, show yourself to the world." For even his brothers did not believe in him. Jesus said to them,** *My time has not yet come, but your time is always here. The world cannot hate you, but it hates me because I testify of it that its works are evil. Go to the feast yourselves; I am not going up to the feast, for my time has not yet fully come.* **So saying, he remained in Galilee. But after his brothers had gone up to the feast, then he also went up, not publicly but in private** (Jn 7:2–10).

While hurling a terrible curse at Jerusalem, Jesus told an extravagant lie, saying that Jerusalem killed all the prophets, including Abel, son of Adam and Eve:

> *I send you prophets and wise men and scribes, some of whom you will kill and crucify and some you will scourge in your synagogues and persecute from town to town, that upon you may come all the righteous blood shed on earth, from the blood of innocent Abel to the blood of Zechariah, the son of Barachiah, whom you murdered between the sanctuary and the altar. Truly I say to you, all this will come upon this generation. O Jerusalem, Jerusalem, killing the*

prophets and stoning those who are sent to you!"
(Mt 23:34–37; cf. Lk 11:51).

At the time Abel was killed, Jerusalem had not yet been founded. And most know that Abel was murdered by his brother Cain. By his sweeping curse and condemnation, Jesus reveals what an extravagant liar he was and how spiteful he could be.

Jesus also condemns Jerusalem for killing the prophet Zechariah, the son of Barachiah. If Jesus meant Zechariah, the son of Berechiah, then he lied again, for that prophet died of old age. Moreover, there is no evidence of prophets being scourged and killed in synagogues.

The church defends Jesus by dismissing his lies as "trifles," saying Jesus was merely trying to make a point, not trying to be factual. To make a point, one cannot make false accusations of murder and dismiss them as trifles. Jesus taught: *Whoever is dishonest in trifles is dishonest in matters of great importance also* (Lk 16:10).

WINNING HEAVEN THROUGH DECEPTION

Jesus presents a devious scheme on how a sinner may attain heaven:

A man accidentally stumbles on treasure in a field. An honest man would run and report his discovery to the owner of the field, and hope for a reward. But Jesus does not advise that. This is what Jesus advises: the man should carefully rebury the treasure, making the earth look undisturbed, and then sell whatever it takes to buy the field. Then as the new landowner, he can dig up the treasure that is now rightfully his:

The kingdom of heaven is like treasure in a field,
which a man found and covered up; then, in his joy,

he goes and sells all that he has and buys that field
(Mt 13:44).

Hasn't Jesus forgotten someone in his scheme? Although the seller of the field was duped, God was not. Jesus is the quintessential example of the kind of person gentiles call "dirty Jew!" One last matter: Does anyone believe that the cheat is actually going to go to heaven?

SELF-SERVING
Jesus was self-serving:

> *A prophet is given honor except in his own country and from his own family* (Mt 13:57).

This famous aphorism is supposed to explain why the Jews including Jesus' family did not believe in him. But the aphorism is not true. The Hebrew prophets were held in high regard by the Jews; a whole section in the Hebrew Scriptures is devoted to them, as the church well knows.

JESUS COMPARED WITH SOCRATES
Socrates, the Greek philosopher who lived five centuries before Jesus, was very different from Jesus: Socrates loved wisdom, dialogue, and questions; Socrates did not insist on his own way; and he went to his death calmly and resolutely.

WISDOM
The church teaches that Jesus of Nazareth is Wisdom itself, but the evidence does not support that.
The Hebrew Scriptures teach the following about wisdom:

Happy the man who fixes his thoughts on wisdom, and uses his brains to think—the man who contemplates wisdom's ways and ponders her secrets (Sirah 14:20–21).

I [Wisdom] speak excellent things. . . . All the words of my mouth are in righteousness; there is nothing crooked or perverse in them. They are all plain to men of understanding. . . . I love those who love me; and those who seek me diligently shall find me. Riches and honor are with me, enduring wealth and prosperity. . . .

The Lord [YHVH] created me at the beginning of his work, the first of his acts of old. I was set up from everlasting, from the beginning, before ever the earth was. . . . By the time he made the heavens, I was there. . . . When he marked out the foundations of the earth, I was by him as a little child; and I was daily his delight, playing always at his side, rejoicing in his inhabited world, delighting in the sons of men.

Now, therefore listen to me, O children; for happy are they who keep my ways. . . . For whoever finds me finds life, and finds favor of the Lord [YHVH]. But whoever rejects me injures his own soul; those who hate me love death (Prov 8:1–36).

And those who are wise shall shine like the brightness of the firmament (Dan 12:1–3).

Jesus frequently did not speak in plain speech. Jesus did not value riches, honor, or property. Jesus did not rejoice in the world or delight in its people. According to the Infancy Gospels, Jesus as a boy did not enjoy playing with other boys and had no friends. As a boy he was somber, severe, cruel, and pitiless; he enjoyed tormenting others and even murdered in revenge for the slightest hurt (*New Testament Apocrypha,* vol. 1, *Gospels and Related Writings*, pp. 388–399).

Jesus despised people of wisdom and hated people of understanding, probably because they rejected him. Jesus prayed:

> ***I thank you, Father, Lord of heaven and earth that you have hidden these things from the wise and understanding*** (Mt 11:25–26; Lk 10:21).

Paul wrote that in embracing Jesus Christ, one had to abandon wisdom and become a fool:

> **If anyone among you thinks that he is wise in this age, let him become a fool that he may become wise. For the wisdom of this world is folly with God** (1 Cor 3:18–20).

THE NOVATION HERESY: JESUS WITHOUT PITY

Novatian was a famous elder of the church of the third century. He professed love of Jesus, but found him lacking in kindness and mercy. Novation said Jesus was pitiless. Novation was condemned, and his writings destroyed. We know what they were about, however, thanks to the fourth century historian Eusebius, who wrote: "Naturally, I feel bitter against Novatian. He has split the church. . . . He impudently suggests that our most kind Lord Jesus Christ was devoid of pity" (Eusebius, *The History of the Church*, 7:9, p. 291).

Many today will be puzzled. What better way to show Jesus' pity than the incident of Jesus and the adulteress? (Jn 8:1–11), That incident, however, did not exist in the gospels in the third century at the time of Novation. We know that for at least three reasons: 1. None of the ante-Nicene church fathers, who cited the gospels copiously, cited that story. 2. Had the story existed, those who opposed Novation would have cited it to prove their case. 3. Had the story existed, Novation would not have spoken of a pitiless Jesus in the first place and thereby would have avoided trial and condemnation.

Once the story of Jesus and the adulteress was written, the gospel redactors did not know where to insert it. So it floated about unanchored for several centuries. Today in Protestant bibles it appears as a footnote to the opening of chapter eight of John's gospel; in Catholic bibles it appears at the opening of chapter eight, which makes it appear as if it had been there all along.

HUMILITY

God loves men of humility:

> **Moses was in fact a man of great humility, the most humble man on earth** (Num 12:3).

> **I dwell in the high and holy place, and also with him who is of a contrite and humble spirit** (Is 57:15).

Jesus was not of contrite and humble spirit. Jesus would perform a miracle in front of great crowds of people, and then, to show his humility, he would tell the throngs to keep the miracle secret!

JESUS' HEAVEN AND HELL

Jesus portrayed heaven as a place where the Father is giving an eternal banquet. The Father sits at the head of the table, and Jesus sits to the Father's right—the place of honor—(Mk 16:19). The Jewish patriarchs are sitting at the table, too: *[I will be] sitting at table with Abraham, Isaac, and Jacob* (Mt 8:11). It is worth noting that Jesus does not have the matriarchs, Sarah, Rebecca, Rachel, and Leah, nor his mother Mary, nor any woman at that table. Where are the women?

If Jesus is sitting at the right of the Father, where does the Holy Spirit sit? Jesus does not say. Perhaps the Holy Spirit is in the form of a dove eternally flying over Jesus' head. If so, that must be disquieting to the banqueters. And what does the dove eat while the Father and the Son and the saints are feasting on roast lamb? Peanuts?

The women in heaven are not sitting at the Father's table. I imagine they are eating by themselves at heaven's kitchen table, after the men have been served. Although Jesus said it was not up to him to assign places at God's banquet table (Mt 20:23: Mk 10:40), the pope infallibly decreed that Mary was at the right hand of her son (Apostolic Constitution, *Munificentissimus Deus*, 1950). That being so, Mary no doubt excuses herself from time to time to join the women in the kitchen. Someone has to supervise the preparation of the meals, the setting of the banquet table, serving the food, pouring the wine, clearing the table, washing the dishes, sweeping up, and scrubbing the golden floors inlaid with precious jewels. Other heavenly women—perhaps the adolescent girls— are taking care of the infants, the toddlers, and the little children. It may have been considerations such as those that prompted St. Therese of Lisieux to declare, "I want to spend my heaven in doing good on earth" (*Autobiography: Story of a Soul*, Epilogue).

As for Jesus' hell, sinners weep incessantly and gnash their teeth from endless suffering and unbearable pain; they are gnawed by worms with insatiable appetites, and are burned in fires that never die. A poor man in heaven must not let a single drop of water fall on the tongue of a rich man in hell lest it assuage for an instant his insatiable thirst (Mt 13:49; 22:13; Mk 9:48; Lk 16:19–26). This is a picture of hell as painted by the man of love and forgiveness.

THE NON-EVERLASTING HEAVEN OF JESUS

Jesus promised eternal life, but his promise is patently false because he says heaven is not eternal:

> ***Heaven and earth will pass away*** (Mt 24:35; Mk 13:31; Lk 21:33).

"MY GOD, MY GOD, WHY HAVE YOU FORSAKEN ME?"

As he hung dying on the cross, Jesus recited Psalm 22. The gospels give only the opening line of the psalm (Mt 27:46; Mk 15:34), not enough to reveal much of its content, so here is a larger excerpt:

> **My God, my God why has thou forsaken me? . . . I am a worm, not a man, and scorned by men, despised by the people. All who see me mock me. . . . They have pierced my hands and my feet. . . . They divide my garments among themselves, and for my robe they cast lots. But Thou, O Lord, be not far off. . . . Save me!** (Ps 22; cf. Ps 31).

On the cross Jesus called himself a "worm" and prayed for God's salvation. The evangelist John alludes to the psalm but has Jesus neutralize it by saying: ***And what shall I say? 'Father, save me from this hour'? No, for this purpose I have come to this hour*** (Jn 12:27).

THE MEANING OF JESUS' LIFE

The life of Jesus of Nazareth was a life of disappointment. Jesus was disappointed in others, and he was disappointed in himself. He taught that he did not know everything and could not do everything. He came to do the will of the Father, but he never really understood or conveyed what the will of the Father was.

On the cross, Jesus prayed that he might escape death, but his prayer went unanswered, and he felt abandoned by God. From that Jesus learned a great lesson all people would do well to learn: God cannot be persuaded to do what God does not wish to do.

ON DISCOVERING THE TRUTH

Jesus of Nazareth apparently thought it was just a matter of time before believers would discover the truth about him, for he said:

> **There is still much that I could say to you, but the burden would be too great** (Jn 16:12–13).

JESUS OF NAZARETH COMPARED WITH THE CHRIST OF THE CHURCH

The real Jesus of Nazareth is not the same as the Christ of the church. Jesus of Nazareth was a highly imperfect man. The Christ of the church is perfect.

The theologians who idealized, idolized, and deified Jesus, and called him perfect did not know him and did not care to know him. In his place they gave us Christ. The Eastern Orthodox Church does not speak of Jesus, but only of Christ. The name Jesus, a Jewish name, would be a constant reminder that their God was a Jew, and the Orthodox Church cannot bear that this Jesus, a strange, homeless, wild and fiery Jew with olive skin, dark hair, dark eyes, hooked nose, prominent ears, Jewish mannerisms, dirty hands, dirty clothes, and body odor, who lied and deceived, and who had little understanding of human nature and the universe.

In Jesus of Nazareth's place, the theologians created a mythological Christ with clean, brushed, long, wavy, auburn hair, blue eyes, a scrubbed and good-looking face, a well-groomed beard, clean hands, and immaculate white clothing, who did not curse or get angry, who never called people names or treated them disrespectfully, who never had to defecate or urinate, who never masturbated or felt lust or had sex with another person.

The church cannot bear Jesus of Nazareth, who disdained miracles, and preached a rather simple and admirable form of Judaism that involved an intimate one-on-one relationship with God, an intimacy that could take place out of doors amidst nature or in one's room as well as in synagogues and the temple:

> **And after [Jesus] had dismissed the crowds, he went up into the hills by himself to pray** (Mt 14:23).

> **And in the morning, a great while before day, he rose and went out to a lonely place, and there he prayed** (Mk 1:35–38).

> **And they went to a place which was called Gethsemane; and he said to his disciples, *Sit here, while I [go elsewhere to] pray*. . . . And going a little farther, he fell on the ground and prayed** (Mk 14:36).

> **[H]e withdrew to the wilderness and prayed** (Lk 5:16).

> **He took with him Peter and John and James, and went up on the mountain to pray** (Lk 9:28).

> *[W]hen you pray, go into your room and shut the door and pray to your Father who is in secret* (Mt 6:6).

The church discarded Jesus of Nazareth's spontaneous and personal form of worship and replaced it with a new religion, resembling the old heathen religions, taking place in great and colossal buildings filled with treasure and images or icons, smelling of incense and smoke, where priests lead the faithful in the recitation of formulaic prayers said by rote and centered on a man-God and to a lesser extent on his human mother and his heavenly Father, and to an even lesser extent on the Holy Spirit and all the saints—a new polytheism, which the church called "monotheism," filled with mysteries, sacraments, rituals, and creeds heaped up with empty phrases.

Jesus of Nazareth would not recognize the mythological Christ and the heathen religion about him.

JESUS OF NAZARETH, THE CHILD

MADONNA AND CHILD

The church worships a young Jewish woman and her Jewish baby boy. To divert attention from that reality, the church calls them "Madonna and Child."

Although the church calls the grown-up Jesus of Nazareth "Perfect" man, it is highly significant that it never calls the young Jesus "Perfect boy." And for good reason. Jesus the boy was a precocious monster.

JESUS OF NAZARETH, THE BOY

When Jesus was twelve years old, he went to Jerusalem with his family and their friends and neighbors to celebrate Passover. When the festival was over, and the entourage departed for home, Jesus, without informing anyone, remained behind.

When Mary and Joseph finally noticed that he was missing after traveling a day's journey—what took them so long?—all the while assuming he was somewhere among the company, they were beside themselves with worry. Three days later, after much searching and anguish, they found the boy in the Temple discussing Scripture with the rabbis. His distraught mother said to him, "**Son, why have you treated us so badly? Your father and I have been looking for you anxiously.**" Jesus retorted insolently, *Did you not know I would be in my Father's house?* (Lk 2:41–52):

> **Now his parents went to Jerusalem every year at the feast of the Passover. And when he was twelve years old, they went up according to custom; and when the feast was ended, as they were returning, the boy Jesus stayed behind in Jerusalem. His parents did not know it, but supposing him to be in the company they went a day's journey, and they sought him among their kinsfolk and acquaintances; and when they did not find him, they returned to Jerusalem, seeking him. After three days they found him in the temple. . . . and his mother said to him, "Son, why have you treated us so [badly]? Behold, your father and I have been looking for you anxiously." And he said to them,** *How is it that you sought me? Did you not know that I must be in my Father's house?* (Lk 2:41–49).

The incident, also found essentially verbatim in the apocryphal Infancy Gospel of Thomas, reveals a disturbed youngster from a disturbed family. Neither Mary nor Joseph noticed that Jesus was missing when they began the return trip home. Why not? Neither Mary nor Joseph, on finding him, embraced him in joy and relief, something an ordinary caring mother and father would do. Life was evidently not happy at the home of the "holy family." Not a single pleasant family interaction is reported in any of the gospels. Joseph is portrayed as weak or remote or absent, and Mary is portrayed as cold, manipulative, and powerful.

THE INFANCY GOSPELS

Although the infancy gospels of Jesus of Nazareth were not included in the canon of New Testament, one gospel is particularly illuminating, for it shows what the author, a devout Christian, thought the childhood of Jesus must have been like, based on his behavior as an adult as recorded in the gospels:

> THE ACCOUNT OF THOMAS THE ISRAELITE PHILOSOPHER CONCERNING THE CHILDHOOD OF THE LORD
>
> I, Thomas the Israelite, tell and make known to you all, brothers from among the Gentiles, all the works of the childhood of our Lord Jesus Christ and his mighty deeds, which he did when he was born in our land. . . .
>
> When the boy Jesus was five years old, he was playing at the ford of a brook, and he, by his word alone, collected into pools the water that flowed by. . . . He made soft clay and fashioned from it twelve sparrows. And it was the sabbath. . . . and there were also many other children playing with him. . . . And when Joseph came to the place and saw the boy Jesus, he cried out to him, saying, "Why do you do on the Sabbath what ought not to be done?" But Jesus clapped his hands . . . and the [clay] sparrows took flight and flew away chirping. The Jews were amazed. . . . But the son of Annas the scribe was standing there with Joseph; and [the boy] took a willow branch and stirred up the water that Jesus had collected. When Jesus saw what he had done, he became enraged and said, "You insolent, god-

less, stupid boy! What harm did the pools of water do to you? See now, you shall wither like a tree" [and the boy did]. . . .

After this Jesus went through the village, and a boy was running and bumped against his shoulder. Jesus was annoyed and said to him, "You shall go no further on your way." And the child immediately dropped dead. . . . And Joseph called the child Jesus aside and admonished him, saying, "Why do you do such things that these people suffer and hate us and persecute us?" Jesus replied, "I know these words are not yours [but are of those who accuse me]" . . . And immediately those [children] who had accused him became blind. . . . And when Joseph saw what Jesus had done, he stood up and took him by the ear and pulled it hard. And the child Jesus was angry [at Joseph, his father] and said to him: . . . . "You have acted most unwisely. Do you not know that I am yours? Do not vex me!"

Now a certain teacher, Zacchaeus by name . . . came over to Joseph and said to him, "You have a clever child. . . . Hand him over to me that he may learn the Greek letters. I will teach them to him, [and I will also teach him the proper way] . . . to greet his elders and to honor them as fathers and grandfathers, and to love those of his own age." And [Zacchaeus took Jesus and] taught him all the letters from *alpha* to *omega*. . . . But Jesus looked at Zacchaeus the teacher and said to him, "How do you, who does not know the *alpha* according to its nature, teach others the *beta*? Hypocrite!" . . . Now when Zacchaeus the teacher heard the many allegorical descriptions of the *alpha* expounded [by the child Jesus], he was perplexed at the boy's reply and great teaching [ability] and said to those present, "Woe is me, I am forced into a quandary, wretch that I am. I have brought shame to myself in becoming this child's teacher." [And he turned to Jesus' father and said:] "Take him away, I beseech you, brother Joseph, for I cannot bear the severity of his look and I cannot make out his speech at all. . . . Woe is me, my friend, he stupefies me. . . . I, an old man, have been overcome by a child. . . . Therefore, I ask you, brother Joseph, take him back to your home. He is something great—a god or an angel or something altogether that I do not know."

And while the Jews were trying to console Zacchaeus, the boy Jesus laughed out loud and said . . . "I have come from above to curse them and call them to the things above, as He who sent me for your sake commanded.". . . And no one after that dared to provoke him, lest Jesus should curse him, and he should become maimed.

Now a few days later, Jesus was playing on the roof of a house, and one of the children who was playing with him fell off the roof and died. . . . And the parents of the dead child came and accused Jesus of having thrown him down. And Jesus replied, "I did not throw him down." . . . Then Jesus leaped down from the roof and stood by the dead child and cried out with a loud voice, "Zenon!"—for that was his name—"Arise and tell me: did I throw you down?" And the boy arose at once and said, "No, Lord, you did not throw me down, but you raised me up." And when [those present] saw it, they were amazed. And the parents of the child glorified God for the miracle that had happened, and worshipped Jesus. . . .

Joseph took the boy Jesus and handed him over to another teacher . . . and Jesus said to the [new teacher], "If you are indeed a teacher, and if you know the Greek letters, then tell me the meaning of *alpha* and I will tell you that of *beta*." And the teacher was annoyed and slapped him on the face, and it hurt. And the child Jesus cursed [the teacher], and he instantly dropped dead. . . . And the child [Jesus] returned to Joseph's house. But Joseph was grieved and gave [the following] orders to [Mary] his mother: "Do not let him go outside, for all those who provoke him die."

After some time had passed, another teacher, a good friend of Joseph's, said to him, "Bring the child to me to school. Perhaps by persuasion I can teach him the letters. And Joseph said to him, "If you have the courage, brother, he's all yours!" . . .

And when he was twelve years old his parents went according to the custom to Jerusalem to the feast of the Passover with their company. And after the Passover they returned to go to their house. And while they were returning, the child Jesus went back to Jerusalem. But his parents supposed that he was in the company. And when they had a gone a day's journey, they sought him among their kinsfolk, and when they did not find him, they were troubled, and returned again to the city seeking him. And after the third day they found him in the temple sitting among the teachers, listening to the law and asking them questions. And all paid attention to him and marveled how he, a child, put to silence the elders and teachers of the people, expounding the sections of the law and sayings of the prophets. And his mother Mary came near and said to him, "Why have you done this to us, child? Behold, we have sought you sorrowing." Jesus said to them, "Why do you seek me? Do you not know that I must be in my Father's house?" But the scribes and Pharisees said, "Are you the mother of this child?" And she said, "I am." And they said to her, "Blessed are you among women, because the Lord has blessed the fruit of your womb. For such glory and such excellence and wisdom we have never seen nor heard." [One cannot help noticing that the church's version of the "Hail Mary" was based, not on any canonical gospel, but on this apocryphal gospel or some similar text.] And Jesus arose and followed his mother and was subject to his parents; but his mother kept (in her heart) all that had taken place. And Jesus increased

in wisdom and stature and grace. To him be glory forever and ever. Amen (*New Testament Apocrypha,*
vol. 1, *Gospels and Related Writings*, pp. 388–399).

LUKE'S TWELVE-YEAR-OLD JESUS

Luke does not name the source of his Passover story, but it
probably came from the infancy gospel of Thomas because it is
almost identical to it, in which case it is highly significant that
Luke did not relate any of the other incidents in that gospel
which portray Jesus as a monster. Although Thomas amelio-
rates Jesus' behavior by saying, "And Jesus increased in wisdom and stature and grace," Luke found it necessary to add
that Jesus thereafter **was obedient to** his parents and also that
he **increased in wisdom and stature, and in favor with God
and man**. In other words, although no one, not even God,
liked Jesus as a child, both God and man liked him better as he
grew older:

> **And [Jesus] went down with [Joseph and Mary] and
> came to Nazareth, and was obedient to them. . . .
> And Jesus increased in wisdom and in stature, and
> in favor with God and man** (Lk 2:51–52).

IS JESUS OF NAZARETH GOD?

CHRISTMAS DAY PRAYER

The church declares in its Christmas Day Prayer:

> O marvelous exchange! Man's Creator has become
> man . . . !

DEFINITIONS OF GOD

God is not defined in the Hebrew Scriptures, for the Jews found God beyond definition. But God is sharply defined in the New Testament:

God is love (ἀγάπη) [*agape*] (1 Jn 4:16).

That definition became Christianity's slogan. Nonetheless, Peter wryly observed:

Love (ἀγάπη) [*agape*] covers a multitude of sins (1 Pet 4:8).

JESUS' TEST OF HIS DIVINITY

Jesus of Nazareth himself provided the test that allows anyone to validate his divinity:

Whatever you ask the Father in my name,
he will give it to you (Jn 15:16–17).

To determine whether Jesus is divine, offer one of the following three prayers and see whether the Father gives it to you:

- Father, give everlasting peace on earth now. This I ask in Jesus' name.

- Father, end all suffering and pain now. This I ask in Jesus' name.

- Father, end all injustice now. This I ask in Jesus' name.

"GOD INCARNATE"

The church teaches that Jesus is "god incarnate" or god made flesh, but Jesus teaches that *God is Spirit* (Jn 4:24). The word *incarnate* does not appear in the New Testament. God incarnate is an invention of the church that makes a mockery of God's Holy Spirit. And Jesus taught, *Whoever speaks against the Holy Spirit will not be forgiven* (Mt 12:32; cf. Lk 12:10).

JESUS COMPARED WITH GOD

If one compares Jesus with God, it readily becomes apparent they are not the same. God is omnipotent, creating the world and everything in it, and called everything he created "good." Jesus created nothing, saw no good in the world, and said:

> *I can do nothing on my own authority* (Jn 5:30).

> *I came to cast fire upon the earth; and would that it were already kindled!* (Lk 12:49).

God is, was, and always will be all-wise. But **Jesus grew in wisdom** (Lk 2:52).

When God wanted something known, it was known; when God wanted something hidden, it was hidden. Jesus had no such power. **Jesus entered a house and did not want anyone to know it. But it could not be hidden** (Mk 7:24).

God is omniscient, but Jesus had highly limited knowledge. Regarding Judgment Day, Jesus said, *But of that day and hour no one knows, not even the angels of heaven, nor the Son, but the Father only* (Mt 24:36; cf. Mk 13:32). Regarding the Son of God, Jesus said, *No one knows who the Son is but the Father* (Lk 10:22).

God has one view of life, Jesus another:

God: **I have set before you life and death . . . choose life**
(Deut 30:4–20).

Jesus: *He who loves his life loses it, and he who hates his
life in this world will keep it for eternal life* (Jn 12:25).

THE QUESTIONS OF JOB

Job poses questions to show the difference between God and
man. Job asks:

> **Have you commanded the morning to come . . . and
> caused the dawn to break in the east?**
>
> **Can you bind the Pleiades? Or unbuckle Orion's
> belt?**
>
> **Can you lead forth the Dog star in its season or
> guide the Great Bear and her children?** (Job 38).

Does anyone believe Jesus could bring forth the dawn or
unbuckle Orion's belt or guide the Great Bear?

GREEK REALITY VS. HEBREW REALITY

The Greeks believed in things rational, tangible, visible,
comprehensible. That was Greek reality. Greek gods were
material and visible—carved in stone or begotten in the flesh
and walking among men. Paul, the Apostle to the Gentiles,
could not accept this Greek idea. Paul was a Jew. He did not
believe in material and visible gods. He believed that the
greatest reality was immaterial, invisible, and spiritual. He
believed that the greatest reality was God. And so:

> When the Greek crowd saw [the miracle that] Paul
> had done, they shouted in their native Greek dialect,
> "The gods have come down to us in the likeness of
> men!" Barnabas they called Zeus, and Paul . . . they
> called Hermes. . . . [Whereupon] . . . Barnabas and
> Paul . . . tore their clothes and rushed into the crowd
> shouting, "Men, why are you doing this? We also
> are men, of like nature with you" (Acts 14:12–15).

GODS WHO WALK AMONG MEN

While Jesus lived, none of his disciples considered him a
god walking among men. They considered him a man walking
among men. In Greek and Roman mythology, however, the
gods frequently walked among men. And so, the Greeks
looked upon powerful Jews who walked among men as gods:

> Herod put on his royal robes, took a seat upon his
> throne, and made a speech. And the [gentiles]
> shouted, "It is a god speaking, not a man!"
> (Acts 12:21–22).

> Now in the city of Lystra, there was . . . a man who
> was a cripple from birth. . . . He listened to Paul
> speak; and Paul, looking intently at him and seeing
> that he had the faith to be cured, said loudly, "Stand
> up!" And the crippled man sprang up and walked.
> When the mob saw what Paul had done, they
> shouted in their own Greek dialect, "The gods have
> come down to us in the likeness of men!" . . . And
> the priest of Zeus . . . wanted to offer sacrifices. But
> when Barnabas and Paul heard of it . . . they rushed
> out among the multitude and cried, "What are you
> doing! We are only men, the same as you! We bring
> you good news, that you should turn away from such
> vain things to the living God who made the heaven

and the earth and the sea and all that is in them"
(Acts 14:8–18).

"OUR LORD AND OUR GOD"

> [The Roman Emperor Domitian] . . . in issuing a circu-
> lating letter . . . began it as follows: "Our Lord and Our
> God bids that this be done!" And so the custom arose
> of henceforth addressing him in no other way (Sueto-
> nius, *Domitian,* 13:5).

For the gentile church to address Jesus with a title less than
that of Emperor Domitian would be unacceptable. The evangelist John has the apostle Thomas, on seeing the newly risen
Jesus, exclaim, **"My Lord and My God!"** (Jn 20:28). Was
Thomas dubbing Jesus with a new title to match the emperor's,
or was he merely expressing astonishment, equivalent to ex-
claiming, "I must be seeing things!" or "What the Devil!" or
"Good God!" or "My Lord and My God!"? Even if Thomas
considered Jesus his Lord and his God, there is no evidence
Thomas was speaking for the other apostles who did not fall on
their knees and exclaim, "My Lord and my God!"

"I AND THE FATHER ARE ONE"
Jesus of Nazareth said:

> *I and the Father are one* (Jn 10:30).

What does Jesus mean? He explains that there is nothing
unique about his unity with the Father. The same unity exists
between Jesus and his disciples:

I am in the Father and the Father in me. . . . I am in my Father, and you [my disciples] are in me, and I am in you (Jn 14:11, 20).

The glory which you [God] have given me I have given to them [my disciples] that they may be one even as we are one, I in them and you in me (Jn 17:21–23).

Near the end of this discourse, Jesus says:

The Father who sent me is greater than I (Jn 14:28).

And then, to be absolutely certain that no one takes him literally, Jesus says:

I have spoken to you in figures of speech (Jn 16:25).

Jesus in the same discourse also states that he is indeed a god, not of the same stature as the Father, but of the same stature as any righteous Jew: *Is it not written in your own Law, "I said, 'You are gods'"?* (Jn 10:34). Jesus is referring to Psalm 82, in which the psalmist states: **You are gods, sons of the Most High, all of you!** (Ps 82:6). The psalmist concludes: **Nonetheless, you shall die like men** (Ps 82:7).

The church, however, disagreed with Jesus and insisted that *I and the Father are one* must be taken literally, not figuratively. The church has its own theology and refuses to let Jesus interfere with it, which is exactly what Dostoyevsky said in the Grand Inquisitor chapter of his famous book *The Brothers Karamazov*.

By the fourth century, Paul's letter to the Hebrews was considered a forgery, and yet, redactors after the Council of Nicea inserted into this well-known forgery the following statement, which had not appeared in the original forgery and did not appear in any of the gospels: **But of the Son [God] says, "Thy**

throne, O God, is forever and ever" (Heb 1:8). None of the church fathers before Nicea cited this passage. Moreover, biblical scholars considered it incredible that Paul, himself an authority on Judaism, would write a letter to his fellow Jews and Hebrew Christians in which God, who is the only God, made such a statement.

PAUL ON GOD AND JESUS

Paul castigated the Greeks for thinking that the gods condescended to walk among men (Acts 14:8–18). He also wrote that the Greeks were wrong to believe in more than one god; for there is only one god who is God, and one Christ who is man:

> **There is no God but one** (1 Cor 8:4).
> **For us there is but one God, the Father. . . .**
> **And there is one Lord, Jesus Christ** (1 Cor 8:6).

> **There is one God, and there is one mediator between God and man—the man Christ Jesus** (1 Tim 2:5).

> **Jesus Christ is in the image of God, but he did not claim to be equal with God** (Phil 2:6).

But Paul prophesied accurately that one day "sound teaching" would give way to mythology:

> **The time is coming when people will not endure sound teaching but, having itchy ears, will turn to teachers that teach them what they want to hear, will turn away from listening to the truth and wander into mythology** (2 Tim 4:3–4).

PHILOSOPHY ENTERS CHRISTIAN THEOLOGY

Jesus, like his fellow Jews, did not engage in Greek philosophy. John the evangelist, however, seemed acquainted with the philosophy of Philo, for John used the term *Logos* or *Word* in the same sense that Philo did, as the link between the spiritual world and the materialistic world. John thereby introduced Greek philosophy into Christian theology. But Jesus never used the terms of Greek philosophy, and it is doubtful he would have understood them. Jesus never spoke of himself as *Logos* or *Word*. Moreover, he never spoke of God, as Christian theologians influenced by Plato and Aristotle came to speak of God, as *Pure Being*, *the Absolute*, or *First Cause*. For Jesus, God was beyond such terms. God was not a philosophical "problem." The idea of a "proof" for the existence of God probably would have sent Jesus flying into a rage. Jesus spoke as one who knew God when he said, ***Hear O Israel: The Lord [YHVH] is our God, the Lord [YHVH] is one,*** and also when he said, ***We [Jews] worship what we know***. The God of Jesus is different from the god of the Greek philosophers, different from the god of the Christian theologians, different from the god of the church.

JESUS DECLARES HIS INFERIORITY TO GOD

Jesus repeatedly proclaims that he is inferior to God:

> ***To sit on my right side or on my left side is not for me to give. It is for those to whom it has already been assigned by my Father*** (Mt 20:23).

> ***Why do you call me good? No one is good but God alone*** (Mk 10:18).

> *But of that Day [of Judgment], of that hour, no one knows, not even the angels in heaven, nor the Son, but only the Father* (Mk 13:32).

> **Some Jews believed that Jesus, in calling God his own Father, was claiming equality with God. To this charge Jesus replied,** *In truth, in very truth, I say to you, The son can do nothing on his own* (Jn 5:18–19).

> *I can do nothing on my own authority* (Jn 5:30).

> *My teaching is not mine but his who sent me* (Jn 7:16).

> *I came not of my own accord, but he sent me* (Jn 8:42).

> *The word which you hear is not mine but the Father's who sent me* (Jn 14:24).

> *The Father is greater than I* (Jn 14:28).

JESUS DECLARES HIS INFERIORITY TO SOME MEN

Jesus taught he was inferior not only to God but even to some men:

> *There is no man born of woman greater than John the Baptist* (Mt 11:11).

> *I tell you, he who has faith in me will do what I am doing; and he will do even greater things* (Jn 14:12).

SUBMISSION TO THE WILL OF THE FATHER

On the cross, the will of Jesus submits to the will of the Father, showing that not only is Jesus inferior to the Father but also their wills are not the same. The church teaches that the

Father had sent Jesus to die by crucifixion to take away the sins of the world, but Jesus prays to escape crucifixion:

> ***Abba, all things are possible for you. Remove this cup from me*** (Mk 14:34–37).

God does not answer Jesus' prayer. Realizing he is going to die, Jesus says in resignation:

> ***Still, not my will but your will be done*** (Mk 14:34–37).

7. THE TEN COMMANDMENTS

THE TEN COMMANDMENTS

Regarding the Ten Commandments, the church teaches:

2057. The Decalogue is a path of life. . . .

2058. "These words the Lord spoke to all your assembly at the mountain out of the midst of the fire, the cloud, and the thick darkness, with a loud voice; and he added no more. And he wrote them upon two tables of stone, and gave them to me" (Deut 5:22). . . .

2059. "The Lord spoke with you face to face at the mountain, out of the midst of the fire" (Deut 5:4). They belong to God's revelation of himself and his glory. The gift of the Commandments is the gift of God himself and his holy will. In making his will known, God reveals himself to his people. . . .

2064. In fidelity to Scripture and in conformity with the example of Jesus, the tradition of the Church has acknowledged the primordial importance and significance of the Decalogue. . . .

2068. The Council of Trent teaches that the Ten Commandments are obligatory for Christians . . . Second Vatican Council confirms . . . "all men may attain salvation through faith, Baptism and the observance of the [Ten] Commandments. . . ."

2071. The commandments of the Decalogue, although accessible to reason alone, have been revealed. To attain a complete and certain understanding of the requirements of the natural law, sinful humanity needed this revelation. . . .

2072. Since they express man's fundamental duties towards God and towards his neighbor, the Ten Commandments reveal, in their primordial content, *grave* obligations. They are fundamentally immutable, and they oblige always and everywhere. No one can dispense from them. The Ten Commandments are engraved by God in the human heart (*Catechism of the Catholic Church*, pp. 499–503).

Let us see just how faithful to the Ten Commandments the church really is. Here they are simply numbered in biblical sequence (Ex 20:1–17; Deut 5:1–21) without making an issue of the numbering disagreement between Catholics, Protestants, and Jews:

1. I AM THE LORD [YHVH] YOUR GOD. . . . YOU SHALL HAVE NO OTHER GODS BEFORE ME

Jesus of Nazareth along with his fellow Jews interpreted this commandment to mean that there is only one God, YHVH. Others interpreted it to mean that gods in addition to YHVH are inferior to YHVH. God himself refuted that interpretation:

[T]here is no god beside me (Deut 32:39).

The prophet Isaiah affirmed this:
I am the Lord [YHVH], and there is no other; beside me, there is no God. . . . there is none besides me; I am the Lord [YHVH], and there is no other (Is 45:1–6).

Jesus also affirmed it:

> ***You shall worship the Lord [YHVH] and him only
> shall you serve*** (Lk 4:8).

Justin Martyr, second century church father, also affirmed it:

> There will be no other God. . . . Nor do we think that
> there is one God for us, another for you. . . . Nor have
> we trusted in another, for there is no other, but in Him
> whom you also have trusted, the God of Abraham, and
> Isaac, and Jacob (*The Ante-Nicene Fathers*, vol. 1, Dia-
> logue with Trypho, chap. 11, p. 199).

In the fourth century, at the Council of Nicea, the church
deified Jesus and established the Trinity, thereby making Jesus
into God equal with YHVH, thereby revoking the commandment. So strike it out!

> ~~I am the Lord [YHVH] your God. . . . You shall have no
> other gods before me~~.

2. YOU SHALL NOT MAKE FOR YOURSELF A GRAVEN IMAGE; YOU SHALL NOT BOW DOWN TO THEM

Paul affirmed this commandment and said it was as binding
on gentile converts to Christianity as it was on Jews:

> **Since we are the children of God, we ought not to
> think that God is like a gold, silver, or stone image
> that comes from the imagination of men. God has
> overlooked your time of past ignorance, but now he**

commands all men everywhere to repent (Acts 17:24–30).

You can be certain of this: no immoral or impure or greedy man—because they are like those who pray before images—has any inheritance in the kingdom of Christ and of God (Eph 5:5).

In the third century, the church father Origen, reaffirmed this:

[T]he making of images . . . takes hold of unintelligent men and drags the eyes of their soul down from God to earth (Chadwick, *Contra Celsum*, 4:31, p. 207).

[Deceived are] people who seek for God in earthly images and do not look up to the real and supreme God (ibid., 7:56, p. 442).

[I]t is quite impossible both to know God and to pray to images (ibid., 7:65, p. 449).

Nonetheless, the Second Council of Nicea in AD 787 declared:

[I]mages of Our Lord and God and Savior, Jesus Christ, and our ever-virgin Lady, the holy Mother of God, and the venerated angels, and all the saints . . . whether painted or made of mosaic or another suitable material, are to be exhibited in the holy churches of God . . . in houses and on streets.

In the sixteenth century, in the Tridentine Profession of Faith, the church further declared:

> [I]mages of Christ and of the Mother of God ever-virgin
> as well as those of the other saints are to be owned and
> kept and due honor and worship should be accorded
> them.

The church justified revoking the commandment against images by saying that God himself had revoked it when he ordered an image of a bronze serpent for Moses (Num 21:4–9), decorative images of angels for the ark of the covenant (Ex 25:10–22), decorative angels, palm trees, and flowers for the temple, and decorative gourds and oxen for the temple fountain (1 Kings 6:23–29; 7:23–26).

Others said God did not command the Jews to worship a bronze serpent, decorative angels, palm trees, flowers, gourds or oxen. Nor did he command the Jews to bow down before them. Jesus went to the temple frequently, but did not bow down before the decorative angels, palm trees, flowers, gourds, and oxen. Neither did he worship them nor tell his disciples to do so. Indeed, Jesus never mentioned them because they were so insignificant to him that he probably did not even notice them.

The church's real reason for venerating icons and images had nothing to do with the brass serpent or the decorations in the temple. The real reason was the Incarnation. The church taught that the Incarnation was a "living image of God." Catechism today teaches: "The veneration of sacred images is based on the mystery of the Incarnation" (*Catechism of the Catholic Church*, p. 518). But the church has it backwards. The Incarnation does not prove that God had a change of heart and approved images. Rather, it is precisely because God forbade images that proves the doctrine of the Incarnation is false. The apostles and disciples never spoke of Jesus Christ as the Incarnation or as the "living image of God." The word *Incarnation* does not appear once in the New Testament.

The prophet Jeremiah said:

> **They have defiled with their loathsome images the house that bears my name** (Jer 7:30).

Paul wrote:

> **They boast of their wisdom but they have made fools of themselves, exchanging the splendor of immortal God for an image shaped like a mortal man** (Rom 1:22–23).

Eusebius, the fourth century church historian, wrote:

> Reason would never allow that the uncreated and immutable substance of Almighty God should be changed into the form of a man (*The History of the Church*, 1:2, p. 35).

Nonetheless, the church revoked God's commandment. So strike it out!

~~You shall not make for yourself a graven image; you shall not bow down to them.~~

3. YOU SHALL NOT TAKE THE LORD [YHVH]'S NAME IN VAIN

The church takes the Lord [YHVH]'s name in vain every time it applies the title *Lord* in English, *Dominus* in Latin, or *Kyrios* in Greek when it appears in the Old Testament to Jesus of Nazareth where that title signifies only the name of God, YHVH.

The church also takes the Lord [YHVH]'s name in vain, by not proclaiming the declaration that must be proclaimed and as Jesus proclaimed it:

> **Hear O Israel, the Lord [YHVH] our God, the Lord [YHVH] is one** (Deut 6:4).

When asked which was the first and greatest commandment, Jesus answered:

> ***Hear O Israel: The Lord [YHVH] our God, the Lord [YHVH] is one*** (Mk 12:29).

The church long ago broke this commandment. Strike it out!

> ~~You shall not take the Lord [YHVH]'s name in vain~~.

4. **REMEMBER THE SABBATH DAY, TO KEEP IT HOLY**

> **Remember the Sabbath day, to keep it holy. Six days you shall labor, and do all your work; but the seventh day is a Sabbath to the Lord [YHVH] your God; in it you shall not do any work . . . for in six days, the Lord made heaven and earth . . . and rested the seventh day** (Ex 20:8–11).

> **Observe the Sabbath day, to keep it holy, as the Lord [YHVH] your God commanded you. . . . The seventh day is a Sabbath to the Lord [YHVH] your God** (Deut 5:12–14).

The church long ago revoked this commandment, and replaced the seventh day with the first day, even though Jesus celebrated the seventh day, not the first day.   The church teaches that celebrating the first day "fulfills the moral command" (*Catechism of the Catholic Church*, p. 525) of celebrating the seventh day, the Sabbath.   The church is mistaken. Celebrating the first day, "The Lord's Day," honors the Resurrection of Jesus Christ and does not fulfill the moral command of celebrating the seventh day, the Sabbath, which honors God [YHVH] and the act of creation and all of God's works of creation.

Jesus celebrated the Sabbath, the seventh day, and taught that it was a festival instituted for man by God:

> ***The Sabbath was made for man*** (Mk 2:27–28).

Had Jesus revoked the Sabbath, as the church teaches, the Jewish leaders would have had reason enough to execute him:

> **Everyone who profanes [the Sabbath] shall be put to death** (Ex 31:14–17).

But Jesus did not revoke the Sabbath.   The church revoked the Sabbath!   So strike it out!

> ~~Observe the Sabbath day, to keep it holy, as the Lord [YHVH] your God commanded you. . . . The seventh day is a Sabbath to the Lord [YHVH] your God~~.

5. HONOR YOUR FATHER AND MOTHER

The church has broken this commandment.   The church dishonors Adam, the father of all humanity, by continuing to teach Original Sin.   The church teaches that Adam's disobedience no less than the color of his eyes has been transmitted to all humanity. Also, the church dishonors Judaism, the mother religion of Christianity, by not acknowledging its mother. The closest the church came was in 1986 when Pope John Paul II said, "Jews are our elder brothers."

Jesus of Nazareth repeatedly broke this commandment. The gospels show that Jesus was disrespectful of his father and mother even when he was a child (Lk 2:41–49). His disrespect toward his family continued into adulthood. At the wedding of Cana, Jesus does not call his mother "Mother" or "Mama" or "My Lady" or even "Mary." He calls her ***Woman!*** And heaping up scorn for her, he says, ***What have I to do with you!*** (Jn 2:4).

Here are other examples of Jesus dishonoring his mother:

> **And his mother and his brothers came; and standing outside they sent to him and called him. And a crowd was sitting about him; and they said to him, "Your mother and your brothers are outside, asking for you." And he replied, *Who are my mother and my brothers?* (Mk 3:31–33).**

Although Mary's cousin Elizabeth honors Mary by calling her blessed, and Mary calls herself blessed, and the church calls Mary blessed, Jesus never called Mary blessed. On the contrary, one day while Jesus was preaching, a woman in the crowd called Mary blessed:

> **Blessed is the woman that bore you and the teats you sucked!**

Jesus, contradicting her, retorted:

> ***Blessed rather are those who hear the Word of God and do it!*** (Lk 11:27–28).

Peace on earth begins with peace in the home. The prophet Malachi said of the Messiah: **And he will turn the hearts of fathers to their children and the hearts of children to their fathers** (Mal 4:5). But Jesus did not turn the hearts of fathers to their children and the hearts of children to their fathers. On the contrary, Jesus taught that he had come to bring discord and divisiveness to the home:

> *Do you think that I have come to give peace on earth? No, I tell you, but rather divisiveness! . . . Father against son, son against father, mother against daughter, daughter against mother!* (Lk 12:49–53).

> *I have come to set a man against his father, and a daughter against her mother* (Mt 10:34–36).

> *If anyone comes to me and does not hate his own father and mother . . . he cannot be my disciple* (Mt 14:26–33).

> *If anyone does not hate his own father and mother . . . he cannot be my disciple!* (Lk 14:26).

Honor your father and mother. The church and Jesus smashed that commandment to smithereens. So strike it out!

~~Honor your father and mother~~.

6. YOU SHALL NOT MURDER

The church long ago broke this commandment. In the name of Jesus, the church murdered heretics and Jews ever since it acquired the power to do so. The church was a willing participant of mass murder of Moslems and Jews during the crusades.

The church tortured heretics and Jews and burned them at the stake during the Spanish Inquisition.

Father Hans Küng, one of the leading Catholic thinkers of the twentieth century, wrote:

> The church preached love while it sowed the seeds of murderous hatred. It proclaimed love, while it prepared the way for atrocities and death. . . (Kung, *The Church*, p. 184).

> An honest and unvarnished admission of guilt for its sins against the freedom of the Children of God [the Jews] is something that the church will constantly have to make. . . (ibid., p. 214).

Perhaps no other institution in the Western World has been responsible for more persecution, torture, and death than the church. Jesus taught: ***You will know them by their fruits*** (Mt 7:16).

You shall not murder? Strike it out!

~~You shall not murder~~!

7. **YOU SHALL NOT COMMIT ADULTERY**

Jesus of Nazareth taught:

> ***You have heard that it was said, You shall not commit adultery. But I say to you that everyone who looks at a woman lustfully has already committed adultery with her in his heart*** (Mt 5:27–28).

Jesus does not discriminate between lust and adultery, between desire and behavior. Elsewhere Jesus makes no distinction between anger and murder. By not differentiating between feelings and behavior, Jesus enchained humanity instead of liberating it. To teach that God-given feelings were equivalent to crimes was not only to defame God but also to place impossible burdens on man. By adding *feelings* of adultery to God's commandment about actual adultery, Jesus broke the following commandment:

> **You shall not add to the word which I command you, nor take from it** (Deut 4: 2).

> **Everything that I command you, you shall be careful to do; you shall not add to it or take from it** (Deut 12:32).

In adding to God's commandment, Jesus broke the commandment against adultery. So strike it out!

~~You shall not commit adultery.~~

8. YOU SHALL NOT STEAL

The church long ago broke this commandment. Leading the list of the church's thefts is its wanton looting of the Hebrew Scriptures, removing passages out of context for the purpose of "proving" its theology. The church plundered the Psalms and the Prophets in their entirety. The church broke this commandment, so strike it out!

~~You shall not steal~~!

9. YOU SHALL NOT BEAR FALSE WITNESS

The church has repeatedly borne false witness against the Hebrew Scriptures and the Jews. Some outstanding examples against the Hebrew Scriptures are: Calling it the Old Testament and stating it has been replaced by the New Testament, and by teaching, apart from the Ten Commandments, it has no value in itself except on its so-called deeper and more spiritual level where it is allegorical for Jesus Christ, the church, and the New Testament; by teaching that it is a "law of bondage" and "the instrument of lust"; by teaching it has no forgiveness or grace; by teaching that the God of the Old Testament is only a God of wrath and justice, not also a God of love and forgiveness.

The church has borne false witness against the Jews by teaching that the Jews collectively—all the Jews of all time—killed Christ instead of teaching that Jesus was a Jew, that his mother was a Jew, that all twelve apostles were Jews—not only Judas Iscariot—and that the earliest church was composed entirely of Jews.

Although Vatican Two attempted to correct some of these errors, not all Christians, not even all Roman Catholics, abide by Vatican Two. So strike the commandment out!

~~You shall not bear false witness~~!

10. YOU SHALL NOT COVET . . .

You shall not covet your neighbor's wife . . . or his manservant or his maidservant . . . or anything that is your neighbor's.

The Ten Commandments concern behavior that is required and behavior that is forbidden, behavior that is right and behavior that is wrong. The Ten Commandments are concerned with "Dos" and "Don'ts" of behavior, not with forbidding feelings over which people have little or no control. Moreover, feelings are not punishable because no one knows what another person is feeling unless the feeling person reveals it. So the Tenth Commandment comes as a surprise. To covet is a feeling, not a behavior, not an action. So something is amiss, and that something is the word *covet* itself.

Covet is a mistranslation. In the original Hebrew, the word in question is *chamad*. Translators have not been confident in translating this Hebrew word because it is used only eight times in the Hebrew Scriptures. Joel Hoffman (*And God Said: How Translations Conceal the Bible's Original Meaning*. New York: Thomas Dunne Books, St. Martin's Press, 2010) recognized that covet was a mistranslation and tried to decode the meaning of *chamad* by means of analytic tools. He settled on the verb *take* only after considering that a "reasonable possibility" would be a "precursor" to the verb *take* but concluding "we don't have a verb in English for 'prepare to take.'"

I suggest we do have such a word, and that word is *touch*, in the sense of *designating or choosing with the intent of taking*, as one might touch an item in a store to signify, "This is the one I want" or "This is the one I'm going to take" or "This is the one I choose." In other words, *chamad* is a form of demonstrative selection. In all cases where the Hebrew word *chamad* appears in the Hebrew Scriptures, the word *touch* in that sense fits. A good fit cannot be said for the word *covet*, the conventional translation, or the word *take*, Hoffman's choice. The Tenth Commandment, using the word *touch* rather than *covet*, becomes: "You shall not touch your neighbor's wife . . . or his manservant or his maidservant . . . or anything that is your neighbor's."

The following shows the seven additional places in the Hebrew Scriptures, where the Hebrew word *chamad* appears, and the various RSV translations of the text are compared with the verb *touch*:

- **. . . . neither shall any man desire your land, when you go up [to Jerusalem]** (Ex 34:24). Notice that the RSV translation rejects *covet* and uses *desire*, which is no improvement because both are words of feeling, not action. *Take* or *touch* are words of action, and both fit, but I think *touch* fits better—"neither shall any man touch your land, when you go up." In other words, no one shall dare to designate your land as his own just because you are temporarily away.

- **The graven images of their gods you shall burn with fire; you shall not covet the silver or the gold that is on them, or take it for yourselves, lest you be ensnared by it; for it is an abomination to the Lord your God** (Deut 7:25). The RSV gives *covet*, which is incorrect. Hoffman's *take* does not work either, for then we would have "you shall not take the silver . . . or take it." *Touch*, however, works nicely: "you shall not touch the silver . . . or take it."

- **. . . . when I saw among the spoils a beautiful mantle from Shinar, and two hundred shekels of silver, and a bar of gold weighing fifty shekels, then I coveted them, and took them** (Josh 7:21). The RSV again gives *covet*. Again, *take* does not work, for we would have "I took them, and took them." *Touch*, however, fits perfectly: "then I touched them, and I took them."

- **Why look you with envy, O many-peaked mountain, at the mount which God desired for his abode, yea, where the Lord will dwell forever?** (Ps 68:16). God does not covet, so the RSV translators resorted again to *desire*. *Take* and *touch* both work, although *take* seems a bit grasping for God, while *touch*, indicative of God's choice, again fits perfectly—"at the mount which God touched (as in *designated*) for his abode."

- **How long, you thoughtless ones, will you love thoughtlessness?** (Prov 1:22). RSV rejected *covet* and instead used *love*, yet a third word for *chamad*. *Love* is not an improvement on *covet*. In this case, both words, even though incorrect, work only because the psalmist assumes he knows how the thoughtless feel and that assumption makes sense. The verb *take* doesn't work. "How long, you thoughtless ones, will you *take* thoughtlessness?" It is awkward at best, nonsensical at worst. Again, *touch* (as in *choose*) works best: "How long, you thoughtless ones, will you *touch* (*choose*) thoughtlessness?" The meaning is clear: How much longer are the thoughtless going to continue to choose to behave thoughtlessly?

- **Lust not after her beauty in your heart** (Prov 6:25). The RSV translators rejected *covet* and instead used a new phrase, *lust after*. The phrase is both gross and concrete. The translators apparently thought a beautiful woman required that. As for *take*, it does not work. "Take not her beauty in your heart"? That is awkward and nonsensical. The verb *touch* works especially well in this case, for it is a poetic metaphor. "Do not touch her beauty in your heart." The meaning is clear: Do not touch her even in your heart.

- **The wicked desire the prey of evil men; but the root of the righteous yield fruit** (Prov 12:12). Once again the RSV rejects *covet* and uses *desire*. In this case, *take* and *touch* work equally well, and from this example alone, one could not choose between them. "The wicked touch (or take) the prey of evil men."

Of the eight times the word *chamad* is used in the Hebrew Scriptures, the word *covet* fits only three times, which demonstrates it is a mistranslation. The word *take* fits only four times, again indicating a mistranslation. But the word *touch* (demonstrative selection or designation) fits all *eight* times. I conclude that the word *touch* is the correct meaning of the verb *chamad*. The commandment is, therefore, best rendered by "You shall not touch your neighbor's wife. . . ." That prohibition is particularly relevant to the history of Christianity because it played a large role in Paul's leaving Judaism. Paul confessed that he could not control himself when it came to touching other people's human property, just as many priests have not been able to resist the inappropriate touching of other people's children. The so-called celibate church has repeatedly broken this commandment, even if one lets the traditional word *covet* stand. So strike it out!

~~You shall not covet your neighbor's wife . . . or anything else that is your neighbor's.~~

In summary, the church, while extolling and exalting the Ten Commandments, has revoked or broken them all!

8. FINAL THOUGHTS

THE HUNTER AND THE FARMER
A FABLE

Once upon a time there was a hunter and a farmer, who, although neighbors, were enemies. They lived near the edge of a forest from which no one who entered could find his way out.

Why were they enemies? The hunter believed in the existence of several gods and wanted the farmer to believe in those gods, too, but the farmer refused. The farmer was certain of the existence of only one god; however, he did not really care what the hunter believed so long as the hunter let him alone and did not harm him. The farmer thought they should be able to live side by side in peace even though they disagreed about the nature of god. But the hunter relentlessly insisted that the farmer believe as the hunter did.

One day the hunter's young son and the farmer's young son wandered into the forest independently of each other. By chance, they met. They were happy to see one another, and forgot their mutual animosity. Somehow seeing a familiar face made the forest seem less frightening.

Night was falling. The boys made a bed of leaves, lay down, and fell asleep. The farmer's boy had a wonderful dream: a spirit appeared and promised to show the boys the way out of the forest and also to make them and their families dwell together in peace. The next morning the farmer's boy—henceforth I shall call him simply the farmer—could hardly wait to tell his dream to the hunter's boy—henceforth I shall call him simply the hunter. The hunter laughed and said, "While we are waiting for your spirit, we better look for food."

Suddenly, a strange young man appeared, who, on learning of the farmer's dream, said, "I am the spirit of your dream." Both boys were amazed. The stranger did not look like a spirit. He was flesh and blood. They spent the day in his company, and he entertained them with wonderful stories and tricks, but he did not show them the way out of the forest.

The hunter was entranced, but the farmer began to grow suspicious. The farmer said, "Although you are a highly entertaining fellow, when are you going to show us the way out of the forest?" The stranger grew angry and began to call the farmer names. Soon they passed a cherry tree without cherries because it was not the season for cherries. The stranger loved cherries and cursed the tree and destroyed it. The hunter was impressed, but the farmer was distressed because he loved trees. Besides, it was not the tree's fault it bore no fruit out of season. He became frightened by the stranger's volatility.

Days passed, and the stranger continued to entertain the boys. One day, wild animals appeared and began to growl ferociously. The boys climbed a tree, but the stranger faced the animals, and even provoked them. He told the boys that the animals could not harm him unless he permitted them to do so. Whereupon the animals attacked him, mortally wounding him, and ran off. The hunter said, "He did that out of love for us." The farmer said, "He used the animals to destroy himself, but that had nothing to do with love of us. He was just as lost and frightened as we were." The hunter hated the farmer for saying that, ending the friendship that had developed between them.

As the stranger lay dying, the farmer said, "Sir, you promised to lead us out of the forest, but you did not do so. I expected you to establish peace between us, but you did not do so. And now you are dying." The stranger said, "Listen to me! Take a piece of my bloody flesh and eat it, and you will live. Believe in me. Love one another. And when at last you die, you will escape the forest and enter the realm of everlasting peace." With that, he died.

The hunter ripped off a piece of the stranger's bloody flesh and ate it, while the farmer looked on in horror. The hunter said, "He promised to show us the way out of the forest, and he has! The way out is to eat him and die. He must be a god!" Night fell, and the boys fell asleep.

The next morning they looked for the stranger's body, but it was nowhere to be found. The hunter said, "He has ascended to heaven!" The farmer said, "The wild beasts dragged him off. But no matter, we are still in the forest." Whereupon the hunter snapped, "My father was right about your family! You don't believe in the gods and not in my new god, either, so I am going to beat you up!" And he did.

The two boys have grown up. The hunter hunts in the thick woods of the forest; the farmer farms in a clearing in the forest. But they still have not found their way out of the forest, and their families still hate one another. The hunter, believing in the promise of his new god, lives with the hope of escaping the forest and finding peace when he dies. The farmer never gives up hope that one day the spirit of his dream will come to show the way out of the forest and the way for their families to live together in peace.

RESPECT FOR OTHERS

Love does not insist on its own way (1 Cor 13:5).

AN ECUMENICAL PRAYER
Abraham is the biological father of the Jews and Moslems and the adopted father of the Christians. Therefore, Abraham is the uniting force of those three religions:

> **God said to Abram [Abraham's birth name], I will
> make of you a great nation, and I will bless you, and
> make your name great. You will be a blessing. I will
> bless those who bless you, and those who curse you,
> I will curse. And by you all the families of the earth
> shall bless themselves** (Gen 12:1–3).

God says that the families of the earth shall bless themselves in
the name of Abraham, not in the name of Jesus Christ. If the
church truly wants universal ecumenism between Christians,
Moslems, and Jews, and blessing from God, why does it not
conclude its prayers thus: "We ask these things in the name of
our common father Abraham"?

THE KORAN AND ECUMENISM

Allah or God in the Koran makes a remarkably ecumenical
statement, more loving than any by the church, and more re-
spectful:

> **48. For each We have appointed a divine law and
> traced-out way. Had Allah willed he could have
> made you one community. But that He may try you
> by that which He hath given you (He hath made you
> as ye are). So vie one with another in good works.
> Unto Allah ye will all return, and He will then in-
> form you of that wherein ye differ** (*The Table
> Spread*).

"HONOR ALL MEN"

Peter wrote: **Honor all men** (1 Pet 2:17).

What does it mean to "honor all men"? Here are some suggestions:

- Every institution should be concerned with defending the right of all people to life, liberty, and the pursuit of happiness. Any institution not concerned with those things and which uses threats, fear, or force is tyrannical and must be opposed.
- If an institution fails to support all the people, whatever their religion, including those with no religion, and fails to treat everyone with dignity, that institution has failed itself and society, and has relinquished its right to exist.
- It is the moral duty of every person to resist tyranny.
- Kidnapping, terrorism, murder, enslavement, rape, child molestation, torture, the preaching of hatred, and attempts at conversions are acts of violence and must not be tolerated.
- No religion can claim exclusivity to truth.

WORDS OF THOMAS JEFFERSON

Intolerance is the principal characteristic of the tyrant, and the church has been among the most intolerant of institutions. Whenever and wherever the church is strong, it does not exhibit tolerance, but whenever and wherever it is weak, it wants the greatest tolerance for itself. But tyranny in any form cannot be tolerated.

Thomas Jefferson's statements against tyranny—tyranny of religion, government, and indeed all institutions—are carved in stone in his monument in Washington, DC:

> I have sworn on the altar of God eternal hostility against every form of tyranny over the mind of man.

> Almighty God hath created the mind free. . . . No man shall be compelled to frequent or support any religious worship or ministry or shall otherwise suffer on account of his religious opinions or belief, but all men shall be

free to profess and by argument to maintain their opinions in matters of religion.

Laws and institutions must go hand in hand with the progress of the human mind as that becomes more developed, more enlightened, as new discoveries are made, new truths discovered and manners and opinions change. With the change of circumstances, institutions must advance also to keep pace with the time. We might as well require a man to wear still the coat which fitted him when a boy as civilized society to remain ever under the regiment of their barbarous ancestors.

REASON

DATA IN SCIENCE VS. DATA IN RELIGION
In science, when data conflict with a hypothesis, scientists reject the hypothesis but keep the data. In the church, when data conflict with dogma, the church rejects the data and keeps the dogma.

FUTILITY OF DIALOGUE
WITH THE UNREASONABLE
Dialogue is futile under certain circumstances and should not be attempted. If a man says, "I believe that plants have extrasensory perception"; or, "The moon is made of cheese"; or, "I was born in the year 1351," is there any point in engaging in dialogue with him? If a woman says, "The earth is flat," will showing her space photographs of the blue spherical planet change her mind? It is the same for someone who says, "I alone hold the truth."

CONVERSION

IDENTIFYING A FALSE RELIGION

A religion may instantly be identified as false if it teaches that it is the True Religion.

THE TRUE AND THE FALSE IN THE GOSPELS

All the mutilations and adulterations of the gospels, all the additions to and subtractions from them, have made it nearly impossible to separate the true from the false, the authentic from the fabricated. Of the sayings of Jesus of Nazareth, it is impossible to be certain which ones Jesus actually said. Scholars have been struggling with that problem since Thomas Jefferson identified it.

In so far as the canonical gospels are biased so as to demonize the Jews and glorify Jesus, one may presume that only statements that portray Jews favorably and Jesus unfavorably actually are authentic. As for the rest, there is only uncertainty.

CAN A RELIGION OF DOUBT CLAIM TO BE TRUE?

Christianity is a religion with many doubts. Can a religion of doubt claim to be true?

The church does not teach two of Jesus' most important statements:

> *Go and learn what this means,* **I desire mercy, and not sacrifice** [Hos 6:5] (Mt 9:13).

Jesus repeats the teaching from the prophet Hosea and expands upon it:

> *And if you had known what this means,* **I desire mercy and not sacrifice,** *you would not have condemned the guiltless* (Mt 12:7).

These statements are not taught because they undermine Christian theology, which is based on the sacrifice of the crucifixion. But Jesus teaches, along with the prophet, God does not want sacrifices; they do not please God, which shows they do not take away sins.

Canonical Matthew draws to a close thus:

> **Now the eleven disciples went to Galilee, to the mountain to which Jesus had directed them. And when they saw him, they worshipped him; but some doubted** (Mt 28:16–18).

"But some doubted" are amazing words. Why did some doubt when they saw him resurrected? Was it not because Jesus had taught he had not wished a sacrifical death because sacrifices do not please God?

Mark's gospel tells the story of a father who asks Jesus to cure his son—"if you can." Jesus retorts, *"If you can!"* **All things are possible to him who believes.** The father replies in a flash of wit, **"I believe. Help my unbelief!"** (Mk 9:17–29). Whereupon, Jesus, with God's help, exorcises the evil spirit dwelling in the son. The story ends without our learning what eventually happened, but elsewhere Jesus teaches the futility of exorcism because it is only temporary; the evil spirit returns with several more spirits, making the condition worse than before. We may, therefore, conclude that the exorcism of the boy was temporary, and that his father would become an even greater doubter than he had been before he met Jesus.

Mark's gospel also tells us that Jesus' family and friends **thought he was out of his mind** (Mk 3:21).

John's gospel says, **Even [Jesus'] brothers did not believe in him** (Jn 7:5).

Paul wrote:

> **If anyone imagines that he knows, he knows nothing** (1 Cor 8:2–3).

> **Let anyone who thinks that he stands take heed lest he fall** (1 Cor 10:12).

> **[I]f justification came through the law, then Christ died to no purpose** (Gal 2:11–21).

> **[I]f Christ has not been raised, then our preaching is in vain and your faith is in vain. We are even found to be misrepresenting God, because we testified of God that he raised Christ, whom he did not raise if it is true that the dead are not raised. For if the dead are not raised, then Christ has not been raised. If Christ has not been raised, your faith is futile and you are still in your sins. Then those also who have fallen asleep in Christ have perished. If for this life only we have hoped in Christ, we are of all men most to be pitied** (1 Cor 15:12–19).

Jesus said, **No one knows who the Son is but the Father** (Lk 10:22). Can a religion with so much doubt boast that it is "the true religion"? Does it have the right to convert others?

THE CRUEL CHURCH

Some people think that today when the Crusades, the Inquisition, torture, burning at the stake, and forced baptism are over, that church cruelty has come to an end. But church cruelty has not come to an end. The church still prohibits divorce and birth control, demands celibacy of its clergy, opposes embryonic stem cell research and other research on life, advocates sexual abstinence outside of marriage, and denounces homosexuality and masturbation. And the church still preaches the everlasting fires of hell.

THE PERVASIVENESS OF CHRISTIANITY

Christianity has reached every corner of the world, which the church asserts demonstrates the persuasiveness of its message. There is, however, another interpretation. Satan promised Jesus of Nazareth the world if only he would worship him (Mt 4:9–11).

AUTHENTIC PRAYER

Prayers of petition are not authentic. No spiritual person would pray for his athletic team to win a game or to get lots of presents for his birthday. No spiritual person would pray for the Jews to convert to Christianity or for God to inflict never-ending punishment on them for "killing God." Authentic prayers are of thanksgiving, or of awe, or of asking for strength in difficult times, or of asking for help in doing what is right when the right is not clear or is dangerous or impossible.

RELIGION AS AN ACCIDENT OF BIRTH

Very few people choose their own religion. It is passed on to them by their parents, as their grandparents passed it on to their parents. Would a loving God reward those who belonged to one religion while punishing those who belonged to another, when the religion they happened to belong to occurred by chance?

A LOVING AND MERCIFUL GOD

I do not believe a loving and merciful god cares whether one believes in him/her or not. Such a god cares only about what one does, especially how one treats one's fellow man and the earth. Any other god is not worthy of worship.

THREE MAJOR FORCES
THAT INDUCE CONVERSION

There are three major forces that induce conversion of the Jews to Christianity. They are jealousy, guilt, and ultimatum.

1. JEALOUSY

Paul taught that the Jews would convert out of jealousy of Christians:

> **So I ask, have the Jews stumbled so as to fall? By no means! Through their trespass, salvation has come to the Gentiles, for the purpose of making Israel jealous. Now if the Jews' trespass means riches for the world, and if their failing means riches for the Gentiles, how much more will their full inclusion mean!** (Rom 11:1–12).

There is no evidence that jealousy was a force in bringing about the conversion of Jews in Paul's day. What was there for the Jews to be jealous of? They already believed they would inherit eternal life without Jesus; and many saw Jesus as a false messiah. However, after Christianity became the dominant religion in the west, envy may have played a role. The desire to assimilate comes about in part through envy of the prevalent culture which includes that culture's religion. Life is easier when one belongs to the prevalent culture and religion.

Envy of Christian culture probably intensified with the arrival of Christmas as we know it—Christmas trees, celebrations, cookies, music. Paul knew nothing about such things because Christmas did not become a Christian holiday until sometime between the fourth and sixth century. It was derived from the Roman holiday the Saturnalia, which occurs at the winter solstice. It is this heathen holiday that helped fix the date of Jesus' birth. Christmas is attractive to the Jews not only because of the concept of the advent of the Messiah, a Jewish idea, but also because the Christmas season is joyous, with parties and warm feelings of cheer and good will. Christians at Christmastime seem to love everyone, even the Jews, unlike at Good Friday or Easter, which tend to bring out feelings of hatred, especially toward the Jews.

2. GUILT

Peter may have been the first to use guilt as a device to make the Jews convert. The strategy is to make the Jews feel responsible and guilty for the crucifixion, and then imply that conversion cures the guilt. After conversion one will never again be accused of killing Christ. On encountering a group of non-believing Jews, Peter gave the following speech:

> **Men of Israel. . . . You crucified and killed Jesus of Nazareth at the hands of lawless men [the Romans] . . . . Now when [these Jews] heard this, they were cut to the heart and said to Peter and the other Apostles, "Brothers, what must we do?" And Peter responded, "Repent and be baptized. . . . The promise is to you.". . . So there were added that day about 3,000 souls** (Acts 2:22).

About three thousand Jews converted in one day. That shows how powerful guilt is as an effective force in the conversion of Jews.

3. ULTIMATUM

The most powerful force of all in conversion prior to the Enlightenment was ultimatum, that is, forced conversion: Convert or die! Spain was unusual in 1492 in giving a third choice: Convert or die or go into exile!

IS THE MAJORITY NECESSARILY RIGHT?

The church justifies conversion on the ground that it alone has the truth. More likely the church is fearful it does not have the truth at all; otherwise it would not be so preoccupied with "truth." Perhaps the church believes the more people it has, the more likely its religion is to be true. But a majority holding a belief does not make the belief true. The majority once believed the earth was flat and the sun revolved around the earth. Jesus of Nazareth said:

> *Enter by the narrow gate; for the gate is wide and the way is easy, that leads to destruction, and those who enter by it are many. For the gate is narrow and the way is hard, that leads to life, and those who find it are few* (Mt 7:13–14).

FINAL QUESTIONS

How can a religion that preaches hatred call itself a religion of love?:

> *But as for these enemies of mine who did not want me to be their king, bring them here and slay them before me* (Lk 19:27).

> *If a man does not abide in me, he is cast forth as a branch is cast forth and dries up. And the branches*

are gathered, thrown into the fire, and burned (Jn 15:5–6).

Who in his right mind would expect a Jew to worship a Jew?

9. SELECTED BIBLIOGRAPHY
Alphabetical Categories

APOCRYPHA
The Apocrypha and Pseudepigrapha of the Old Testament. Vol. 2, *Pseudepigrapha*. Edited by R. H. Charles. Oxford: Clarendon Press, 1913, 1977.

New Testament Apocrypha. Vol. 1, *Gospels and Related Writings*. Edited by Edgar Hennecke. Tübingen, Germany: 1959. English translation edited by R. McL. Wilson. Philadelphia: Westminster Press, 1963.

BIBLES
Biblia Sacra, Iuxta Vulgatam Clementinam. Madrid: Biblioteca de Autores Christianos, 1977.

The Holy Bible, Revised Standard Version. New York: Thomas Nelson & Sons, 1946, 1952.

The Holy Scriptures. English text revised and edited by Harold Fisch. Jerusalem: Koren Publishers, 1992.

The New English Bible with Apocrypha. Oxford: Oxford University Press; Cambridge: Cambridge University Press, 1970.

Novum Testamentum Graece [Ἡ Καινή Διαθήκη]. Stuttgart, Germany: Verlag und Druck der Privileg, 1952.

The Septuagint with [Old Testament] Apocrypha: Greek and English. Translated by Sir Lancelot C. L. Brenton. London: Samuel Bagster & Sons, 1851; Grand Rapids, MI: Zondervan Publishing House, Regency Reference Library, 1885, 1911.

The Soncino Books of the Bible. 14 vols. Vol. 1, *The Soncino Chumash*. English text edited by A. Cohen. London: Soncino Press, 1947, 1979.

————Vol. 5, *Isaiah*, English translation by I. W. Slotki. London: Soncino Press, 1949, 1980.

CATECHISMS OF THE ROMAN CATHOLIC CHURCH

An American Catholic Catechism. Edited by G. J. Dyer. New York: Seabury Press, Crossroad Book, 1975.

Catechism of the Catholic Church. Citta del Vaticano [Vatican City]: Libreria Editrice Vaticana; Liguori, MO: Liguori Publications, 1994.

Catechism of Christian Doctrine (*Baltimore Catechism #3*). Rockford, IL: Benziger Bros., Tan Books and Publishers, 1885, 1974.

New Catechism: Catholic Faith for Adults (Authorized Edition of the Dutch Catechism). New York: Seabury Press, Crossroad Book, 1969.

The Teaching of Christ: A Catholic Catechism for Adults. Edited by Donald W. Wuerl, Ronald Lawler, Thomas Comerford, and Kris D. Stubna, Huntington, IN: Our Sunday Visitor, 1976, 2005.

CHURCH FATHERS

The Ante-Nicene Fathers. 9 vols. Edited by Alexander Roberts and James Donaldson. Edinburgh: T. & T. Clark; American reprint of the Edinburgh edition, revised by A. Cleveland Coxe. Grand Rapids, MI: Wm. B. Eerdmans Publishing Co., 1990, 1993.

The Nicene and Post-Nicene Fathers. First Series. 14 vols. Edited by Philip Schaff. Edinburgh: T. & T. Clark; Grand Rapids, MI: Wm. B. Eerdmans Publishing Co., 1989, 1994.

The Nicene and Post-Nicene Fathers. Second Series. 14 vols. Edited by Philip Schaff and Henry Wace. Edinburgh: T. & T. Clark; Grand Rapids, MI: Wm. B. Eerdmans Publishing Co., 1989, 1991.

COMMENTARIES ON JESUS OF NAZARETH, EARLY CHRISTIANITY, AND THE NEW TESTAMENT

Bundy, Walter E. *The Psychic Health of Jesus*. New York: Macmillan, 1922.

————*The Religion of Jesus*. Indianapolis: Bobbs-Merrill, 1928.

————*A Syllabus and Synopsis of the First Three Gospels*. Indianapolis: Bobbs-Merrill, 1932.

The Five Gospels: The Search for the Authentic Words of Jesus. Translation and commentary by R. W. Funk, R. W. Hoover, and the Jesus Seminar. New York: Macmillan, 1993.

Origen. *Contra Celsum [Against Celsus*, which contains excerpts from Celsus's book *The True Doctrine.]* Translated by Henry Chadwick. Cambridge: Cambridge University Press, 1953.

Tyson, Joseph B. *A Study of Early Christianity*. New York: Macmillan, 1973.

CRITICISM OF THE ROMAN CATHOLIC CHURCH

Hoffer, Eric. *The True Believer: Thoughts on the Nature of Mass Movements*. New York: Harper & Row, Perennial Library, 1951, 1966.

Isaac, Jules. *The Teaching of Contempt: Christian Roots of Anti-Semitism*. New York: Holt, Rinehart & Winston, 1964.

Julian. *Against the Galileans*. Cambridge, MA: Harvard University Press, Loeb Classical Library, 1923, 1961.

Küng, Hans. *The Church*. Garden City, NY: Doubleday, Image Books, 1967, 1976.

Russell, Bertrand. *What I Believe: Why I Am Not a Christian and Other Essays on Religion and Related Subjects*. Edited by Paul Edwards. New York: Simon & Schuster, Touchstone Book, 1957.

Twain, Mark. *The Complete Essays of Mark Twain*. Edited by Charles Neider. Garden City, NY: Doubleday, 1963.

DIASPORA
Keller, Werner. *Diaspora: The Post-Biblical History of the Jews*. New York: Harcourt, Brace & World, 1969.

DOCUMENTS OF THE CHRISTIAN CHURCH AND OF THE ROMAN CATHOLIC CHURCH
Documents of the Christian Church. Edited by Henry Bettenson. Oxford: Oxford University Press, 1963.

The Documents of Vatican II. Edited by A. P. Flannery. New York: Costello Publishing Co., Pyramid Communications, Pillar Books, 1975.

The teaching [sic] *of the Catholic Church as Contained in Her Documents*. Prepared by J. Neuner and J. H. Roos, edited by K. Rahner, and translated by G. Stevens. New York: Mercier Press, Alba House, Society of St. Paul, 1967.

HISTORIES OF THE CHURCH
Chadwick, Henry. *The Early Church*. Penguin Books, 1967, 1978.

Durant, Will. *Caesar and Christ: A History of Roman Civilization and Christianity from Their Beginnings to A.D. 325*. New York: Simon and Schuster, 1944.

Eusebius. *The History of the Church* [from Christ to Constantine]. Translated by G. A. Williamson. Penguin Books, 1965, 1984.

————*Life of Constantine*. Edited by P. Schaff and H. Wace. A Select Library of the Nicene and Post-Nicene Fathers of the Christian Church, Second Series, Vol 1. Edinburgh: T. & T. Clark; Grand Rapids, MI: Wm. B. Eerdmans, 1991.

Harrison, Everett F. *The Apostolic Church.* Grand Rapids, MI: Wm. B. Eerdmans, 1985.

Hefele, Charles Joseph. *A History of the Christian Councils, from the Original Documents, to the Close of the Council of Nicaea, A.D. 325.* Translated and edited by William R. Clark. Edinburgh: T. & T. Clark, 1871.

Tacitus. *Histories*, Vols. 4–5; *Annals*, Vols. 1–3, 13–16. Cambridge, MA: Harvard University Press, Loeb Classical Library, 1937, 1951.

HISTORIES BY JEWISH HISTORIANS AT THE TIMES OF JESUS AND PAUL

Josephus. *Jewish Antiquities.* Books 12, 14, 18, 19, 20. Cambridge, MA: Harvard University Press, Loeb Classical Library, 1933, 1939.

———[*My*] *Life. Against Apion.* Cambridge, MA: Harvard University Press, Loeb Classical Library, 1926, 1976.

———*The Jewish War.* Books 1–6. Cambridge, MA: Harvard University Press, Loeb Classical Library, 1927, 1956.

Philo. *Embassy to Gaius.* Cambridge, MA: Harvard University Press, Loeb Classical Library, 1962, 1971.

JEWISH COMMENTARY ABOUT JESUS IN THE MIDDLE AGES

Schäfer, Peter. *Jesus in the Talmud.* Princeton, NJ: Princeton University Press, 2007.

JUDAISM AT THE TIME OF JESUS

The Mishnah. Translated by H. Danby. London: Oxford University Press, 1933.

Moore, George Foot. *Judaism in the First Centuries of the Christian Era.* Vols. 1–2. Cambridge, MA: Harvard University Press, 1927, 1955.

KORAN [QURAN]
The Meaning of the Glorious Koran, An explanatory translation by Marmaduke Pickthall. New York: Alfred A. Knopf, Everyman's Library, 1909, 1930, 1992.

MEIN KAMPF
Hitler, Adolf. *Mein Kampf [My Struggle]*. Translated by Ralph Manheim. Boston: Houghton Mifflin Company, 1943.

NEW TESTAMENT BACKGROUND
Barrett, C. A. *The New Testament Background: Selected Documents.* New York: Harper & Row, Torchbook, 1961.

Euripides. *Bacchae.* Translated by A. S. Way. Cambridge, MA: Harvard University Press, Loeb Classical Library, 1912, 1979.

Smith, Morton. *Clement of Alexandria and a Secret Gospel of Mark.* Cambridge, MA: Harvard University Press, 1973.

———*The Secret Gospel: The Discovery and Interpretation of the Secret Gospel According to Mark.* New York: Harper & Row, 1973.

WRITINGS OF POPE JOHN PAUL I
Luciani, Albino. *Illustrissimi: Letters from Pope John Paul I.* Translated from the Italian by William Weaver. Padua: Edizioni Messaggero, 1976, 1978; USA & Canada: Little, Brown & Company, 1978.